PASSIVE SOLAR ARCHITECTURE

Heating, Cooling, Ventilation, Daylighting, and More Using Natural Flows

DAVID A. BAINBRIDGE ■ KEN HAGGARD

With contributions from Rachel Aljilani, Alfredo Fernandez-Gonzales, Pliny Fisk, Aerial Fisk, Steve Herckeroth, Richard Levine, and Erin Scholl

CHELSEA GREEN PUBLISHING

the politics and practice of sustainable living

CHELSEA GREEN PUBLISHING

White River Junction, Vermont

Project Manager: Patricia Stone
Developmental Editor: Cannon Labrie
Copy Editor: Laura Jorstad
Proofreader: Susan Barnett
Indexer: Shana Milkie
Designer: Maureen Forys, Happenstance Type-O-Rama

Printed in the United States of America
First printing July, 2011
10 9 8 7 6 5 4 3 2 1   11 12 13

OUR COMMITMENT TO GREEN PUBLISHING

Chelsea Green sees publishing as a tool for cultural change and ecological stewardship. We strive to align our book manufacturing practices with our editorial mission and to reduce the impact of our business enterprise in the environment. We print our books and catalogs on chlorine-free recycled paper, using vegetable-based inks whenever possible. This book may cost slightly more because we use recycled paper, and we hope you'll agree that it's worth it. Chelsea Green is a member of the Green Press Initiative (www.greenpressinitiative.org), a nonprofit coalition of publishers, manufacturers, and authors working to protect the world's endangered forests and conserve natural resources. *Passive Solar Architecture* was printed on FSC®-certified paper supplied by RR Donnelley that contains at least 10-percent postconsumer recycled fiber and less than 1 percent of the material in this book is not FSC®-certified.

LIBRARY OF CONGRESS CATALOGING-IN-PUBLICATION DATA

Bainbridge, David A.
  Passive solar architecture : heating, cooling, ventilation, daylighting and more using natural flows / David Bainbridge and Ken Haggard.
    p. cm.
  ISBN 978-1-60358-296-4
1. Solar energy—Passive systems. 2. Architecture and energy conservation. I. Haggard, Kenneth L. II. Title.

TH7413.B345 2010
690'.8370472--dc22

2010030052

Chelsea Green Publishing Company
Post Office Box 428
White River Junction, VT 05001
(802) 295-6300
www.chelseagreen.com

MIX
Paper from
responsible sources
FSC® C101537

green
press
INITIATIVE

Chelsea Green Publishing is committed to preserving ancient forests and natural resources. We elected to print this title on FSC®-certified paper containing at least 10% postconsumer recycled fiber, processed chlorine-free. As a result, for this printing, we have saved:

17 Trees (40' tall and 6-8" diameter)
7,542 Gallons of Wastewater
7 million BTUs Total Energy
478 Pounds of Solid Waste
1,672 Pounds of Greenhouse Gases

Chelsea Green Publishing made this paper choice because we are a member of the Green Press Initiative, a nonprofit program dedicated to supporting authors, publishers, and suppliers in their efforts to reduce their use of fiber obtained from endangered forests. For more information, visit www.greenpressinitiative.org.

Environmental impact estimates were made using the Environmental Defense Paper Calculator. For more information visit: www.papercalculator.org.

CONTENTS

PREFACE

Sick building syndrome is a term used to describe situations in which building occupants experience discomfort and even acute health problems that appear to be related to time spent in the building.

—MOHAMED BOUBEKRI, 2008

BUILDINGS MATTER. We spend more and more of our lives inside them, and poorly designed, built, and maintained buildings are a common cause of human suffering, illness, and death. People are too often hot in summer, cold in winter, and face real danger if the power goes off. Many more suffer at work or at home from poor air quality. Sealed buildings, flawed building materials, and poor design lead to leaks and mold unless installation and maintenance are perfect—and they rarely are. In 1998, World Health Organization research suggested that 30 percent of all the new and remodeled buildings in the world were afflicted with sick building syndrome. The annual cost of poor indoor air quality in the United States alone has been estimated at $160 billion by the Department of Energy, more than the gross national product of most countries. In contrast, sustainable buildings, to those who live and work in them, pay large dividends as human comfort and health improve and productivity increases. The value of productivity gains alone is often a hundred times greater than energy savings.

Buildings are also a major user of materials and energy. They account for as much as a third of all the flow of materials (water, metals, minerals, et cetera) each year in the United States and are also responsible for 40 percent of the country's greenhouse gas emissions. And this is not just a local problem. When Stefan Bringezu and co-workers computed the resource intensity of the fifty-eight sectors of the German economy, they concluded that buildings and dwellings consumed between 25 and 30 percent of the total nonrenewable material flow in Germany.

Buildings not only are material-intensive but also require massive amounts of energy and water and are a source of many toxic and ecotoxic materials, including paints, plastics, cleaning solutions, pesticides, garbage streams, and copper, zinc, and lead leaching from roofing and pipes. Floods and fires release a wide range of toxins from buildings. Air pollution from buildings and from the power generation needed to heat and cool them causes far-reaching ecosystem damage and disruption locally, across the country, and around the world.

Why have we been so fuelish? As Amory Lovins and others have noted, small but important signals and incentives make it most profitable for designers, engineers, builders, and installers to create inefficient, costly, and unhealthful developments and buildings. This has been compounded by poor training in schools, particularly in architecture and engineering, lack of training for builders, and government subsidies that artificially reduce the cost of energy, water, and building materials.

Almost all of the adverse impacts of building can be avoided by good design and construction. New buildings in any climate can be solar-oriented, naturally heated and cooled, naturally lit, naturally ventilated, and made with renewable materials.

In most climates, proper building orientation can dramatically reduce building energy demand for heating and cooling at no cost increase. In a study of more sustainable home design (validated by actually building the home) in Davis, California, the home summer peak energy demand dropped from 3.6 kilowatt-hours (kWh) to 2 kWh, and annual energy use for heating and cooling dropped 67 percent. This improvement didn't cost anything; in fact, it reduced the cost of construction.

The goal of the sustainable building (also called green building) movement is to improve the comfort and health of the built environment while maximizing use of renewable resources and reducing operating and life-cycle costs. The savings are particularly important for retirees and for institutions that cannot count on increasing income in the future to offset projected large increases in cost for energy, water, and other resources. Comfort and health, security and safety in power outages, energy and water use, waste, recyclability, and cost are key issues. Systems considerations are critical in siting buildings, building orientation, design, and operation, but they are usually ignored.

Buildings Matter for Ill...

THE IMPORTANCE OF SEEMINGLY SIMPLE CHOICES

The simple choice of window orientation can have large implications for cost, energy use, and comfort, yet these implications are rarely considered. Most attention in building codes is on reducing energy use for winter heating, but in many areas cooling is equally or even more important. Fortunately, design for passive solar heating in winter can reduce summer cooling demand as well, since facing south allows easy solar control in the summer with overhangs. The most common failing of building design is not orienting the house properly, something that has been well understood for more than two thousand years. As the Greek writer Aeschylus noted of the barbarians, "They lacked the knowledge of houses turned to face the sun."

Besides discomfort, poor orientation is expensive to building owners, society, and the planet. The cost of a 50-square-foot west-facing window in Sacramento, California, is calculated to be $40,000 over a thirty-year period if you add up the added air-conditioning cost, the additional utility cost, and the related environmental cost of such a simple choice. If the three million houses built in California since 1980 had been well designed with regard to the simple problem of orientation, we could have reduced the critical summer peak energy demand by 3,000 to 6,000 megawatts at no additional cost. Sustainable design can pay big dividends!

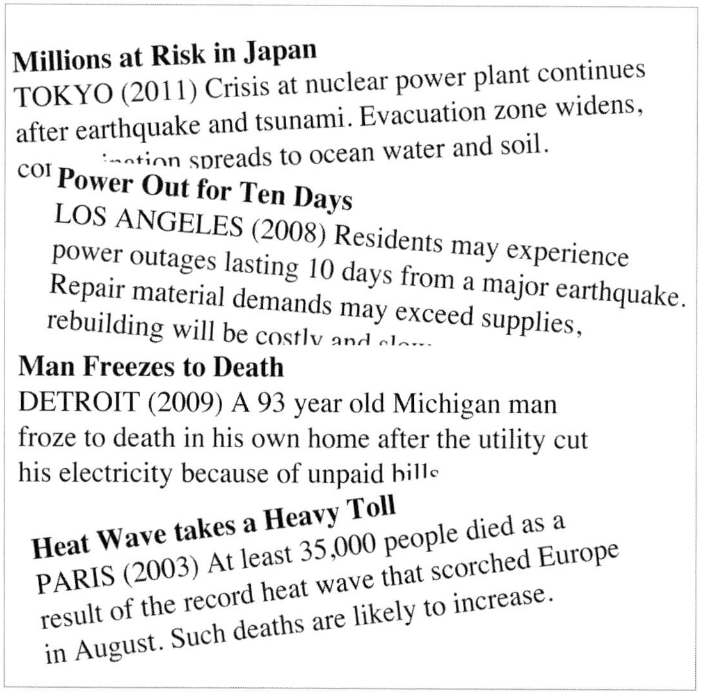

Millions at Risk in Japan
TOKYO (2011) Crisis at nuclear power plant continues after earthquake and tsunami. Evacuation zone widens, con~~tamin~~ation spreads to ocean water and soil.

Power Out for Ten Days
LOS ANGELES (2008) Residents may experience power outages lasting 10 days from a major earthquake. Repair material demands may exceed supplies, rebuilding will be costly and slow.

Man Freezes to Death
DETROIT (2009) A 93 year old Michigan man froze to death in his own home after the utility cut his electricity because of unpaid bills.

Heat Wave takes a Heavy Toll
PARIS (2003) At least 35,000 people died as a result of the record heat wave that scorched Europe in August. Such deaths are likely to increase.

Fig. 0.1

Fig. 0.2. *Even when the power is off, a sustainably designed building works well.*

. . . or for Good

In a sustainable culture buildings will once again be seen as part of a beautiful place from planetary biomes to specific sites. These buildings will be part of a cyclic flow of materials and energy in an environment without seams or waste.

—ROBERT HAGGARD

THE VILLAGE HOMES subdivision in Davis, California, used proper solar orientation to reduce energy use for heating and cooling 50 percent back in the 1970s. The 500,000-square-foot ING bank in the Netherlands cost little more than conventional construction, but uses less than one-tenth as much energy, and absenteeism is 15 percent lower. A sustainably designed factory complex helped double worker productivity for the Herman Miller Corporation in Holland, Michigan. A very modest retrofit of a standard office building in San Diego reduced seasonal energy use for heating and cooling 70 percent and improved the comfort of those working there.

Increasing attention has been paid to sustainable building as a result of the US Green Building Council's Leadership in Energy and

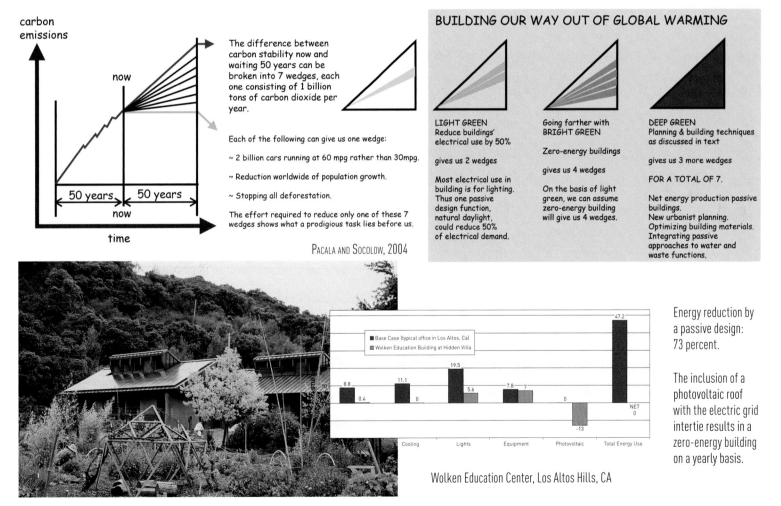

carbon emissions

now

50 years | 50 years
now

time

The difference between carbon stability now and waiting 50 years can be broken into 7 wedges, each one consisting of 1 billion tons of carbon dioxide per year.

Each of the following can give us one wedge:

~ 2 billion cars running at 60 mpg rather than 30mpg.

~ Reduction worldwide of population growth.

~ Stopping all deforestation.

The effort required to reduce only one of these 7 wedges shows what a prodigious task lies before us.

PACALA AND SOCOLOW, 2004

BUILDING OUR WAY OUT OF GLOBAL WARMING

LIGHT GREEN
Reduce buildings' electrical use by 50%

gives us 2 wedges

Most electrical use in building is for lighting. Thus one passive design function, natural daylight, could reduce 50% of electrical demand.

Going farther with
BRIGHT GREEN

Zero-energy buildings

gives us 4 wedges

On the basis of light green, we can assume zero-energy building will give us 4 wedges.

DEEP GREEN
Planning & building techniques as discussed in text

gives us 3 more wedges

FOR A TOTAL OF 7.

Net energy production passive buildings.
New urbanist planning.
Optimizing building materials.
Integrating passive approaches to water and waste functions.

■ Base Case (typical office in Los Altos, Cal
▨ Wolken Education Building at Hidden Villa

8.8 | 0.4 | 11.1 | 0 | 19.5 | 5.6 | 7.8 | 7 | 0 | -13 | 47.2 | NET 0

Cooling | Lights | Equipment | Photovoltaic | Total Energy Use

Wolken Education Center, Los Altos Hills, CA

Energy reduction by a passive design: 73 percent.

The inclusion of a photovoltaic roof with the electric grid intertie results in a zero-energy building on a yearly basis.

Fig. 0.3. *We all use buildings, and if they are designed right they can improve health and security and provide an effective and proactive approach to reducing global climate disruption.*

Environmental Design (LEED) program and other green building evaluation programs. While more green buildings are being built, they are only pale green and often perform little better than the buildings they replace, for they often neglect the most elementary feature of sustainable design: using the sun and climate resources for heating and cooling.

The benefits of sustainable design include comfort, health, economy, security and safety during power outages, as well as reduced impact on the planet. A well-designed building will keep its occupants warm in winter and cool in summer even when the power goes off. A sustainably designed building will also be able to provide emergency water supplies from its rainwater harvesting systems during a water-main break or natural disaster. And a passive solar water heater will provide hot water for showers and cleaning even when the power is off.

Building sustainable buildings has never been easier. Improved sensors and control systems can increase building thermal performance and resource use by better managing fans, pumps, valves, vents, shades, lights, and blinds, as well as making it easier to monitor buildings. Replacing the hidden mechanical meters used for energy and water with highly visible and easy-to-read water and energy meters in the lobby, living room, or as a display on your computer makes it much easier to understand and optimize building performance.

Better accounting that takes the true costs of a building—throughout its life cycle—into consideration is critical to make it clear that sustainable buildings are the best choice. When health and productivity are added to the mix, sustainable buildings are the best buy! Improving accounting for all costs is not going to be easy, as those who benefit from current subsidies are loath to give them up. But growing awareness of global warming, resource shortages, and energy insecurity are adding pressure for change.

A well-designed and well-constructed building should require minimal mechanical cooling, heating, and ventilation systems and limited artificial light during the day. And it can be built with renewable, locally sourced materials, which in turn can be manufactured and maintained without toxic chemicals. The built environment can become a source of satisfaction and joy rather than a polluting and often toxic prison. People enjoy sustainable buildings. They improve the quality of life. And sustainable designs add value from increased productivity from improved working and learning conditions. This book will help you find your path to sustainability!

ABOUT THIS BOOK

OUR GOAL in writing this book is to provide a comprehensive introduction and guide to the subject of passive solar architecture, a field the two of us have been working in for the past forty years. Our hope is to revive the name *passive architecture* as an umbrella term that includes in its purview all dimensions of green building and sustainability in the built environment.

Our paths first crossed in the 1970s. We were each working in one of the four passive solar "hot spots" in the country, Ken in San Luis Obispo and David at the University of California–Davis. (The other two were at Los Alamos and on the East Coast at MIT and Princeton.) By the 1980s, *passive* was a common term, and hundreds of passive buildings had been built. Performance and prediction modeling were developed, so that the application of various architectural elements could be evaluated before construction to determine optimum design features.

However, with the election of Ronald Reagan in 1980, most federal support for solar energy was removed, an oil glut developed, energy prices shrank, and the United States drifted backward toward its old wasteful energy ways. The passive architectural movement lost its immediacy, and most of the research and development was picked up by European countries, particularly the United Kingdom and Germany.

By the end of the first decade of this century, neglect and indulgence with regard to energy and building financing caught up with us in the form of the worst recession since the Great Depression. In addition, some began to recognize that looming problems such as the peak in fossil fuels, global climate disruption, and resource wars could only be addressed by shifting to a green economy.

At present, *green architecture* is very broadly defined and can mean different things to different people. Smart-growth concepts, healthy interiors, sustainably produced materials, energy conservation, life-cycle costs, new urbanism—all these and more are considerations for a green building. Stricter definition and quantification of green buildings is starting to occur with certification programs such as LEED (Leadership in Energy and Environmental Design), Green Globes, Living Buildings, and others. These programs are based on checklists of prescribed points given for various green characteristics. With this situation, is the term *passive architecture* still relevant?

There are several reasons why the term *passive* is even more relevant than ever. One is that because of the breadth of green building and the greater difficulty that designers have in conceptualizing energy aspects than they do other green aspects, energy concerns in green buildings can often take second place, which is what happened in the early LEED checklists. There was a tendency to lump energy concerns under "energy efficiency" where they could be more easily dealt with by prescriptive standards. This type of simplified categorization misses the whole point of good passive architecture, which is *a method of energy production* as well as energy efficiency. Providing natural light by a well-designed atrium is energy production just as much as providing the same amount of light by electricity produced from a distant coal plant, except the passive approach is healthier and does not involve line loss to transport the energy, pollution, and other embedded costs. An energy-efficient building is a necessary prerequisite for a passive building, but energy efficiency by itself does not make a passive building. Therefore, we still need a term that allows the emphasis on producing thermal effects with building elements. *Passive architecture* fits the bill.

Green building really consists of three major concerns: sustainability, passive solar design, and triple-bottom-line accounting. All three topics and their interrelatedness are discussed in chapter 1. These are not static concerns, but a set of evolving techniques, all critical to obtaining the synthesis we call green building. Passive design must be a core consideration in a green building. We explore the latest developments and techniques for passive heating, passive cooling and ventilation, and natural lighting in chapters 2, 3, and 4, which are the heart of this book.

We see the shift to sustainable thinking and building as a continuum that contains starts, stops, and temporary reverses, but in general remains an evolution of building design and technology. Passive design is a necessary core element in green building because it embodies a shift from lightly differentiated design where discrete parts perform discrete functions to highly integrated design where one part contributes to many functions. This shift in the design process allows for dynamic synergy, where the whole is more than the sum of the parts, and the parts all contribute to the whole. Synergy is more biological than mechanical; synergy is what will allow a sustainable culture where there is greater health, wealth, and equity because in the final analysis, systems with high synergy are more effective, reliant, and efficient.

The passive approach to building is not a fixed practice. If we look at its development over time, we see more and more functions being accomplished on-site using building elements. First there was heating, then cooling using the same building elements, then lighting, then electricity production. Now advanced passive buildings are going for water collection, carbon dioxide sequestration, and waste processing. What we are striving for is combining more and more

production and use at the scale of the individual building. The harvesting of on-site resources is the focus of chapter 5.

In chapter 6, we invite some other voices to join us in looking at the big picture and at reimagining the present and the future. It is at the macro scale—where we can reconnect perceptions and assumptions about production and use—that passive architecture finds its cultural relevance. When building users can once again be more than just inhabitants of sealed boxes where energy production is out of sight and out of mind, then we can regenerate the awareness of energy and resources that is a necessary part of our transition from an industrial to a sustainable society.

Oily wasteful wolf and practical passive pig will help illustrate this story.

ONE SUSTAINABLE BUILDINGS

Green buildings provide greater health and well-being by integrating principles of sustainability, passive design, and triple-bottom-line accounting.

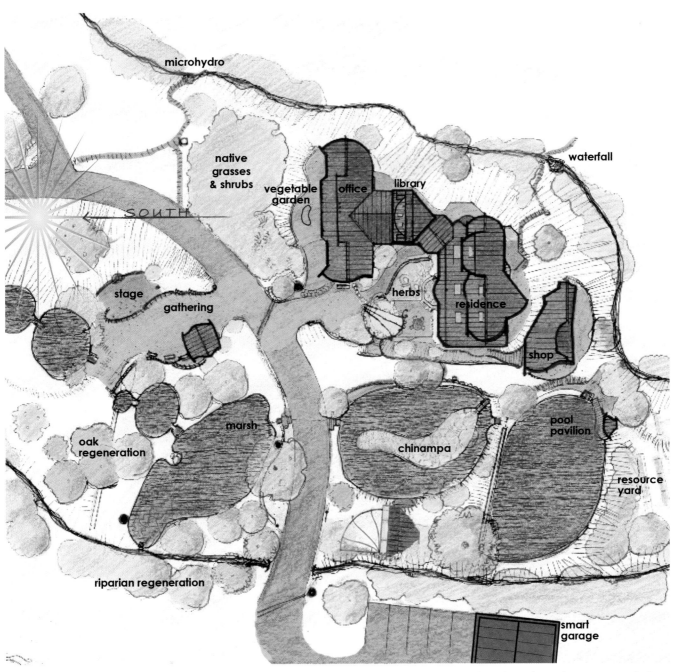

This mixed use complex is passively heated and cooled and all electricity needed is produced on-site. It is constructed of straw bales and wood milled on-site from trees killed in a wildfire. Landscape regeneration and habitat conservation were integral elements of the design.

Building sustainable and joyful buildings is not difficult or costly, but it does require a different approach. Designing and building good buildings demands a detailed understanding of the site and its microclimate, the orientation of the building and site with respect to the sun, and choosing and using materials, resources, and energy sustainably and wisely. This book works through the steps that are required for sustainable design, beginning with a definition of *sustainability*, fundamentals of energy and buildings, understanding site opportunities and constraints, and client requirements. The primary focus of this book is on using natural energy flows to meet the needs for heating, cooling, ventilation, and lighting, but supplemental materials extend the consideration of sustainability into materials, community, and other essential resource needs that can be met in full or in part by on-site resource capture.

Sustainability was defined at the United Nations Conference on the Environment in 1987 as "the ability to meet the needs of the present without compromising the needs of future generations." More expansive goals were discussed, but this was the most that could be agreed upon. While the UN definition is widely used, it still isn't specific enough. A working definition of sustainability must recognize that the environment and human activity are an interconnected, co-evolutionary whole. It is not just the protection of the environment that defines sustainability; the term must also encompass culture, economy, community, and family. As part of the whole, we must take into account how human activities affect natural processes and see how nature and natural flows are critically linked to our health and prosperity. Our contribution and participation in these processes must be restructured to sustain ourselves, other species, and the planet. Sustainability is local, regional, national, and global, and includes considerations of past, present, and future.

Sustainability is sometimes used in a narrow sense—as in "sustainable means profitable"—but we believe that a simple, single definition is not adequate to the task. Instead,

to help shape and improve our designs we propose a working definition that is multidisciplinary. Sustainability must be understood by planning and design teams, citizens, and policy makers. A single definition won't do, because sustainability is simple and complex, local and global, and based on actions taken today, past decisions and behavior, and the impacts and results from these choices extending for hundreds of years into the future. We have found it helpful to develop a working definition of *sustainability* with a spectrum of issues and ideas from relatively simple to more complex definitions (see figure 1.1).

For human survival and a livable future, the idea and application of sustainability must become part of an epochal cultural shift. The greatest barriers to understanding and embracing sustainability are residual biases from the fossil-fueled industrial era, when failed accounting and disconnection from nature led to potential catastrophe. It can be as hard for us to imagine what a sustainable culture of tomorrow might be as it was for the residents of a small horse-dominated farming town in Illinois in 1890 to envision the coming car-based culture of 1950. Their vision was restricted by their experience, and so is ours.

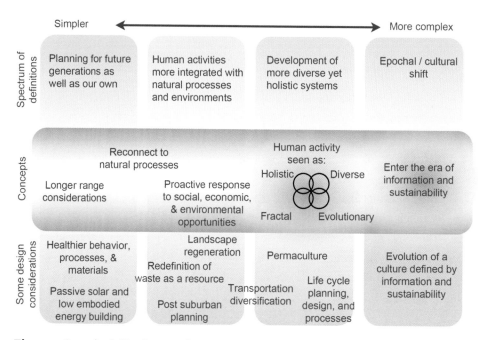

Fig. 1.1. *Sustainability is a continuum, as seen in this working definition of the term for planning and design.*

We can learn a great deal from studying and experiencing first-hand the best practices and communities that exist today. We can also learn from examining previous epochal shifts in cultural attitudes such as the transition from gathering and hunting to agriculture and more recently the abolition of slavery and voting rights for all. We can find good examples of sustainable management of local resources, notably a recent book by Arby Brown* on the Edo period in Japan, but this and other studies are far different in scale and perspective from the challenges we face in developing a sustainable global community. Failures of imagination can lead to philosophical traps; some of the most common are related to questions such as our place in nature, our interdependence with other cultures and ecosystems around the world, and the challenge of living within our means.

The question of our place in nature is critical. Aldo Leopold* was one of the first to address the problem:

> *In short, a land ethic changes the role of Homo sapiens from a conqueror of the land-community to plain member and citizen of it. It implies respect for his fellow members, and also respect for the community as such. In human history we have learned that the conqueror role is eventually self-defeating. Why? Because it is implicit in such a role that conqueror knows, ex cathedra, what makes the community clock tick and just what and who is valuable, and what and who is worthless, in community life. It always turns out that he knows neither, and this is why his conquests eventually defeat themselves.*

This is a critical step, but will not come easily to many people who have ignored and remain disconnected from the world.

Many people who have started to make this shift develop a sense of hopelessness, believing that we as a species are "bad" for the environment and that the slowness of our response to real and imagined crises dooms us. To them, humans are detrimental to nature—a species out of control—guilty just for being human. Many feel either that nothing can be done about our failures, leading to despair, or that we must sacrifice to atone for our sins. We should shiver in the dark, eat only beans and rice, and use less of everything. This view is equally flawed.

* Sources mentioned or cited in the text are marked with an asterisk, and full citations are listed in appendix C, "References and Further Reading."

The problem is not us, but our ignorance and failure of imagination to understand how we could do better. We can be more comfortable, healthier, and secure by working with nature instead of fighting to subdue and conquer it. We have enough successful examples to show that by working with natural flows, renewable materials, and ecologically sound practices, we can exceed our current expectations with only 10 percent of the current negative impact or, better yet, with impacts that are positive. We know we need to change, but it is hard to get started. Guilt has never been an effective tool for driving change. Joy and satisfaction lead to more successful outcomes, and financial signals from true-cost accounting encourage rapid improvement.

Balance, like sustainability, is a seemingly simple idea but in practice can be very complex. Our first impulse is to believe that a static balance must be achieved between humans and nature, our appetites and impact, and our economy and ecology. But what we need is dynamic balance and resilience to ensure the long-term stability of the complex systems that support us recover from perturbation. Certainly much of the industrial era has progressed with very little thought for consequences, and as William McDonough* has argued, we could hardly have done worse if we deliberately set out to do things as badly as possible, with the result being an out-of-control juggernaut of unbalanced, unhealthy, and destructive practices.

We need to be careful about how we define *balance* to avoid being caught in outdated attitudes or too narrow a focus. Balance is often defined by an accounting of inputs and outputs across the boundaries of a closed system that can be quantified, but an accurate accounting can be quite difficult to achieve for the complex world we live in. It is easy to fall for a single indicator that leads us astray. For example, the focus on energy conservation and stable interior temperatures in the 1970s led to sealed buildings that now cost the country billions of dollars a year in lost productivity and ill health.

Considering the complexity of living organisms and living systems, it should come as no surprise that achieving balance is complex and challenging. We need to focus more on our goal of healthy, happy, and productive people in a vital and resilient ecosystem—rather than oversimplifying indicators of balance, whether it is the temperature in a room or total global carbon emissions. Ecological systems, communities, families, landscapes, and heartbeats all dance to complex, collective, and often chaotic rhythm ("chaotic" in the modern scientific sense of unpredictable variations within prescribed limits, not in the literal sense of fearful disorder).

Passive Design

The pursuit of human comfort illustrates the flaw of seeking stability in inherently dynamic systems. We evolved in environments that varied in temperature, humidity, light, and wind conditions. Our activity levels, clothing, state of mind, mood, and other factors can also change, either inadvertently or deliberately. The development that began about 1950 of mechanical systems for heating and cooling buildings with heavily subsidized fossil fuels led to building standards that reflected the goals of the manufacturers of this equipment to sell more equipment, rather than the goal of meeting human needs. The ideal temperature was considered to be 72°F (see figure 1.2), and mechanical-systems controls were designed with the idea of making the balance between cold and hot as constant as possible. The buildings in which these mechanical systems were applied were not efficient. They were not well insulated, had very little thermal mass, and were oriented to minimize street, utility, and construction costs rather than to respond to sun angles or wind patterns. Therefore, the air conditioner or furnace had to come on fairly often to bring things back to the "ideal." In reality, this type of temperature control is actually far from stable, as shown in figure 1.3.

Early attempts to provide natural conditioning of buildings with passive solar architecture ran up against the barrier of the static ideal enshrined in the building codes, which dictated that a building must be able to maintain a constant air temperature. The reality is of course far different, as any post-construction analysis will show, but this was ignored by codes and standards enforcement. The design of one of the first large passive solar buildings in California was blocked by interpretation of this static idea, despite the monitoring of existing buildings that showed air temperatures in offices in adjacent buildings were very unstable and often uncomfortable. In contrast, environmentally responsive passive solar buildings dance within prescribed limits of comfort, as shown in figure 1.4. The temperatures that dip outside the comfort zone can be eliminated by a very small backup mechanical system that is far less expensive in cost and energy use than that required to repeatedly adjust temperature as shown in figure 1.3.

Eventually, some regulators accepted the fact that temperature could be allowed to swing within a temperature band defined as the comfort zone, and passive solar buildings became more acceptable. A passive building is an integrated design approach that uses on-site energy sources and sinks to condition the interior by architectural rather than mechanical means. Experience around the world has demonstrated that we can provide most of the thermal conditioning needs of a majority of buildings with passive design.

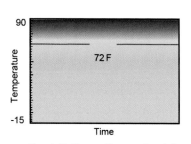

The static theory of temperature balance's "ideal."

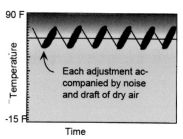

The reality for mechanical systems.

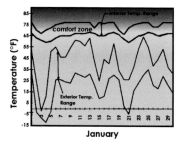

The predicted interior temps of an optimized passive solar residence without backup heat in Denver, Colorado

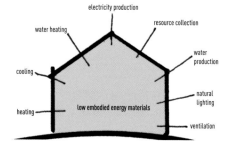

Passive design provides all the above functions via architectural form.

Figs. 1.2–1.5. *Passive design provides comfort without consuming nonrenewable resources in an effort to meet a flawed and unobtainable static ideal.*

Triple-Bottom-Line Accounting

The failure of the current worldwide economic system is in large part a failure of accounting.

How did we get here? Many of our most pressing problems are the result of a mind-set that emphasizes parts and the short term at the expense of the whole and the long term. This bias creates specialized concentration on single-purpose concerns, often with disastrous consequences. This mind-set also contributes to the perverse incentives and distorting effects we list here; addressing these will encourage sustainable building.

- Recent architectural approaches evolved within a narrow framework that ignored the integration of multiple parts to achieve a whole. For example, Beaux Arts architecture of the nineteenth century emphasized art and history, and the resultant buildings all too often became shallow copies of the past rather than a response to contemporary needs. In the twentieth century, modernism became preoccupied with the function of space and circulation, but ignored human comfort and health, energy, and environmental impacts. Modern architecture became as narrow and fragmented as Beaux Arts design and as unsustainable, often driven by abstract formulas and theories. The distorted view of architecture as sculpture has also contributed to the failure to embrace integrated, site-adapted designs that focus on health, comfort, and satisfaction. These may look good on paper or from a helicopter, but they can be untenable for occupants. The architect often plays the artist, and engineers are used to make the sculpture livable. The lighting engineer might be directed to design the lighting for minimal installed cost without considering possible use of daylighting (determined by the architect's window decisions) or the cost of cooling to offset lighting heat gain (a problem for the mechanical engineer). The architect would often design the building without consulting anyone about the implications for natural heating, cooling, or daylighting. User comfort, health, and productivity are rarely an issue, a concern thought to be handled in the codes. Prospective occupants are rarely surveyed, and post-construction analysis is not done.

Reimagining architecture as a complex team effort that integrates art and engineering from the start to meet human and environmental needs and embracing sustainability is critical and will result in a new green architecture as different from modern architecture as modernism was from Beaux Arts.

Like architecture, economics has also devolved into a highly fragmented endeavor where many complexities and costs can be ignored by exiling them to the public and environmental realm as "externalities." At the same time, obsolete subsidies from the past have become frozen through the dominance of lobbies and political contributions. The result is a rapidly crumbling economic edifice of flawed accounting, wasted resources, inefficiencies, obsolete subsidies, and the misplaced focus on financial manipulation and wasteful marketing. The effect of all of this on architecture and building is to further accentuate the disconnection between building impacts and costs described above.

- Given current financial pressures, a developer in the United States must often focus on minimal first cost without considering life-cycle costs, health, comfort, and productivity. Building owners usually pass all energy costs to leaseholders and feel little pressure to improve efficiency. Many large buildings are poorly operated and maintained. Building operation is not a highly valued or rewarding profession, and operators are often not treated well or given the resources they need to do their jobs well. Managers of flawed buildings often assume the energy demands are immutable and may reduce or fire maintenance staff to save money, further increasing life-cycle cost as poorly maintained mechanical systems add pollutants to indoor spaces and the moisture buildup and leaks lead to mold, rot, and increasing risk to health and productivity. The difference in building service life between the United States and Europe is related to differing economic incentives. Buildings in Europe have a lifetime that is typically double, but often four times as long as, that of a comparable building in the United States.

- Subsidized power and material costs are also important. The estimated subsidies ($45 billion per year) for nonrenewable fuels have biased the market against renewable energy sources. If energy costs reflected real costs, electricity would cost four times as much as it does today. The separation of users from production costs also has encouraged poor design and very wasteful operation.

■ Planning is still dominated by the post–World War II auto-based suburban model that ignores sustainability concerns despite the high and increasingly expensive infrastructural cost of building. This approach to planning can severely limit options for solar orientation, natural cooling, and meeting infrastructure needs on-site. Good planning requires an intimate understanding of the site, microclimate, airshed, watershed, and bioregion.

■ Incentives for minimal innovation are incorporated in percentage-based fees common for architects and engineers. These are often fixed percentages and encourage use of standard plans and details that are acceptable, but unoptimized. Liability fears common in our litigious society may cause engineers to oversize equipment to avoid lawsuits and callbacks, where a contractor has to come back to respond to complaints of inadequate heating, cooling, ventilation, or lighting. Although more challenging to put into practice, performance-based contracting fees related to savings over base-case conditions can drive design innovation.

■ Failure to follow up on building performance is also pervasive. Building commissioning provides a critical first step and is now required for LEED-rated buildings, but remains rare. Building commissioning provides training for the new occupants and managers and a management guidebook, just like commissioning a naval vessel. Building performance after completion is seldom monitored, although it is easy to do this now that inexpensive automated sensors and recorders are readily available. A recent review of rated LEED buildings showed that many were not meeting performance expectations, illustrating the importance of monitoring.

■ It's ironic that with our high level of education and massive use of information technology, ignorance of some very basic things is still so widespread in the design professions. Topics such as solar orientation and natural lighting are not complex or difficult, but our society's general level of abstraction and disassociation have taken these commonsense relationships out of use. It used to be rare for architecture students to visit or see a sustainable building or to work with sustainable building materials.

Many of these problems will be alleviated as we shift from a one-dimensional economic viewpoint with a flawed accounting system to a three-dimensional economic viewpoint with the more accurate accounting we are now capable of undertaking. This is possible owing to our greater ability to process, model, and evaluate information. This new way of factoring costs is called triple-bottom-line accounting, a concept developed by UK business consultant John Elkington in 1997. Triple-bottom-line economics differs from conventional accounting because it attempts to include ecological and cultural costs and benefits, as shown in figure 1.6. In a healthy society, these factors should not remain in opposition to one another, but should reinforce sustainable behavior, health, and happiness (Bainbridge, 2009*). The use of triple-bottom-line accounting in life-cycle design is most clearly articulated by William McDonough and Michael Braungart,* who developed the diagram shown in figure 1.6. This diagram, when shown as a fractal, expresses the complexity of the issues, the potential for integrated solutions, and the infinite diversity of response that humans are capable of making.

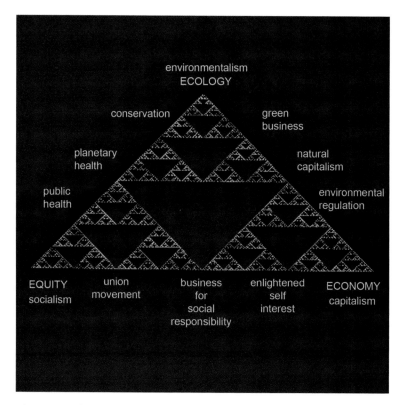

Fig. 1.6. *Triple-bottom-line accounting. The figure illustrates the complexity of the balancing act required to integrate ecology, economy, and social equity. Every little decision has implications for all three.*

Green Architecture

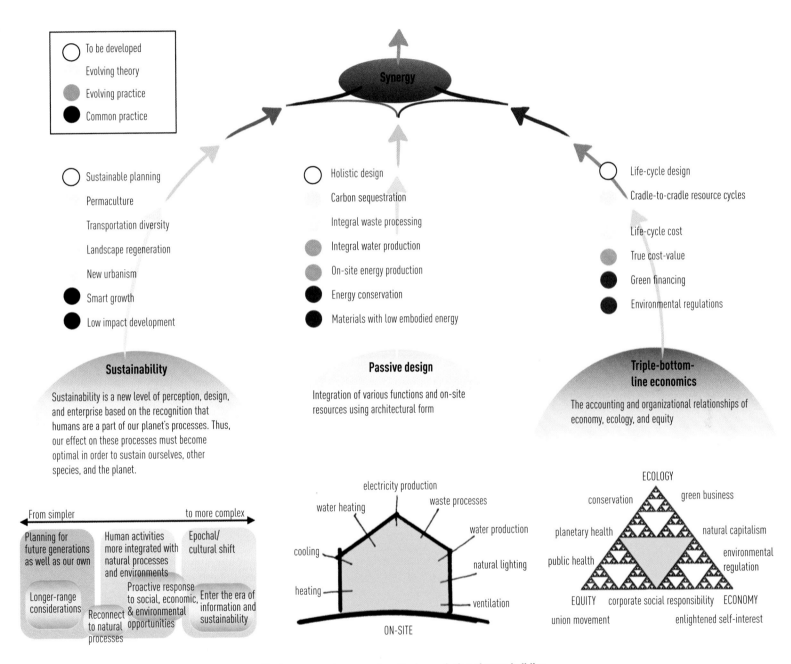

○	To be developed
	Evolving theory
⬤ (grey)	Evolving practice
⬤ (black)	Common practice

Synergy

○ Sustainable planning
Permaculture
Transportation diversity
Landscape regeneration
New urbanism
⬤ Smart growth
⬤ Low impact development

○ Holistic design
Carbon sequestration
Integral waste processing
⬤ Integral water production
⬤ On-site energy production
⬤ Energy conservation
⬤ Materials with low embodied energy

○ Life-cycle design
Cradle-to-cradle resource cycles
Life-cycle cost
⬤ True cost-value
⬤ Green financing
⬤ Environmental regulations

Sustainability

Sustainability is a new level of perception, design, and enterprise based on the recognition that humans are a part of our planet's processes. Thus, our effect on these processes must become optimal in order to sustain ourselves, other species, and the planet.

Passive design

Integration of various functions and on-site resources using architectural form

Triple-bottom-line economics

The accounting and organizational relationships of economy, ecology, and equity

From simpler → to more complex

Planning for future generations as well as our own	Human activities more integrated with natural processes and environments	Epochal/cultural shift
Longer-range considerations	Proactive response to social, economic, & environmental opportunities	Enter the era of information and sustainability
	Reconnect to natural processes	

electricity production
water heating
waste processes
water production
cooling
natural lighting
heating
ventilation
ON-SITE

ECOLOGY
conservation
green business
planetary health
natural capitalism
public health
environmental regulation
EQUITY
corporate social responsibility
ECONOMY
union movement
enlightened self-interest

Roots, common terms, and continuing evolution of green building

Fig. 1.7. *Green architecture. This diagram shows the roots, common terms, and continuing evolution of green building. The roots of the green building movement are sustainability, passive design, and triple-bottom-line accounting. This diagram shows the continuing evolution of concerns and techniques growing out of these roots and through synergetic design, becoming green architecture and sustainable building.*

To address the problems with architecture and building, triple-bottom-line accounting means that costing must be revised to include all life-cycle costs over the thirty-, fifty-, or one-hundred-plus years of service life for construction, operation, and maintenance. All health and environmental costs created by hazardous materials and pollution, from production to construction and on through disposal or reuse of building materials, must be included. It should also include pollution-related costs from energy and water use and the impact of other material flows for maintenance and operation. With creative design and true-cost accounting, we will find that some of these costs are negative—but some can be positive. Life-cycle costing can lead to life-cycle design where savings can be achieved by developing synergies. Synergy occurs when the advantages of the whole far exceed the advantages of the parts. This is why a sustainable society offers greater wealth, health, justice, comfort, and joy.

The adverse impacts of our current way of doing things can be evaluated by periodically examining the ecological footprint of our planet, nations, communities, families, buildings, and materials. Mathis Wackernagel* and William Rees developed the concept of an ecological footprint to demonstrate the impact of our way of living through the amount of land area it takes to maintain present industrial lifestyles. We can do this at a very simple level by calculating our ecological footprint online using an eco-footprint calculator (see, for example, www.myfootprint.org).

Cultural Shift

Our goal in building sustainable buildings must always be to improve the comfort, health, and security of people. To do this, we need to rethink our approach to design and operation of the built environment while maximizing use of renewable resources and minimizing life-cycle costs. Improving comfort and health yield the biggest dividends. Energy and water use, waste minimization and recycling, ecosystem protection, and first cost are also important. Integrating systems is critical to meet multiple needs and goals, maximize benefits, and minimize costs. Optimizing design at the earliest stages can often dramatically improve performance at little or no additional cost.

The first step is proper orientation for solar heating and natural cooling. If possible, insulation should be placed outside the thermal mass. The only exception is in hot, humid climates where light frame or open buildings with optimized ventilation are the key to human comfort. Traditional homes in hot, humid areas often were placed on stilts to get more wind for ventilation cooling, or they had very high ceilings and paddle fans to keep air moving and double roofs to keep solar heating to a minimum.

A review of passive buildings using performance simulations showed that annual energy use for heating and cooling dropped from 54,000 BTU to 900 BTU per square foot per year (98 percent) for a super-insulated roof pond (98 percent) in El Centro, California, and from 48,500 BTU to 4,800 BTU (90 percent) for a super-insulated solar building in Denver with appropriate thermal mass (see table 1.1).

Table 1.1. *Sustainable building performance, as measured by energy use for heating and cooling in BTU per square foot per year.*

		Nonsolar Stick-built	Solar Stick-built	Solar Straw bale (SB)	Percent reduction
Denver, CO **[5673HDD, 625CDD]**	Cooling BTU	7,450	2,686	1,816	76
	Heating BTU	41,075	13,474	3,016	93
	Heating and cooling	48,525	16,160	4,832	90
			Sb int* adobe	Roof pond	
El Centro, CA **[4370CDD, 1010HDD]**	Cooling BTU	49,898	11,387	553	99
	Heating BTU	3,904	0	351	91
	Heating and cooling	53,802	11,387	904	189

Calculations by J. Rennick and SLSG
*Straw bale with adobe interior for mass

A building with just good insulation and sufficient thermal mass usually achieves a 50 to 70 percent energy savings, but with good orientation and window placement, it can reach 80 to 90 percent.

The choice of materials also matters. They should be, insofar as possible, local, natural, and renewable. As Arne Naess* notes, "The degree of self-reliance for individuals and local communities diminishes in proportion to the extent a technique or technology transcends the abilities and resources of the particular individuals or local communities. Passivity, helplessness and dependence upon 'megasociety' and the world market increase." Self-reliance is critical, as the building challenge is not simply for the developed countries—although their use of resources is disproportionately large—but must also include the billions of people who remain in poverty.

Application of sustainable design principles can improve the lives of people in Geneva, London, Cape Town, Sydney, Los Angeles, and Lima, as well as the favelas and slums of the world's growing megacities. The oldest occupied communities in the United States, the pueblos of New Mexico, reflect the importance of local, sustainable, and understandable materials. Building systems that employ locally available, safe, and easy-to-use materials such as straw bales and earth deserve special recognition because everyone in the community, including kids, can participate in construction. Community building through straw bale building workshops has created added benefits for this very efficient, sustainable building material (figure 1.8).

Fig. 1.8. *To construct a small straw bale cottage in San Diego County, many people help a family create a new living space, while learning the techniques for building with straw bales and becoming part of a burgeoning sustainable building community.*

There are many benefits to changing our cultural attitudes to planning and building, but to start, we would emphasize three key concerns: health, security, and economy.

Sustainable buildings are healthier: Fewer sick days, reduced allergies and irritations, fewer doctor visits, reduced medical expenditures, and better sleep—all these add value. Comfort adds quality to life, and comfort and health add to productivity gains in the office or factory. As Ken found in surveys for a state office building design, people are aware of the problems and flaws in buildings. Many related how they hated their current space and were trying to transfer to different units where offices had more daylight and better ventilation.

More sustainable buildings also provide security and freedom from fear. Even if the power goes out in an ice storm, earthquake, hurricane, political dispute, or power-grid failure, homes will remain comfortable and livable. Commercial and industrial buildings remain inhabitable even when the power goes off, and workers can wrap up their work rather than groping their way through a dark and unpleasant building to get to safety outside.

The most important reason for change is for long-term prosperity. Better design can save money now and as long as the building is used. Money can be spent on more productive activities rather than simply going to the utility company. As the California blackouts of 2001 showed, we can't count on nonrenewable energy resources. They will be more expensive in the future—perhaps much more expensive.

Energy costs for operating a sustainable building are low, and will remain low. This can be critical for retired people and institutions and is important for families and most businesses. Heating and cooling costs can be kept below $50 per month, in contrast with the rapidly rising utility bills many people experience today.

Sustainable buildings increase the quality of life. They improve health, speed learning (schools), increase sales (retail), improve patient outcomes (hospitals), and improve productivity (manufacturing and services). In commercial buildings, the return on investment for improvements on air quality alone has been estimated to be 60:1. In central California, the revised design of a tract home led to reduced construction costs and a seasonal energy savings for heating and cooling of 70 percent. Rather than "freezing in the dark," as the fossil-fool-funded opponents of renewable energy have argued, occupants and workers in sustainable buildings will be dancing in the sunlight!

ONE SUSTAINABLE BUILDINGS

It is sometimes helpful to go back and look at what was done before mechanical systems and energy consumption ruled the building comfort universe. Today you make the HVAC system whatever size is needed and buy the amount of energy required. The problem is today soon becomes tomorrow. Energy availability and cost will change. I am betting that some of these old lessons will become the basis for tomorrow's buildings.

—JOSEPH LSTIBUREK, 2008

The physics of comfort and building performance are relatively straightforward. Unfortunately, most designers and builders have ignored these principles in recent years and simply added fossil-fueled space-conditioning systems to force bad buildings to provide reasonably tolerable conditions. We can do much better when we work with the sun and on-site climatic resources. To do that we need to start by understanding and reconsidering some basic assumptions. The first of these is the elementary relationship among energy production, use, and efficiency.

Energy Production, Use, and Efficiency

Our society has so isolated production and use that very few people think about the impacts of their use of energy. We flip the light switch without considering the long chain of responsibility that leads back to the power plant, open-pit mine, and ravaged countryside. While we've become more efficient on the production side,

we've become extremely wasteful on the use side. Just look around and notice all the high-quality energy being wasted by the massive use of electric lighting during the day inside buildings and often outside as well. We are not only lighting a majority of the earth at night, we are attempting to do the same during the day.

Passive design at this most basic level is the reuniting of these three: production, use, and efficiency at the scale of the building site. A *passive building* is defined as a building that:

1. Uses on-site energy sinks and sources.

2. Relies on natural energy flows with a minimum of moving parts.

3. Includes energy production as an integral part of the building design.

When we fail to consider the implications of our actions, we often do harm to others or the planet. Sometimes the simplest, most basic relationships become confused as we deal with complex social concerns such as energy regulations. For example, California's

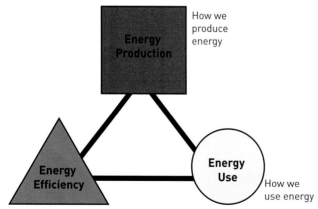

Fig. 1.9. *Energy production and energy use must both operate with a minimum of waste to achieve efficiency.*

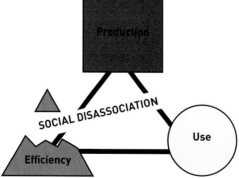

Fig. 1.10. *Social disassociation between production and use. Most people have no idea where the energy they use comes from or how low the efficiency of use is.*

Fig. 1.11. *Passive design integration. In passive design use, production and efficiency are integrated on-site.*

well-regarded Title 24 building energy regulations have emphasized efficiency to the neglect of on-site production produced by passive means. Hence this code, the strongest in the nation, has not given credit for the most basic passive strategies such as thermal mass or night ventilation cooling. Likewise, the national LEED green building rating system with its linear checklist has an unintended bias against highly integrated passive design. Using linear analysis to evaluate a connected synergetic product will not work. Fortunately, both of these programs are evolving over time and will eventually be corrected to allow the basic relationships among production, use, and efficiency to be more accurately evaluated.

Building Metabolism

The scale of our buildings and artifacts on the earth have now gotten so large that we must now think of them more like living organisms that are part of ecological systems if we are to be a healthy part of the planet and not some self destructive parasite.

—IAN MCHARG

On a particular site, energy sources and sinks suggest how much energy is available for use in a building. It may seem that once the building's use is determined, it should be relatively easy to determine the energy needed—the building's load. In fact, however,

determining load is one of the more challenging aspects of natural space conditioning. Loads are a product of the relationships of the building's scale, metabolism, form, and human behavior. This is a complex problem because the relationship of these factors is not linear. To understand this complexity, consider the thermal loads of two different animals, a hummingbird and an elephant (see figure 1.13).

Animals, like buildings, need to maintain a relatively constant temperature. Heat to maintain this temperature is provided by the animal's metabolism, and heat loss occurs mostly through the animal's skin. Heat loss is therefore related to the skin's surface area. A hummingbird is a very small animal, and the ratio of skin area to the volume of its body is very large. The hummingbird loses heat rapidly and must have a high corresponding metabolism to maintain a high enough interior temperature. Hummingbirds feed on the nectar of flowers, one of the most concentrated foods available in the natural world, and must eat often. In contrast, elephants, though vastly larger, have a low skin-area-to-volume ratio, with correspondingly lower heat loss. Thus, elephants can survive with less frequent meals of low-energy food like plant leaves.

Buildings act the same way. There are buildings like the hummingbird, with a large skin-to-volume ratio. These are called skin-dominated buildings, that is, buildings in which the building envelope dominates the thermal loads. Corresponding to the elephant are the interior-load-dominated buildings, which are large

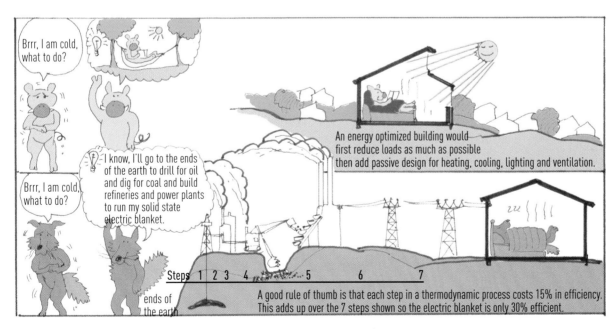

Fig. 1.12. *Systems considerations and impacts must be considered.*

enough for the internal loads to dominate their thermal character. Knowing these rather simple relationships destroys one of the myths of passive heating: that it is easier to heat small buildings than large buildings. Actually, in most temperate zones, the reverse is true. Heating larger buildings is usually easier because they produce much more internal heat, and their skin-to-volume ratio is small. Thus, if properly designed, they can often heat themselves largely by their own internal metabolism—*metabolism* being defined as heat generated inside the building by lighting, equipment, and people. Cooling, however, presents another set of challenges for large buildings.

In most temperate zones, heating, cooling, or combinations of the two are the limiting design factors for skin-dominated buildings. In interior-load-dominated buildings, heating is generally easier to accomplish than cooling, particularly if artificial lighting is not overused. Artificial lighting produces a great deal of heat, which is added to the cooling load. In many large, thick industrial-era buildings, lack of natural lighting is usually the limiting condition.

The recent bias has generally been toward interior-load-dominated buildings because they lend themselves to a single goal—maximum rental area for the lowest first cost. However, from an aesthetic, social, health, productivity, and environmental viewpoint, the typical interior-load-dominated building of the industrial era is disastrous. Skin-dominated buildings are usually more appropriate in temperate zones, because balanced natural heating, cooling, and lighting are easier to achieve within these buildings.

In addition, social relationships are better when users feel less cut off from the exterior environment. They are also easier to daylight, and studies have shown they are healthier and more productive. The perceived density advantages of big, interior-load-dominated buildings are illusions, except to the building developer.

Energy-Efficient Building

Integration of many factors is the essential character of sustainable buildings. A passive sustainable building is one that is efficient enough to use the energy available from the sun and microclimate of the site to meet its needs. A sustainable building integrates production, use, and efficiency at the building site. Keeping integration in mind, this section deals with energy efficiency, an aspect of building, design, and construction that is a necessary prerequisite for a successful passive building. However, energy efficiency in itself does not create a passive building. The key is on-site energy production. This distinction is very important to avoid the confusion that exists with our present regulatory and evaluation structures, which recognize energy efficiency but do not consider energy capture or production at the building scale.

An efficient building must minimize heat loss or gain depending upon the season and its internal metabolism. Achieving this involves siting and orientation, which both affect solar use and control and air movement and control. It also requires energy-efficient construction with careful weatherization and appropriate construction materials.

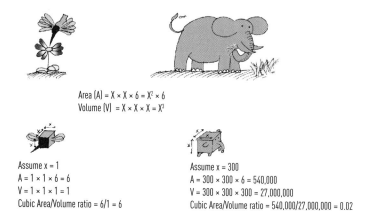

Fig. 1.13. *Thermal loads related to form: skin-dominated animal versus load-dominated animal.*

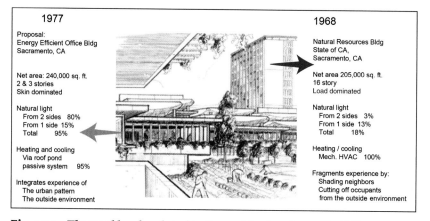

Fig. 1.14. *Thermal loads related to form: skin-dominated building versus load-dominated building.*

Siting and Orientation: The Best Orientation? Face the Equator!

Many designers find it uncomfortable to acknowledge the importance of facing the equator (south for the Northern Hemisphere, north for the Southern Hemisphere). This is because they feel this is an affront to their creativity. However, we would argue that this is an immutable cosmic relationship with multiple advantages. Failure to use these advantages is not an act of design freedom but a failure of the designer's creativity and unwillingness to acknowledge the implications of his or her choices on the planet and future generations. Creative design can resolve design problems even for odd-shaped sites with important views in other directions or with other site limitations without giving up important advantages of good orientation.

There are three reasons for this cardinal rule:

1. If you wish to utilize solar radiation for heating or daylighting, facing the equator gives the best solar access. Horizontal sun from the east in the morning and the west in the evening is not very effective except for producing uncomfortable glare and summer overheating.

2. Conversely, if you wish to control solar radiation in the summer or fall, the same orientation is optimal because the sun is high in the summer and low in the winter and can therefore be easily controlled with simple horizontal overhangs that still allow the sun in during the winter.

3. If your site is in the tropics, the sun from the equatorial direction is very high year-round—and the climate is likely to be hot year-round as well. Therefore solar control is the main concern, and it's still most easily done with horizontal overhangs on the side facing the equator.

Sun from the east and west is very difficult to control owing to its lower angles, which cannot be blocked by simple overhangs. The control of east or west sun is better accomplished through vertical fins, wing walls, louvered screens, or landscaping.

In this section, we concentrate on energy efficiency, but remember that orientation principles are important for energy production in passive solar buildings, for heating, daylighting, or electrical production.

Making optimum orientation a part of the design process is not difficult, but there are some basic things to consider. These are shown in detail on page 26.

Winter

Summer

Fig. 1.15. *This south-facing building in the Northern Hemisphere collects solar radiation in the cold winter and yet is fully shaded on a hot summer day. Low horizontal sunlight in the morning and late afternoon is intercepted by wing walls below and vertical fins on the south-facing dormer.*

Insulation

The second step in building or remodeling for energy efficiency is reducing unwanted conductive heat loss (or gain). Insulation is the key—not only for the walls and ceiling, but also for the foundation or slab perimeter, windows, doors, and the people inside. Most homes are woefully under-insulated. Typical wall-insulation levels are still R-13 to R-19 in many areas of the country, but they should be at minimum R-30, and R-50+ is much better. Straw bale buildings can offer R-40 walls at about the same cost as conventional buildings with R-19. Double-wall systems with cellulose insulation can also reach R-40 easily. Foam sheathing inside, outside, or both in- and outside of a wood-framed wall can also reach adequate levels of insulation, but sustainability and moisture questions remain. Insulation on massive walls of stone, concrete, brick, or earth should always be on the outside.

Ceiling or roof insulation is relatively easy to install and should generally be R-50+ in most temperate areas. Installation detailing is critical to avoid fire risks, properly ventilate attics and roof spaces, and ensure adequate weatherization.

Scrimping on insulation is penny-wise and pound-foolish because insulation is the least expensive component of standard construction. Adding more later is much more costly. The expensive part of upping insulation levels is not the insulation itself but creating the added cavity space required. It is also usually desirable to provide a small but vented airspace above high levels of insulation in ceilings to avoid moisture buildup that can lead to mold problems. This is advisable even in relatively dry climates where this traditionally is not done with lower levels of insulation. The greater the amount of insulation, the greater the potential will be for condensation on its upper surface: Condensation occurs on the coldest surface.

Double-pane windows are commonly used, and high-performance windows or double-pane plus storm windows are usually cost-effective. Doubled single-pane windows might be the lowest-cost long-life window system in some parts of the world. Argon-filled high-performance windows are worth considering, as are the transparent insulating materials that can reach R-20, but these can be hard to obtain and costly in many areas.

Insulated drapes, blinds, and shutters are very effective on windows and skylights if they are well sealed. Interior shutters may cause overheating and failure of plastic skylight glazing or double-pane window seals. Exterior insulated blinds and shutters are preferred but more challenging to find (except in Europe) and more costly to build.

Weatherization

Infiltration losses are as important as conductive losses, and careful weatherizing is necessary. This includes both the obvious problems of weatherstripping doors and windows and also the more general problems of caulking and sealing building joints, access holes, and other areas where unwanted infiltration occurs. Infiltration may easily account for half of the heat loss in a well-insulated but poorly weatherized house. The infiltration rate on a typical house may be 1.5 air changes per hour, but can go significantly higher if the wind is blowing. With careful attention to detail the air exchange can be reduced to 0.2 changes/hour.

This low rate of air exchange can be unhealthy, especially if materials and operations inside the building include semi-toxic materials (deodorants, cleaning materials, smoking, off-gassing furniture and carpet, fixtures, decorations, air fresheners, and so on). The goal is to have controlled ventilation so the air comes in when and where you want it and is fresh and healthy. A super-insulated solar house will perform so well, it is often possible to have several windows slightly open almost all winter. In Europe, small trickle vents are being installed for fresh air. In very cold areas, an air-to-air heat exchanger is desirable for ventilation during the coldest periods. The heat exchanger warms the incoming fresh air with warm stale outgoing air. The low cost and efficiency (up to 90 percent) of this type of heat exchanger, coupled with very good insulation and a very tight building, allows a level of efficiency so high that residences in the difficult winter climates of Northern Europe can be heated by internal heat and solar gain.

Well-insulated, high-thermal-mass buildings were pioneered by Emslie Morgan, who designed the St. George's School in Wallasey, England, in 1961. This building was heated for many years with only south-facing windows and energy from the students. In the 1980s with the advent of inexpensive air-to-air heat exchangers, super-insulated and super-weatherized buildings were built in Alaska, Canada, the continental United States, and Denmark. The rapidly growing *Passivhaus* movement in Germany and Northern Europe has demonstrated that super-insulated, super-weatherized buildings with heat-exchange ventilation can reduce heating costs 80 to 90 percent and cost only 5 to 7 percent more to build than standard residences. More than twenty thousand have been built in Northern Europe to date.

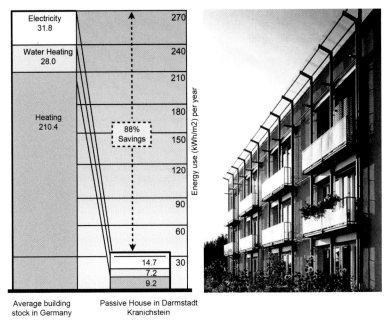

Electricity 31.8	270
Water Heating 28.0	240
	210
Heating 210.4	180
88% Savings	150
	120
	90
	60
14.7	30
7.2	
9.2	

Energy use (kWh/m2) per year

Average building stock in Germany   Passive House in Darmstadt Kranichstein

Fig. 1.16. *The exterior and the performance of a solar-oriented, super-insulated, super-weatherized passive house in Darmstadt, Germany.*

Energy-Efficient Materials

Most conventional building materials come with a very high life-cycle energy cost. Most are damaging to the environment, require the use of dangerous ingredients as well as massive amounts of energy and water, and have only a limited lifetime. But it doesn't have to be this way if we consider buildings, materials, and construction in the context of energy and resource efficiency and on-site energy production. We need to understand three aspects of materials: their thermal characteristics, the embodied resources they contain, and their relation to the carbon cycle.

Thermal Characteristics of Building Materials

The most important thermal characteristics are insulation and thermal mass. These two are often confused, but the differences are critical to understanding energy flows in buildings. Insulation is the ability to resist heat flow. This is accomplished by providing trapped airspaces that reduce convection or reflective foils that slow radiation transfers across dead airspaces. Insulation effectiveness is measured in R-value, with the *R* standing for "resistance to heat flow." Materials with high R-values are necessary for buildings to retain heat when the exterior temperature is cold or to retain "coolth" when the exterior temperature is hot.

Thermal mass provides the ability to store heat or coolth so that the interior temperature swings of the building are dampened. The measurement of a building's response to both thermal mass and insulation is measured by a building's time constant in hours. The time constant is the characteristic time it takes for the inside of a building to approach ambient conditions. The time constant of an uninsulated wood-framed house with gypsum wallboard is about half an hour, a passive building twelve hours, and a better passive building twenty-four hours; a totally optimized passive building might reach a time constant of eighty hours.

For skin-dominated buildings in temperate climates, both insulation and thermal mass are needed. One without the other will not produce an optimized building. Generally speaking, the building envelope should be well insulated, and interior surfaces and elements should have thermal mass. The trend for energy-efficient buildings has been to develop composite wall systems that have highly insulated exterior surfaces, and interior surfaces that provide thermal mass.

This is the opposite of traditional construction with heavy exterior walls, limited insulation often on the inside, and very lightweight interior walls.

Embodied Resources of Materials

Building materials not only influence the energy requirements of a building but also require energy and resources for their creation, shipping, and application. The energy costs of collection, processing, and transportation are called the embodied energy of a material, and can be determined by accounting for the energy requirements in sourcing, transporting, processing, distributing, using, maintaining, and eventually recycling the material. Materials such as aluminum and Portland cement have high embodied energy as a result of the considerable energy used in their production, while others like gypsum and earthen materials have low embodied energy.

In addition to embodied energy, building materials also require other resources and create other problems such as deforestation and air and water pollution. These factors are all considered in the Wuppertal Institute's studies of the material intensity of the German economy (Schmidt-Bleek, 2000*). In Germany, buildings and dwellings accounted for 25 to 30 percent of the material flow of the economy. We don't have this information for much of the US economy, but the figure is probably larger.

Fig. 1.17. *Burning rice fields aggravates asthma for local residents, increases health care costs, and generates greenhouse gases. A waste of an excellent building material.*

Dealing with true costs as discussed above requires a careful accounting for all the embodied costs of materials and is an important part of what's called the life-cycle assessment of a building. There are two ways to look at life cycles. One is cradle-to-grave life cycle, in which we look at all the costs of materials through one complete cycle of use to disposal. The second is cradle-to-cradle resource cycles through several uses (McDonough and Braungart,

2002*). We design the building material to optimize the whole by adding value to cost, including value for the next cycles of use and/or supplementary values in the process of manufacture. This approach is referred to as life-cycle design and is an important part of the transformation of our industrial waste-based economy to a sustainable one. This more integrated approach can often find new uses for what are currently considered wastes. Rice straw is a good example of a waste that can be used to build high-performance passive solar buildings.

Carbon Sequestration

The climate crisis is upon us, caused by our profligate use of fossil fuels for more than 150 years. Our unfortunate delay in addressing this massive threat now forces us to respond with far-reaching efforts to avoid a catastrophe affecting everyone on the planet. There have been proposals for removing carbon dioxide from the atmosphere by scrubbing it from coal plants and burying it deep underground in geological formations that have been emptied by oil production, or by building gigantic scrubbing antennas into the sky, or by seeding large parts of the ocean with iron powder to produce plankton blooms that will take up carbon dioxide. The risk and expense of such schemes indicate the difficulty in which we find ourselves, but also reflect the reductionist industrial-era mind-set that perceives separate operations as a solution to an integrated systems problem.

It makes more sense to include the sequestration of carbon as a part of an existing human activity—building. To quote an old Chinese saying, "Why not ride the horse in the direction it is going?" We could start sequestering carbon at a rate far exceeding these expensive schemes to isolate or hide carbon at far less cost by making it an integral part of our building activity. Straw has a very low embodied energy cost and high carbon content, is presently considered a waste material, and is most commonly disposed of by field burning. By using straw in buildings, we improve building performance and reduce greenhouse gas emissions, reduce emissions from field burning (figure 1.17), and reduce methane emissions from rice straw decomposition in wet fields. This is a perfect example of a sustainable life-cycle design solution. By changing building design, we will have added a new value to construction addressing the climate problem while simultaneously creating less expensive, healthier buildings and reducing the pollution impacts of the field burning of straw.

Traditional Materials

The concern for sustainable buildings is changing the way we select and specify building materials and increasing the variety of available materials. The development of new, more sustainable materials is also proceeding rapidly. The desirability of traditional industrial materials such as steel, concrete, glass, milled lumber, gypsum board, and ceramics is being reevaluated. Steel has fared pretty well because much of it is recycled. Concrete has become less desirable because producing cement adds a large amount of CO_2 to the atmosphere (up to 15 percent of human-made greenhouse gases). The appropriate use of wood depends upon how it is grown and harvested, and certified wood should be considered. Aluminum is frowned upon because of its high embodied energy, but it is easily recycled. Vinyl and PVC plastics are avoided because of the toxic by-products emitted during their creation and when they burn in fires, and difficulties involved in reusing and recycling them. Gypsum wallboard has a bad reputation because it can become moldy

Fig. 1.18. *Rammed earth is well suited for passive solar buildings. This passive solar house was built in Greeley, Colorado, in 1950. The top image shows the construction phase. Designed by solar pioneer J. Palmer Boggs and built by Lydia and David Miller.*

if damp, but it has low embodied energy. Although it is relatively lightweight, it's cheap enough to allow adding additional layers for greater thermal mass when needed. Wallboard with phase-change materials incorporated may offer the benefit of much-improved thermal storage. Straw board can be an excellent material for interior walls, but is not readily available in most of the world.

Traditional pre-industrial materials are being reconsidered because they have very low embodied energy and resources and high thermal-mass capabilities. These include the following materials.

- **Rammed earth:** Soil is the building material in rammed earth construction (see figure 1.18). Selected soils are moistened, placed in forms, and rammed to a high density and strength. This method of construction has been used for thousands of years. Parts of the Great Wall of China are rammed earth. The technique can be used for multistory buildings if done carefully. In modern times, rammed earth systems have been refined in France (called *pisé*) and other parts of Europe, where thousands of such buildings are found. The Miller passive solar house in Denver made good use of rammed earth in 1950. More recently, innovative builders like David Easton in California have developed methods of spraying on the dirt at high pressure to speed construction, but rammed earth walls can also be built with simple hand tools. The result is high-mass buildings with thick, dense walls 12 to 24 inches thick that are quiet and durable, with a beautiful finished surface.

- **Adobe:** The tradition of building with dried mud blocks, called adobe, also goes back thousands of years. Adobe walls are often very thick for larger buildings (between 36 and 72 inches) and between 14 and 24 inches for residential-scale buildings. Builders in Yemen reach up to ten stories with straw-reinforced

Fig. 1.19. *Adobe building in San Luis Obispo by Roger Marshall.*

adobe blocks. Adobe blocks have also been used to build domes and arched structures in many areas. There are perhaps seventy-five thousand adobe homes in New Mexico, a relatively stable seismic zone. There are millions of adobe buildings in China, the Mideast, and Africa that, unfortunately, are not so seismically safe. Although techniques for seismic reinforcement have been developed, they are not widely used outside the United States. Thermal performance of adobe can be improved by adding more straw. The cost of building with adobe is high in the United States because it is so labor-intensive—often double the cost of a comparable straw bale wall.

- **Straw bale:** Building with straw bales has been a marvelous success, far beyond what we imagined at the first straw bale building workshop in Elgin, Arizona, in 1989. The straw bale revival began after historic buildings from the early 1900s were rediscovered in the Great Plains. Straw bale buildings are surprisingly fire resistant once plastered, provide superior insulation (R-30 to R-45+), provide distributed thermal mass with their thick interior plaster skin, and create living spaces that are quiet and economical. In addition, straw bale buildings sequester carbon and are fairly easy to make earthquake-resistant. For these reasons, thousands have been built recently both at commercial and residential scales around the world. Natural plasters of mud and clay mixed with straw can be used in many circumstances for the finish surfaces on the bales, particularly on interior walls.

In the enthusiasm of rediscovery, there has been some misuse of these traditional materials. Keep the basic requirement for energy-efficient buildings in mind. Rammed earth and adobe have wonderful thermal mass but provide very little insulation, so in climates with wide external temperature variation they need to be insulated on the exterior. The most common method for doing this is to add a layer of polystyrene foam at the exterior surface just behind the weather skin.

Rammed earth and adobe walls are most effective thermally when used as interior walls within a well-insulated shell where their thermal mass is best utilized. From an energy- and resource-efficiency viewpoint, the optimum use of these materials is to have exterior walls of straw bale construction and interior walls of adobe or rammed earth. This has been validated by computer simulation studies of this arrangement for a variety of climates across the United States (Haggard et al., 2005*).

Fig. 1.20. *Straw bale construction before adding interior plaster.*

Fig. 1.21. *California's first permitted straw bale building, Owens Valley, 1992.*

New Materials

Along with the rediscovery of traditional materials has come the development of a host of new materials for sustainable building. Nanotechnology has allowed the manufacture of microscopic containers of paraffin at the scale of the finest grade of sand. When paraffin melts or solidifies, the phase change enables large amounts of energy to be stored or released. These nanoparticles can be also added to concrete or plaster to create high-thermal-mass components that don't weigh very much. This material can also be added to gypsum so that lowly gypsum board can now become very inexpensive effective-thermal-mass interior material. Long-term studies of the health and ecological risks of nanoparticles have still not been done, but the hope is that they will prove safe.

The creation of new types of transparent insulation systems (see figure 1.22) that allow solar gain (insolation) and yet provide good insulation with the same material are also noteworthy. Advances in the development of new glazings allow for either heat-rejecting glass or heat-receiving glass. Glazing with greater insulation value than ever before still retains visual characteristics needed for natural lighting. Aerogels allow very high insulation values yet still allow solar energy to pass through. There is also glazing that can change opacity with temperature, creating an automatic response to thermal conditions. Increasingly, there are photovoltaic materials that are also building components, and some can be custom-designed to produce different degrees of transparency while still producing electricity. Advances in waterproofing materials and techniques now allow the incorporation of landscape as a direct part of the building for green roofs, although detailing remains critical to avoid costly, bothersome leaks. Finally, with improvements in plastics we have the opportunity to more economically add water for desired thermal mass in tubes, tanks, or other containers. Beautiful tiles and ceramics can be created from a host of recycled material like crushed glass or various scrap.

As more appropriate technologies develop and we evolve a sustainable design culture, a range of materials, both old and new, will make the narrow vocabulary of the late industrial period look mundane and boring.

Fig. 1.23. *Photovoltaic trellis, green roof, and natural lighting on the California Academy of Science, San Francisco.*

Fig. 1.22. *Transparent insulation.*

Fig. 1.24. *Thin tiles containing nanoscale capsules of phase-change paraffin provide lightweight thermal mass while acting as a light-diffusing element for a library.*

Fig. 1.25. *Glazing capable of changing from clear to opaque, controlled by electric current.*

Scales of Place

With the first mission to the moon, we were able to see the earth in a new way for the first time. Today we can see the surface in remarkable detail by simply pulling up Google Earth on our computers. We have a fully integrated worldwide economy for the first time. We are for the first time just starting to realize we are changing the world's climate in ways that are likely to be very costly.

To develop more sustainable designs, we need to start with this perspective of spaceship earth. We begin by considering our place in the biosphere and working down through smaller and smaller systems until we reach the site. Integrated understanding of the relationships among these inter-nested systems is our goal and a key element in creating sustainable designs. Terms of reference:

Biosphere: The realm of life on earth. From the upper atmosphere to deep in the ocean and inside the earth's surface, life exists and thrives in an area larger than previously thought.

Biomes: The major types of natural environments. Each biome consists of similar climatic, geological, and ecological characteristics that are considered unique. UNESCO's Biosphere Reserve Program lists fourteen terrestrial biomes; the Köppen system of world climates lists seventeen.

Bioregions: Biomes further differentiated by topography, hydrology, smaller climate variation, or other factors are called bioregions.

Watersheds: The area drained by a particular drainage system is called a watershed. Large watersheds contain progressively smaller watersheds. Water is such a critical element for life that watersheds should be a very important design consideration.

Airsheds: An area determined by topography and wind patterns, much like a watershed. Humidity, temperature, pollen, and pollution flow and concentration are all affected by airshed characteristics.

Ecosystem: This is a much more specific area describing particular flora and fauna of a biome or bioregion.

Ecotone: The overlapping area where ecological communities meet is called the ecotone. Ecotones are important because they are usually biologically richer than a single ecological community, due to the edge effect.

Landscape: The visual surroundings as perceived by a viewer. In this context, it refers to the perceptual whole rather than just vegetation, and includes the effects of human activity.

Settlement pattern: Human settlement patterns have been more diverse than the industrial standards of a city, suburb, and country. Thus, the use of the term is more generic.

Settlement: A particular part of the general settlement pattern, usually politically or spatially defined.

Complex: A group of buildings, open space, and infrastructure creating a recognizable unit.

Architecture: Buildings and their adjacent spaces.

Artifacts: Human-made objects.

Materials: That which a place or object is constructed from.

Compounds: Building blocks of materials.

Elements: Building blocks of compounds. Compounds and elements can be in solid, liquid, or gaseous forms and can thus flow back into larger entities. If done in a nondesigned, careless way, this can be in the form of waste or pollution. If done in an optimized design, they can take the form of a useful resource.

Biomimicry: A growing field of research that will play an increasing role in sustainable building design and construction; nature is seen as model, measure, and mentor.

Global industrialization has tended to homogenize place. One of the main tenets of modern architecture was that the same design could happen anywhere, which is why it's sometimes called "international architecture." To reconnect to place, we need to start with the recognition of the differences in place. We can begin by understanding biomes. A biome is an ecological community of plants and animals extending over a large natural area. As can be seen in figure 1.27, different biomes are largely the result of temperatures and rainfall, although topography and geology can play a role as well. To design sustainable architecture, we need to have an intimate feeling for the biome in which we are designing.

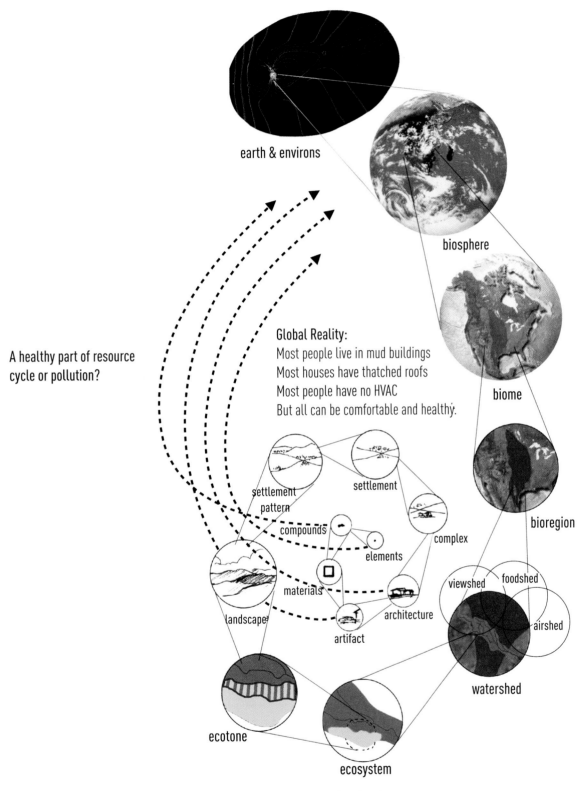

earth & environs

biosphere

biome

bioregion

A healthy part of resource
cycle or pollution?

Global Reality:
Most people live in mud buildings
Most houses have thatched roofs
Most people have no HVAC
But all can be comfortable and healthy.

settlement
pattern

settlement

compounds

complex

elements

materials

viewshed   foodshed

landscape

architecture

airshed

artifact

watershed

ecotone

ecosystem

Fig. 1.26 *The progression from the micro to macro level of site development*

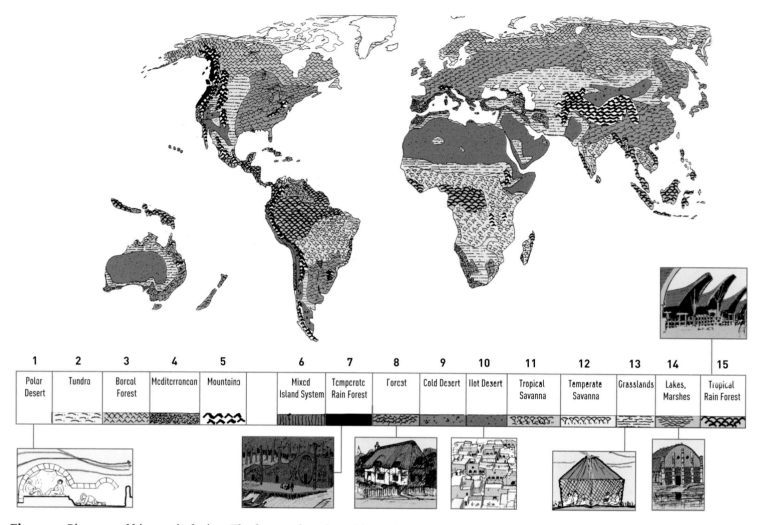

Fig. 1.27. *Biomes and biometric design. The factors that shape biomes help determine building response to environment.*

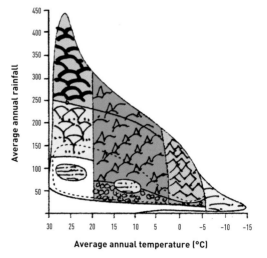

Fig. 1.28. *Rainfall and temperature are the main variables in defining a biome.*

Bio-Climatic Design

By comparing the indigenous architecture of similar biomes in different parts of the world, we can discover the traditional response to climate and place that are often remarkably alike despite different cultural traditions. Understanding our particular biome will help reveal natural resources that are available for green design. Straw bale construction was invented in the North American temperate grassland biome where trees are scarce and sandy soils formed weak turf and where native people created efficient buildings with native prairie grasses.

Bioregions

Within most biomes are smaller bioregions where place is further differentiated by topography, hydrology, microclimatic variation, and other factors. Bioregions usually contain a series of inter-nested watersheds and variations of plant communities caused by slope, soil variations, and human activities. The boundaries between these are called ecotones, which are generally biologically richer than the adjacent plant communities owing to edge effects where the two communities are interlaced.

The microclimate interacts with the region's geological foundation to shape the soils and vegetation that create the local bioregion. The bioregion may play a key role in siting, design, and construction. If the bioregion resources include rice, oat, or wheat straw, then a straw bale building may be more appropriate than a wood-framed or "stick-built" home. If adobe soils are common, and climates are warm in winter and cool in summer, then an adobe or rammed earth building may be a better choice.

If local streams run year-round, a microhydro generator may make more sense than a photovoltaic system. If it is windy, a wind turbine may make more sense. The bioregion will also influence water-use decisions, food production choices, and landscaping. The better the fit to the bioregion, the more sustainable the building will be.

This is the scale where human settlement patterns and community infrastructure start to become a factor. Transportation corridors, water systems, power plants, transmission lines, and waste disposal are common examples of community infrastructure. Up until recently, the cost of all these was relatively well hidden by subsidies at the federal and state level. However, with soaring costs of energy, scarcities of resources, impacts from climate change, and collapsing government budgets, these costs have not only increased dramatically but become more visible. At the same time, the adverse impact and disruption to various bioregions have become more dramatic and visible. Infrastructure costs are not trivial and are often greater than the construction costs of many projects they serve. All these factors are behind the increasing resistance of local communities to physical growth. Development has been destructive, but can be reshaped to restore ecosystems and communities, as shown in figure 1.29.

Green design (as defined on page 7) has the capability to dramatically reduce infrastructure costs by producing most of the energy needed on-site through passive design, conserving and producing water on-site, and potentially handling much of the waste on-site. As sustainable planning, appropriate technology, and green design are joined, they can also reduce transportation requirements, avoid disruption to the landscape, and even help with landscape and hence bioregional regeneration.

Fig. 1.29. *Attitudes toward building can affect a bioregion's prosperity and future.*

There is a common myth that sustainable design costs more. This is only true so long as costs such as infrastructure requirements remain hidden. In reality, with all things considered, sustainable design costs less. As more of these infrastructure costs become more apparent, green design will be seen to cost less and become more common. Sustainable design must integrate the large scales of biomes and bioregions as well as the small scale of materials and construction. This can be done no mater how restricted or constrained the building site is, because all sites have a natural history and all have a microclimate.

Microclimate

Solar radiation, topography, wind, rainfall, and vegetation all interact and help shape the local microclimate. Even when architects and engineers try to consider climate factors, they often fail to acknowledge the wide variations in microclimate that may occur within a relatively small area—as seen in a study in Ohio, comparing a small valley with the state.

Table. 1.2. *Microclimate Matters*

Microclimate Factor	109 stations, Neotoma valley (0.6 km sq)	88 stations, Ohio (113,000 km sq)	Max difference, Neotoma to Ohio
Highest temperature	75°F to 113°F	91°F to 102°F	–16 to +11°F
January low	14°F to –26°F	–6°F to –20°F	–6 to +20°F
Frost-free days	124 to 276	138 to 197	14–79
	Wolfe et al., 1949*		

The enormous differences in microclimate within this small valley illustrate the need to understand your local site. If the nearest weather station data is used, it may be off by 20 to 30°F in winter and summer, and solar radiation may be very different as well. A sustainably designed building that should work well can fail if it is not adjusted to suit local microclimate differences.

Radiation is usually the most important determinant of the microclimate. Both solar radiation and the heat radiated back to space are important. The radiation balance of a particular site will be determined by the sun's path (a function of latitude), the topography (slope aspect and elevation), the landscape, the color and type of the land cover and surface, and the possible shading and wind modification from structures on bordering properties.

An east-facing slope will warm rapidly in the morning and then cool off in the afternoon, while a west-facing slope will be warmest in the afternoon and early evening. In fact, the west-facing slope will generally be the warmest part of the site since radiation is high at the same time the air temperature is high.

As a rough rule of thumb, you can displace the site in latitude by the angle of its north or south slope. For example, a south-facing 10° slope at 40°N latitude would have a solar potential similar to that of a flat site at 30°N latitude. Conversely, a north-facing 10° slope at 40°N latitude would have a microclimate similar to that of a flat site at 50°N latitude.

At higher elevations, the thinner atmosphere increases the radiation flux and can let more heat escape to space. The net effect is a cooling of between 3° and 4°F per 1,000 feet. The key factor that blocks outgoing radiation is water vapor. Clouds can increase night heat retention, while clear nights can lead to rapid cooling. Cold, dry nights and hot, dry days in the desert are the result of an atmosphere with very little moisture to block radiation flows.

Clouds and fog will limit heat gain. If morning fog is common, it can limit heat gain from east-facing windows in spring or fall during cool mornings. This may influence window and thermal-mass placement. Or summer coastal fog may provide considerable beneficial cooling during otherwise hot weather. If cloudy periods or fog are common in winter, then solar gain may be limited when it is needed most demanding more insulation and thermal mass.

Plants can intercept almost all the sun's energy before it reaches the ground, keeping the soil relatively cool all summer. Even leafless deciduous trees may block 40 to 70 percent of the sun's energy in winter. Vegetation also blocks outgoing radiation, reducing nighttime cooling. The color and nature of the earth's surface determine solar absorption and reflection. In 1809, Samuel Williams of Vermont demonstrated the changes in temperature and humidity in cleared and forested areas; the forests were 10°F cooler in summer and warmer in winter. Water evaporated 1.5 times faster in the open areas (Thoreau, 1993*).

The actual amount of direct radiation received on any spot will vary with the atmospheric content, cloudiness, and solar angles, which determine the sun path length. An average of about a third of the extraterrestrial radiation that hits the outside of the earth's atmosphere reaches the earth's surface as direct solar radiation.

Solar radiation that reaches the earth after reflection or refraction is known as diffuse radiation. The amount will vary with the atmospheric content, cloudiness, and solar angles. On average, about a quarter of the extraterrestrial solar radiation reaches the earth as diffuse radiation. On a cloudy day, diffuse radiation may account for almost all of the energy received at the surface. It is often assumed to be uniformly distributed over the sky for simplicity, but the distribution is in fact far from uniform; diffuse radiation is usually much stronger near the sun disk's position in the sky. On a clear, bright day with a few big clouds, radiation may reach a peak as direct solar radiation is augmented with reflection from bright clouds.

The total of the diffuse and direct components of solar radiation, figure 1.30, reaching the ground is known as the *global radiation*.

Reflection occurs when radiation bounces off a surface. This can be either specular or diffuse reflection, figure 1.31. A mirror or still water exhibits specular reflection, while snow or white paint exhibits diffuse reflection. The term *reflectance* is used to describe the ability of a given surface to reflect radiation. The reflectance of a surface is generally given as a ratio of the reflected to the incident radiation,

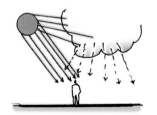

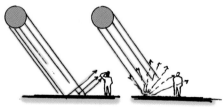

Fig. 1.30. *Direct and diffuse radiation.*

Fig. 1.31. *Specular and diffuse reflection.*

expressed as a percentage. Reflectance is often different for specular and diffuse radiation. Table 1.3 lists specular and diffuse reflectance of common surfaces in visible wavelengths. Fresh snow can improve south-window-wall performance significantly—often important during the cold, clear days that often follow a big winter storm.

Table 1.3 *Direct and diffuse reflection vary by surface.*

Specular	Surface	Diffuse
	Fresh snow	75–95%
	Old snow	40–70%
65–95%*	Dry sand	35–45%
60%*	Wet sand	40%
60%*	Water	40%
	Meadow	12–30%
	Grass	25%
	Dark soil	7–10%
	Concrete	40%
	Red brick	45%
	Tarpaper	7%
85%	Aluminum foil	15%
	White paint (new)	75–80%
	White paint (old)	55%

* Low angle

Adding the direct and diffuse and reflected radiation gives us the *total solar radiation*. This is particularly important for natural heating systems in the higher latitudes where a snowy surface in front of the south-wall collector may add 30 percent to the total solar radiation in the winter.

The reflectivity of the surface determines how much radiation is absorbed. But the type of surface and its moisture content determine what the effect of heat radiation will be. A walk around town after sunset illustrates this clearly. The parking lots and west-facing walls of concrete buildings have stored much of the sun's energy and will re-radiate it for several hours, but the west walls of wood-framed buildings are soon cool. Buildings with ivy-covered west walls will remain even cooler, thanks to the solar control and evaporative cooling by the plants. Trees shade the ground and also absorb energy for photosynthesis and transpire large quantities of water vapor. Temperature differences of 10°F or more may occur between areas with and without trees.

Design with Climate

Many architects will put the same house or commercial building design in any climate and simply change the size of the mechanical systems. Sustainable design, however, must consider the local site, microclimate, and bioregion.

A sustainable building for Phoenix, Arizona, won't be the same as one for Denver, Colorado, because of obvious climatic and bioregional differences. It may also be built differently because the most appropriate locally available building materials are not the same.

Sun Path and Orientation

Solar radiation is the dominant factor in almost all sustainable building designs. It is critical in heating, cooling, and daylighting. To use solar energy effectively, we use our knowledge of the sun's path and the nature of solar radiation to capture heat when we want it, shed heat when we don't, and gather light.

Solar Geometry

Through years of teaching and practice we have found the most important, basic, simple things are often the most neglected. This is too often true with solar geometry. Therefore, we have put on one page all you need to know to deal with solar geometry in design besides standard orthographic projection.

Wind and Airflow

The orientation of slopes also influences local wind patterns, which in turn help determine temperature. Winds driven by convective currents during the day help to cool valley slopes. At night, dense colder air settles to valley floors. Cold-air drainage can create very cold areas, and houses located in these spots may have very high heating demand compared with neighbors 20 feet higher. Buildings and fences in cold-air drainages must be carefully designed to prevent damming the flow and creating a reservoir of freezing air that can lead to damage to landscape plants and crops and higher heating bills.

Water bodies, which absorb and store solar radiation well, help to stabilize the surrounding microclimate. The leeward side of a lake is always milder than the windward side. This influence is minor for small bodies of water, and even for Lake Michigan the 10°F temperature reduction extends inland less than a mile. But cool ocean breezes can reach far inland during the summer.

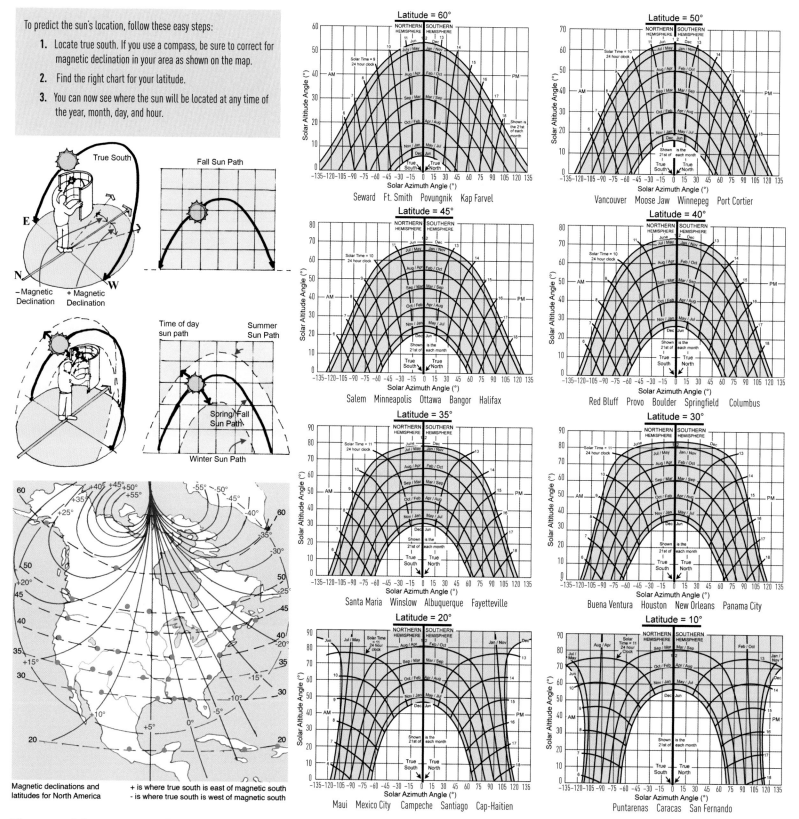

To predict the sun's location, follow these easy steps:

1. Locate true south. If you use a compass, be sure to correct for magnetic declination in your area as shown on the map.

2. Find the right chart for your latitude.

3. You can now see where the sun will be located at any time of the year, month, day, and hour.

Magnetic declinations and latitudes for North America

+ is where true south is east of magnetic south
- is where true south is west of magnetic south

Fig. 1.32. *Solar geometry. The sun altitude is the elevation. The azimuth angle is in relation to the equator.*

Topography is a major factor in determining site wind patterns. Hilltop homes experience the highest wind speeds. They are also most vulnerable to wildfires. A house on a hillcrest will be more exposed to cooling breezes in the summer, but also to winter gales. The choice of house location, window type and placement, roof shape and overhangs, and even building materials are influenced by the site topography, wind speeds, and patterns.

If a cold strong northwest wind blows across your region in winter, then building your house in a northeast–southwest valley may be a good idea. Or if a cooling sea breeze approaches from the southwest in a very hot climate, then a site that channels this wind to the site will make it easier to keep cool. Low places can be subject to cold-air drainage and flooding.

Analyze Your Own Site

You can learn a lot by simply being observant, looking at and feeling the environment of your site. Visit as often as possible, in both fair weather and storms. Which direction is the wind blowing from? What is the wind speed? What is the temperature? When does the last snow melt? Where does the frost remain in the morning? It's easy to install your own weather station on-site using data loggers and weather instruments. Then compare your temperature and wind with the local meteorological station—you may be surprised to see how different your microclimate is from the "standard."

A basic instrument package might include a temperature data logger (as low as $40 from Lascar) and a handheld wind recorder (as low as $50 from LaCrosse) or a complete weather station for $1,000 to $2,000. This might seem like a large investment, but the potential savings far exceed even the highest-cost weather station. An infrared thermometer ($80 to $100), which reads the temperature of surfaces, can be very informative as well. Use it to better understand the influence of radiation, orientation, and moisture on radiant surface temperatures.

The development of a local site climate profile begins with a study of existing climate data. These are increasingly available online, from NOAA, individual states, and others. This background information is helpful, but then you need to do your own detective work. How does your site compare with the nearest weather station? Tuning into the uniqueness of your site is critical.

Site Selection

The choice of building site should take into account microclimate and other specific site characteristics. Shown in figure 1.33 are many of these aspects for choosing a site for residential-scale construction. The specific criteria for a given site will depend on the use, occupants, regulations and code requirements, material availability and cost, microclimate resources, ecosystems, and many other factors. Each chapter includes a discussion of site-related considerations.

A common mistake in residential site selection is to locate the building at the highest spot. The top of the hill is the worst location because it increases weather exposure and wildfire risk, maximizes noise dispersal and impact from others, and is most visually disruptive for others. The military crest or, as Frank Lloyd Wright called it, the Taliesin ("shining brow" in Welsh) is a better location with reduced fire risk, less extreme winds, and reduced visual and noise impact.

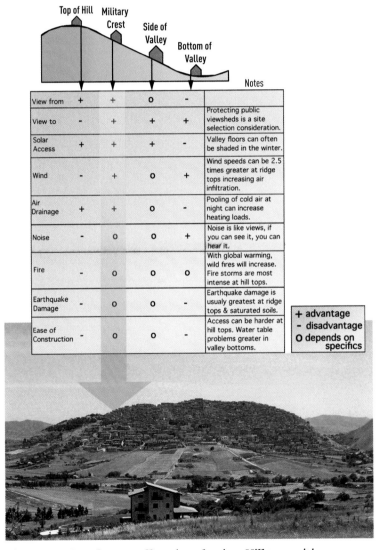

	Top of Hill	Military Crest	Side of Valley	Bottom of Valley	Notes
View from	+	+	o	-	
View to	-	+	+	+	Protecting public viewsheds is a site selection consideration.
Solar Access	+	+	+	-	Valley floors can often be shaded in the winter.
Wind	-	+	o	+	Wind speeds can be 2.5 times greater at ridge tops increasing air infiltration.
Air Drainage	+	+	o	-	Pooling of cold air at night can increase heating loads.
Noise	-	o	o	+	Noise is like views, if you can see it, you can hear it.
Fire	-	o	o	o	With global warming, wild fires will increase. Fire storms are most intense at hill tops.
Earthquake Damage	-	o	o	-	Earthquake damage is usualy greatest at ridge tops & saturated soils.
Ease of Construction	-	o	o	-	Access can be harder at hill tops. Water table problems greater in valley bottoms.

+ advantage
- disadvantage
o depends on specifics

Fig. 1.33. *Many factors affect site selection. Hill town siting recognizes many of these considerations. This is Gangi, central Sicily.*

Human Comfort

We build structures to improve our comfort by controlling our personal microclimate. The goal is to be much more comfortable and healthy than we would be living under a tree or in a cave. This has not always been the case with modern buildings, but naturally heated, cooled, daylit, and ventilated buildings can provide this level of comfort, health, and mental well-being. They also improve our ability to learn (in schools), to heal (hospitals), and to work (offices and manufacturing facilities).

Yet all too frequently buildings are not comfortable, healthy, or joyful. Some buildings we have looked at over the years actually would provide fewer hours within the comfort range over the course of a year than you could enjoy by living outside under a tree. These terrible buildings may decrease the temperature extremes, but they store the day's heat to make hot summer nights unbearable; or they retain the night's cold in winter long after the sun is up and it has become comfortable outside. Few people will find joy working in a cubicle in a room with no windows, a sealed air system delivering a steady stream of smelly plasticizers and chemicals from the outgassing of building materials, furniture, and fixtures, as well as fungal spores and decay by-products and other allergens.

Although the simple term *human comfort* covers a complex subject, involving all the methods of heat transfer (radiation, conduction, convection, evaporation) as well as many psychological and physiological factors, it's not that hard to get it right. Human comfort for this book is defined as "that range of microclimate conditions under which a person feels good." The comfort range varies depending on the type of activity engaged in, health, clothing, past experience and adaptation, expectations, and body type.

A resident in a rural area may find lower temperatures more comfortable than an urban dweller. And a thin, inactive elderly man may feel cold and uncomfortable in a room described as very comfortable by a young, fit woman. Living rooms may feel comfortable when much cooler than bathrooms, particularly when the bathroom floor is tile and feels cold. Not everyone will want the same conditions, so the goal is to provide individual controls and opportunities for everyone to be as comfortable as possible.

Human comfort also is influenced by and influences our thermoregulation systems, involving a complex interaction of autonomic and voluntary responses, mental attitude, and clothing. These govern the rate of heat loss or gain from the body and the rate of heat production. The comfort condition is usually met when these are balanced. Our regulatory systems are also influenced by many factors including temperature, humidity, radiation, air movement, clothing, metabolism, and acclimation. Comfort or discomfort can be created in many ways.

On a winter night, for example, large single-pane cold windows and leaky walls can create chills in the living room even when the air temperature is 75°F. The same room could be very comfortable

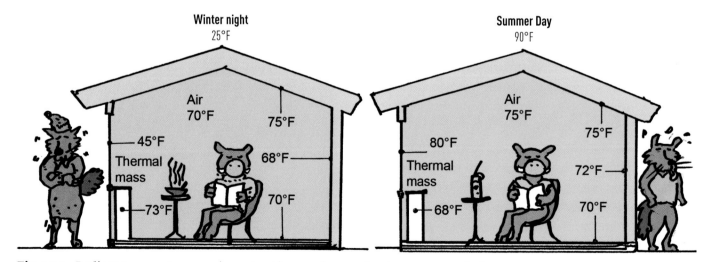

Fig. 1.34. *Radiant temperatures are important in ensuring comfort in summer and winter.*

at 65°F if the radiant temperatures of interior surfaces are warm, a high-performance window is used, and the building is draft-free.

Comfort in summer depends on the same interactions, only in summer we would like low radiant temperatures for interior surfaces, quiet but steady air circulation, low humidity to improve evaporation, and no heating from direct sunlight. Effective use of microclimate resources can provide summer comfort with natural forces in virtually any environment, even in the hottest deserts.

If a house is working well enough to provide comfort for the clothes that the owner wishes to wear and the activities planned, then it is a comfortable home. By wearing shorts and a light shirt in summer or a vest in winter, the comfort range can be extended. Table 1.4 shows that clothes make a big difference, and many of the perceived comfort differences between men and women are related to the clothes they are expected to wear. A commercial building will have to be cooler in summer to provide comfort for men who wear suits and ties, but these lower temperatures can cause women in skirts and lighter blouses to be continually cold and perhaps to sneak in an electric heater under their desks.

Table 1.4. *Chart of clo values for common clothing options. Clothing thermal properties are described by a unit called the **clo**, a dimensionless number equal to the total thermal resistance of the clothing from the skin to the outer surface of the clothing.*

Attire	clo value
Nude	0
Shorts	0.1
Shorts, open-neck short sleeve shirt, sandals, light socks	0.3–0.4
Long trousers, open-neck short sleeve shirt	0.5
Typical business suit	1
European heavy suit, vest, cotton long underwear	1.5
Chinese winter wear	2
Outdoor winter wear	3–4+

In winter, warmer clothes make it possible for a building to be cooler, yet still remain comfortable. Chinese rural residents found indoor winter temperatures of 52.7°F comfortable, while urban Chinese felt 57°F was better. These compare with temperatures of 71.4°F in urban Iran, 71.2°F in Italy, and the historic US goal of 72°F. These

differences reflect differing expectations, adaptation, and clothing. Lower interior winter temperatures can help reduce the stress of going outside on a cold winter day. One of the worst feelings after trudging through the snow and cold is entering a building that is blistering hot, which results in sweating, evaporative cooling, and perhaps a chill.

In summer, 80 percent of the people may feel comfortable at 86°F in tropical climates with outdoor mean monthly air temperatures of 95°F, according to revised thermal comfort standards based on field research by Brager and de Dear (2000*).

Clothes make the man, so the saying goes. But clothes often make discomfort the rule or demand high energy inputs for cooling and heating. More appropriate clothing choices can make a big dent in our national energy bill. President Obama has set an excellent example by wearing less formal clothing and being shown without his suit jacket.

Shifting to business attire that allows businessmen to wear shorts (like Bermuda does), or polo shirts and slacks could significantly reduce energy costs for cooling around the world. Eliminate the wool or polyester business suit and tie and shift to linen, bamboo, or silk fabric.

Furniture also matters. A mesh chair will provide more comfortable conditions on a hot day, while a deep padded chair will reduce heat loss on a cold winter day. In hot climates, a mesh chair is more appropriate; in a colder climate a deep padded chair will be better. In temperate climates, the choice of chair type may be made to suit individual preference.

Air temperature is most commonly talked about as the determinant of comfort, but it is just part of the comfort equation. As a general rule, in dwellings thermal radiation will be about equal in importance to the combined effects of air temperature, humidity, and air motion. The influence of thermal radiation explains why natural heating, cooling, and ventilation systems are so delightful.

The ideal system for human comfort is one with radiant temperature in the comfort range on all surfaces. This has been known for a very long time and was practiced by the Romans and Chinese in buildings with radiant walls, floors, and ceilings heated by air. These hypocaust systems are being used again in Europe. Ancient Persian systems provided very effective cooling with natural energy flows, wind catchers, and evaporation from fountains to provide uniform temperatures in protected spaces. Courtyards and fountains provide many of the same benefits today in Italy, Spain, and the Middle East.

The renewed interest in cooling and heating panels for radiant temperature control is also encouraging. Changing the radiant temperatures can be more effective in providing comfort than simply working with air temperature. The fiction that a fixed air temperature is a provider of comfort never made sense, and although codes still focus on air temperature, the concerns are beginning to shift toward comfort instead. Not everyone can be comfortable, but with good design the predicted mean comfort vote (PMV) can be maximized and the predicted percentage of dissatisfied people (PPD) can be minimized.

A natural heating, cooling, and ventilation system will typically include only a couple of surfaces that are directly heated by the sun, but radiant exchange within the building and across distributed thermal mass help deliver very stable temperatures that allow internal radiant exchange to equilibrate. These uniform radiant temperatures can provide comfort even if the air temperature varies considerably from 72°F. In fact, with good radiant temperatures it may be comfortable with air temperatures in the low 60s in winter or in the low 80s in the summer.

Comfort zones also vary depending on adaptation, experience, and expectation. In figures 1.35 and 1.36, you can see the changes for residents of different zones. As these show, in hotter climates, the comfort zone can be displaced up as much as 18°F. In colder climates, this can be displaced down an equivalent or greater amount, and Arctic dwellers may work outside in shirtsleeves when the temperature is far below freezing.

Natural variation in perceived comfort is common, and is characterized by a normal distribution, with most people clustered in the same area. There are outliers, and some people can feel comfortable far outside the norms. For clients of custom homes, it is always good to determine what they prefer. Skin and basal temperatures can be a good quick check. David, for example, has a consistent body temperature near 96.6°F instead of 98.6°F. This is just a 2°F difference, but if we compare the differences between basal air temperature of 72°F, it is 8 percent different, a significant difference.

Comfort Range

Our comfort range also varies with our activities, health, nutrition (low iron can lead to cold hands and feet), when we last ate, age, and time of day. However, in some tests there has been very little difference between young and elderly subjects when the activity levels are comparable. Sensitivity to cold in elderly people may reflect reduced activity more often than increased sensitivity. A good salsa CD and some dancing around the house could be just the ticket to warm up on a winter day. A hyperkinetic person may be much warmer than a meditative and very still person.

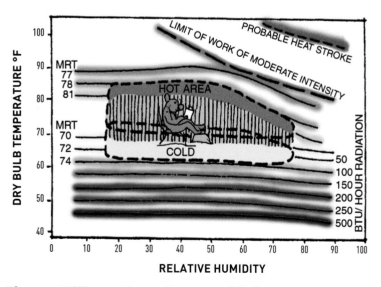

Fig. 1.35. *Differences in comfort zones with climate.*

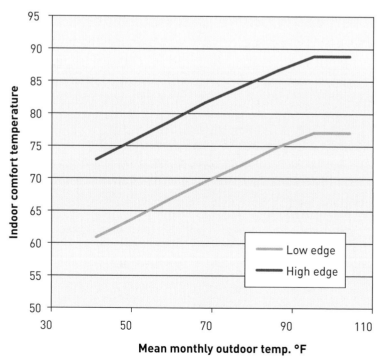

Fig. 1.36. *The indoor comfort zone related to mean monthly outdoor temperature.*

When we are sleeping, many people prefer cooler temperatures and a good comforter, and can be quite comfortable at 60°F or less. By adding bed curtains and canopies, sleepers in the old days stayed warm even in very cold, damp, and breezy homes and castles. The canopies limited drafts, captured air warmed by sleepers, and improved the radiant environment. These same features can help improve comfort in homes where thermal performance is less than ideal and where whole-house retrofits would be too costly.

If we graph our comfort zone over a winter day, it might look something like the diagram in figure 1.37. This assumes winter clothing is being worn: pants, long sleeves, warm socks, and a vest.

With solar orientation, sufficient thermal mass and an efficient building shell, natural heating, and ventilation can provide full comfort in most climates without using any fossil fuels. Natural heating without fans, boilers, and furnaces can also improve the quality of indoor air and eliminate unwanted noise, vibration, and cost!

In a well-designed naturally heated building the balance of solar gain, thermal mass, and insulation will usually provide such good performance that windows can be left open to provide sufficient fresh air for those who wish it on all but the coldest days. This also allows different family members or workers to adjust their space to their desired comfort condition. This sense of control also adds to the feeling of comfort, even when it does not provide fully comfortable conditions. This same sense of control is more difficult to provide in a sealed building. However, just as with lighting, surveys show that most people prefer operable windows and will use them wisely, but some people are too passive and will rarely operate windows or even blinds.

Natural cooling with solar orientation, solar control, and microclimate-adapted cooling (radiant, evaporative, or convective) can provide cooling almost everywhere on a summer day. Using the cooling strategies in this book can improve comfort throughout the cooling season.

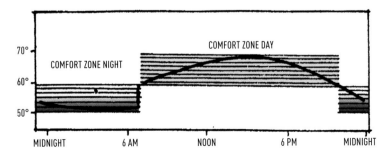

Fig. 1.37. *Daily variation in comfort expectations.*

This comfort is readily apparent and is usually one of the first comments a visitor will make during a visit to a naturally heated, cooled, and ventilated building. This comfort and quiet is in marked contrast with mechanical or artificial space-conditioning systems.

Comfort Problems with Artificial Heating and Cooling

Heating

Forced-air heating systems are most common in the United States. While they may theoretically be able to maintain the air temperature at 72°F, they often have trouble reaching all areas of a building. The resulting cold pockets and hot pockets lead to discomfort. In addition, the hot air quickly rises to the ceiling, leaving the floor too cool and the ceiling too warm with resulting imbalance in radiant temperatures, often 15°F or more. A large cold window in a room heated with air temperatures above 75°F may still be uncomfortable to someone sitting nearby. Tall glass-walled office buildings create even more difficult conditions to balance temperatures. Workers on the lower floors on the north side may be freezing while occupants of south and west upper floors are baked in the afternoon.

Forced-air heating increases convective cooling of occupants as well as providing an irritating, drying wind (more colds), noise (more stress and less sleep), vibration, and breezes. The ducts and the air movement also stir up dust and can bring mold into the living space from ducts and return pathways in walls, attics, and basements.

Radiant heating systems are usually more comfortable, although they also suffer from problems absent in natural systems. The most common variant is the radiant floor, which is usually run with hot water. This type of system works fairly well and is considered one of the more comfortable systems by people who have never experienced natural heating and cooling. But leaks and repairs can be costly and frustrating to fix.

Radiant ceilings are also used, often using electric resistance heating panels, and while they are often more comfortable than forced-air systems, here the problems are worse than for a radiant floor. The overheated area is near the head (one of the dominant heat-exchange areas for humans) while the floor remains cool. In addition, air heated on the surface has nowhere to go, so it forms a pool of hot air near the ceiling.

Cooling

Air conditioners work well for cooling and moving air, but it takes a great deal of energy to do it. They also provide a very cool stream of air that may be too cool to be comfortable if you are in it. In many cases they cannot cool the room enough to lower the radiant temperatures of the walls, ceiling, and windows, so the room is noisy and breezy, but not comfortable. Oversizing of air conditioners often leads to repeated on–off cycling that is irritating and inefficient. Air-conditioning is also expensive, requiring power at the most expensive peak period. As time-of-use billing becomes more common, this will dramatically increase the cost of air-conditioning. Air conditioners condense out water, and stopped drains often lead to mold problems. And air conditioners leak CFCs and HCFCs, gases that are both implicated in global warming and attack the atmospheric ozone layer, leaving us more vulnerable to potentially deadly UV radiation.

Evaporative coolers (sometimes pejoratively called swamp coolers) use evaporation of water across a pad/filter to reduce outside air temperatures to a comfortable level for indoor comfort. These can be very effective in areas with low humidity, and may be run with solar panels. But on hot humid days, they provide little relief. Indirect evaporative coolers are better and are finally becoming more available on the market. Some of these are twice as efficient as an air conditioner, and because they do not add moisture to the air they provide better comfort even in humid areas.

Ultimate Comfort

There is no doubt that a building with a very energy efficient shell and natural heating, cooling, and ventilation systems (if well designed) is the most comfortable building possible. People who get to visit, live, or work in one of these buildings will often exclaim they are "More comfortable than ever before." They are not mistaken. Comfort is good for health, and the human body recognizes what is good for it. Balanced radiant temperatures are ideal for health. The quiet comfort of naturally heated and cooled homes can improve sleep quality, and research has revealed how important sleep is for health and mental well-being.

Natural light is increasingly recognized as important for health as well. Daylight can help minimize problems with seasonal affective disorder. Daylighting has been shown to improve students' learning performance in schools, speed recovery of people in hospitals, and increase worker productivity. The "Greenhouse" factory of the Herman Miller Corporation in Holland, Michigan, helped double productivity and paid the additional cost of good design back in a matter of months. Good building design also increases shopper satisfaction, and large retailers and others are starting to adopt better building practices to improve profitability

Natural heating, cooling, and ventilation should be used for all new buildings, and a retrofit effort needs to be started for the many appallingly bad buildings we now live and work in. Windows, solar tubes for daylighting, roof monitors, and other features can bring light and fresher air into dark sealed buildings and improve the quality of life. Solar and climatically adapted retrofits can reduce heating and cooling costs and improve comfort in almost any building.

Health

The benefits of good building can be realized with improved health. Less stress, less drying air in winter, less mold, fewer allergens, and better sleep add up to better health all year. When more comprehensive studies are finally done on the benefits of good design, they will be as dramatic as the benefits found in analyses of daylighting on learning and productivity. In sustainable buildings, fewer days are lost to absenteeism and ill health. It is not uncommon to see sick days decline 12 to 20 percent.

Joy

If you feel very comfortable and are healthy, it is easier to feel joy. Naturally heated and cooled buildings are more joyful buildings. They are quiet, feel good, and help harried parents, children, and workers recover from the day's stressful activities and the bad buildings we now work in, go to school in, or shop in. Working hard and effectively is much easier and more satisfying in a comfortable and enjoyable building.

Comfort Outside

The same principles determine the comfort conditions outside. Good design can improve comfort outside and can improve conditions for pedestrians and bicycle commuters. This can encourage more commuters to choose these more sustainable options. Solar orientation can create comfortable winter spaces, and effective use of microclimate resources can create cool havens in summer. This helps keep people outside and interacting in the community. The mean radiant temperature is very important outside and should be a factor for all landscape and city design.

Many traditional designs of outdoor space were effective for improving comfort. From the shaded streets and souks of desert cities to the *toldos,* fountains, and landscaping of courtyards in Italy and Spain, we can find excellent examples of solutions for outdoor comfort. Sadly, most American cities have been built for cars, not people, and microclimate has not been considered in design and development.

Occupant Program and Preferences

Rather than to exclude people from making design decisions because they are ignorant, the most feasible solution is to educate them.

—ROBERT SOMMER

The most important factor in building design should be the comfort, security, and happiness of the occupants. Sadly this is usually neglected when the client is not the occupant—and even when clients will be occupants, they are often not consulted on critical factors. The growing number of studies on productivity and health benefits of sustainable buildings is encouraging more careful consideration of the occupants even when the client is a developer with first cost and financing pressure as a primary concern. Working to meet client desires or preferences can be challenging even when the client will be the occupant, and the architect and designer is concerned about meeting needs and wants. Anyone with much project experience can recognize the challenge, which includes developing a program that clarifies client preferences, needs, and wants. See the "Program Considerations" sidebar.

The development of the program for the building should be thorough, articulated clearly, and refined as the project progresses. In most cases it will take time to educate the clients, clarify preferences and requirements, and isolate important drivers of design decisions. Arranging visits to both very good and very poor designs can be helpful in clarifying client needs and preferences. Monitoring performance of existing spaces where clients live or work can also be instructive.

PROGRAM CONSIDERATIONS

- Use patterns—annual, season, vacation only.
- Living pattern—cooking, relaxing, working, sleeping, interacting, individual time.
- Daily-use pattern—early riser, late sleeper, night owl.
- Temperature and clothing preferences.
- Bedding choices and preferences.
- Lighting preferences.
- Bathing preferences, time and type (shower, tub, furo, inside/outside).
- Privacy preferences.
- Sound preferences.
- Ventilation preferences.
- Security preferences.
- Ceiling height.

- Clothes washing and drying (clothesline?).
- Building-material/color preferences.
- Flooring preferences. Tile or carpet? Can floor mass be effective or not?
- Landscaping preferences—gardening, flowers, colors, food production.
- Waste management preferences, recycling, composting.
- Storage requirements.
- Rainwater harvesting.
- Gray-water use.
- Desired involvement in building operation—none to intensive.
- Allergies and asthma issues—ventilation/building-material choices.

Program Example

Figure 1.38 shows an example of sustainable issues as an integral part of programming for the zero-energy building illustrated in the preface on page v.

Six basic issues regarding sustainability based on the idea of cyclic rather than linear processes are included. A key question is always:

How much does the client wish to push to advance the state of the art of sustainable design? Some techniques to allow efficient cycles at this scale exist and have been tested exhaustively (marked with ⊛ on the chart). Others are developed but are not common enough to be available without extra expense (marked by ◐). And finally, there are some that, although examples exist, are more adventuresome from a technical and regulatory viewpoint (marked by ▣).

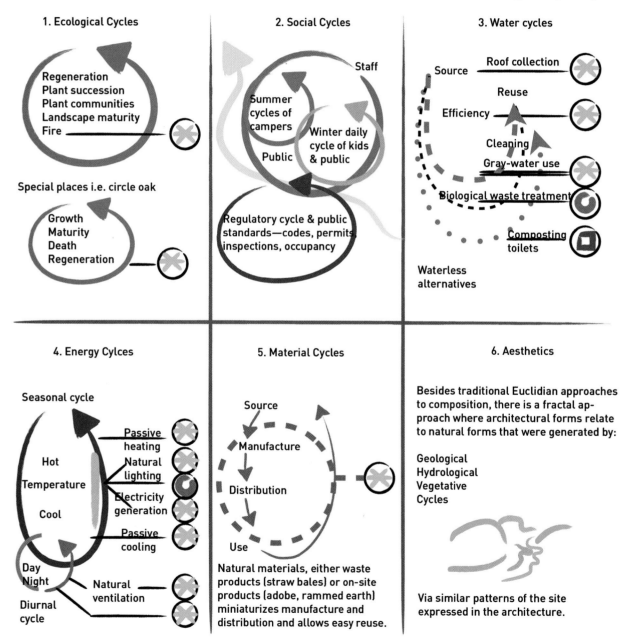

Fig. 1.38. *Programming based on cyclic rather than linear processes for sustainable design.*

Passive Considerations in Programming

Passive considerations for heating, cooling, ventilation, and day-lighting need to be part of each phase of work, starting with programming. Leaving passive considerations out of the early phases of work and attempting to graft them on later (figure 1.39) results in less cost-effective integration. Attempting to add passive solar and sustainability elements at the end of a project's design or construction often hinders success and is like adding a sail to a powerboat after the boat has been launched.

The myth that passive solar buildings cost more to build has been fueled by this lack of attention and commitment to passive strategies throughout the design and construction process. In reality, passive solar buildings can be similar in cost to conventional buildings and may cost less because they can reduce the need for expensive mechanical systems, which can make up to a third of the total cost of a building. Reducing mechanical systems to a backup role saves in up-front capital costs as well as operating costs.

The importance of the programming phase of work as a prerequisite to the later phases cannot be overestimated, as it greatly affects each successive decision.

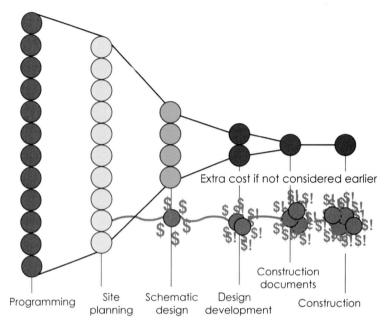

Fig. 1.39. *The cost of incorporating sustainability concerns at different phases of design and implementation.*

Cost Savings and Aesthetics

Costs

When green design considerations are integrated at the beginning of the design process, there may be no premium in construction first cost and dramatic savings in life-cycle cost. This is illustrated in the example on pages 131–132.

Passive solar systems can often reduce the cost of a building by utilizing components that are already in the budget (windows, overhangs, mass) and minimizing or eliminating the mechanical support systems that are needed in a nonsolar or anti-passive solar building. To realize these savings passive solar design should be a key factor in city street layout and subdivision design.

Within any section of this book, the cost for a given result will depend on the skill of the designer and the client's choices. A low-cost canvas or shade cloth cover to control summer overheating from a west-facing window might cost less than $1/square foot, while a high-end motorized exterior shutter might cost $36/square foot or more.

As we tell clients, overall building costs vary as much or more. Straw bale passive solar homes have been built for less than $10/square foot (in areas without building codes) and for more than $300/square foot. Typically, they will cost about the same as a conventional custom building—less than a super-insulated building made using double-stud or truss walls, and considerably less than an adobe house.

California's Sustainable Building Task Force quantified the value of resource savings in table 1.5 (Kats et al., 2003*). In October 2002, the David and Lucille Packard Foundation* released their Sustainability Matrix and Sustainability Report, developed to consider environmental goals for a new 90,000-square-foot office facility. The study found that with each increasing level of sustainability (including various levels of LEED), short-term costs increased, but long-term costs decreased dramatically.

A second, older study conducted by Xenergy* for the City of Portland identified a 15 percent life-cycle savings associated with bringing three standard buildings up to USGBC LEED certification levels (with primary opportunities to save money associated with energy efficiency, water efficiency, and use of salvaged materials).

Table 1.5. *Financial benefits of green buildings per square foot.*

Category	20 year NPV
Energy Value	$ 5.79
Emissions Value	$ 1.18
Water Value	$ 0.51
Waste Value (construction only) - 1 year	$ 0.03
Commissioning O&M Value	$ 8.47
Productivity & Health Value (Certified & Silver)	$ 36.89
Productivity & Health Value (Gold & Platinum)	$ 55.33
Less Green Cost Premium	$ (4.00)
Total 20-year NPV (Certified & Silver)	$ 48.87
Total 20-year NPV (Gold & Platinum)	$ 67.31

Life-Cycle Costs

The most important savings from passive solar design comes in reduced life-cycle costs (LCC). Energy savings of 70 to 90 percent at little or no added construction cost can quickly become significant. If we add in the avoided external costs, the savings go up even faster.

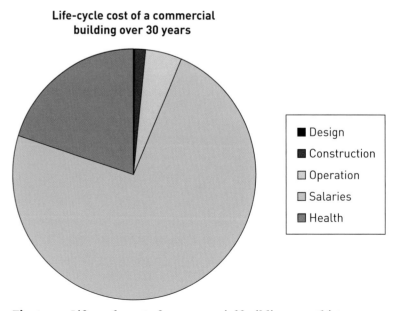

Life-cycle cost of a commercial building over 30 years

- ■ Design
- ■ Construction
- □ Operation
- □ Salaries
- ▨ Health

Fig. 1.40. *Life-cycle cost of a commercial building over thirty years.*

For example, a typical American home used more than 50 mBTUs for heating every year. If this is one of the thirty-one million all-electric homes, the direct cost would be somewhere around $1,600 a year for a nonsolar house with almost $200 of external costs for emissions of carbon dioxide, nitrogen oxides, sulfur oxides, and particulate matter less than 10 microns. Over a hundred years, the all-electric nonsolar home would cost $180,000, while the passive solar homeowner would save $172,000.

Savings in commercial buildings are comparable, but the advantages are even greater. A daylit, comfortable, health-giving passive solar building will increase sales and productivity. In many cases, the productivity gains outweigh energy savings 20:1 or more.

Substantial research supports the health and productivity benefits of green features, such as daylighting, increased natural air ventilation and moisture reduction, and the use of low-emitting floor carpets, glues, paints, and other interior finishes and furnishings. In the United States, the annual cost of building-related sickness is estimated to be $58 billion. According to researchers, green building has the potential to generate an additional $200 billion annually in the United States in worker performance by creating offices with improved indoor air quality (CEC, 2008*).

Note that $200 billion is larger than the size of the entire Canadian construction market, which was $156 billion in 2006. As this potential benefit becomes more widely understood, countries with a comprehensive range of green products will have a competitive advantage in the global marketplace.

Aesthetics

Passive solar design is architecture, and architecture is involved with aesthetics. The question of what aesthetics is has been asked for a long time, from Plato to Tolstoy to Wright to Hundertwasser (see Haggard, Cooper, and Gyovai 2006). Plato felt that aesthetics dealt with perfection, which could exist only in the mind. The more modern interpretation by Tolstoy was that aesthetics was the result of honest emotion, an approach more related to ours. Frank Lloyd Wright championed organic architecture as a reinterpretation of nature's rules to suit humans, and to provide harmony with the materials chosen and the site. And Hundertwasser argued that aesthetics came from using organic forms and reconciling humans with nature. All steps along the way to integrated, sustainable design. So the question continues, what are the aesthetics of *passive solar architecture*? Historically, architectural aesthetics have dealt with three qualities: harmony, proportion, and scale. These three have been used to create architecture composed of:

Sequence: *The movement of things.*

Rhythm: *The repetition of things.*

Order: *The constructive nature of things.*

Form: *The shape of things.*

Theme: *The primary story told by the composition.*

Feeling: *The emotion conveyed by the story.*

Clarity: *The clear communication of any or all of the above.*

The aesthetic goal in any composition is to achieve synergy, where all the elements are so well composed that the whole exceeds the sum of its parts, giving the composition a transcendent quality. This quality has been achieved by all great architecture.

The theme for passive solar architecture could be comfort, which is discussed throughout this book. However, the next level of comfort would be health: personal health, community health, and planetary health.

With comfort and health comes the feeling of rightness, rightness that supports health and comfort. Successful passive solar design can create comfort and contribute to health. In addition to being successful aesthetically, it must be clear in its communication of these qualities through its feeling of rightness.

Aesthetically successful passive buildings have an intense but peaceful feeling of this rightness that is communicated by the building itself without words or description.

Modern architecture using the theme of industrial progress became the architecture of the twentieth century. Passive solar architecture using the theme of comfort, health, economy, and sustainability is becoming the architecture of the twenty-first century.

Trout Farm kitchen

Trout Farm dining room

Trout Farm living room

Trout Farm office

San Luis Obispo Botanical Garden Education Center

Co-housing dining area, common house

Trout Farm 1 Tool Temple

Residence

Sanctuary of Beth David Synagogue

Beth David Synagogue

Fig. 1.41. *Sustainable design can be beautiful as well as comfortable, healthful, and economical.*

TWO PASSIVE HEATING

We now have the ability to provide 60 to 90 percent of the heating needs in buildings by utilizing different passive strategies tuned to the microclimate of the place.

Basics of Passive Heating

Heating Load

Heating demands vary greatly with the "metabolism" of a building as described in chapter 1. Even in the same climate a small skin-dominated house can have a high heating demand, a moderate-density apartment a lower demand, a high-density apartment complex a much smaller heating need, and a large internal-load building no heating load at all. In fact, the large building could be dominated by cooling, ventilation, and lighting demand. These variations result from the skin-to-volume ratio of the building. For large buildings, the heat generated by the building's occupants, equipment, computers, and lights, which are called internal loads, can play a major role in meeting heating needs.

The climatic heating load for a building is usually measured by the number of heating degree days, which is defined as the difference between the average daily temperature on the site and a base temperature of 65°F. The spectrum of heating degree days ranges from Resolute Bay, Canada, 74°N, at 15,356 HDD (SI units 8,542 HDD); to 52 HDD (SI units 29 HDD) for Key West, Florida, 24°N.

Internal Loads

The temperature in a building is affected by internal heat from occupants, cooking, computers, machinery, and lights. These heat sources can be a benefit in winter and a problem in summer. In a typical home with inefficient appliances, the largest sources of heat gain can be the refrigerator and freezer, clothes dryer, and water heater. Cooking, lights, and even people (100 watts each) also contribute to heat gain. The contribution from cooking heat depends almost entirely on use patterns; a baker and a nonbaker will have very different internal heat gains in the same house. The heat gain will be less if the water heater, clothes dryer, or washer is in an unconditioned space like the garage. Much of water heater's energy goes down the drain with the hot water and the dryer's heat is vented outside.

We can get a sense of relative importance of these by looking at the energy consumption for a typical 1,500-square-foot all-electric house in the Southwest of the United States, shown in table 2.1.

Computers, game players, printers, televisions, and other electronics can also add heat. Even on standby, many appliances,

electronic systems, and charging systems for cell phones and PDAs add small but continuous loads. In larger buildings with more people and equipment, internal loads may dominate building metabolism.

Table 2.1. *Family energy use in the southwestern United States.*

	KWH	*3413 = BTU	USD/ yr at 13.7¢ / kwh
Water heating	4595	15,682,735	$ 629.52
Refrigerator	1200	4,095,600	$ 164.40
Clothes dryer	1111	3,791,843	$ 152.21
Range / oven	700	2,389,100	$ 95.90
Dishwasher	337	1,150,181	$ 46.17
Clothes washer	170	580,210	$ 23.29
Lighting, TV, computer	155	529,015	$ 21.35
Total	8113	28,218,684	$ 1,132.84

Heat Sources

Internal heat loads and solar radiation are the primary heat sources for passive heating in sustainable buildings. The goal is to reduce energy needed at the site enough so that a small mechanical backup system will suffice.

Heat distribution with a standard mechanical system is usually done by moving heated air with fans. This results in people and air

Fig. 2.1. *Convective heat transfer versus radiative heat transfer.*

being heated by convection and cooled by evaporation at the same time. In passive systems, the approach is to warm thermal mass, which in turn heats the occupants by radiation. The effects of these two methods of heat transfer are quite different. Convection heating can be uneven; it's often noisy, and the air is often uncomfortably dry. The comfort and health advantages of radiant heating are readily apparent to anyone who has experienced both systems.

Term	Definition	Units	Conversion
Heating Degree Days (HDD)	Thermal needs on site for comfort most often measured as the difference between average daily temperature and a base temperature of 18°C (65°F) or 23°C (74°F)	HDD 18°C (65°F)	DD (SI) = 0.555 DD (US)
Cooling Degree Days (CDD)		CDD 18°C (65°F) CDD 23°C (74°F)	DD (US) = 1.8 DD (SI)

Fig. 2.2. *Degree day (DD) definitions.*

Radiation in Passive Heating

Radiation

Since radiative transfer of heat is one of the main elements of passive design, you need to understand some of its characteristics.

Any object at a temperature greater than absolute zero (−273°C) emits radiation, with the wavelength and intensity dependent on temperature. Radiation will always flow from a warmer object to a cooler object and will ultimately result in thermal equilibrium if no other energy is added or taken away from the objects. Radiation from the sun is in the form of short-wave radiation, while radiation from warm objects in a room is by long-wave radiation, as shown in figure 2.3a.

Overlapping figures 2.3a and 2.3b in figure 2.3c shows how the solar gain aspect of passive solar design works. Solar radiation enters through the transparent elements of the building and heats material in the interior, ideally optimized thermal mass. This material re-radiates at long wavelengths. At this long wavelength glass is opaque, therefore heat is retained within the interior space. This condition is called the greenhouse effect. When we tune a building to this condition, with optimum orientation and quantity of transparency, optimum amount of thermal mass,

a method of providing control to respond to seasonal variation, and a spatial form and order that allows all of these to transfer heat to the occupants, then we have designed a good passively heated building.

Responses to Radiation

When radiation strikes a surface, it can be reflected, absorbed, or transmitted. The properties of various materials may be quite different, and materials must be chosen to ensure that the desired performance is achieved. The angle at which direct solar radiation strikes a surface is known as the angle of incidence. This is particularly important when we consider the absorption, reflection, and transmission of solar energy. In general, the more acute the angle of incidence is, the greater the reflection, while absorption will be minimized.

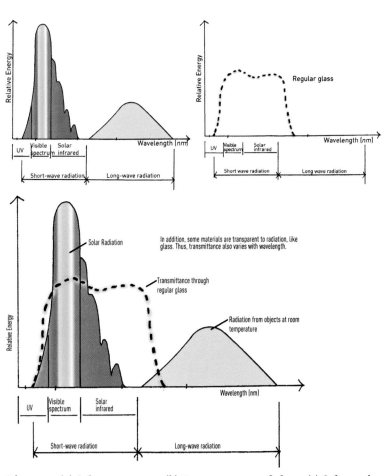

Fig. 2.3. *(a) Solar spectrum. (b) Transparency of glass. (c) Solar gain through glass, figs. a and b overlaid.*

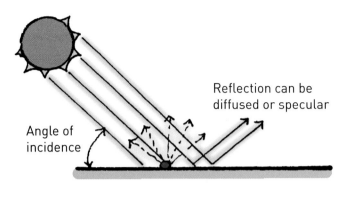

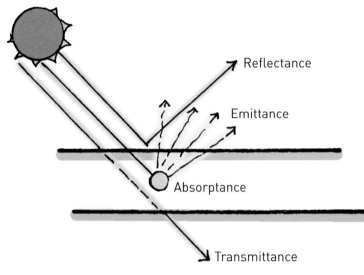

Fig. 2.4. *Reflectance, absorbtance, and emittance.*

Table 2.2. *Absorptvity and emissivity of common materials.*

	Material	% Absorbed
Absorption	Flat black paint	96%
	Black tar paper	93%
	Galvanized steel	65%
	Concrete	60%
	Brick (red)	55%

	Material	% Emitted
Emittance	Rough concrete	97%
	White plaster	91%
	White enamel on galv. iron	90%
	Concrete	88%
	Black paint on aluminum	88%
	Galvanized iron (old)	28%
	Galvanized iron (new)	10%

This table also shows why in hot climates it is far better to paint galvanized metal roofs than leave them bare, achieving a 90 percent emissivity, rather than just 28 percent. This is also why metal tools left out in the sun get so hot.

Absorptivity and Emissivity

Once the energy is absorbed by a material, it will be re-radiated or emitted. Building materials such as plaster, glass, plastic, concrete, and aluminum differ in their ability to absorb, transfer, and emit radiation, as shown in table 2.2. These properties may also vary with wavelength. The emissivity of materials is important in many designs—particularly those that rely on both short- and long-wave radiation for heating and cooling. Materials that collect energy effectively yet emit little energy are known as selective surfaces.

You can see why a selective surface is often used in collectors: The emissivity can drop from 90 percent to 10 percent. These selective surfaces may be created by direct deposition on metal (best) or deposition on a thin film of metal foil that can be stuck on the collector surface (good); or they can be applied as a paint (not as effective).

Elements of Passive Heating

In passive buildings we use solar radiation, internal loads, and architectural elements to provide the majority of a building's heating requirements. Success is achieved by optimally tuning the whole building to respond to the elements (figure 2.5).

How these elements respond can be understood better by examining some extreme architectural types, what we've called tin boxes, thermos bottles, pyramids, and chicken coops. Response to the environment is visualized using the concept of sol-air temperature (T_o). The sol-air temperature is a fictitious exterior temperature that would have the same effect on the building as the combined affects of the on-site sources and sinks of its immediate setting, such as air temperatures, solar radiation, and radiation to the night sky.

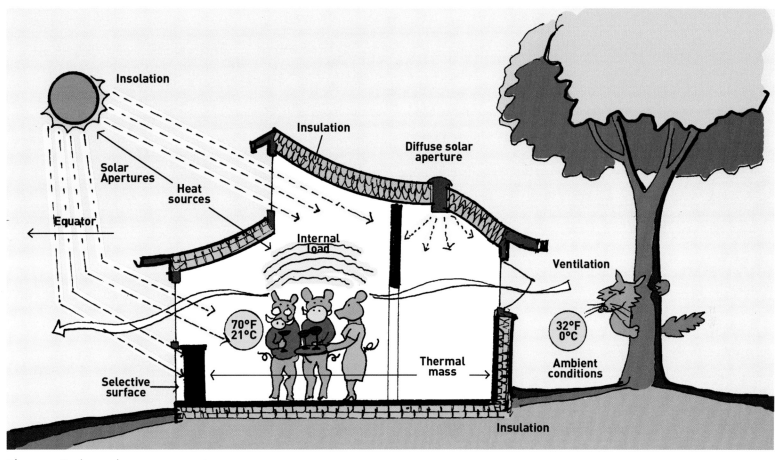

Fig. 2.5. *Basic passive arrangements.*

Tin Boxes

For a climate with hot days and cold nights, typical of temperate zones in fall and spring, the worst building we could build thermally would be a tin box with no insulation. During the day, its shaded walls would quickly warm to the temperature of the exterior air, and walls and roof exposed to the sun would become even hotter. Since the inside temperature (T_i) is a combination of these, our building would be hotter than the outside temperature. After dark, the walls would radiate heat to the clear night sky and soon would drop below air temperature. The roof would drop to an even lower temperature because it has better exposure to the whole dome of the night sky. Thus, the interior temperature of our tin box would cycle from warmer than the outside in the day to colder than the outside at night. The tin building closely follows the sol-air temperature of its environment. This building accentuates exterior temperature swings, which results in it being more uncomfortable inside than outside.

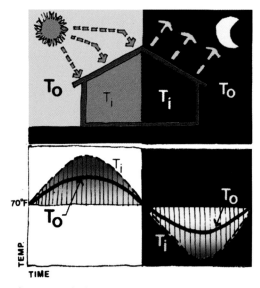

Fig. 2.6. *Tin box.*

Thermos Bottles

Here we still have lightweight construction, but now our building is extremely well insulated. This reduces the heat gain and loss but does not affect gain and loss through windows or gain from internal loads. The result would be the same as wearing a bulky overcoat no matter what our activity. At times we would be comfortable, but at other times not, unless we could bring in external energy. The extensive insulation can increase the efficiency of our energy use but does not in itself optimize comfort. The thermos bottle can gradually get cooler and cooler if it is not augmented with heat. This is why energy efficiency, while a necessary prerequisite to passive conditioning, is related to but different from passive energy production, as described in chapter 1.

Fig. 2.7. *Thermos bottle.*

Pyramids

Consider what happens with a thick building made of very heavy materials. In contrast with the tin box or thermos bottle, the temperature variation inside a heavily massed building will be less severe. The indoor temperature will still oscillate with the daily sol-air temperature, but the oscillation is dampened. This is because the heavy material will slowly store heat during the day that is released to warm the building at night. In an extreme architectural version of this type of building, such as an Egyptian pyramid, the interior temperature remains almost constant. This is why heavy buildings are an indigenous response to climates where the mean sol-air temperature is about 75°F.

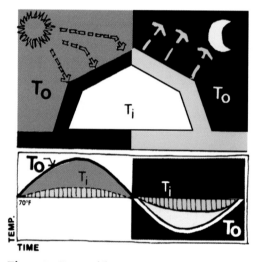

Fig. 2.8. *Pyramid.*

Chicken Coops

High-mass buildings are not appropriate for all situations. In hot humid climates, for example, the heat sink of the night sky is much reduced by the water vapor of the surrounding air, so the high sol-air temperature stays relatively constant. In this case, the only cooling mechanism available passively is evaporation from a wet surface. The most readily available and effective surface is the occupant's skin if we can provide the necessary airflow with building design or form. The appropriate building form is a building with a roof designed for maximum shade and no walls to allow optimum air passage—essentially a chicken coop.

Fig. 2.9. *Chicken coop.*

"Classic" Passive Types

In the period following the first oil crisis in 1973, six approaches to passive conditioning were formalized into classic passive types. These consisted of three generic categories, each of which has two distinct approaches. The generic category was based on the relationship between the thermal collector—or, in the case of cooling, thermal dissipater—and the interior space of the building.

In direct systems, thermal transfer occurs inside the interior of the building. In indirect systems, thermal transfer occurs at the building envelope, and in isolated gain systems the thermal transfers occur outside the building envelope via a separate architectural element.

More specific classifications, of which there are two under each generic approach, are based on particular types of thermal mass for direct systems or the particular architectural elements in which thermal functions occur for indirect and isolated systems. Although in practical application passive buildings are usually a mixture of these approaches, there is much to be learned from looking at them separately, as discussed on pages 56–77.

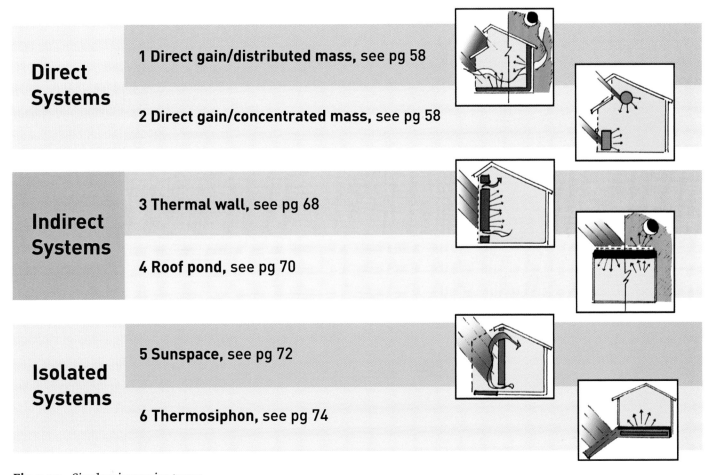

Direct Systems

1 Direct gain/distributed mass, see pg 58

2 Direct gain/concentrated mass, see pg 58

Indirect Systems

3 Thermal wall, see pg 68

4 Roof pond, see pg 70

Isolated Systems

5 Sunspace, see pg 72

6 Thermosiphon, see pg 74

Fig. 2.10. *Six classic passive types.*

PASSIVE HEATING—A LONG HISTORY

Passive heating was not invented in the 1970s—it has a long history. Before HVAC systems became so pervasive in the 1950s, most buildings were passive. Although comfort standards were different, many of these buildings were amazingly effective for their time and culture. There is a historical overview at the bottom of the following pages that illustrates the evolution of passive heating over the last several thousand years.

It is interesting to consider some historical examples that are extreme in that performance often made the difference between life and death. These examples use internal loads to heat in extreme climatic conditions.

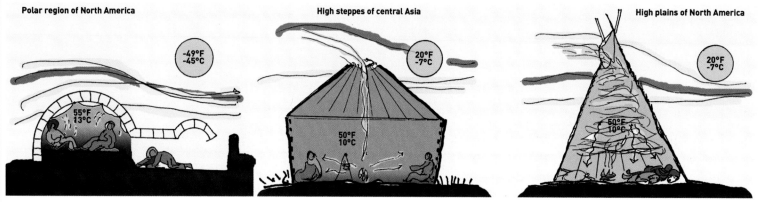

Fig. 2.11. *(a) Polar region of North America: The use of ice for structure and insulation allowed survival in emergencies with only body heat as the internal heating source. (b) High steppes of Central Asia: A highly mobile yurt with a collapsible frame and felt covering allowed survival using only internal loads and a small dung fire, provided by the animals in this herding culture. (c) High plains of North America: A light frame and buffalo hide tepee could work under blizzard conditions using a trapped layer of smoke from a very small fire and an enhanced internal load (a "three-dog night").*

1970

Fig. 2.12.

History is important because it gives context and inspiration, but can be misused. Most modern yurts illustrate the problem. Yurts have a romantic attraction due to their roundness, structural integrity, and low cost for the volume achieved. But sadly, most modern yurts are thermal disasters.

Instead of thick felt walls and roof, which provided insulation in the historic yurts, they are often made of canvas that provides no insulation. Instead of the steady central fire fueled by dung from the animals of a herding culture vented by a central aperture they have a plastic dome in the center. This accentuates high summer sun for overheating and loses heat during the winter without admitting the low winter sun—just the reverse of what is needed.

The interior temperature in the modern yurt may be higher than the exterior during summer and colder than the exterior in winter like the tin box (see page 43). The result is the devolution of an elegant passive shelter for a harsh steppe environment to a design that is "hip" and economical but not efficient or comfortable.

Prerequisites for Passive Heating

A passive building must first be an energy-conserving building. This prerequisite allows passive design to take the next step to on-site energy production. Energy conservation begins with the building envelope. Three aspects of an energy-conserving envelope are insulation, reduction of air infiltration, and energy-efficient construction.

The major consideration of an energy-conserving envelope is the conductive value of the skin of the building.

An Energy-Efficient Building

The flow of heat from molecule to molecule is called conduction and can be a very important design consideration in sustainable buildings. If you hold a poker in the fire, it will gradually heat up until you can no longer hold it; the handle is transferring energy by conduction. Insulation has low conductance and slows down heat gain or loss. Several terms are used to describe various aspects of conduction in a building or clothing system. The major terms are:

U: *Conductivity, per thickness*

$\textbf{U}_t$**:** *Conductivity, total value for unit*

R: *Resistance to heat flow per thickness*

$\textbf{R}_t$**:** *Total resistance for unit*

A: *Area*

$\mathbf{\Delta T}$**:** *Difference between temperature inside and outside*

If we take each component of the building's weather skin and add up the thermal conductivity of the area of each element, we can calculate the building's overall heat gain/loss coefficient, usually signified by the letter Q. Thus $Q = \sum U A \Delta T$, described in the United States by BTU/hr°F and everywhere else by Watts/°C. *BTU* stands for "British Thermal Unit," the energy required to raise one pound of water 1°F, about the energy of a wooden match when burned.

2010

It is possible to design and construct a modern yurt that is thermally acceptable if we apply basic passive design principles for our time and capability, as the originators of this design did for their time and situation. We could use for the walls and roof lightweight materials that provide more insulation. Modern material technology offers us this opportunity with very lightweight layers of highly reflective fabric or insulating fiberfill (as used in sleeping bags). Both would be more appropriate than one layer of canvas. In addition, the central aperture could be geometrically modified to optimize the solar radiation situation based on the site and season. Side windows or a glass door could be added for additional solar gain if needed.

Fig. 2.13.

Table 2.3. *R-values of common envelope materials.*

Insulation Type (Note: Value may very with installation method)	RSI per cm thickness	R [US] per inch thickness	RSI per thickness indicated	R [US] per thickness indicated
Blanket or Batt mineral fiber 8.6 cm [3.5"]			2	11
14 cm [5.6"]			3.3	19
19 cm [7.5"]			4	22
24 cm [9.5"]			5.3	30
28 cm [11"]			7	38
38 cm [15"]			8.8	50
Boards and Slabs Polystyrene (extruded)	0.35	5		
Cellular Polyurethane	0.4	6		
Cellular Polyisocyanurate	0.49	5.6–7		
Loose Fill Cellulosic Insulation	0.23	3.4		
Perlite Expanded	0.23	3.4		
Perlite Dense	0.18	2.6		
Pumice	0.14	2		
Rice Hulls	0.14–0.20	2–3		
Vermiculite	0.14	2.1		
Spray Applied Aircrete	0.27	3.9		
Polyurethane Foam	0.4	6		
Cellulosic Fiber	0.22	3.8		
Glass Fiber	0.26	3.8		
Reflective Insulation Reflective material in center of air cavity			0.6	3.2
Transparent Insulation Honeycomb Polycarbonate 50 mm			0.5	2.8
Honeycomb Polycarbonate 100 mm			0.9	5.3
Capillaries Polycarbonate 100 mm			1	5.9
Capillaries Acrylic Glass 100 mm			1.1	6.3
Aerogel between Dual Glazing 35 mm			5.8	36.3
Vacuum Panel 2.5cm [1"]			3.4	50

Recent concerns about indoor air quality in tight buildings has generated the increased use of nontoxic, natural products for insulation.

	RSI per cm thickness	R [US] per inch thickness	RSI per thickness indicated	R [US] per thickness indicated
Wool Fiber	0.27	3.8		
Wool Felt	0.23	3.3		
Hemp	0.21	3		
Cotton	2.5	3.5		
Flax	0.21	3		
Cork	0.22	3.2		
Straw bale 46 cm [18"]	0.10–0.20	1.5–2.0	2.8	33

It is unfortunate that the United States uses different units than the rest of the world and that energy units are more complex than simpler measurements like length, area, and volume, but fortunately online conversions are available.

This book uses US units, and sometimes we also give the metric or SI units.

Reduce Heat Loss Through the Building's Skin

The thermal resistance of materials (R) is defined as 1/conductance. R-value is described in BTU/Hr/ft²/°F. The thermal resistance of a material also depends on the airflow across the surface. Air films at the surface can increase the R-value as much at 0.07 on a vertical surface when the air is still. Moving air will drop this as low as 0.02. All wall sections should be calculated together to consider all the materials and airspaces.

Reducing Heat Loss Through the Building's Glazing

Windows are a primary concern because their total resistance to heat flow may be only 0.9 for a single-glazed window. Dual-pane windows may achieve 1.8—still only one-tenth the value of a well-insulated wall and one twenty-fifth that of a super-insulated wall. Due to the dominance of windows in the conductive heat transfer situation, considerable work has been done to increase the efficiency of windows. The first step in this process was the use of dual-glazed windows, perhaps initially in ancient Rome. At first, modern double-pane windows had a propensity for the seal that joined the two panes to fail, especially if installed on a slope, causing more innovative passive designers to use a variation on the old storm window. These are two separate windows with a 2- to 3-inch airspace between them. Window technology has advanced enough for dual-glazed windows to become the standard application, although seal failure will still occur in many windows after ten to twenty years. It has now become hard to find new single-glazed windows without paying extra for a custom configuration.

Triple-glazed windows with argon gas between panes have become available with an R-value of up to 4.35. These are used in areas with high heating loads such as northern North America and Northern Europe.

The advent of low-emissivity (low-E) glazing led to another leap in window efficiency with increased insulation capability, but this also complicated design by requiring specification of different glasses for different orientations. Manufacturers have responded by reducing the availability of higher solar heat gain glass.

Low-E window technology uses a metallic film that reduces radiant heat flow through the glazing by reflecting radiation back in the direction from which it came. This may be applied to the glass or a plastic film between glass layers. The plastic film can be used to create a triple glazing. These windows can reflect much of the long-wave infrared part of solar radiation (good for cooling) while still transmitting the visible component, and can also reflect back the radiation from the warm interior surface of the glass (good for heating). This approach is good enough to essentially make low-E double glazing as good as triple glazing without the low-E coating. There are several types of low-E glazing that do different things—which is the tricky part for the passive designer interested in heating, because these are not equally available. For now, let us say if we want to passively heat, but we choose the most commonly available low-E glazing, we could do everything else correctly but still fail miserably, as illustrated in figure 2.14. In addition to the R-value of the glass, we must also consider its solar heat gain expressed in its solar heat gain coefficient (SHGC). The SHGC is a measure of how much heat flows through the glass to the interior of the building compared with amount that strikes it, usually ranging from 0.2 to 0.9. For passive solar heating, a higher SHGC is desirable but becoming harder to find; efforts have focused on conservation rather than energy capture and production with passive solar systems.

Fig. 2.14. *A section through two identical passive buildings except for the type of low-E glazing. The building that doesn't capture the winter sun will be uncomfortable and require more costly heating.*

This problem with glazing illustrates a basic rule in passive design, which is that single-purpose functions and reductionist thinking are the biggest enemy to accomplishing our goals. If we look at glazing facing the equator as only good for energy conservation and do not take into account energy production at the same time (as described on page 10), we can design an energy-efficient building but not achieve the next step, a passive solar energy-producing building.

Optimized Air Infiltration

Weatherization

Infiltration losses can be just as great as conductive losses and may easily account for half of the winter heat loss in a well-insulated but poorly weatherized building. Weatherstripping doors and windows and caulking and sealing building joints, access holes, and other areas will reduce unwanted infiltration.

Recent improvements in insulation and glazing techniques have made air infiltration the prime contributor to winter heat loss; however, complications arise in buildings that are so tight that the flow of fresh air to maintain the health of its occupants is compromised.

A fresh-air intake should be provided for any fireplace, stove, or furnace. Chemical properties of interior materials and their behavior will affect the fresh-air needs of the occupants. Nontoxic materials, finishes, and furnishings are preferable. Proximity to smoking areas, perfumes, and other odors contribute to air-quality and ventilation needs as well.

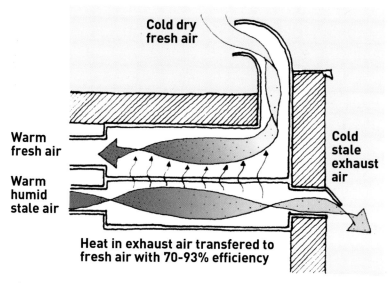

Fig. 2.15. *Air-to-air heat exchanger.*

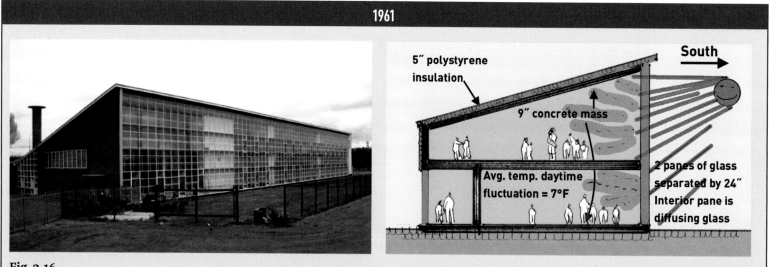

Fig. 2.16.

St. George's School near Wallasey, England. This highly glazed, highly massed, and highly insulated school provided 100 percent of the heating without a furnace. Designed by Emslie A. Morgan, an unsung passive hero, the design provides 50 percent of the heating by solar insolation and 50 percent from internal loads (34 percent lighting, 16 percent from occupants).

Fresh-Air Needs

Advances in materials technology allow for a much more energy-efficient envelope with regard to both convection and air infiltration. When these are correctly understood and applied, buildings can heat themselves even in difficult climates with a small amount of solar insolation and heat internally generated by people, light, and electrical equipment.

This was first demonstrated at St. George's School in Wallasey, England (latitude 52.5°N). This building operated successfully without a mechanical heating system for many years, relying on heat from the students and the sun. Eventually changing use patterns (fewer students and less internal gain) and codes led to retrofitting with a mechanical system. In the 1980s, residences with high levels of insulation and weatherization in Saskatchewan were also heated almost completely by solar energy and internal loads. These techniques of minimizing heat loss enough to allow very large solar heating fractions are most recently being applied at a much larger scale in the *Passivhaus* movement in Northern Europe, particularly Germany, as described on page 14.

Table 2.4. *Approaches to air infiltration and fresh-air needs.*

Fresh air occurs by default	Traditionally, the air change per hour (ACH) of residential scale buildings was such that fresh air needs were provided by infiltration only. This usually averaged about one ACH. This is still the case for passive cooling in humid climates utilizing ventilation cooling see passive cooling section.
High-efficiency passive solar building	In contrast to mechanical conditioned buildings with sealed windows and little individual control the goal is to allow control of ventilation by the occupant. A super-insulated passive house should perform so well that it is possible to have some windows slightly open almost all winter, integrating individual choice, control, and air infiltration.
Hybrid system (passive–active)	The envelope is very tight with ACH between 0.25 and 0.50. Fresh air needs are provided by a ventilation system using an efficient air-to-air heat exchanger similar to fig. 2.15.

1988

Fig. 2.17. *An example of second-wave straw bale construction. Demonstration blueprint farm Laredo, Texas, 1988, by the Center for Maximum Potential Building Systems (CMPBS).*

The first residential building to demonstrate the value of super-insulation in conjunction with air-to-air heat exchangers for air supply was the Saskatchewan house built in Regina in 1977 by the National Research Council of Canada. It provided 100 percent of the heating needs in this severe climate without an installed furnace. Because of its success, similar buildings were built in Massachusetts and Montana in the 1980s, but further activity in the United States was stopped by the oil glut that occurred in the mid-1980s and the influence of the fossil-fuel industry on national policy.

Straw bale construction, first used in the upper Great Plains of North America in the 1890s, was rediscovered at this time because it was an inexpensive way of providing R-30 insulation using what was considered a waste product.

Utilizing Energy-Efficient Construction

It is generally not appreciated how recently energy-efficient construction practices were adopted. However, if you get involved with many remodeling projects, it becomes clear. Insulation may not be found in many buildings built before the 1960s. Even as late as the 1970s, insulation was pretty minimal in California—only R-11 fiberglass in the roof cavity and no insulation in the walls. Even in very cold places such as Anchorage, Alaska (10,500 HDD base 65°F), the common wall was often only 2-by-4 studs with fiberglass insulation with a nominal value of R-11, but actually much less considering conduction through the wall framing.

Good insulation and weatherization did not really become a serious concern in the United States until after the energy crisis during the 1973 oil embargo. Efforts to create more energy-efficient buildings at the time often created their own problems. Increasing insulation in the roof beyond R-19 and making tighter buildings created the need for venting air cavities above roof insulation, but this was not common practice in residential construction. The improved insulation created more potential for condensation on the cold inner surface of the roof and could result in mold and rot with inappropriate detailing.

The health problems associated with the growth of mold were important. Tightening buildings to reduce air infiltration coincided with the explosion of newer artificial materials used for furnishings, fixtures, and household products with increased off-gassing of toxic materials. The result was the identification of sick building syndrome (SBS), which became a large problem in the 1980s and continues today, accentuated by sealed buildings, poorly maintained HVAC systems, and interior materials susceptible to the growth of molds or emitting harmful gases. As a result of the high costs associated with SBS, new green building standards are concerned about indoor air quality (IAQ).

With modeling and optimization studies from the 1980s to the present, a better understanding of optimal insulation levels and rules of when to use enhanced ventilation utilizing air-to-air heat exchangers become clearer for passive solar buildings. These developments are summarized in table 2.5.

Nominal insulation value stated on insulation material is typically much higher than the actual value of a wall because of conduction through framing and less-than-perfect installation. Added framing

for openings, joints, fire breaks, or seismic resistance can reduce insulation values 10 to 25 percent. Insulation performance can also be degraded by moisture buildup, so placement of a vapor barrier is important and will vary depending on climate. Venting the cold surface of insulated walls or simplifying moisture control with closed-cell-foam-type insulation can minimize these losses. However, the production process, useful life, disposal, and the potential for hazardous off-gassing in a fire are life-cycle considerations for insulation. Certain insulation materials such as straw bales should be allowed to breathe water vapor, rather than seal in vapor with a barrier. In this case, providing weep screens at the bottom of the wall is important.

Table 2.5. *The range of insulation values in RSI (R in the United States) for a passive skin-dominated building.*

Biome	Subtropical	Temperate	Cold *	Very cold *
Roofs	3.3 [19]	8 [45]	10.5 [60]	17.6 [100]
Walls	7 [11]	5.3 [30]	7 [40]	17.6 [100]

* Fresh air enhancement via air-to-air heat exchanger systems.

Proper Orientation

One of the earliest design decisions essential for passive heating is the orientation of the building to the sun. As shown on page 13, orientation to the equator is best. This has been known, exploited, forgotten, ignored, rediscovered, and exploited again many times throughout history. Knowing this and really utilizing it in the design process are two different things. It's easy to get distracted with other aspects of site planning such as views, property lines, circulation, access, and regulatory requirements. However, a really good designer should be able to take all these factors into account and not lose proper solar orientation in the process. Over-abstraction of the design process makes it too easy to ignore basics like orientation. We've consulted with architects who are into working drawings and still do not know which way south is, much less the nuances of magnetic declination and sun angles as shown on page 26. We recommend showing the equatorial direction on plans to continually remind ourselves of this important aspect. Therefore, in North America and Europe use south

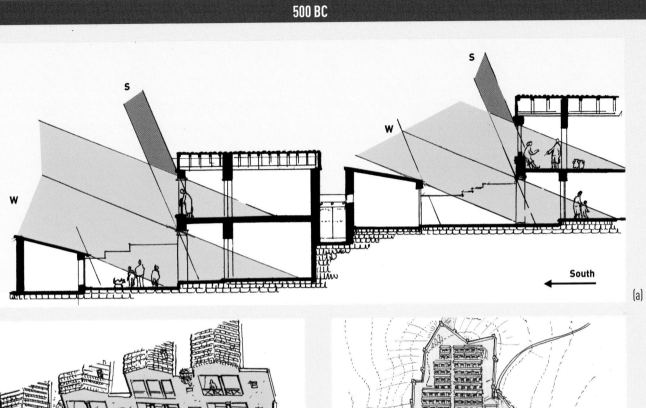

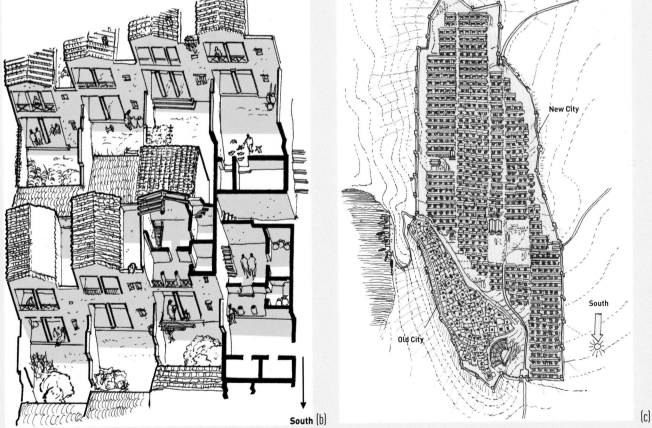

Fig. 2.18. *(a, b) Section and isometric of the solar city of Priene in Asia Minor. (c) Many Hellenistic cities at this period were enlarged using the solar planning principles of Hippodamus. This example on the right is the city plan of Olynthus in Northern Greece.*

There are many ways of determining insolation patterns on and in buildings. You can draw multiple sections using descriptive geometry or use computer programs that can quickly show sun patterns—*if* you ask the right questions.

Since passive design is essentially holistic design with an emphasis on integration, we have found that it's best to investigate insolation patterns in the most direct and easily visualized way in relation to the building's overall form. For this reason, we are very partial to models. Three-dimensional models allow better integration, because the user can visualize the whole building and site without the tediousness of drawing multiple sections or relying on the often hidden black-box assumptions of the computer program. These are better used later in the design process when more accuracy is required. It is very easy to change a 3-D model into a 4-D model (the addition of time) with the use of the sun-peg diagrams shown in figures 2.19 and 2.20. These can be used to essentially turn your model into a personal heliodon. The steps in using sun-peg diagrams are:

1. Find the chart nearest your latitude.

2. Make a copy of the chart (expanding it on a copier or computer if desired).

3. Make a peg whose height above the chart's surface equals that shown on the chart. Mount this peg where noted. It must stand perfectly vertical relative to the model.

4. Mount your copy of the chart with attached peg on the model. The chart must be perfectly horizontal

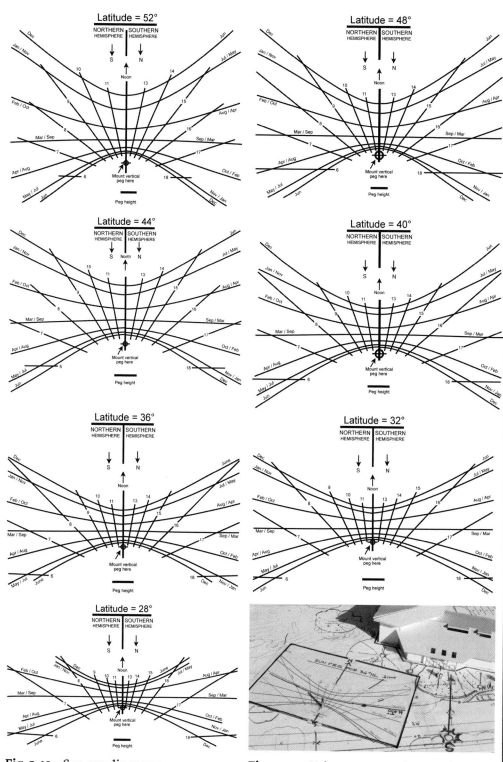

Fig. 2.19. *Sun-peg diagrams.*

Fig. 2.20. *Using a sun-peg chart to determine insolation on October 19.*

over its entire surface, and the true south arrow must be the same as true south on the model.

5. Choose a test time and date. Take your model out into direct sunlight and tilt the model until the shadow of the peg points to the chosen time and date. When the end of the peg's shadow touches this point, your model will show the correct sun and shadow patterns for this date and time.

Solar access is also important. Solar access was first given legal standing in Greek and Roman times. It was rediscovered in the 1970s. Some cities and many states now provide some type of protection for solar access (www.solarabcs.org/ solaraccess). It is important to determine your solar access rights to avoid building a lovely passive solar building that is shaded by a neighboring home, shopping center, or line of trees.

arrows to orient drawings and plans. This may sound trivial, but it serves as a constant reminder of the primacy of proper orientation as the design progresses and multiple designers become involved.

How much leeway do we have with regard to orientation? Up to 15° off south is usually not too much of a problem. Even slipping orientation 20 to 25° off may not be disastrous. However, beyond this the building's relationship to solar radiation gets increasingly difficult, not just for heating but more critically in the control of unwanted radiation from the east and west and during fall and summer.

South–north sections are often the most important drawing in visualizing passive design, as shown in figure 2.21. Visualization is made more difficult when the building is not oriented to the equator. This makes layout of sunlight and sun patterns in the section drawings a geometry problem because the rays of sunlight at the most important times are not seen at true angles as they would be with better orientation. A designer has to do more calculations to use profile angles to visualize interior light and insolation patterns. A profile angle is the angle a line appears in a view that is not perpendicular to the line in question—in this case the ray of sunlight penetrating the building.

A device that is very helpful in dealing with site orientation questions is a solar site selector (figure 2.22). This simple device allows you to determine the effect of barriers like adjacent buildings, trees, and the like on available solar radiation.

Fig. 2.22. *Using a solar site selector.*

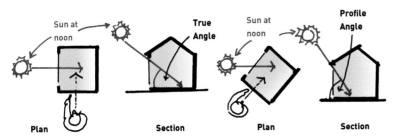

Fig. 2.21. *True angle and profile angle.*

Classic Approaches to Passive Heating

Direct-Gain Systems

The six classic approaches to passive heating (see page 45) are so pure as to be caricatures. Their application in the 1980s showed that they are usually best considered as components that can be used in various combinations rather than as pure systems. However, it is helpful to look at them independently to be able to explore some of the principles involved before looking at combinations.

Each approach must provide three functions: (1) thermal collection; (2) thermal storage; (3) thermal transfer and control. In direct systems, these three functions are accomplished in the interior space of the building. Collection is accomplished by apertures that allow sunlight directly into the interior space, and thermal storage is accomplished by elements within this space. Thermal transfer is accomplished by radiation from this storage, and control is also accomplished spatially. Because of this intimate relationship to interior space, direct-gain systems are also natural lighting systems (covered in depth in chapter 4). However, some aspects must be discussed here as well since direct gain and natural lighting are so intimately interconnected.

Looking at seven hundred years of architectural history, we can see the sequential developments that were necessary to be able to achieve direct-gain passive solar heating. These are (1) the development of glazing systems that allowed natural light to become a major architectural consideration; (2) the rediscovery of orientation and control aspects that allowed better use of this light; (3) the development and availability of better-quality insulation; and (4) the conscious use of thermal mass. Most important, however, once these things were available, was the correct configuration and sizing of all these features into an integrated whole that could optimize the building's response to the thermal environment. This became easier to achieve with the development of computer-aided simulation models in the 1980s.

1300

Sainte Chapelle, Paris (a)

1850 (f)

Crystal Palace, World's Fair, London

1500

Blue Mosque, Istanbul (b)

1900

Casa Batlló, Barcelona (c)
north elevation

Casa Batlló, Barcelona (d)
south elevation

Casa Batlló, Barcelona interior light (e)

Fig. 2.23. *(a, b) Gothic and later Ottoman architecture incorporated glass as a major architectural element. (c, d, e, f) Improvements in glass manufacturing and mass production of glazing systems allowed large public buildings to be made of glass. (c, d, e) Optimizing orientation and control, this famous building by Antoni Gaudí differentiates north and south by the type and amount of glass to provide optimum orientation and seasonal solar control. As a high-mass building of stone, masonry, and tile, it has all the elements of a good direct-gain building except for good insulation, which was not available at the time.*

1920 Nebühl, Switzerland, Solar Housing Estate.

In Northern Europe, there was much emphasis on improving health by large solar developments. Germany led in this effort, which was cut short by World War II. After some false starts, south was rediscovered to be the optimum orientation.

1940 Solar buildings by George Fred Keck, Chicago, Illinois.

Libby Owens Ford developed the first commercially available double glazing, which stimulated solar designs in the United States. Insulation, however, was minimal, thermal mass unknown, and most designs overglazed, so performance was not up to its potential.

1946 Prefabricated solar house, Camden, New Jersey.

1946 Prefabricated solar house, Camden, New Jersey.

Fig. 2.24.

1952 Frank Lloyd Wright's Solar Hemisphere, Madison, Wisconsin.

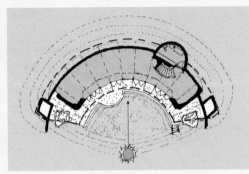

As usual, Frank Lloyd Wright led in innovation. This house has good orientation, some mass on the north wall, is bermed on the north, and has good solar control. Insulation was still inadequate and the house is undermassed and overglazed, but it was a step up from conventional housing.

1961 St. George's School, Wallasey, England.

An obscure architect, Emslie A. Morgan, builds a very close to optimum passive building in a challenging climate (see also page 50). Overglazing and overheating could be a problem, but the building is not occupied in the summer during school recess.

1972 Sunscoop House, Santa Fe, New Mexico, by David Wright (no relation to FLW).

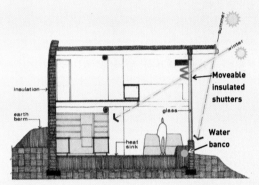

This was probably the first close to optimized direct-gain building besides St. George's School. It is highly massed by adobe walls, insulated on the exterior with polystyrene foam, masonry floors, and water bancos. Sizing, while improving, is still a guess; in hindsight, it is probably overglazed.

1980 Development of simulation models.

Phil Niles in California and Doug Balcomb in New Mexico develop the first performance-based passive models allowing optimized sizing of components. Many simulation programs exist, and a list can be found at www.eere.energy.gov.

System 1: Direct Gain/Distributed Mass

In the simplest direct-gain system, thermal mass is spread around in relatively thin layers throughout the interior space. Transfer of heat from sunlight to the mass is by radiation if directly in sunlight, or by re-radiation or convection from warmer areas. Radiation coupling for all thermal mass is desirable, but it is not possible without overglazing a building; convectively coupled mass works, however, and can be used to good effect. It's usually best for this distributed mass to be a light color. While this reduces direct absorption, it helps reflect light onto a greater surface of the distributed mass. In addition, light colors are also much better for natural lighting, reducing the glare that comes with dark interiors contrasting too greatly with large bright openings.

Distributed mass is best for balanced heating and cooling conditions. Night ventilation cooling over distributed mass allows greater surface area for heat dissipation by convection to the cool night air vented over the mass during the cooling mode.

System 2: Direct Gain/Concentrated Mass

In this approach, the thermal mass is more concentrated, perhaps as a water tank or masonry wall. The concentrated mass allows greater efficiency for heating but diminished effectiveness for night ventilation cooling. Water in tanks, tubes, or containers is one of the most effective thermal-mass materials since it is 2.7 times as effective at storing energy as concrete by volume and 6 times more effective by weight. Thick masonry elements such as heavy walls, floor slabs, or structural elements made of stone, rammed earth, adobe, or concrete can also be used as concentrated mass.

Concentrated mass is usually smaller in surface area and can be darker and therefore more absorptive without creating a dark interior. Re-radiation at long wavelengths (see page 41), however, is less dependent upon color, so surfaces not radiatively coupled can be a light color to help with natural lighting.

Details for System 1: Direct Gain/Distributed Mass

APERTURE

Ideally, each room should have an equator-facing solar aperture of the size shown. This is rarely practical, and thought should be given to which rooms should have aperture priority. Usually, rooms used the most face the equator, with less used spaces behind.

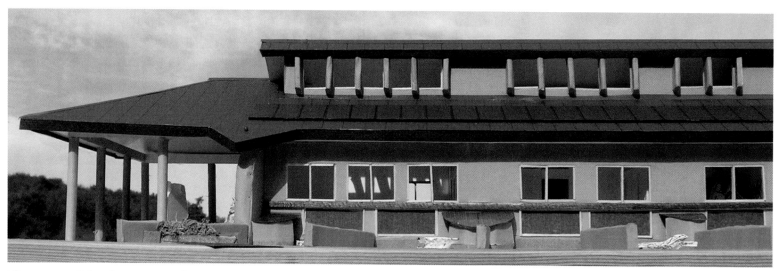

Fig. 2.25a. *Solar dormer, exterior. A dormer or roof monitor has the advantage of putting sunlight high in the middle of the room, helping reduce glare, fading of fabric, and so on. It can also add to the roof structure with fins to better reflect light around the space.*

Fig. 2.25b. *Interior. An optimized dormer prevents unwanted sun in summer by utilizing a horizontal overhang to shade high sun and small wing walls to shade early-morning and late-afternoon horizontal sun.*

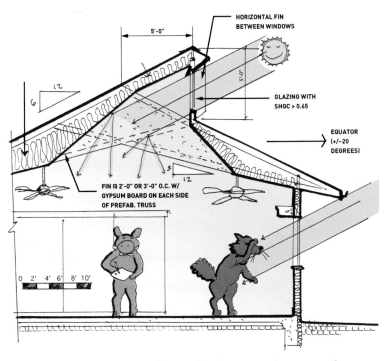

Fig. 2.25c. *Section. Control is easy for the seasonal extremes, but more complex in spring and fall. Early spring usually requires heating and early fall requires cooling, yet the sun angles are equal. Thus it is desirable to adjust the horizontal overhang as shown on page 61.*

THERMAL MASS

More distributed mass is needed than is usually imagined. It must be spread over such a large part of the building's interior; while some areas can be radiatively coupled to available insolation, others have to be convectively coupled.

The most common materials used are shown here. Their heat capacity in bulk and in their most common usage is shown in table 2.6.

Table 2.6. *Heat capacity of common building materials in bulk and by common application.*

	Heat Capacity Bulk		Heat Capacity of Common Application	
	BTU/ft³ °F	kJ/m³ °C	BTU/ft² °F	kJ/m² °C
Concrete	22.5	1,507	7	144
Masonry	18.7	1,253	3.2	65
Gypsum plaster	10.5	703	0.33	7
Phase change	210	14,000	30	600

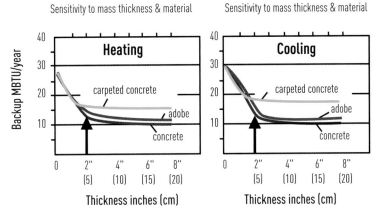

Fig. 2.26a. *An advantage of direct-gain/distributed-mass systems is that the mass is equally helpful for heating and night ventilation cooling, as shown in the sensitivity charts for Fresno, California (latitude 37°N).*

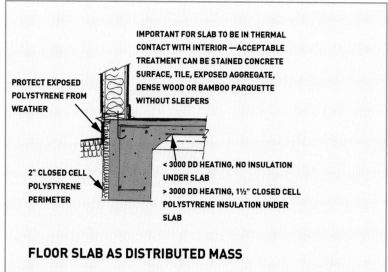

PROTECT EXPOSED POLYSTYRENE FROM WEATHER

IMPORTANT FOR SLAB TO BE IN THERMAL CONTACT WITH INTERIOR —ACCEPTABLE TREATMENT CAN BE STAINED CONCRETE SURFACE, TILE, EXPOSED AGGREGATE, DENSE WOOD OR BAMBOO PARQUETTE WITHOUT SLEEPERS

2" CLOSED CELL POLYSTYRENE PERIMETER

< 3000 DD HEATING, NO INSULATION UNDER SLAB
> 3000 DD HEATING, 1½" CLOSED CELL POLYSTYRENE INSULATION UNDER SLAB

FLOOR SLAB AS DISTRIBUTED MASS

Fig. 2.26b. *In passive systems, often the thermal mass is the only added expense beyond a standard well-insulated building. Therefore it's helpful to be careful and efficient in regard to the mass provided. Free mass is usually available in the floor slab if it is not insulated from the interior space by carpet and is insulated from the exterior.*

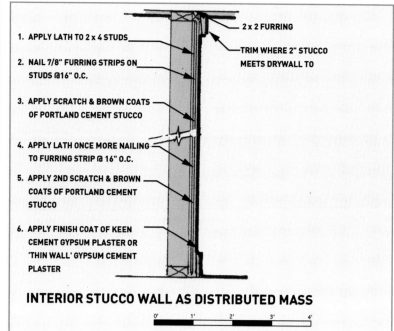

1. APPLY LATH TO 2 x 4 STUDS
2. NAIL 7/8" FURRING STRIPS ON STUDS @16" O.C.
3. APPLY SCRATCH & BROWN COATS OF PORTLAND CEMENT STUCCO
4. APPLY LATH ONCE MORE NAILING TO FURRING STRIP @ 16" O.C.
5. APPLY 2ND SCRATCH & BROWN COATS OF PORTLAND CEMENT STUCCO
6. APPLY FINISH COAT OF KEEN CEMENT GYPSUM PLASTER OR 'THIN WALL' GYPSUM CEMENT PLASTER

2 x 2 FURRING

TRIM WHERE 2" STUCCO MEETS DRYWALL TO

INTERIOR STUCCO WALL AS DISTRIBUTED MASS

Fig. 2.26c. *The slab plus additional mass on interior wall surfaces is usually enough to meet the mass requirements.*

SIZING

Rules of thumb are used to size these components to develop a preliminary design allowing 50 to 60 percent performance. Design refinement using a performance simulation model should then allow an additional 20 to 25 percent improvement in heating performance.

As can be seen from the sensitivity charts above, on a diurnal basis concrete and masonry aren't much more effective beyond 2 inches in thickness. Gypsum plaster or wallboard can be used as cheap distributed mass in two 5/8-inch layers but has less heat capacity, so divide wallboard area by 4.

More Details

These details are typical for residential and light commercial buildings at a mid-latitude temperate climate with balanced heating and cooling loads.

Table 2.7. *Rules of thumb for areas of solar aperture and thermal mass for direct-gain/distributed-mass systems.*

Climate	Very Cold	Cold		Temperature		Tropical Dry	Tropical Wet
Thermal Load	Heating only	Heating only	Heating and some cooling	Balanced heating and cooling	Cooling and some heating	Cooling w/ small heating	Cooling only
Area of aperture per floor area %	10–20%	10–25%	14–20%	9–15%	8–13%	6–11%	0%
Area of mass per area of aperture	5–10%	6–11%	8–12%	9–14%	9–14%	9–14%	9–14%

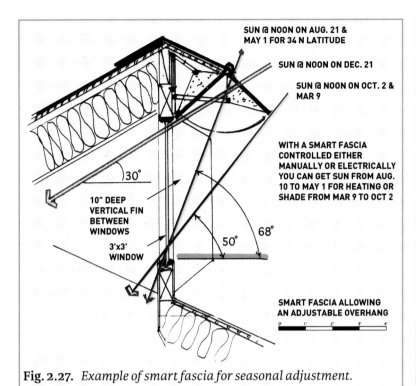

SUN @ NOON ON AUG. 21 &
MAY 1 FOR 34 N LATITUDE

SUN @ NOON ON DEC. 21

SUN @ NOON ON OCT. 2 &
MAR 9

WITH A SMART FASCIA
CONTROLLED EITHER
MANUALLY OR ELECTRICALLY
YOU CAN GET SUN FROM AUG.
10 TO MAY 1 FOR HEATING OR
SHADE FROM MAR 9 TO OCT 2

30°

10" DEEP
VERTICAL FIN
BETWEEN
WINDOWS

3'x3'
WINDOW

50°

68°

SMART FASCIA ALLOWING
AN ADJUSTABLE OVERHANG

Fig. 2.27. *Example of smart fascia for seasonal adjustment.*

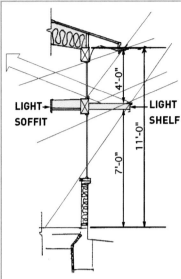

LIGHT
SOFFIT

LIGHT
SHELF

4'-0"

11'-0"

7'-0"

Fig. 2.29. *For higher spaces, the equatorial wall becomes difficult to shade in the summer and still receive sunlight in the winter. A common approach is to use two horizontal overhangs. The lower one provides control to the lower part of the wall and can also act as a light shelf to reflect light deeper into the space. This has additional advantages for improving natural lighting.*

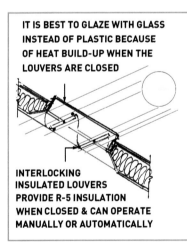

IT IS BEST TO GLAZE WITH GLASS
INSTEAD OF PLASTIC BECAUSE
OF HEAT BUILD-UP WHEN THE
LOUVERS ARE CLOSED

INTERLOCKING
INSULATED LOUVERS
PROVIDE R-5 INSULATION
WHEN CLOSED & CAN OPERATE
MANUALLY OR AUTOMATICALLY

Fig. 2.28. *Skylights accentuate high summer sun gain and overheating and increase nighttime heat losses in winter and are not very effective in gathering low winter sun. If they are steep enough with operable louvers, however, they can be effective and have the advantage of being able to adjust to spring and fall seasonal variations.*

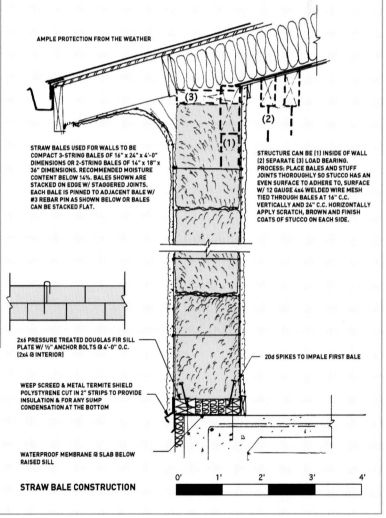

AMPLE PROTECTION FROM THE WEATHER

(3)

(2)

(1)

STRAW BALES USED FOR WALLS TO BE
COMPACT 3-STRING BALES OF 16" x 24" x 4'-0"
DIMENSIONS OR 2-STRING BALES OF 14" x 18" x
36" DIMENSIONS. RECOMMENDED MOISTURE
CONTENT BELOW 14%. BALES SHOWN ARE
STACKED ON EDGE W/ STAGGERED JOINTS.
EACH BALE IS PINNED TO ADJACENT BALE W/
#3 REBAR PIN AS SHOWN BELOW OR BALES
CAN BE STACKED FLAT.

STRUCTURE CAN BE (1) INSIDE OF WALL
(2) SEPARATE (3) LOAD BEARING.
PROCESS: PLACE BALES AND STUFF
JOINTS THOROUGHLY SO STUCCO HAS AN
EVEN SURFACE TO ADHERE TO. SURFACE
W/ 12 GAUGE 4x4 WELDED WIRE MESH
TIED THROUGH BALES AT 16" C.C.
VERTICALLY AND 24" C.C. HORIZONTALLY
APPLY SCRATCH, BROWN AND FINISH
COATS OF STUCCO ON EACH SIDE.

2x6 PRESSURE TREATED DOUGLAS FIR SILL
PLATE W/ ½" ANCHOR BOLTS @ 4'-0" O.C.
(2x4 @ INTERIOR)

20d SPIKES TO IMPALE FIRST BALE

WEEP SCREED & METAL TERMITE SHIELD
POLYSTYRENE CUT IN 2" STRIPS TO PROVIDE
INSULATION & FOR ANY SUMP
CONDENSATION AT THE BOTTOM

WATERPROOF MEMBRANE @ SLAB BELOW
RAISED SILL

STRAW BALE CONSTRUCTION

0'   1'   2'   3'   4'

Fig. 2.30. *The rediscovery of straw bale construction as mentioned on page 18 was a boon for the direct-gain/distributed-mass approach. Bale walls provide greater insulation than most wall systems, and the stucco or plaster applied to the wall surfaces is the right thickness to act as optimized distributed mass, as shown on page 59. The result is a composite wall system that is an excellent fit for the needs of a direct-gain/distributed-mass passive system. It is a prime example of achieving synergy in design, where the whole is greater than a sum of the parts.*

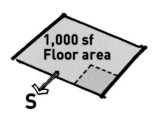

Sample rule-of-thumb calculation balanced heating and cooling of a direct-gain/distributed-mass system in the Northern Hemisphere.

From page 60 south-facing aperture needs to be 9–15% of floor area. Use 12%, 1,000 x .12 = 120 sq. ft.

Dormer with 4 3x3 lights = 36 sq.ft.
South wall windows
   3 4x6 windows = 72 sq.ft.
   1 3X6 window = 18 sq. ft.
total south-facing glass = 126 sq. ft.

From page 60 mass = 10–14 sq.ft./sq. ft.south glass
Use 12%, 126 x 12 = **1,512 sq. ft. mass**

Thermally exposed floor slab minus area covered by walls, closets, cabinets, etc. = 800 sq.ft.

Interior skin of straw bale walls minus windows and area covered by cabinets etc. = 500 sq. ft.

Double 5/8″ gypsum board ceilings
1,200 sq. ft./4 = 125 sq. ft.

total distributed mass = 1,600 sq. ft.

As you can see getting enough mass is the largest challenge with this system which is why the developments described below are so important.

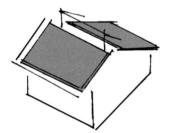

Fig. 2.31. *A sample rule-of-thumb calculation for balanced heating and cooling of a direct-gain/distributed-mass system in the Northern Hemisphere.*

New developments promise to increase the capability of direct-gain/distributed-mass systems while also reducing their cost. These include transparent insulation (see page 19) and phase-change thermal mass (see page 59). Transparent insulation can allow more aperture with less conductive heat loss and hence greater spread of sunlight to distributed mass without adding to conductive heat loss, which has been the limit on glazing to date. Phase-change thermal mass can be used as an additive to masonry or gypsum wallboard to appreciably increase distributed thermal storage capability.

With these recent developments, the direct-gain/distributed-mass approach to passive heating and cooling becomes a much more viable option for many situations than ever before.

Details for System 2: Direct Gain/Concentrated Mass

The difference with concentrated-mass designs is not so much about aperture or spatial relationships but with thermal-mass placement. Here mass is more concentrated, allowing greater efficiency especially for heating. The most efficient thermal mass short of phase-change material is water. Therefore direct-gain/concentrated-mass designs have traditionally been approaches that use large amounts of water in architectural configurations.

Early applications, because of a concern with leaks, used off-the-shelf items that had proven watertight characteristics. However, these components often were not optimally shaped in relation to desired mass and aperture relationships. With performance modeling, later applications were able to better optimize this relationship, often as custom steel water tanks used below the standard window-sill on the south wall.

Fig. 2.32c. *Early large-scale waterwalls 1976.*

Fig. 2.32a. *First modern waterwall by Steve Baer. Corrales, New Mexico, 1970.*

Fig. 2.32b. *Corrugated culverts as waterwalls 1975, Living Systems.*

Fig. 2.32d. *Since 1976, Kalwall Corporation (now Solar Components) has manufactured fiberglass tubes that offer many advantages as translucent waterwalls.w*

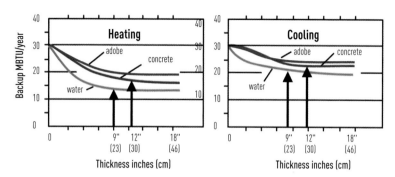

Fig. 2.33. *Sensitivity analysis of concentrated -thermal mass for heating and cooling.*

Table 2.8. *Common concentrated-mass materials.*

	Heat Capacity Bulk		Heat Capacity of Common Application	
	BTU/ft^3 °F	kJ/m^3 °C	BTU/ft^2 °F	kJ/m^2 °C
Masonry	18.7	1253	3.2	65
Water	62.4	4181	46.8	950

The advantages of water can be seen in these sensitivity charts for both heating and cooling for Fresno, California (latitude 37°N). For heating, water has a higher heat capacity and is also able to redistribute heat within the container by convection currents. For cooling via night ventilation, larger surface areas needed for conductive transfer from cool air to the mass diminish somewhat the advantage of concentrated mass for this function. The corrugated surface on culvert-type containers helps by exposing more surface area to cooling air currents.

SIZING

We've only begun to explore water as an architectural material. This effort is important because water has wonderful heat capacity and amazing aesthetic potential, and it's potentially the cheapest and most available material for thermal-mass purposes. We live on a watery planet. If we are to really develop an earth-expressive architecture, water as architectural material will be a part of this evolution.

Fig. 2.34a. *2006 application of a waterwall to a social hall.*

Table 2.9. *Rules of thumb for thermal mass for direct-gain/concentrated-mass systems.*

Climate	Very Cold	Cold		Temperature		Tropical Dry	Tropical Wet
Thermal Load	Heating only	Heating only	Heating and some cooling	Balanced heating and cooling	Cooling and some heating	Cooling w/ small heating	Cooling only
Area of mass per area of aperture	5–10%	6–11%	8–12%	9–12%	8–12%	10–14%	0%

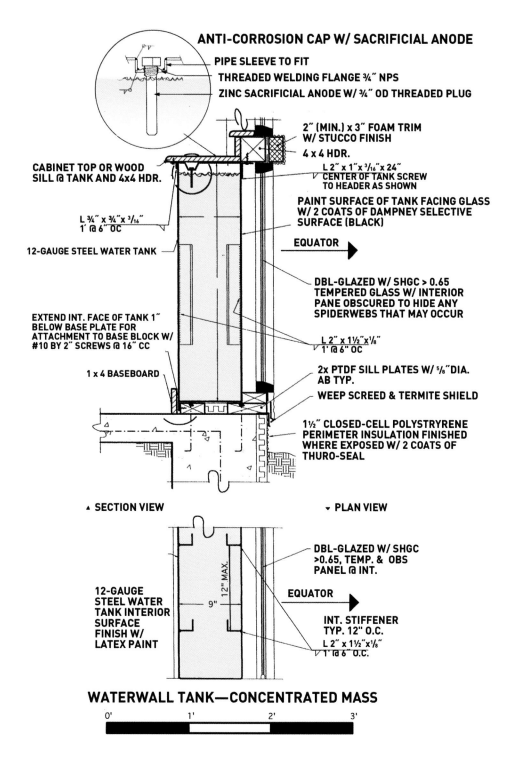

ANTI-CORROSION CAP W/ SACRIFICIAL ANODE

PIPE SLEEVE TO FIT

THREADED WELDING FLANGE ¾" NPS

ZINC SACRIFICIAL ANODE W/ ¾" OD THREADED PLUG

2" (MIN.) x 3" FOAM TRIM W/ STUCCO FINISH

4 x 4 HDR.

L 2" x 1" x ³/₁₆" x 24" CENTER OF TANK SCREW TO HEADER AS SHOWN

CABINET TOP OR WOOD SILL @ TANK AND 4x4 HDR.

PAINT SURFACE OF TANK FACING GLASS W/ 2 COATS OF DAMPNEY SELECTIVE SURFACE (BLACK)

EQUATOR

L ¾" x ¾" x ³/₁₆" 1' @ 6" OC

12-GAUGE STEEL WATER TANK

DBL-GLAZED W/ SHGC > 0.65 TEMPERED GLASS W/ INTERIOR PANE OBSCURED TO HIDE ANY SPIDERWEBS THAT MAY OCCUR

EXTEND INT. FACE OF TANK 1" BELOW BASE PLATE FOR ATTACHMENT TO BASE BLOCK W/ #10 BY 2" SCREWS @ 16" CC

L 2" x 1½" x ⅛" 1' @ 6" OC

1 x 4 BASEBOARD

2x PTDF SILL PLATES W/ ⅝" DIA. AB TYP.

WEEP SCREED & TERMITE SHIELD

1½" CLOSED-CELL POLYSTRYRENE PERIMETER INSULATION FINISHED WHERE EXPOSED W/ 2 COATS OF THURO-SEAL

▲ SECTION VIEW

▼ PLAN VIEW

DBL-GLAZED W/ SHGC >0.65, TEMP. & OBS PANEL @ INT.

12-GAUGE STEEL WATER TANK INTERIOR SURFACE FINISH W/ LATEX PAINT

12" MAX.

9"

EQUATOR

INT. STIFFENER TYP. 12" O.C.

L 2" x 1½" x ⅛" 1' @ 6" O.C.

WATERWALL TANK—CONCENTRATED MASS

0'   1'   2'   3'

Fig. 2.34b. *Waterwall tank: concentrated-mass detail.*

1800

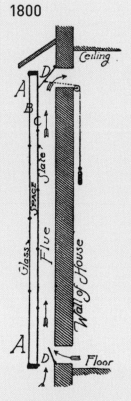

Professor Edward Morse of Salem, Massachusetts, patents a solar heating system made of a glazed wall and air vents. Unfortunately the uninsulated buildings of this era were not efficient enough to make very good use of such a system.

1947

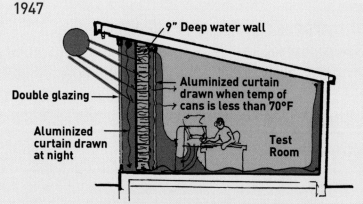

9" Deep water wall
Double glazing
Aluminized curtain drawn when temp of cans is less than 70°F
Aluminized curtain drawn at night
Test Room

From 1938 to 1958, MIT developed and tested four solar houses funded by solar enthusiast Godfrey Lowell Cabot. Most of these were active systems using flat-plate collectors and isolated storage. However the second study done in 1947 was a passive direct-gain system. Great effort was made to make the test rooms the same as a standard "well-insulated" house of the time, which was about R-12, neglecting the prerequisite to passive design discussed on pages 47–49. As a result, performance was disappointing and this approach was prematurely abandoned.

1967

Air vent
12" thick concrete wall
Double glazing
Air vent

Félix Trombe, a French scientist, creates a wall that uses the thermal mass of 12 inches of masonry as a solar heater, allowing a lag of heat flow so that the wall warms the space at night. Heat radiating from the storage wall is supplemented by air vents that allow faster heat transfer to the conditioned space by convection. In passive circles, this design became known a Trombe wall and found widespread use in the 1970s.

1981

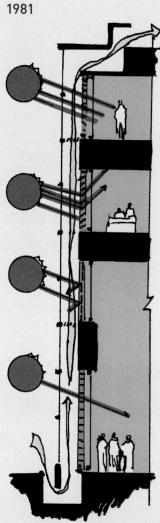

Beginning in the 1950s, modern architecture became plagued by the all-glass curtain wall that—although visually exciting—was thermally disastrous. Using a concept developed by Richard Levine, the Hooker Building in Buffalo, New York, created a thermal wall utilizing curtain-wall technology, an air plenum, and insulated louvers. Since then, this double-skin thermal wall approach has been utilized in many larger buildings, particularly in Northern Europe.

Fig. 2.35. *System 3: History of thermal walls.*

Indirect-Gain Systems

In indirect-gain passive systems, some part of the building's weather skin is evolved to provide the thermal collection, storage, transfer, and control function. For indirect cooling, we would add thermal dissipation, described in the next chapter. Although there are many variations for indirect gain, there are two major approaches. In the first, the exterior wall becomes the passive system, hence the name *thermal wall*. The second approach uses the roof as the passive system This has traditionally been called a roof-pond system since most approaches have used water-pond roofs; however, high-mass solid materials or phase-change materials can also be used. Therefore, the most generic term would be *thermal roof system*. Although to date these have been separate systems, combinations of the two are possible.

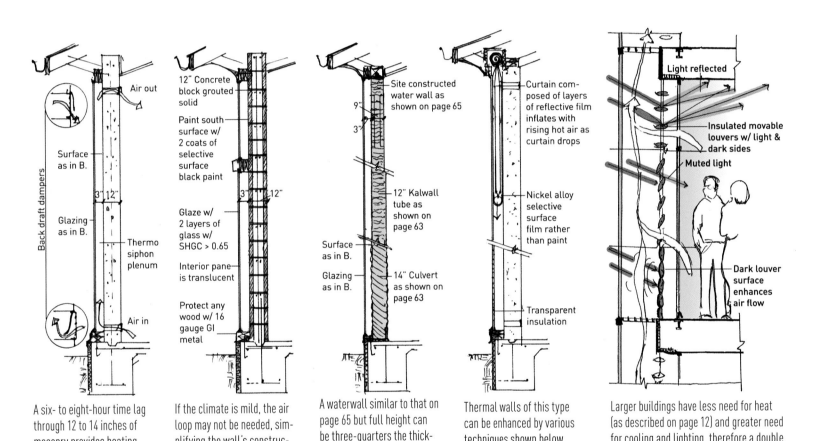

A six- to eight-hour time lag through 12 to 14 inches of masonry provides heating after sunset. Vents create a thermal siphon air loop, providing early-morning heating while keeping the south surface of the wall cooler and thus a more efficient solar collector.

If the climate is mild, the air loop may not be needed, simplifying the wall's construction. A rule of thumb is that an unvented thermal wall can be used if the average January temperature is 50°F or over with good insolation.

A waterwall similar to that on page 65 but full height can be three-quarters the thickness of a masonry wall and has no need for the air loop, since water mixes itself by stratification.

Thermal walls of this type can be enhanced by various techniques shown below.

Larger buildings have less need for heat (as described on page 12) and greater need for cooling and lighting, therefore a double thermal wall can be used that can control heat gain, enhance natural ventilation, and provide better lighting for high buildings.

Fig. 2.36. *Variations in the evolution of thermal walls.*

System 3: Indirect Gain/Thermal Wall

The history of indirect systems shown on pages 66–67 provides the basis of the definition of system 3 (and sometimes system 4) in the classic passive nomenclature. However, progress in Europe with Foster's evolution of the thermal wall into a thermal envelope suggests that a more up-to-date term for system 3 should be *thermal envelope.*

Details for System 3: Indirect Gain/Thermal Walls and Thermal Envelopes

In recent years, innovation in passive design has moved from the United States to Europe. There the evolution of the thermal wall into thermal envelopes with expanded functions of daylighting and natural ventilation have become more common.

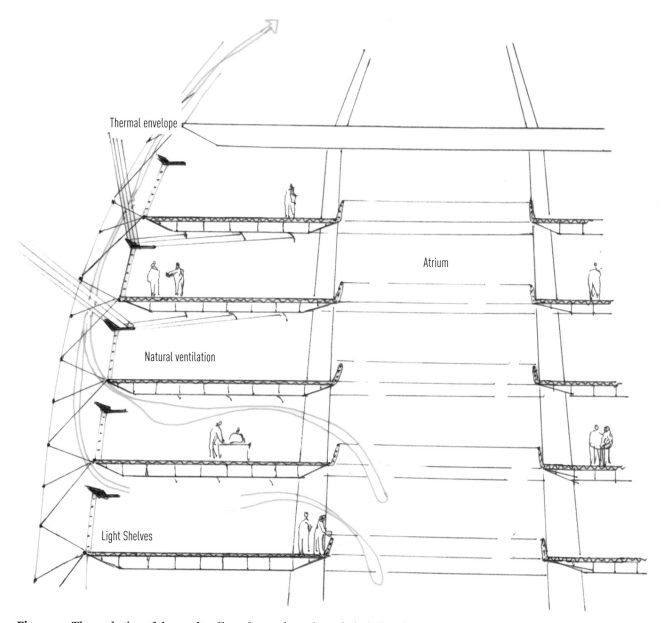

Fig. 2.37. *The evolution of thermal walls to thermal envelopes in buildings in Germany by Norman Foster and engineers Battle and McCarty.*

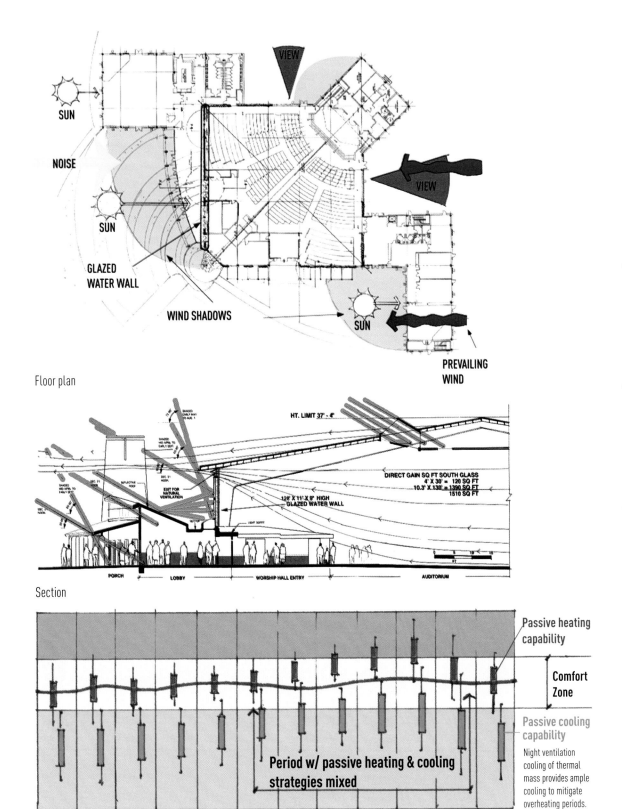

Floor plan

Section

Passive cooling and heating capability to achieve thermal comfort.

Passive heating capability

Comfort Zone

Passive cooling capability

Night ventilation cooling of thermal mass provides ample cooling to mitigate overheating periods.

Period w/ passive heating & cooling strategies mixed

Fig. 2.38.
An example of the waterwall approach. The size of this assembly space (140-foot span) made it very economical to use a pre-engineered rigid steel frame. However, it is difficult to get the amount of solar aperture and mass needed for passive conditioning within this structure. Therefore the passive component was decoupled from the structure by creating a 128-foot-long waterwall on the entire south face above the lobby space. Heating is done by this 1,365-square-foot waterwall, leaving only 112 square feet of direct gain in the roof. The performance model for this building uses the Energy 10 performance prediction model. Cooling is done by night ventilation over high-mass floors and the waterwall. Each type of thermal wall has its unique character that can be used for other functions in an integrated design. Illustrated here is a situation where the massive barrier-like qualities of a large waterwall are used as sound protection and space definition, and for movement of cool night air when needed.

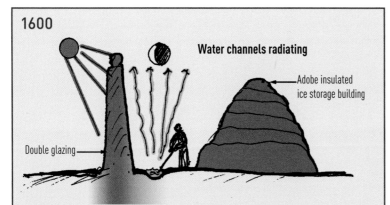

1600

Water channels radiating

Adobe insulated
ice storage building

Double glazing

Yakh-chal (ice wall) ice-making structure in Iran.

1969

Harold Hay, the inventor of this system, with roof pond test cell in Phoenix, Arizona.

1973

Atascadero Roof Pond Prototype. Insulation retracted exposing the ponds. Insulation extended covering the ponds. This system provided 100 percent of the residential heating and cooling requirements.
Fig. 2.39.

Details for System 4: Indirect-Gain/Roof Pond and Thermal Roof Details

Roof ponds are very simple in concept but can be tricky in application. A large amount of thermal mass on a radiative roof (usually an inexpensive steel deck) is shaded by movable insulation during the night in winter and exposed during the day, allowing indirect-gain solar heating. By shading the mass during the day in the summer and exposing it at night, the same system achieves effective indirect loss cooling to the night sky. Although roof ponds are the top performers of the six classic passive types, they have been the least used. There are several reasons for this situation. Until recently this system was stalled by patent and licensing issues, and industrial design development of the system components has not been done. People are also afraid of water overhead, but with new materials the roof pond might be replaced with a phase-change material. Of the classic approaches, this requires the most integration with architecture, which goes against the grain of a reductionist-thinking culture that emphasizes parts over wholes.

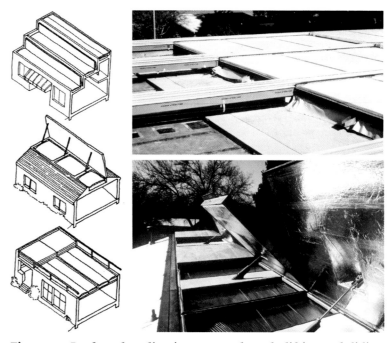

Fig. 2.40. *Roof pond applications, stepped ponds, lifting and sliding insulated covers.*

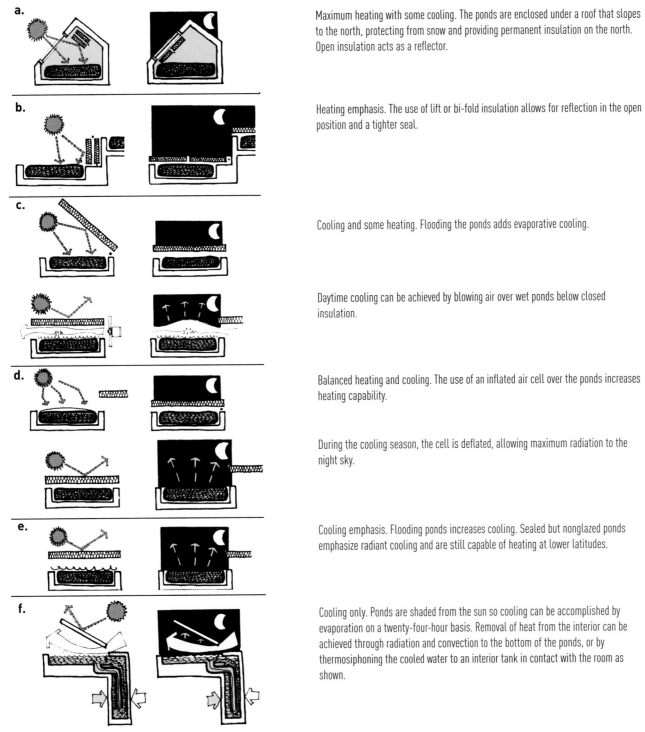

a. Maximum heating with some cooling. The ponds are enclosed under a roof that slopes to the north, protecting from snow and providing permanent insulation on the north. Open insulation acts as a reflector.

b. Heating emphasis. The use of lift or bi-fold insulation allows for reflection in the open position and a tighter seal.

c. Cooling and some heating. Flooding the ponds adds evaporative cooling.

Daytime cooling can be achieved by blowing air over wet ponds below closed insulation.

d. Balanced heating and cooling. The use of an inflated air cell over the ponds increases heating capability.

During the cooling season, the cell is deflated, allowing maximum radiation to the night sky.

e. Cooling emphasis. Flooding ponds increases cooling. Sealed but nonglazed ponds emphasize radiant cooling and are still capable of heating at lower latitudes.

f. Cooling only. Ponds are shaded from the sun so cooling can be accomplished by evaporation on a twenty-four-hour basis. Removal of heat from the interior can be achieved through radiation and convection to the bottom of the ponds, or by thermosiphoning the cooled water to an interior tank in contact with the room as shown.

Fig. 2.41. *The adaptation of roof ponds in various climates can be accomplished by changing the roof configuration and the type of movable insulation.*

Fig. 2.42. *Adaptation of roof ponds to a multistory urban situation. This design was predicted to provide 100 percent heating and cooling in Sacramento, California.*

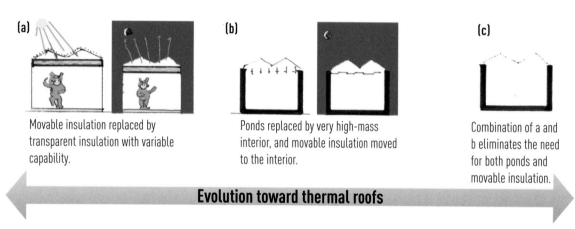

(a) Movable insulation replaced by transparent insulation with variable capability.

(b) Ponds replaced by very high-mass interior, and movable insulation moved to the interior.

(c) Combination of a and b eliminates the need for both ponds and movable insulation.

Evolution toward thermal roofs

Fig. 2.43. *Evolution toward thermal roofs employing no moving parts.*

More holistic design will lead to widespread use of this approach. New developments in insulation and thermal mass can allow for the reduction of redundancies and greater simplification of this proven and highly efficient approach to passive heating and cooling.

Isolated-Gain Passive Heating and Sunspaces

Isolated-Gain Heating

Isolated or indirect solar heating systems can also be installed on new or, more commonly, existing buildings. These may be called a sunspace, solarium, sunroom, solar greenhouse, or thermosiphon air system. We consider four general types: sunspace, seasonal sunspace, solar greenhouse, and thermosiphon.

Sunspace

A sunspace, solarium, or conservatory typically is on the equator-facing side of the building. It adds window area for added solar gain, but buffers loss because it can commonly be closed off from the house at night. The mostly vertical glass can be shaded in summer to reduce overheating. Thermal mass can be added to reduce temperature swings to protect plants in the sunspace, but for maximum heating less mass may be preferable.

The essential details for an effective sunspace are sufficient vent areas for effective air exchange with the conditioned building space. This means large vents up high to move hot air into the house and low vents for cooler return air. In a suspended-floor building this may be by an underfloor plenum (channel for airflow) from the polar side. The sunspace floor can be set below building-floor level to reduce backflow of cold air into the building. A photovoltaic-panel-driven fan or normal fan can be used to increase heat flow into the building. High-efficiency low-voltage motors and propellers from electric model airplanes may prove very useful for moving the air.

In summer, vents, roll-down shades, or landscaping is needed to reduce overheating. Again, vents should be high for venting and low for intake. The intake air may be pulled from outside or from the house, to provide ventilation flow.

Thermal mass is optional. In many cases, it will be desirable to temper the microclimate in the sunspace throughout the year. This is particularly important if it will be used to grow plants, or will be open to the house for much of the year. Sunspaces are often very pleasant, and people and pets tend to spend more time in them than might be expected.

SEASONAL SUNSPACE

A seasonal sunspace may be very effective for retrofitting existing buildings. It can add the considerable solar energy needed to warm an under-insulated building. One of the best strategies is adding seasonal glazing to an existing porch, wall, or patio area. This can be as simple or sophisticated as design and budget allow. Twin- or triple-wall polycarbonate panels offer a very strong, light method of glazing. You might consider such panels as large storm windows for the porch.

The most effective orientation is equator-facing, but east- or west-facing porches can also be very useful heaters in winter, early spring, and late fall. An east-facing porch can pop the building temperature early in the morning, and a west-facing porch can give a nice boost in the afternoon, but both will be heaters in the summer unless shaded. In very cold climates, the sunspace may be used in the warmer months of the year but insulated in the cold dark months. It will still act as a buffer space and wall-insulation upgrade. The keys are glazing, vent area and placement, and supplemental fans as needed. Thermal mass may be desirable as well, and isolating it is usually important.

Fig. 2.44. *This open-porch-to-sunspace retrofit in Berkeley, California, dramatically improved thermal performance and created additional living space.*

Fig. 2.45. *A sunspace from the exterior and interior in Cambria, California.*

Fig. 2.46. *A solar greenhouse in central California.*

SOLAR GREENHOUSE

A solar greenhouse typically has much more glazing, including sloped glazing overhead. This adds more light and heat, but also adds risk of leaks and increases heat loss at night. Solar greenhouses are also known for summer overheating.

Solar greenhouses were once considered a good way to add the large glazing areas needed to provide sufficient heat for an under-insulated building. It usually makes more sense to improve the building shell—particularly for a new building. For existing buildings, a solar greenhouse can make sense. Or if the building owner plans to grow food or use plants as part of a biofilter or treatment system, a greenhouse may be worthwhile.

The biggest challenge is to avoid overheating in summer. This typically requires a roll-down shade cloth or awning, large vent areas to the outside (low and high), and often a supplemental PV fan. A very simple integral solar water heater can be placed in the solar greenhouse.

Making good use of winter solar heat demands a good vent system to the house (low and high), perhaps a supplemental fan, and in some cases thermal mass. Insulated curtains or shades can help reduce night heat loss. Insulated doors or shutters for vent openings are desirable.

Thermosiphon

Air and water density changes with temperature, and this makes it possible to create a circulating system without fans or pumps. These have been used on a wide range of buildings. Air systems are easier to work with, but are most favorable on hillsides or two-story homes where the collector can be placed below the living space. A wall-mounted unit can also be made, but the warm air is delivered at the ceiling instead of near the floor, and a small fan may be needed to help circulate the warm air.

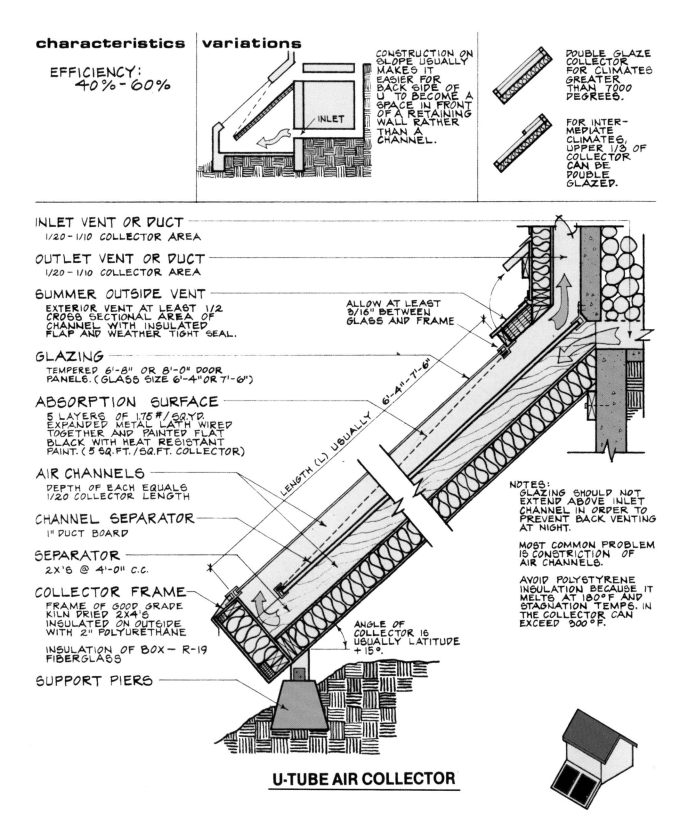

characteristics | variations

EFFICIENCY: 40% – 60%

CONSTRUCTION ON SLOPE USUALLY MAKES IT EASIER FOR BACK SIDE OF U TO BECOME A SPACE IN FRONT OF A RETAINING WALL RATHER THAN A CHANNEL.

INLET

DOUBLE GLAZE COLLECTOR FOR CLIMATES GREATER THAN 7000 DEGREES.

FOR INTERMEDIATE CLIMATES, UPPER 1/3 OF COLLECTOR CAN BE DOUBLE GLAZED.

INLET VENT OR DUCT
1/20 – 1/10 COLLECTOR AREA

OUTLET VENT OR DUCT
1/20 – 1/10 COLLECTOR AREA

SUMMER OUTSIDE VENT
EXTERIOR VENT AT LEAST 1/2 CROSS SECTIONAL AREA OF CHANNEL WITH INSULATED FLAP AND WEATHER TIGHT SEAL.

GLAZING
TEMPERED 6'-8" OR 8'-0" DOOR PANELS. (GLASS SIZE 6'-4" OR 7'-6")

ABSORPTION SURFACE
5 LAYERS OF 1.75 #/SQ.YD. EXPANDED METAL LATH WIRED TOGETHER AND PAINTED FLAT BLACK WITH HEAT RESISTANT PAINT. (5 SQ.FT./SQ.FT. COLLECTOR)

AIR CHANNELS
DEPTH OF EACH EQUALS 1/20 COLLECTOR LENGTH

CHANNEL SEPARATOR
1" DUCT BOARD

SEPARATOR
2X'S @ 4'-0" C.C.

COLLECTOR FRAME
FRAME OF GOOD GRADE KILN DRIED 2X4'S INSULATED ON OUTSIDE WITH 2" POLYURETHANE
INSULATION OF BOX — R-19 FIBERGLASS

SUPPORT PIERS

ALLOW AT LEAST 3/16" BETWEEN GLASS AND FRAME

LENGTH (L) USUALLY 6'-4" – 7'-6"

ANGLE OF COLLECTOR IS USUALLY LATITUDE + 15°.

NOTES:
GLAZING SHOULD NOT EXTEND ABOVE INLET CHANNEL IN ORDER TO PREVENT BACK VENTING AT NIGHT.

MOST COMMON PROBLEM IS CONSTRICTION OF AIR CHANNELS.

AVOID POLYSTYRENE INSULATION BECAUSE IT MELTS AT 180°F AND STAGNATION TEMPS. IN THE COLLECTOR CAN EXCEED 300°F.

U-TUBE AIR COLLECTOR

Fig. 2.47a. *U-tube air collector.*

characteristics

EFFICIENCY 40%-60%. DUE TO DOUBLE GLAZING SITUATION, THIS COLLECTOR GETS BETTER RESULTS UNDER HARSHER CONDITIONS THAN STANDARD U-TUBE COLLECTOR.

variations

BACK VENTING AIR COLLECTORS CAN BE APPLIED TO SEVERAL VARIATIONS.

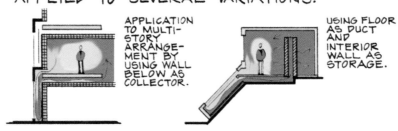

APPLICATION TO MULTI-STORY ARRANGEMENT BY USING WALL BELOW AS COLLECTOR.

USING FLOOR AS DUCT AND INTERIOR WALL AS STORAGE.

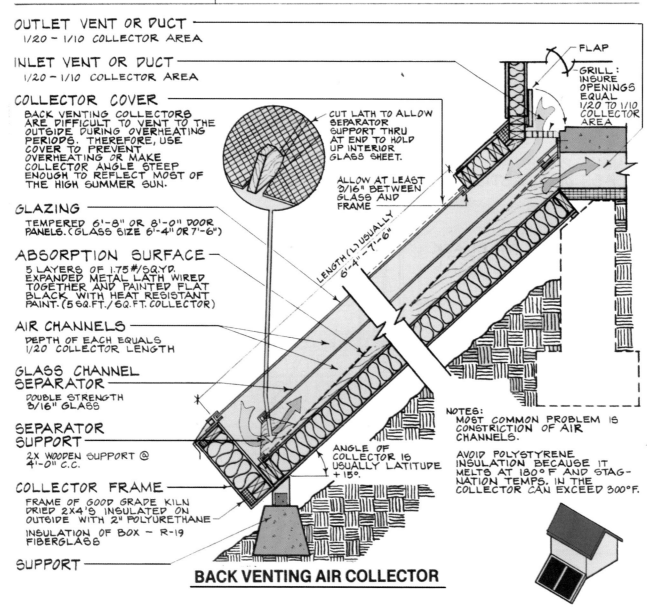

OUTLET VENT OR DUCT
1/20 – 1/10 COLLECTOR AREA

INLET VENT OR DUCT
1/20 – 1/10 COLLECTOR AREA

COLLECTOR COVER
BACK VENTING COLLECTORS ARE DIFFICULT TO VENT TO THE OUTSIDE DURING OVERHEATING PERIODS. THEREFORE, USE COVER TO PREVENT OVERHEATING OR MAKE COLLECTOR ANGLE STEEP ENOUGH TO REFLECT MOST OF THE HIGH SUMMER SUN.

GLAZING
TEMPERED 6'-8" OR 8'-0" DOOR PANELS. (GLASS SIZE 6'-4" OR 7'-6")

ABSORPTION SURFACE
5 LAYERS OF 1.75#/SQ.YD. EXPANDED METAL LATH WIRED TOGETHER AND PAINTED FLAT BLACK WITH HEAT RESISTANT PAINT. (5 SQ.FT./SQ.FT. COLLECTOR)

AIR CHANNELS
DEPTH OF EACH EQUALS 1/20 COLLECTOR LENGTH

GLASS CHANNEL SEPARATOR
DOUBLE STRENGTH 3/16" GLASS

SEPARATOR SUPPORT
2X WOODEN SUPPORT @ 4'-0" C.C.

COLLECTOR FRAME
FRAME OF GOOD GRADE KILN DRIED 2X4'S INSULATED ON OUTSIDE WITH 2" POLYURETHANE INSULATION OF BOX – R-19 FIBERGLASS

SUPPORT

CUT LATH TO ALLOW SEPARATOR SUPPORT THRU AT END TO HOLD UP INTERIOR GLASS SHEET.

ALLOW AT LEAST 3/16" BETWEEN GLASS AND FRAME

FLAP

GRILL: INSURE OPENINGS EQUAL 1/20 TO 1/10 COLLECTOR AREA

LENGTH (L) USUALLY 6'-4"-7'-6"

ANGLE OF COLLECTOR IS USUALLY LATITUDE + 15°.

NOTES:
MOST COMMON PROBLEM IS CONSTRICTION OF AIR CHANNELS.

AVOID POLYSTYRENE INSULATION BECAUSE IT MELTS AT 180°F AND STAGNATION TEMPS. IN THE COLLECTOR CAN EXCEED 300°F.

BACK VENTING AIR COLLECTOR

Fig. 2.47b. *Back-venting air collector.*

Air collectors can use mesh or solid collectors (often black-painted metal roofing is used under double glazing), and the heated air can pass through the mesh or in front of or behind the collector plate. Air gaps should be generous, ½ inch to 2 inches or more to allow free flow. Large vent areas, smooth duct runs, and free-flow collector spaces can improve performance. Back-flow preventer flaps can prevent reverse action at night. Seal joints and connections carefully to avoid cold-air leaks. Insulated shutters can also be helpful.

Thermal-mass storage has been used with some thermosiphon systems. Rockbeds appeared promising for air systems, but problems with mold and pests have occurred in some cases. Using high-mass floors or distributed phase-change mass may be safer and more effective. You might also use pavers over a sand floor with concrete-block air channels (as used by New Mexico solar pioneer Peter van Dresser).

A small window-box air heater can be added to almost any window if you need a heat boost or would like to take a baby solar step before doing a major retrofit. A larger wall-mounted unit can provide heated air that circulates across the building under a high-mass floor, rises to the second story, and then is returned as cool air to the collector.

Example of Integrated Design for Passive Heating

Integrated Holistic Design

You may have noticed in the last several pages the difficulty of keeping heating separate from other functions such as cooling, lighting, and ventilation. This is because the most characteristic aspect of passive design is that it is integral to architecture—not only to other thermal functions but also to aesthetic, social, and cultural functions and expressions. The material in this book is organized to emphasize particular functions but should always be considered in the complete context of passive design for heating, cooling, lighting, and ventilation.

Integration is important because it is a change society needs to make if we are to critically respond to the problems and opportunities of this unique period of history, when we must make the transition from reductionist to holistic thinking.

One way to clarify this issue is to review the literature about how we should respond to the massive threat of global climate change. In this debate, what's striking is the size, complexity, and cost of many climate correction proposals, such as:

1. Injecting SO_2 into the upper atmosphere to reduce solar insolation.

2. Seeding the ocean with massive amounts of iron to increase plankton blooms to take up CO_2.

3. Sequestering CO_2 from burning coal by pumping it into underground geological strata to contain it.

4. Creating huge satellite photovoltaic arrays in space where sunlight is more intense, then microwaving this energy to earth to replace fossil fuels.

Green planning and passive solar architecture are rarely mentioned, being the proverbial elephant in the room that our myopic society can't see. Since buildings and communities are the primary source of global warming gases, it might be expected they would be a large part of this debate. The reason they are not is related to the conceptual problem of reductionist versus holistic thinking. Reductionist thinking breaks a problem into discrete parts, and solutions are sought at that level; synergetic thinking strives for solutions at the level of the whole. Because a synergetic whole is far more efficient than the sum of its parts, integral thinking is the most effective approach. Our industrial culture values reductionist thinking and often fails to understand or value synergy.

The geo-engineering approaches described above are examples of reductionist thinking. They are single-purpose, linear processes that exist in isolation with unknown side effects. They are emergency responses that treat the symptoms, not the disease. In contrast, green environmental design and construction with passive design address the causes, are multipurpose, provide multiple benefits, and are connected intimately to our settlement patterns, which are causing much of the problem.

In the integrated-design section of each chapter, we will offer examples of passive systems that are integrated enough into the environmental, community, and architectural context to become synergetic in character.

State Office Building for an Era of Transitions

Historical and Urban Patterns

The site is downtown Sacramento, California. This inland city has much of the character of the Middle West. It was platted with large square city blocks that have wide streets with large trees. In contrast with late modern state office buildings, the goal for this project is to become an integral part of the existing city layout and character.

The program required that the building contribute to urban street life and provide clear circulation to the public. This low-rise building achieves this by creating a series of storefront offices fronted by ample sidewalks and street landscaping. Government offices have the traditional street address. From the street, the building is structured along a "publicness gradient" to open into a series of interior-block open spaces more related to employees than to the general public.

Historical Architectural Patterns

An analysis of the state buildings of the capital area revealed a variety of building styles from eclectic 1920s to art deco 1930s, monumental 1950s, Le Corbusier–inspired slabs from the 1960s, and corporate towers of the 1970s. Despite this variation, there was a consistent progression of buildings becoming increasingly large in scale, disconnected from the outside, and unpopular to work in; and each was accompanied by a large increase in energy use per square foot. The architectural goal for new state office building was to recover the scale of the earliest buildings in the area, to reverse this trend of resource intensity, and to utilize natural energy through passive design. The plan reduces the building's imported energy use while providing a healthier and more pleasant working environment.

The new state office building is designed to serve work groups of six to twelve and work clusters of approximately one hundred people. The result is a series of modular pavilions and mezzanines that interlock at split levels along the publicness gradient spine. Each module provides space for one work group on each level. The thermal roof provides thermal control, natural lighting, and a sound-diffusing shape in the central work space. The scale achieved is closer to that of a large residence than that of the newer state office buildings. On the interior, the scale is more like the earliest state office building. This scale would better serve the six-to-twelve-person work groups and more likely stimulate user control and responsibility mentioned in the program. Groups of three and four modules combine to form the work clusters that serve about a hundred people each.

Structural System

The structural system for the roof evolved from the thermal and acoustical factors plus the desire to use thin steel as efficiently as possible. The result is a shape generated by translating one circular arc polygon over another, creating equal-sided parallelograms that also act as shear panels. The result in an extremely stable structure using 16-gauge sheet steel to support 54 tons of water for each module.

Natural Lighting

The lighting design was based on using artificial light only in a supplementary capacity to daylight. Daylight was calculated to provide 75 to 100 percent of the background illumination and up to 50 percent of task illumination in all interior spaces.

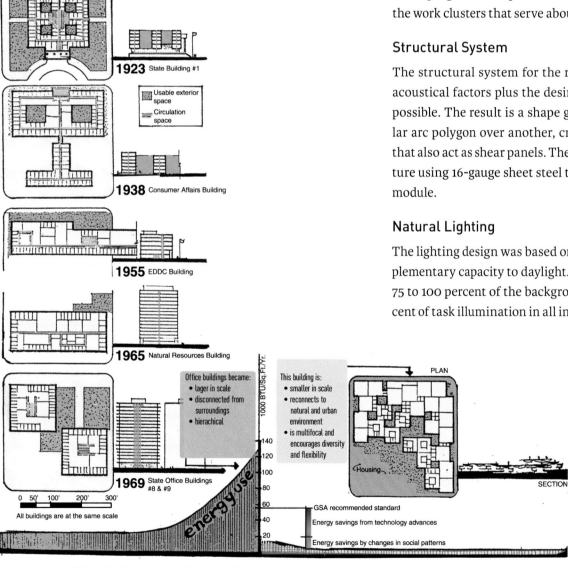

Figure 2.48. *Historical patterns of land and energy use.*

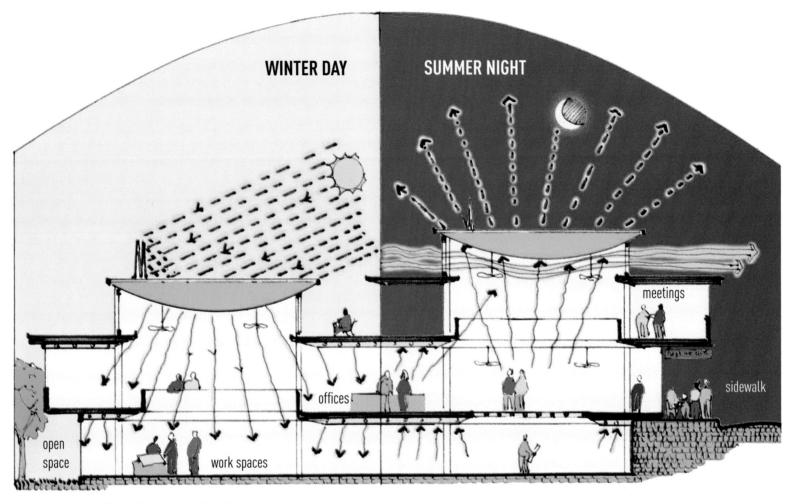

Fig. 2.49a. *Detail section, day and night.*

Fig. 2.49b, c. *Exterior perspective sketches.*

Fig. 2.49d. *Interior perspective sketch.*

Thermal Patterns and Architectural Form

The modular form of the pavilions lend themselves to the roof pond system of heating and cooling, which is by definition modular, while achieving 240,000 square feet of office space on a 152,000-square-foot site without exceeding three stories in height. Thermal control is provided by roof ponds and movable insulation coupled with ceiling coils that provide heat and coolth from the ponds to the perimeter of the modules and to lower floors not so affected by direct radiation from the ponds. Night ventilation cooling of the ponds can be accentuated by allowing air to flow over both the top and the exposed conductive bottom surfaces of the ponds while venting the warmer air from the interior space.

The ratio of interior floor area served by the roof pond is slightly less than 4:1. Dynamic-response modeling was done by the admittance method, and predictions for 100 percent heating in December (except during extended fog conditions) and 100 percent cooling in July were obtained. Since evaporation was not needed for cooling, this thermal control was achieved without adversely modifying the exterior environment. This is an important urban design consideration because in a high-density urban setting, small modifications to the exterior environment by many buildings add up rapidly to create environment modifications such as heat islands.

In this application, resulting savings due to passive solar heating and night sky cooling were predicted to be 4,292 therms/year for an average module or 188,900 therms/year for the whole building for a reduction of 1,134 tons of CO_2 per year.

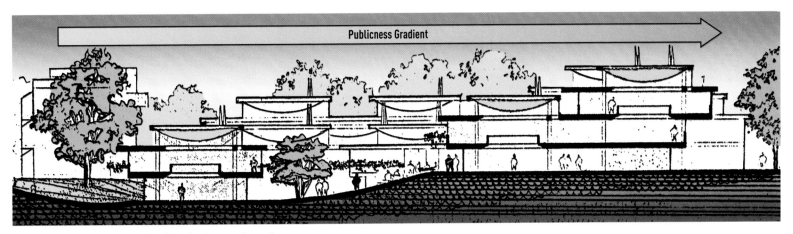

Fig. 2.49e. *Overall section in relation to the urban context.*

Backup for Passive Heating

It's interesting to note that only in the year 1976 did the energy produced by nuclear power in the US as a whole equal that produced by firewood.

—PETER VAN DRESSER, 1977

Although we've described and illustrated some 100 percent passive systems, generally the passive approach, unless super-insulated and with heat-exchange ventilation, will not be able to ride through more than two to three days of cloudy weather, and backup heating will be required. The question is how big this backup system must be. A good passive building in most temperate climates should be able to provide 60 to 90 percent of its heating needs, and the backup need is far less than the heating equipment of a standard building. This is an important point, for it is here that first cost savings can be achieved. It is important to recognize that the backup is just that, a smaller supplementary system.

Too often clients we've had can't bring themselves to trust the passive approach enough to not demand a full-on supplementary conditioning system because they have no experience with living in a passive building. Most often such a large system is not well suited to the backup needs of a passive building.

A popular choice in residences is to ask for a radiant hydronic system in the floor slab. Such a system is the ultimate in comfort because, like the passive approach, a radiant slab is the most uniform and comfortable approach to mechanical heating. However, the radiant floor slab charged by a natural gas or fuel-oil boiler is not an ideal backup system for a passive building because it's a slow-response system when what is needed is a fast-response system just for intermittent extreme events or cloudy periods. It's also an expensive large system when a small-scale inexpensive system is all that is needed.

We've found that small natural-gas- or propane-fueled heaters do the trick even for commercial-scaled buildings. Usually, the smallest commercially available heater is all that's needed, 30,000 to 50,000 BTUs/hour.

Other systems worth considering include installing a small solar hydronic heating system using the solar hot-water heater and its backup natural gas water heater as supply for radiators or a fan coil. With very low heating demand in super-insulated passive buildings, this type of system can work well. They are becoming more common in Europe. These systems also work well with district heating.

Another option is a hot-air system modeled on the Roman hypocaust. Hot air from a heater or solar system is used to heat internal walls and thermal mass. There is no risk of leaks (as there is in the hydronic system) in this approach.

Wood pellets and woodstoves are still a good option if they burn clean enough, but air pollution can be a problem if everyone uses wood or yard wastes for heat. Efficient wood fire heaters will allow the remaining demand to be met by a local small woodlot. This woodlot should be composed of a mix of trees, with preference given to nitrogen-fixing edible tree crops. With a sustained yield of 0.4 ton/acre/year, the need for heating can be met from less than ½ acre. Compost heat can also be used for supplemental heating.

The high-mass masonry stoves used in Russia, Finland, Korea, and other cold areas are excellent for winter comfort and are becoming more common in the United States and Canada. The fire in these high-mass systems can be burned hot and clean for a relatively short time; then the thermal mass will provide warmth for many hours. The drawback is that they are slow response and they are best used in a passive house in the far north, in very cold climates, or in situations with long cloudy periods. For further information, see *Masonry Heaters: Designing, Building, and Living with a Piece of the Sun* by Ken Matesz.

Summary: Passive Heating

The primary focus in passive heating is hoarding internal heat gain and capturing the sun's energy. The challenges include keeping this heat for use at night and on cloudy days and avoiding overheating on sunny days. These are not difficult, but take care and attention. Many of the solar homes built in the 1970s, flush with solar excitement, weren't very good at controlling overheating or saving energy for use at night. They were overglazed, under-insulated, and often had insufficient mass. We know better today.

Although we have shown the spectrum of passive systems for heating for residential application in temperate climates, there is much to be said for simple, easy-to-operate passive designs. For most situations, we've found the solution is a very well-insulated building with direct gain and both distributed and concentrated mass. Many other options have been tried, including rock and gravel beds, massive underground water tanks, and many other strange and wonderful creations. These may be useful for some extreme sites, but they have proved more challenging to make foolproof and long-lived.

Larger buildings are a different animal; rather than heating, the need for lighting and cooling is dominant, so we refer you to chapter 3 on passive cooling and chapter 4 on natural lighting.

This prototype roof pond system in Atascadero, California, was the first passive system to give equal emphasis to cooling and heating (1975).

Basics of Passive Cooling

Passive cooling considerations are important in building design. A building that gets too cool in winter is a problem, but occupants can add a vest or jacket and be comfortable even with temperatures in the 50s. A building that overheats in summer is more problematic, for even with minimal clothing it is hard to stay comfortable as the temperature rises above 80 to 85°F. Passive cooling strategies for new and existing buildings will become increasingly important as global warming causes many more heat waves and increases the need for cooling for comfort in buildings that were historically comfortable in summer—but are no longer.

Building Metabolism and Cooling Demand

Cooling demands vary widely with the orientation of the building windows, the metabolism of the building (see page 12), and occupant behavior. Cooling loads are strongly influenced by unwanted solar heat gain in summer and by internal loads. The opportunities for passive cooling are influenced by building type and size, but good design can bring passive cooling to small-scale skin-dominated buildings and large buildings with low skin-to-volume ratios.

Climate-based cooling loads are usually described in cooling degree days, the difference between the average daily temperature and the base temperature. These may be base 65°F or 80°F. In hot tropical areas where people are adapted to higher temperatures (see

page 30), base 80°F will often be used. Cooling degree days, base 65°F, range from 4,200 at Yuma, Arizona, to 162 in Seattle.

A new Web site, www.degreedays.net, generates degree days to the base temperature you set almost anywhere in the world.

Cooling degree days alone are not enough for building design development. Humidity and wind speed are very important for passive cooling and comfort. Relative humidity (by hour) and average wind speed and direction are often reported and are helpful to know.

External Loads

In smaller skin-dominated buildings, the external loads commonly dominate the cooling load. Building and window orientation are critical to reduce unwanted heat gain in summer. Fortunately, the best orientation for cooling is also best for passive heating in winter.

In the mid-latitudes, the equator-facing windows have the best winter heat gain and the lowest summer heat gain. By adding an overhang, the equator-window gain in summer can be reduced further. East- and west-facing windows cause overheating in summer, late spring, and fall. They often benefit from lower solar heat gain factor glazing, but equator-facing windows should have high solar heat gain glazing for winter heating.

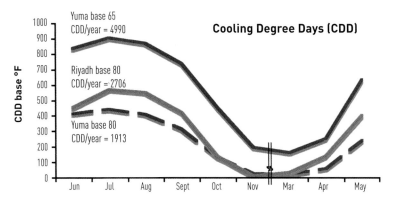

Fig. 3.1. *This chart shows the cooling degree days for Yuma, Arizona (base 65°F and 80°F) and Riyadh, Saudi Arabia. In June (30 days) the average temperature is about 95°F in Yuma (900 CDD/30 days = 30°F, 30°F + Base 65°F = 95°F).*

Fig. 3.2. *Louvered shades allow ventilation and control the sun.*

THREE PASSIVE COOLING AND VENTILATION

Solar control with light-colored walls and roofs, window overhangs, shutters, screens, and shades is inexpensive and very effective. Landscaping can also be used to reduce external loads. Shade trees, green screens, and even living roofs can reduce heat gain. Neighborhoods with extensive landscaping and trees can be 10°F to 15°F cooler than those without.

Internal Loads

Internal heat load must also be managed carefully to reduce cooling demand. As noted on page 40, internal heat gain can be significant. In larger buildings, these internal loads often dominate the cooling demand. An efficient refrigerator provides a double bonus for homeowners by reducing both energy use and cooling cost. In office and commercial buildings, the use of daylighting can reduce unwanted heat gain from lights. More efficient lights also reduce heat gain. Careful placement of large heat producers such as refrigerators, freezers, and computer servers can reduce heat gain in conditioned spaces and help drive ventilation flows.

Passive Cooling Opportunities

Compared with the two passive heating sources of sunlight and internal heat gain, passive cooling is a bit more complex but equally achievable in all climates. The sources for passive cooling are the three thermal sinks of cool night air, night sky radiation, and evaporation from wet surfaces.

The use of these sinks is very dependent upon humidity. Humidity in the atmosphere produces a thermal blanket that reduces the temperature differences between day and night, thus reducing the ability to cool with night air. Humidity also substantially reduces the amount of night sky radiation. Passive cooling strategies in hot-dry climates and hot-wet climates are very different. Hot-dry climates have more night sky radiational cooling that can create cooler night air or can be used directly by a building's elements and configuration. The high humidity of hot-wet climates limits cooling resources, and tropical and subtropical hot-wet climates are considered the most difficult passive cooling situations. However, there are many successful passively cooled buildings in these climates.

The main thermal sink to use in humid climates is wet surfaces. Human skin is admirably designed for cooling if enough airflow is provided. Strategies for passive cooling for these climates include minimizing solar and thermal loads while maximizing ventilation during the day and night.

Natural ventilation is an integral part of the use of two of these sinks, cooling with night air, and cooling by wet surfaces. Ventilation is an important element of almost all passive cooling designs and is covered in more detail on pages 117–129.

These sinks used singly or in combinations can provide sufficient cooling for full comfort in virtually any climate. Passive cooling can eliminate or minimize the use of electricity while providing more comfortable and healthier living conditions.

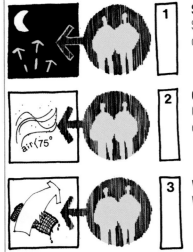

The principal sinks that can be used to cool are

Sky and Space
Sky and space are among the principal sinks that can be used to cool. Some heat is always radiated from a building out to the sky. Under certain circumstances, the upper atmosphere and space can act as an appreciable sink.

Outside Air
Outside air that is cooler than about 75°F can act as a heat sink. This is typically the case in coastal California during our usually cool nights.

Wet Surfaces
Wet surfaces provide on-site sinks because heat is absorbed when water evaporates.

Fig. 3.3. *Cooling sources.*

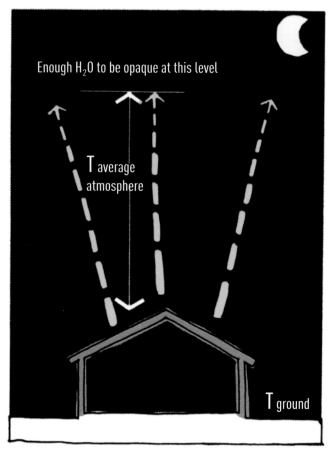

Fig. 3.4. *Terrestrial surfaces radiate energy to anything colder than they are. Therefore, a building at 75°F will radiate heat upward to the cooler sky and space. This radiant energy will travel until it hits a nontransparent barrier that absorbs radiation. In the sky, this barrier is mainly atmospheric water vapor. In dry climates, it takes several thousand feet of atmosphere to contain enough water to be thermally opaque to this upward radiation. The average temperature of the night sky is typically 10°F to 50°F lower than the air temperature near the ground; therefore heat is always radiated from a building out to the sky. The drier the night air, the lower the effective sky temperature and the greater the heat-sink effect. This is why deserts can be cool or even cold at night.*

Cooling Considerations

Passive cooling, just like passive heating, works best in an efficient shell. This entails not solar-heating the building during the cooling period by giving careful consideration to solar control and minimizing internal heat gain that could add to the cooling load. The first of these prerequisites is covered here under solar control. The major factor for internal heat reduction is lighting. Replacing electric lighting with natural lighting is in most cases the best way to reduce internal heat gain. Natural lighting is so important that it has its own chapter (chapter 4).

The cooling-load relationships vary depending upon a building's metabolism, which is related to the size of the building as discussed on page 12. For passive heating, the thermal load decreased with the size of the building because of larger internal loads. For passive cooling, the opposite occurs. Generally speaking, passive cooling and ventilation loads increase as the size and complexity of the building increases, as shown in figure 3.5. Assembly spaces that have peak periods with very large numbers of people add special challenges from the heat of the people, humidity, and carbon dioxide.

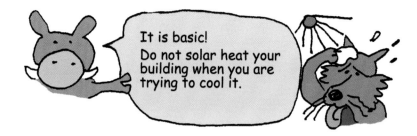

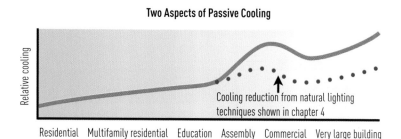

Fig. 3.5. *(1.) Metabolism: Unlike passive heating, passive cooling and ventilation demands increase as the size and complexity of the building increases, with the exception of assembly spaces. (2.) Scale of cooling and heating needs: Passive cooling capability varies distinctly with humidity. In dry-hot climates, clear night skies allow night radiation and convective cooling with cool night air. In hot-wet climates, the only thermal sinks available are wet surfaces that can cool through evaporation.*

Prerequisites for Passive Cooling

Careful orientation of buildings and windows and solar control strategies can block the unwanted heat from the summer sun, yet still allow the sun in for winter heating and daylighting. The critical first step is keeping windows in the shade during the summer. This is easiest for a new building, where summer shading can often be achieved at little or no cost, but it can be done for almost any building even as a retrofit. (Refer to pages 26 and 54 for a reminder of the sun path and radiation characteristics, and page 47 for energy-efficient design.)

Orientation matters most, and a clear understanding of radiation impacts can help you pick the best placement for windows or the best place in an apartment or office complex. Studies in Davis, California, showed that the worst orientation of apartments (east top) in one complex in summer had energy bills that were ten times higher than the best (north bottom) and twice the south-facing apartments (Hammond et al., 1974*).

We want to start with a very efficient building shell, but then we need to remember that the sun's energy is concentrated on the east and west walls and windows on summer days in the mid-latitudes while the equator-facing and north sides receive considerably less radiation. Direct radiation is most important, but diffuse radiation and reflected radiation must also be considered.

Table 3.1. *Solar heat gain for unshaded windows at 40°NL. By comparison the conduction through a light-colored R-40 wall with a temperature of 95°F outside and 75°F inside will be only 12 BTU/ft²/day.*

BTU/ft² day	21-Dec	21-Jun
N	98	484
NE or NW	103	894
E or W	430	1200
SE or SW	1104	1007
S	1562	622

Conduction through a light colored R-40 wall with an outside 95°F and inside temperature of 75°F = 12 BTU / ft²/ day

In the summer, unshaded east- and west-facing windows can add more than a hundred times as much energy as a super-insulated wall per square foot and twice as much unwanted solar energy as an equator-facing window. With windows in the right places, a building will be much more comfortable and economical in the summer and winter.

Building Shape and Orientation

A striking example of what can happen if solar control is ignored is demonstrated in the building shown in figure 3.6. This is an exhibition and visitor facility for the ancient Greek city of Selinunte in southern Sicily. It's a clear design concept with ample parking leading into a sloping plaza and an underground exhibition hall and ticket and sales areas that set the stage for the magnificent ruins. However, it has one fatal flaw—the lack of solar control. The front facade facing southeast below the bermed roof is all glass with no solar control. Direct solar gain is accentuated by reflection from the sloping light-colored plaza. As a result, what is potentially a powerful design is made very uncomfortable by the harsh sun. This glaring

Fig. 3.6. *Building shape and orientation in Selinunte, Sicily, 37.5°N latitude.*

sun has also faded out very large expensive drawings of the original city, a huge model of the site, and is slowly destroying the building itself. The very large glass sheets on the front facade are cracking, doors are ripping off their hinges from the constant expansion and contraction, and the concrete surfaces are spalling. The moral of the story is that sunshine can be a wonderful thing, but it can also be a monster if ignored.

Solar Control

The easiest control device is a horizontal overhang. Overhangs can be very effective for apertures that face the equator because the sun path is high in the summer and low in the winter. Additional challenges to solar control come from east–west orientation, but a variety of shading devices can be used to reduce overheating.

Unfortunately horizontal overhangs do not work well for windows oriented more than 15° east or west of equator facing. Wing walls, louvers, or fins can be used to protect these orientations but must be carefully designed for appearance and durability. Movable fins are best but can be costly and complex to build and maintain. These may be easier to build and maintain if they are included within a double facade.

Shading Devices

There are many approaches to providing shade, privacy, security, and flexibility to windows and doors, as shown in figure 3.8. These fall into two general categories, exterior and interior shading devices.

Exterior shading devices are usually better because once the sun enters a window, heat has effectively entered the house, and although its impact can be reduced with an interior shade that is well sealed, some heat trapped between the shade and the window will still pass into the room.

In traditional management of courtyard buildings in the Mediterranean region, a *toldo* or fabric shade may be closed over a courtyard when it is hot. These shades are often made of fabric that is open weave or translucent to allow light in but reduce heat gain. John Reynolds found that these could reduce temperature more than 30°F. A large courtyard in San Diego's Balboa Park was transformed from a hot-in-summer, cold-in-winter space to a very pleasant environment by adding a permanent translucent fabric cover.

Fig. 3.7. *Toldo system of sun control. (a) Retracted. (b) Extended.*

An exterior porch that gets too hot in summer, particularly east- or west-facing ones, can be shaded with homemade vertical sun screens hung at the end of the porch. These can be louvers, shade screen, shade cloth, or diagonally crisscrossed wood strips, such as plaster lath, set into a frame; or woven willows, bamboo, or cane. These will still admit enough light so the porch won't be dull and dim, but will keep the porch and the building much cooler. Motorized or mechanical awnings can be used to provide sun when wanted and shade when needed. Those developed for the recreational vehicle market are very robust.

The ultimate design of a total exterior shading retrofit may include a mix of the options discussed here, depending on the many variables of orientation, window placement, available space (for wings and fences), and certainly on how the retrofits will affect your building's appearance.

Additional Approaches to Thermal Control

Cool Roofs

Although insulated ceilings can reduce heat gain from a hot roof, it is desirable to further reduce gains with light-colored roofing. Light colors can reduce roof temperature dramatically, keeping the building cooler and extending the life of the roof. Certain roofing materials also naturally "run cooler" than others. Tarred roofs, dark metal roofs, and asphalt shingles are among the hottest roofs, while living roofs are the coolest.

Measurements of roof temperatures in Davis, California, found that black roofing reached 162°F, two coats of aluminum paint reached only 143°F, and smooth white paint topped out at 117°F, a cooling benefit of 45°F essentially for free.

There is, however, an aesthetic nuance here that should be discussed. Light-colored buildings are much more visually intrusive in most landscapes than dark-colored. Most landscapes, at least in temperate biomes, are dominated by green, so darker buildings and roofs fit in much better. If the roof can be seen from public spaces and you still want it to be as cool as possible, you should consider "cool roof" technology. By using tricks with emissivity, you can look dark and yet act light and stay cool.

Ten Approaches to Shading

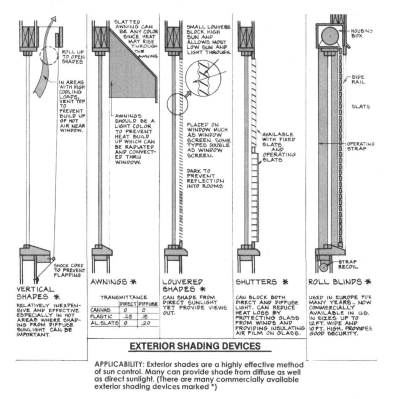

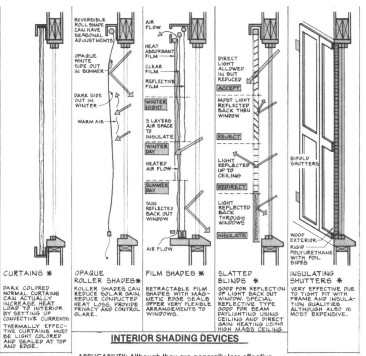

Fig. 3.8. *(a) Exterior shading devices. (b) Interior shading devices.*

Fig. 3.9. *Be discreet: Fit the building into the environment.*

A double roof may make sense in the hot desert or the tropics. Double roofs were included on early Land Rovers for tropical use for this reason. The upper roof should be light in color and well vented so that the heat buildup between the two roofs sets up a convection airflow to exhaust hot air.

Landscaping

Landscape elements can help a great deal with solar control. Plants on an arbor can provide different solar control between spring and fall, but arbors are often made with such large elements they block too much of the winter sun. A tension arbor made of wire works very well. A wire arbor can provide good support and almost full sun in the winter after the vines or plants are pruned. If wood or metal elements are used for an arbor, keep the structural members as small as possible so they won't cast shadows on equator-facing windows in the winter.

Trees, vines, and shrubs are attractive and can provide very effective control for roofs, walls, and windows. Trees can have a shading coefficient of 0.2, which is the same as an overhang. However, care must be taken to minimize unwanted shading in the winter. A deciduous tree to the south can shade in the winter as well as the summer because limbs, bare branches, and twigs can block much of the desired sun. Placing deciduous trees to the southeast and southwest instead of directly toward the equator can allow summer shading and unimpeded winter sun.

Landscaping is also perfect for providing needed shade for windows or walls that face east or west. An arbor or netting should be held back from the window or wall 2 to 3 feet, if possible, to allow for better ventilation and to avoid damage to the siding. A small misting system that uses a high-pressure nozzle to create a mist of water on the outside of the vines can add additional cooling.

A solar-control landscape plan for a house or commercial building might include tall trees to the southeast and southwest for wall and roof shade, deciduous vines for shade on a horizontal arbor above the equator-facing windows, a low-growing darker green ground cover on the equator-facing side to reduce ground reflection and heat buildup, hedges to the east and west to shield those walls and windows, and shrubs or small trees on the polar side to the east or west to block late-evening and early-morning sun in the hottest period of the summer. Shade plants also contribute to a cooler building environment, especially compared with artificial grass, concrete, asphalt, or gravel surfaces. These high-mass surfaces get very hot and retain heat late into the evening or night.

Not only does landscaping cool the house and yard, it also makes a quieter, cleaner, and more satisfactory environment. In Sacramento, California, cutting down trees in one neighborhood resulted in a 10°F jump in ambient summer air temperature and considerably increased cooling loads in adjacent homes.

Improved Glazing

Attempts to use tinted glass in the past were often not very effective. Much of the glass used cut down on the light transmission in the visual spectrum but not the UV or infrared, so the occupants got less light and still much of the heat. It would have been better just to use less glass. However, the advent of heat-reducing low-e glass has corrected this situation, allowing in much more of the visual spectrum and much less heat. But do not use this glass on south windows where passive heating is wanted in the winter.

Space Planning

For more extreme cooling conditions like the tropics and semitropics it can pay to zone the heat-producing parts of the building so they don't contribute cooling load to the rest of the building; kitchens, laundry, and utility rooms are the most common offenders in residences. You can see an example of zoning to move heat producing activities out of the living space in figure 3.15 on page 97.

Fig. 3.10. *Solar control options include, solar control glass screens, most expensive, exterior operable blinds, roll-down awnings, and awnings.*

Classic Approaches to Passive Cooling

Passive cooling has a long-established history dating back thousands of years with a legacy of very sophisticated techniques. Recent improvements have come with new materials, more sophisticated analysis, and the development of performance-prediction techniques for the four systems shown in figure 3.11.

All of these cooling approaches are affected by local climate and microclimate. The choice among different systems is based on the humidity levels and temperatures throughout the year, as noted in the introduction. Places with low humidity have much more potential for night sky radiation and accompanying cool night air. This allows cooling with system 1 or 3.

QUIET AND COOL

Fan noise can be an issue with cooling fans. If the fans are noisy, they won't be used as often or feel as cool. A quiet ceiling fan should be less than 60 dB. An average 18-inch hall fan emits 76 dB on high, 66 dB medium, and 53 dB low, while a 7-inch fan puts out 56 dB on high and 48 dB on low. Sound ratings may also be given in sones (a subjective measure of sound intensity as heard by humans)—get the lowest you can find. Panasonic makes an 80 cfm bathroom fan that is only 0.3 sone.

High humidity acts as an obscuring blanket for night radiation and keeps night temperatures relatively high. This reduces the capability of approach 1 and 3. For this reason, tropical and subtropical hot-wet climates are considered the most difficult passive cooling situations. Still, there are many successful passively cooled buildings in these climates utilizing systems 2 (evaporative cooling by air flowing over the skin) and/or 4 (architectural-based systems utilizing cool towers or landscape elements such as fountains).

Combinations of many of these systems are possible.

System 1: Night Ventilation Cooling

This approach is most applicable to dry climates with cool night air. It is essentially the same as the direct-gain/distributed-mass system for passive heating described on page 58. These components work equally well for heating and cooling. Therefore, the details and sizing information on page 60 apply here as well—with the addition that for cooling, we need to provide good airflow over the distributed mass at night. Information on these techniques is covered under the ventilation section of this chapter on pages 117–129.

System 2: Ventilation Cooling

This approach is most applicable to hot humid climates such as the Gulf Coast of the United States, much of South America, and South Asia. Owing to high humidity, cool night air and night sky radiation are less available for cooling, and we need to rely on airflow over moist skin both day and night for cooling. This approach has been used successfully for thousands of years. The key to success, other than total protection from the sun, is getting sufficient airflow. Ideally, you want on the order of thirty to sixty air changes per hour. Thermal mass is of less help, although thermal lag through roof elements can help reduce peak afternoon temperatures. Walls need to be highly porous to improve airflow.

The traditional approaches shown in figure 3.12 have large overhangs for protection from the hot sun and either no walls at all or walls that are highly porous to air. Screened porches offer large free-flowing surfaces. Traditional materials such as thatch roofs and woven-fabric walls perform well because they shed water but also breathe, which helps with ventilation and minimizes the development of mold problems in wet and humid environments. Traditional Mayan homes with thatched roofs remained comfortable in summer, but when the switch was made to black corrugated roofing they became very uncomfortable.

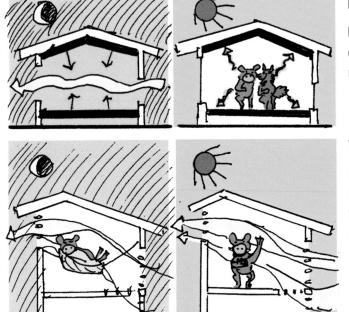

Night Vent Cooling

(System #1) Enough thermal mass is cooled by cool night air to ride over the following hot day when the building is kept closed up except for ventilation required for health. Thermal mass with large surface area helps in the transfer of coolth from vented air to the mass.

Ventilation Cooling

(System #2) The main thermal sinks in hot humid climates are wet surfaces that utilize evaporation to cool. A gentle breeze across our skin is very effective for this purpose. Therefore, this strategy minimizes solar and other thermal loads while maximizing ventilation during the day and night. Thermal mass isn't much help in this situation.

Radiation Cooling

(System #3) In relatively dry climates with clear skies, it is possible to directly tap into night-sky outgoing radiation as described on page 101 to provide cooling.

Evaporative Cooling

(System #4) Evaporation from wet surfaces can cool air, which in turn is used to cool the building. This approach can take the form of landscape elements (such as fountains) architectural elements (cool towers), or mechanical devices.

Fig. 3.11. *Classic passive cooling systems.*

1200

Fig. 3.12. *Traditional ventilation cooling responses in the vernacular architecture of the tropics. Tall ceilings, porous but insulated roofs, and large openings for ventilation all facilitate cooling. Shown are examples in the Amazon Basin and the South Pacific that use highly developed organic fabric construction techniques.*

1500

Fig. 3.13. *The medieval architecture of Japan evolved a responsive hot-humid-climate architecture of highly modular construction, sliding walls, sophisticated use of wood and thatch, and maximum airflow day and night, with large openings to the outside and large openings for internal circulation and cross-ventilation.*

1600

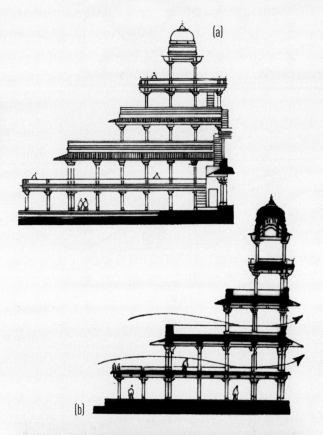

Fig. 3.14. *The formal architecture of Mogul India evolved wonderful methods of ventilation cooling while also accomplishing a high degree of privacy. (a) At Fatehpur Sikri, near Agra, crossventilation was achieved by eliminating walls; (b) in the harem at Fatehpur Sikri, privacy was obtained by screens similar to those shown in (c) at the Red Fort.*

With our over-reliance on mechanical air-conditioning, cooling for hot, humid conditions has almost become a lost art. It is instructive to look at successful historical examples. One of the best is the staff housing built in Gamboa, Panama, built by the United States for the families of the engineers creating the Panama Canal. These houses were built in 1906 before the availability of mechanical air-conditioning, so passive cooling was the basis of the designs using the following architectural techniques:

- Three stories high with living facilities on the higher levels, where breezes are stronger and more accessible.

- A ground level used mostly for services and largely open.

- Long, thin buildings carefully designed for maximum cross-ventilation. Interior walls, where they exist, have open grilles above privacy walls.

- Large, well-ventilated attic spaces and ample overhangs at each floor for shading from the always high tropical sun.

- Ample banks of screened casement windows on all sides.

- Strict zoning separating heat-producing areas such as bathrooms, kitchens, and laundry rooms.

- Provision of ceiling fans as an integral part of each room.

PROVEN PERFORMANCE IN THE TROPICS

1906

Fig. 3.15. *Staff Housing Gamboa, Panama. With the return of the Panama Canal facilities to Panama, Gamboa is now a resort run by the Panamanians. If you visit, rent a suite in these facilities, shut off the noisy wheezing window air conditioner that's been recently added, open the casement windows wide, smell the fragrant tropical breeze, listen to the sounds of exotic birds, turn on the ceiling fan, sit back in the wicker furniture, and pour yourself a cool gin and tonic. (a, b, c) The small structure on the ground floor is the laundry room. (d) Typical interior. (e) Kitchens, bathrooms, and laundry are thermally isolated.*

Ventilation Cooling, Recent Examples

Taiwan is an example of a hot, humid climate where the dogma is that you need mechanical air-conditioning to survive. Shown are three examples that help demonstrate that modern versions of passive cooling by ventilation are applicable in the hot humid climates of the world.

CLASSROOMS FOR DHARMA DRUM UNIVERSITY

Dharma Drum is a new Buddhist university being built on the northern coast of Taiwan. Shown here are studies done to illustrate the passive cooling capability for high-density classroom buildings. These long, thin buildings utilize enhanced cross-ventilation, natural lighting, and ceiling fans powered directly by photovoltaic panels.

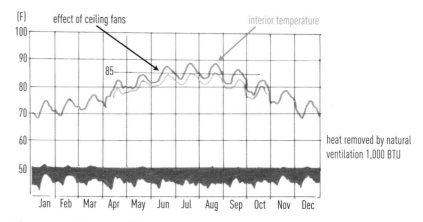

Fig. 3.16a. *Ventilated classroom energy analysis using Energy10 modeling software (continuous vent @ 2 cfm/sq. ft. work and non-work days).*

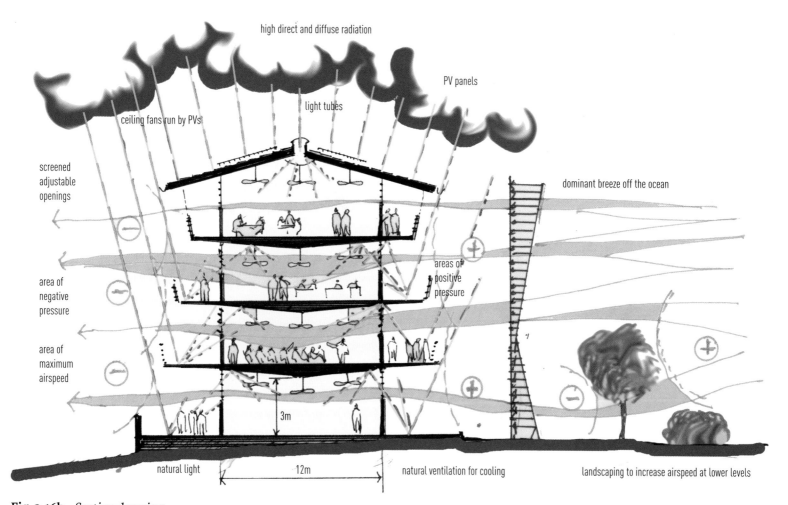

Fig. 3.16b. *Section drawing.*

CHI FAMILY COMPOUND IN DRAGON WELL

The Chi family wanted a traditional house without air-conditioning, which they found uncomfortable. The plan shows some of the ventilation studies used to create a passively cooled building. It was constructed in 2003 and has successfully operated as a passively cooled building.

TREASURE HILL

As one of the last post–World War II squatter settlements, Treasure Hill in Taipei is now considered a cultural resource. This retrofit of two abandoned hovels into the Community Planning Center involved making it passively cooled by utilizing the breezes from the adjacent riverfront, as well as adding openings, ventilation cowls, and insulation.

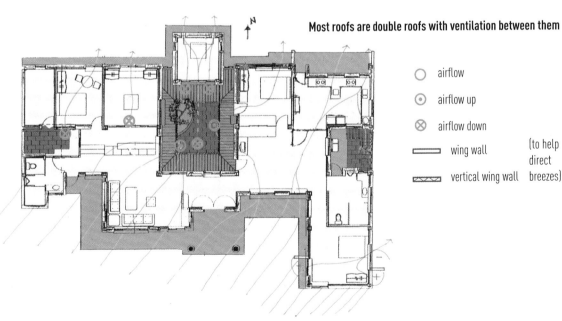

Most roofs are double roofs with ventilation between them

○ airflow

◉ airflow up

⊗ airflow down

▭ wing wall

▨ vertical wing wall

(to help direct breezes)

Fig. 3.17. *Chi family compound exterior and interior (above). Plan showing ventilation (below).*

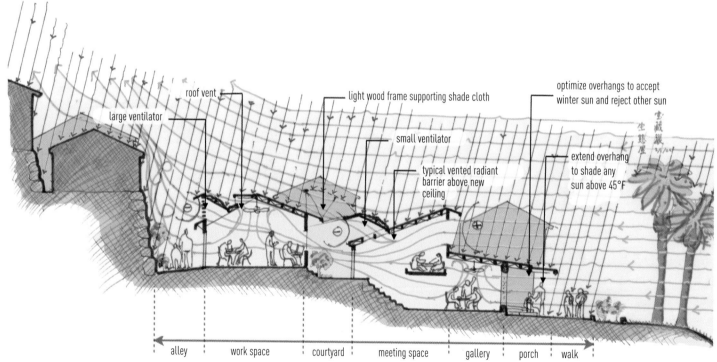

large ventilator

roof vent

light wood frame supporting shade cloth

optimize overhangs to accept winter sun and reject other sun

small ventilator

typical vented radiant barrier above new ceiling

extend overhang to shade any sun above 45°F

alley | work space | courtyard | meeting space | gallery | porch | walk

Fig. 3.18. *Cooling retrofit for Treasure Hill.*

System 3: Radiant Cooling

Radiant Cooling Design

High mass roofs with operable insulation, either of concrete or with roof ponds, provide the functions of cold collection and storage with one element and, therefore, these types of radiant cooling are effecting in providing daylight cooling, practically at any region with low cloudiness at night, regardless of the air humidity.

—BARUCH GIVONI, 1991

The potential for natural cooling using cold night sky and cool north sky in the day has received much less attention than it deserves. Although these microclimate/site resources are not as powerful as evaporative cooling, they can be used as important elements in natural cooling design, particularly in areas with clear skies and lower humidity. The rapid chilling in the desert after a hot day results from the powerful effect of night sky radiant cooling.

The cooling potential of the night sky was first utilized by societies many centuries ago. In Iran, night sky radiant cooling was used in the *yakh-chal* to produce ice, even when ambient air temperatures fail to drop below freezing (see figure 3.19). A tall U-shaped mud wall facing north was used to fully shade a small shallow trough of water. The cooling effect of the north sky in the day and the colder sky at night allowed ice to form. The ice was then collected and stored for use during the hot days that follow. Similar practices have been used in the desert of Chile and with ice pits in the West Indies.

Radiant cooling works because sky temperatures may be 10 to 40°F below air temperature. Frederick A. Brooks reported a night radiant-cooling-driven air temperature observation of 28°F over straw-covered ground near Sacramento after a daytime high of 98°F. The heat loss may be on the order of 20 BTU per square foot per hour (sf/hr) with a clear sky and low humidity, although peak losses in the desert have been measured at 30+ BTU/sf/hr; the nighttime loss under clear dry skies can be even higher.

Radiant cooling results when the incoming direct and indirect radiation is less than the energy radiated to the sky vault. During the daytime, the short-wave radiation from the sun dominates, but at night long-wave radiation from earth exceeds the counter-radiation from molecules and particles in the atmosphere. This loss is referred to as the net outgoing radiation and is primarily at wavelengths between 7 and 14 microns. Most of the net outgoing radiation occurs to the cold night sky, but radiation to space also occurs during the day. If this outgoing long-wave radiation was not taking place, the earth would get warmer and warmer; and if the losses were not reduced by water vapor and carbon dioxide in the atmosphere the surface of the earth would get very cold at night.

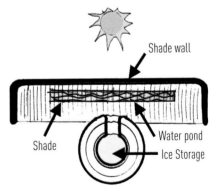

Fig. 3.19. *(a) Yakhchal, a place for making ice by radiant cooling. (b) Plan drawing.*

The rate of outgoing radiation is not uniform across the sky vault. Research has been done on the variation in radiation across the cold night sky. At night the greatest radiation loss occurs directly overhead.

Table 3.2 *Net outgoing radiation. FA Brooks, 1959.*

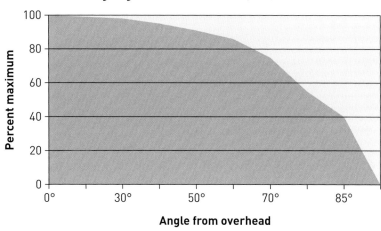

The radiation losses also vary with the nature of the sky view. Trees, walls, clouds, or structures can decrease night sky cooling, but more than 80 percent of the outgoing radiation flows to area of the sky vault above 30° from the horizon, so relatively low obstructions can be ignored. Trees and taller nearby structures should be considered, however. You can see this with the pattern of frost or dew formation on car windows. The windows protected by being near a building or under a tree will be free of frost or dew because the radiant loss has been reduced.

Observations on radiant cooling to the sky by Tod Neubauer,* Richard Cramer, and N. R. Ittner added more insight on the cool day sky. In a comprehensive test in Davis, California, the nighttime and daytime radiant exchanges across the sky dome were measured. The average nighttime temperature for a horizontal black panel was 10°F below air temperature, and even vertical walls with sky exposure were 5°F below air temperature. White panels were considerably cooler during the day, but similar at night—as would be expected with paints with comparable emissivity. White panels sloped facing north at 60° and 70° stayed below air temperature throughout the day. Further studies identified 65° as the coolest spot, as shown in figure 3.20.

Tests in the very hot Imperial Valley identified the cool spot in the north sky at 60°N in August. This cool spot had previously been noted as a minimum at a compass point opposite the sun and approximately at a right angle. The cool spot was 40°F cooler than air temperature at 3:30 PM, 23°F cooler at 6 PM, and 13°F cooler at 2 PM. Observations of animals suggest they are able to detect the cool spot in how they locate themselves in relation to shelter.

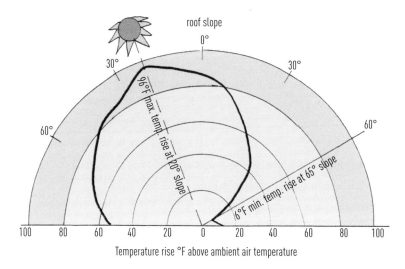

Fig. 3.20. *Day sky cool spot: Relation of roof plane to temperature rise on a typical summer day in August. Neubauer and Cramer, 1965.*

Increasing moisture in the atmosphere 30 percent can reduce outgoing radiation as much as 15 percent, while cutting it in half can increase cooling by 25 percent. Increasing moisture content can reduce the radiant losses as the angle away from the zenith increases. The strongest radiant cooling will be achieved with horizontal surfaces exposed to unobstructed, dry, and cloudless skies. Cooling may also be enhanced by convective cooling if cool breezes are blowing; but these may reduce radiant-cooling benefits if the cool air from a radiating surface is carried away instead of being captured by the building.

Even in more humid areas, cooling rates up to 50 percent of those in low humidity areas are possible, which means that up to 100 to 150 BTU per square foot per day of cooling effect may still occur on a clear night. Although radiant sky cooling is more effective in the drier areas, it can be worthwhile elsewhere when combined with evaporation, convective cooling, or ventilation.

Design Techniques

Many traditional buildings with high-mass roofs benefit from night sky cooling. Without it they would become ovens. The thermal lag provided by the slow energy transfer through a thick roof can make a classroom or office more livable during the late afternoon, but will add unwanted heat later at night. If the high-mass roof could be insulated in the day, it will work better. But faster energy transfer is desirable.

Harold Hay resolved this problem in his development of the Skytherm houses. These use bags of water on the roof covered with movable insulation to take advantage of radiant night sky cooling. These systems have been very effective. The water for the roof pond is typically placed in bags on a metal roof support system that doubles as a ceiling for the room below. This ensures excellent radiant transfer from the water bags to the room. In summer, the roof insulation panels are drawn back at night to initiate cooling by night sky radiation and then closed during the day to retain the coolth. Open water, sprinkling, or misting can be added to provide the added benefit of evaporative cooling. The roof water bags can also be used for heating by reversing the operation, opening the covers during the day in winter to collect solar heat and closing them at night.

The radiant transfer with a high-mass ceiling makes for very uniform and comfortable temperatures. A test facility in Phoenix, Arizona, and then a house in Atascadero, California, demonstrated the year-round performance of this design. The problem remained the management of the horizontal insulation panels. (See the Atascadero prototype on the section title page.)

These problems were resolved with the Winters house designed by Jon Hammond. This used hydraulic rams to tilt up a reflective, insulated roof panel over the water bags. This is more robust and develops a much better seal. Performance fully met the expectations of the clients, who were from Alaska and wanted a cool home in summer. This building is shown on figure 3.21.

Fig. 3.21. *The Winters House, Jon Hammond, Living Systems.*

Water roof ponds have been used because they have good thermal capacity and by circulation move the warmest water to the radiant surface. But concrete, phase-change materials, or other high-mass materials can also be used.

Radiant Cooling Details

The widespread use of high-mass roofs in developing countries offers a great opportunity in developing further options for low-cost movable insulation retrofits to improve radiant cooling. An insulated louver system may be a good solution for a reliable and robust system that would work for both heating and cooling as shown below.

Steve Baer, always the most practical idealist, was also influenced by Harold Hay (see page 103) and developed what he calls the Double Play System essentially doing what Hay's roof ponds did but using off-the-shelf components that have been time-tested—components like 12-inch-diameter PVC pipe as water containers inside the building and polypropylene swimming pool solar collectors as the radiator/absorber. The result is a system of passive heating and radiant cooling that is simple, inexpensive, easy to understand, and easy to maintain.

Baruch Givoni, working in the Negev Desert, has developed a range of approaches for using radiant cooling using air systems rather than water systems.

Other more exotic cooling systems that use the combined effects of evaporation and night sky radiation are the wetted roof pond, the cool pool, and heat exchangers coupled to a shaded pool or swimming pool, shown on page 112.

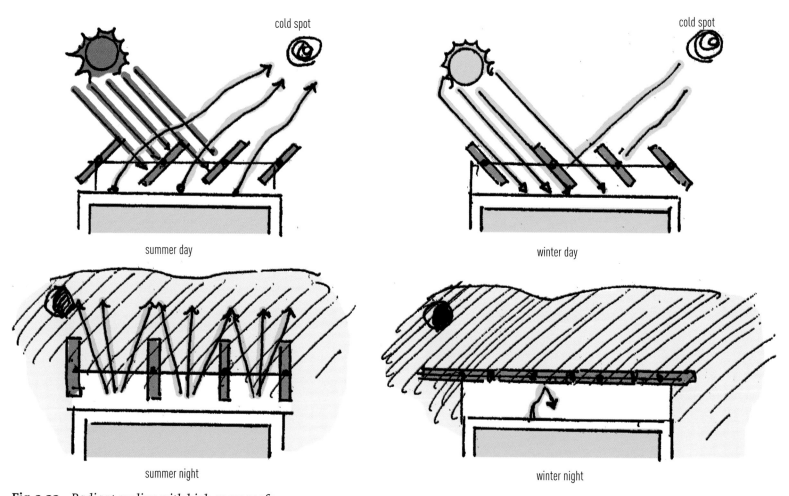

Fig. 3.22. *Radiant cooling with high-mass roofs.*

"Night sky" cool roof systems that pump water to a white roof for evaporation and night sky radiant cooling can also be effective. Several options were developed by the Davis Energy Group. A manufacturing facility in Vacaville found that this system provided a 67 percent cost saving with a payback of 2.5 years. In Australia, this type of system is being used to provide cooling through floor slabs and ceiling beams.

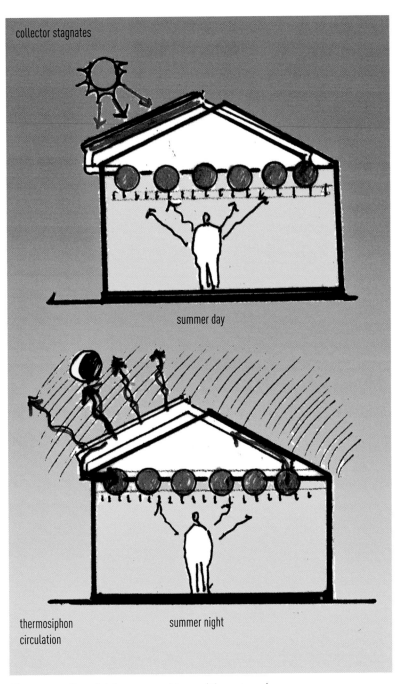

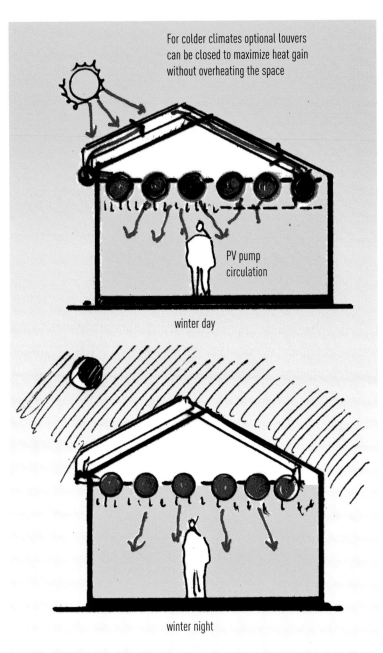

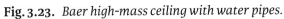

Fig. 3.23. *Baer high-mass ceiling with water pipes.*

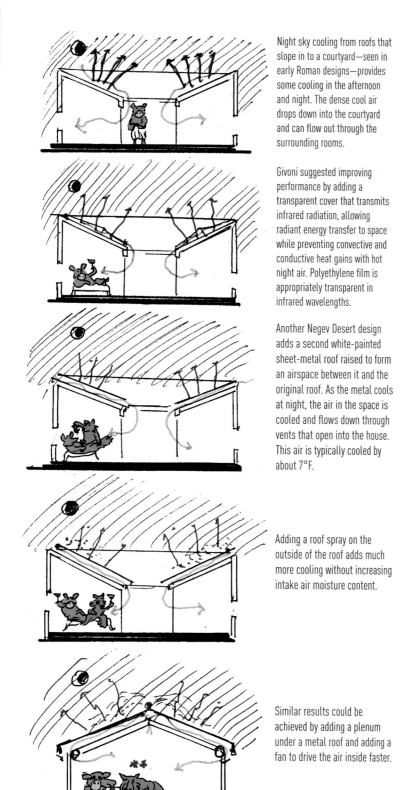

Night sky cooling from roofs that slope in to a courtyard—seen in early Roman designs—provides some cooling in the afternoon and night. The dense cool air drops down into the courtyard and can flow out through the surrounding rooms.

Givoni suggested improving performance by adding a transparent cover that transmits infrared radiation, allowing radiant energy transfer to space while preventing convective and conductive heat gains with hot night air. Polyethylene film is appropriately transparent in infrared wavelengths.

Another Negev Desert design adds a second white-painted sheet-metal roof raised to form an airspace between it and the original roof. As the metal cools at night, the air in the space is cooled and flows down through vents that open into the house. This air is typically cooled by about 7°F.

Adding a roof spray on the outside of the roof adds much more cooling without increasing intake air moisture content.

Similar results could be achieved by adding a plenum under a metal roof and adding a fan to drive the air inside faster.

Fig. 3.24

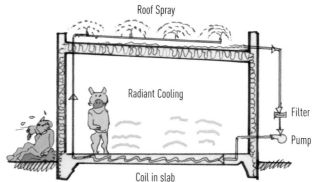

Fig. 3.25. *White Cap F System for nighttime cooling.*

Calculations

The rate of heat loss can be calculated using any one of the formulas developed for calculating outgoing radiation at night. These generally provide reasonable agreement with observed data. Geiger* provides a graphic solution that accounts for humidity, relative temperatures, and water vapor. Radiant losses are increased when the radiator is warmer than air temperature. They can be reduced up to 30 percent by high humidity, but there are two frequency windows in the atmosphere where moisture content doesn't affect radiation loss so they can work even in more humid areas.

The relative humidity equation developed by MacDonald* develops estimates for night sky cooling. It uses readily available information and it may be the easiest formula to use. ε is the emissivity of the surface, which would typically be around 0.95 to 0.99.

$$I_o = \varepsilon \, (0.165 - 0.000769 \; RH) \; \text{langley/minute}$$

With ε assumed to be 0.95, and relative humidity of 20 percent, this estimates net radiant loss at 0.16 ly/min or 34.7 BTU/sf/hr.

The Passive Solar Research Group in Omaha explored different methods for calculating radiant losses. One approach was possible when an upward-facing infrared thermometer (165° aperture) was used to determine sky temperature. The equation for radiant loss then becomes

$$R = \varepsilon_r \, (\sigma T_{pond}{}^4 - \sigma T_{sky}{}^4) \; \text{w/m}^2$$

ε_r = roof pond emissivity (perhaps 0.95)

σ = Stefan-Boltzman constant (5.7×10^{-8} watts/meter^2/°K)

If the sky temperature is 15°C and the roof pond is 20°C, then the radiant heat loss will be about 7 watts/m²/hr or 20 BTU/sf/hr.

Clouds can reduce net night sky radiation by blocking radiant loss and increasing the counter-radiation. We feel this effect when thick cloud cover at night reduces heat loss to space, moderating a winter night, or when clouds reduce cooling effects on a hot summer night. Even if there are no clouds, increasing the moisture reduces heat loss to space, but when very dry atmosphere conditions develop the heat loss can increase, helping us keep a house cool in summer.

Most of the long-wave-radiation blocking occurs very close to the earth. Dense fog can reduce outgoing radiation to zero; high thin cirrus might reduce radiation loss only 10 percent. Relatively little work has been done to provide tables for calculating impact of different cloud types on outgoing radiation. The formula for calculating the effect of clouds on outgoing radiation is: $I = I_0(1 - kn^m)$, where k, n, and m are constants with different values calculated by different investigators. For general estimates, n and m can be around to equal 1 and the formula becomes: $I = I_0 (1 - k)$. The table below presents experimentally determined values for $1 - k$.

Table 3.3. *The impact of clouds on outgoing radiation.*

Effect of clouds on outgoing radiation

Value of I-k	Cloud type	Cloud elevation (m)	Feet
0.84	Cirrus	12,200	40000
0.68	Cirrostratus	8,390	27500
0.34	Altocumulus	3,660	12000
0.2	Altostratus	2,140	7000
0.12	Stratocumulus	1,220	4000
0.04	Stratus	460	1500
0.01	Nimbostratus	92	300
0	Fog	0	0

Sellers, 1965

The radiant cooling rates observed are typically 10 to 50 BTU/sf/hr, but in the desert with very high temperatures and dry, clear skies the rate may be higher. Even with more commonly observed rates, a 1,200-square-foot roof would provide 12,000 to 60,000 BTUs of cooling per hour and perhaps 100,000 to 500,000 BTUs each night, more than enough for an energy-efficient building shell to perform well. Still higher radiant-cooling rates may be possible with selective surfaces and better isolation of cooling surfaces from conductive and convective heat gain.

Cooling a high-mass roof surface that is exposed to the room below works well, and collecting cool- or cold-air drainage has shown some promise. Radiant cooling has great potential and has been demonstrated in many buildings, but commercialization of this approach is still lagging. This is a result of limited development of movable insulation systems and the ease of installing low-cost air-conditioning made possible by heavily subsidized nonrenewable-fuel-based generation of electricity and no payment for external costs of air pollution and global climate change. As prices for electricity climb and fees for climate change impact are added, or in places where electricity is not available, these radiant systems will be more widely used. They can improve security because they can work well even when power supplies are interrupted.

System 4: Evaporation

Evaporating water has a very powerful cooling effect. The phase change from water to water vapor, the latent heat of vaporization, takes considerable energy—about 1,050 BTUs per pound of water at 75°F. Evaporating a cubic foot of water will provide about 65,000 BTUs of cooling for a passive building. Many traditional building systems used evaporation-based cooling to great advantage, perhaps with a pool or fountain in the courtyard or building, sprinkling the tile or floor with water, or utilizing the evapotranspiration from landscaping to provide cooling. With most evaporative systems airflow is important, so refining the ventilation design is important, as is protecting cooling breezes. These remain among the most important cooling options for the world's hot climates because they can often minimize or eliminate air-conditioning systems.

Lessons from these historic cooling options can be used to improve comfort for the five hundred million people who live in warm climates but earn less than a dollar a day. In ancient Rome, for example, villas would often have a shallow landscaped pond for summer cooling. The *maziara* of the Middle East uses terracotta water jars in the wind flow to add evaporative cooling to a building. Frescoes from Egypt show slaves fanning terra-cotta jars full of water to cool the room. In traditional Iranian designs, many buildings have running water in areas with ventilating towers, called *badgirs*, above to improve airflow. Wetted fabric or fiber can also be used for cooling. In parts of India, the solid doors were removed in summer and tatties or a thermantidote made of dried *khusskhuss* grass was installed. These fiber nets over a framework are wetted to create a cool airflow by sprinkling or with an automatic drip or tipping trough that rolls over when full to wet the pad. Similar practices can be found in Iran and other parts of the Middle East. In Rajasthan, a grille was wetted with rosewater and used in place of a door. The blades of the large ceiling fans in India were sometimes wetted as well. Tents were also wetted to keep occupants more comfortable.

The evaporative cooler using excelsior pads (aspen fiber) developed from these simple systems. Indirect evaporative coolers, which offer cooling without humidity, are once again reaching the market. These are very energy-efficient and with improved heat exchangers can reach temperatures below the wet bulb temperature.

Landscaping with larger trees can provide very powerful evaporative cooling and solar control. Tests have showed temperature reductions of 22°F with full tree shade, dropping temperatures from 108° to 86°F in a test trailer. The cooling effect of landscaping can be enhanced by spraying or sprinkling. Peter the Great reportedly used a similar system to add water from pipes to the outer foliage of a tree to increase summer cooling at his residence.

Evaporative cooling doesn't leak ozone-layer-killing or global warming gases like air conditioners do. The most economical systems involve simple evaporation from fountains, landscaping, or mist systems. More complex evaporation-based cooling systems with tanks or pools that add night sky radiation cooling as well can provide comfort even in the most extreme deserts.

How Much Cooling Can We Expect?

The evaporative cooling that can be expected for a building site can be estimated from the nearest evaporation pan data. Standard daily pan evaporation is measured using a 4-foot-diameter Class A evaporation pan. Class A pans offer actual measured evaporation rates and integrate wind, humidity, and temperature. Although the pans are smaller than cooling system tanks or ponds would typically be, they suggest the potential for evaporative cooling pretty clearly, as shown in figure 3.26.

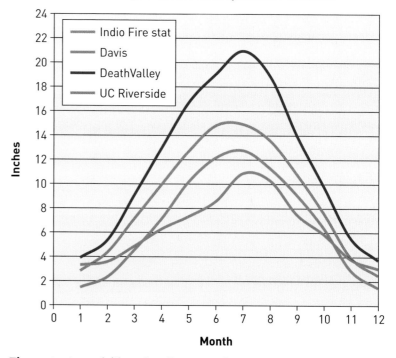

Fig. 3.26. *A rough idea of cooling potential can be estimated by calculating the evaporation per square foot per month. This is shown for Yuma, Arizona, in figure 3.27. If the evaporation is 12 inches, then 1 cubic foot per square foot of water surface is evaporating every month. This provides 65,000 BTUs per square foot of cooling per month, or about 2,000 BTUs per square foot of pond per day. More typically, cooling rates will be in the range of 300 to 700 BTU/sf/night. In an energy-efficient building with good solar control, this will be enough to provide cooling for comfort with many evaporative cooling systems.*

KEY TERMS

- **Dry bulb temperature:** the air temperature measured with a bare thermometer.

- **Wet bulb temperature:** the air temperature measured with a thermometer bulb with a wetted fabric sleeve exposed to rapidly moving air (often done on a sling).

- **Relative humidity:** the percent of moisture in the air compared with the maximum possible.

- **Dew point temperature:** the temperature to which a surface must be cooled to condense water. This can be determined with a metal cup full of ice water and a thermometer. Pour cool water into the cup and add ice. Measure the temperature periodically until drops form on the outside of the cup.

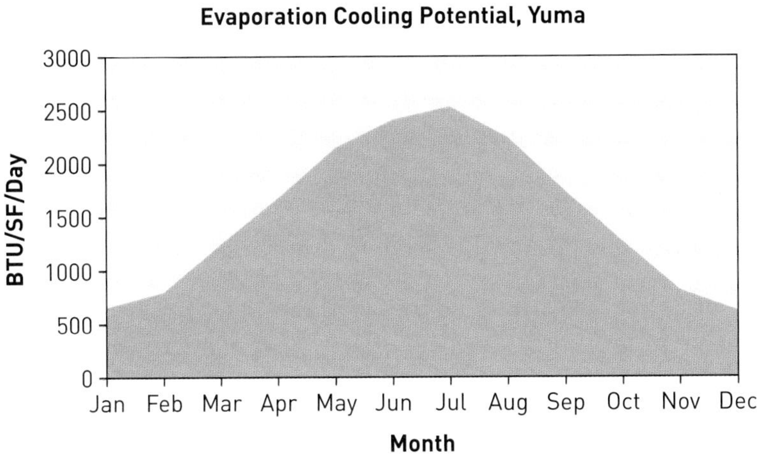

Evaporation Cooling Potential, Yuma

Fig. 3.27. *Evaporation cooling potential for Yuma, Arizona.*

The potential for evaporative cooling is related to the site microclimate. Humidity and wind affect evaporation rate. Evaporation is most powerful in arid environments but can be helpful in more humid environments if it is indirect and does not increase the humidity levels where the people are living. Evaporation can be used to cool the air in a building, around the building, or the thermal mass. Common options include cooling towers, misters, sprinkling the tile or concrete, fountains, pools, or landscaping. Indirect cooling options include roof ponds and roof sprays.

Cooling Towers

The Environmental Research Lab at the University of Arizona–Tucson developed a very effective cooling-tower design for buildings using evaporation. This modern version of a Persian wind tower was a better investment than a solar chimney for cooling. More recently, evaporative cooling has been added to traditional wind towers in the Middle East to improve cooling. These experiments have included pads, wetted curtains, and clay pipes. Airflow has been slightly reduced but cooling has been increased. The cooling towers developed by ERL use a pad or set of evaporative pads at the top of the tower. The intake air is cooled and the denser air falls down the tower and into the building. Systems have been built for both homes and greenhouses and performed very well.

The tower is 6 feet by 6 feet in cross section and 25 feet tall. A 4-inch-thick vertically placed evaporation pad of cellulose sits at the top and is kept wet with a 1/25-horsepower pump. A high-quality mister might provide the same benefits, but would probably require more careful control and maintenance. A plywood X-baffle in the tower helps collects wind from any direction. Adding the wind effect improves tower performance significantly, reducing the size needed. With a 4-meter-per-second wind, the tower downdraft doubles. A test system installed on a home provided good comfort, never exceeding 78°F inside, despite air temperatures reaching 108°F. The inside air temperature was held to within a couple of degrees of the outdoor wet bulb temperature.

Cooling towers can be easily incorporated in new buildings (see figure 3.30), but are not hard to retrofit to some existing buildings. The cool draft should flow into the building through a large inlet and perhaps into a hallway or central room with good airflow paths to other rooms. A solar chimney or stack effect may be used to help draw cool air through the building. Greenhouses with a solar chimney at one end and cooling tower at the other allow for passively generated cross-ventilation with cool air.

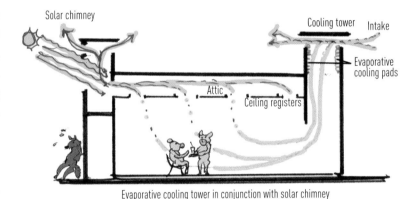

Evaporative cooling tower in conjunction with solar chimney

Fig. 3.28a. *Evaporative cooling tower with solar chimney for exhaust.*

Fig. 3.28b. *Cooling-tower house.*

Cooling-tower-house performance

Temperature °F

- Outside air
- Interior air
- Wet bulb

8/19/85　8/20/85　8/21/85　8/22/85　8/23/85

Date

Fig. 3.29. *Cooling-tower thermal performance.*

Fig. 3.30. *Two passive downdraft cooling towers at Zion Visitors Center, Zion National Park, Springdale, Utah.*

Additional Cooling Techniques

MISTERS

Misters can provide evaporative cooling for outside spaces and intake air. They come in a range of prices and effectiveness. The best systems use very high pressure and metal fittings to produce a very fine fog. The cheapest systems are all-plastic and use just standard water pressure; they make big drops and are not as reliable. The best compromise is often a medium-priced system with a booster pump and metal fittings, running at 100 to 200 psi.

Misting systems can provide cooling comfort for a courtyard or exterior space as well as cooling for the building.

Fig. 3.31. *Misters cooling the Audubon Center in Los Angeles.*

SPRINKLING INTERIORS

Many traditional buildings used evaporative cooling from sprinkling the tiles or floor. This can be effective in a building or in a courtyard. Temperatures can be dropped 20 to 60°F in a matter of minutes. The lower radiant temperatures and cooler air both improve comfort.

FOUNTAINS

Traditional buildings often incorporated a fountain to cool spaces. The effect comes from evaporation primarily, but the psychological benefits of the sound of running water are also important. For maximum cooling, the fountain should create small water particles. A fountain in a pool can help keep pool temperatures down. This cooled water could be used in a radiant cooling system or fan coils. Waterfall features can also be used inside or outside to increase cooling.

LANDSCAPING

Plants evaporate water as part of transpiration. A courtyard tree can provide delightful shade and considerable evaporative cooling for a building. A green wall or screen can provide evaporative cooling and solar control. Arbors, vines, and other landscaping can also provide evaporative cooling. The evapotranspiration of water from plants provides very significant cooling. This can be augmented by sprinkling the vegetation with water. A weeping hose or sprinkling hose can be threaded through a hedge or tree to improve cooling.

GREEN ROOFS

A green roof is a roof that is partially or completely covered with vegetation and soil, or with a growing medium, planted over a waterproof membrane. Also known as living roofs, eco-roofs, *oikosteges*, and vegetated roofs, green roofs can also reduce ceiling or attic temperatures and stormwater runoff. Effective design and choice of plant material is critical. The challenge is developing a lightweight soil mixture and secure waterproofing system. The soil layer can improve roof material lifetimes by shielding them from UV radiation and extreme temperatures. Maintenance is also required for most living roofs. Some cities are supporting these living roofs with financial incentives to help reduce stormwater runoff and water-quality problems.

Fig. 3.32. *Green walls and arbors can provide effective cooling.*

Green roofs can be categorized as intensive or extensive, depending on the depth of planting medium and the amount of maintenance required. Intensive roofs typically have deeper soil and require more maintenance and irrigation.

Green Roof Cross Section

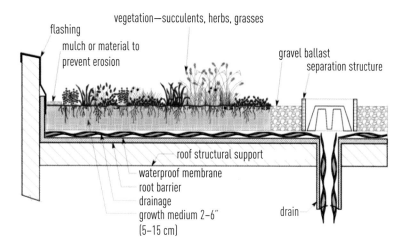

Green Roof Thermal Performance

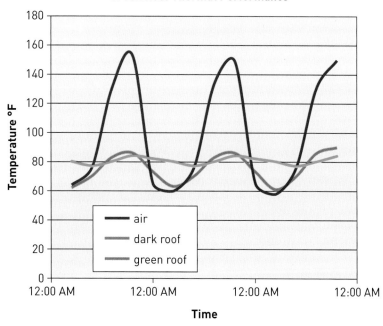

Fig. 3.33. *(a) Green roof diagram. (b) Comparison of dark roof and green roof surface temperature at 40°N latitude.*

Hybrid Applications

COOL ROOFS

A light-colored roof is cooler than a dark roof, but roof temperatures can be dropped even more by sprinkling or misting, which lowers the temperature of the roofing material, which in turn helps to reduce attic temperatures in poorly insulated roof systems.

Evaporation on the roof can also be used to cool water in a reservoir for daytime cooling. A pump can be used to move water at night to a white roof, where evaporation and night sky radiation chill the water for use in cooling during the day. These systems are discussed in more detail in the section on radiant cooling.

A traditional sleeping room in the desert was sometimes made using a lightweight metal shell with a sprinkler running on the outside, creating a desert submarine. Not only did it sound cool, but it was cool. The monsoon or rain palaces of Asia could be updated to create a cool room. A lightweight metal roof would be chilled with a flow of water dropping off the eaves into a trough or pond and recirculated to the roof.

COOL POOLS

A roof pond that is fully shaded all the time and has an open surface for evaporation is called a cool pool. These systems are well suited for areas where temperatures are very high in summer. They are noteworthy because they can provide indirect evaporative cooling and can work even in more humid climates. Cool-pool performance tests in California's low hot desert showed that they can provide comfort under extreme conditions. One of the test cells included a heat load simulating internal heat gains, and it showed very little change in temperature, for as water temperature increases so do evaporation and cooling. The importance of shading is clearly shown, with the sun-exposed pond getting very hot.

A cool pool with a water pond over the ceiling coupled to a vertical waterwall was extremely effective and maintained comfort even in the middle of a very hot parking lot at the state fairgrounds in Sacramento. This configuration provides low radiant temperatures on two surfaces, improving comfort. The demonstration unit by Living Systems maintained cool temperatures even though it only used plastic flap doors and experienced considerable human traffic (letting in hot outside air) with daytime temperatures exceeding 100°F.

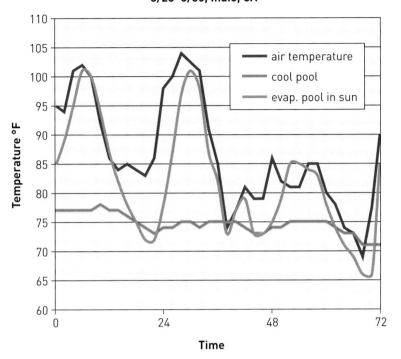

**Cool pool performance
8/28–8/30, Indio, CA**

air temperature
cool pool
evap. pool in sun

Fig. 3.34. *Cool-pool performance, Indio test.*

ROOF POND AND COOL-POOL PERFORMANCE

Not many studies of cool pools, roofs wetted at night, and flooded roof ponds have been done, so the relation between climate and cooling potential is not well developed. If average wind speeds from the nearest station are used to calculate the cooling rate for a cool-pool house, the cooling potential may be underestimated because the wind speed is generally highest when the relative humidity is lower. Conversely, if average wind speed is used to estimate cooling for a misted water bags in a Skytherm house with insulated lids closed in the day, it will tend to overestimate evaporation because the pond is being exposed at night when wind speed and relative humidity are higher.

A ground-mounted cool pool, a swimming pool, lake, pond, or the ocean, can also be used as a source of cool water for radiant cooling within a building if the transfer distance is short. The cool water is pumped through radiant tubing in the ceiling, walls, or floor to cool the space. But adding pumps and controls adds to the cost, complexity, and unreliability. An existing swimming pool could be converted to a cool pool by adding a screened shade. This large mass could be kept cool and used in a radiant cooling system or fan-coil system.

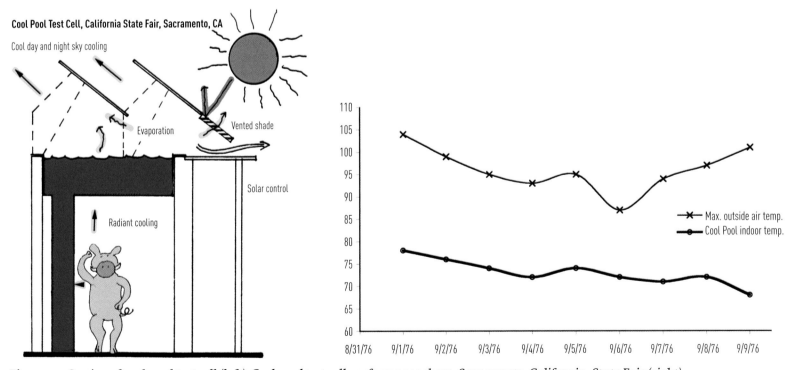

Fig. 3.35. *Section of cool-pool test cell (left). Cool-pool test cell performance chart, Sacramento, California, State Fair (right).*

Supplemental Cooling

There are three basic types of mechanical systems for adding cooling: direct and indirect evaporative coolers and air conditioners. Air conditioners are commonly used and well understood, but direct and indirect evaporative coolers are more efficient, delivering comparable cooling capacity for one-quarter to one-half the energy cost of an air conditioner.

The direct evaporative cooler or "swamp cooler" draws outside air through wetted pads and blows the cooled air through the house or building. These were first used extensively in New England and the southeastern seaboard to cool large mill buildings. They worked there, but they are more effective in drier climates where the added humidity won't be a problem. Models with the fan driven by a photovoltaic panel are available.

The indirect evaporative cooler couples evaporative cooling with a heat exchanger. It may draw air from the building through evaporative pads and exhaust it through a heat exchanger, dumping the now cooler but humid air to the atmosphere. Or it may use fresh air for both the cooling and the makeup air. A second fan draws drier exterior air through a heat exchanger, where it is cooled off and blown into the building. These were first used in Arizona and California in the 1930s on both homes and larger buildings. These are less efficient than a direct evaporative cooler, but they don't add humidity to the living space, and they improve comfort. Indirect evaporative coolers were once sold by several manufacturers and were also widely used on commercial buildings. Neal A. Pennington developed a commercially sold home system in the early 1940s that was bulky but effective (see figure 3.36).

COOLING EFFICIENCY

The energy-efficiency ratio of an air conditioner is its British thermal units rating over its wattage. For example, if a 10,000 BTU air conditioner consumes 1,200 watts, its EER is 8.3 (10,000 BTU/1,200 watts). Air conditioners with EERs ranging from 9 to 16 for central systems are available; and more efficient models, EER 20, use a groundwater source heat pump. In contrast, the EER may reach 40-plus for indirect evaporative coolers. These units offer double the efficiency, and are typically quieter than air conditioners.

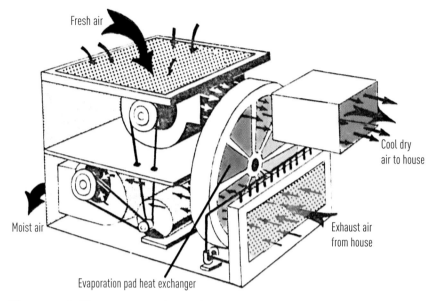

Fig. 3.36. *Indirect evaporative cooler, 1940s.*

Cool and Comfortable

Large Buildings

Direct and indirect evaporative systems can be included in large-building design. Fountains, waterfalls, and pools can be included in lobbies and large rooms. Large-scale roof ponds and cool pools have not been built, but as noted before indirect evaporative systems were once widely used in large commercial buildings. Both approaches will be considered and used more frequently in the years to come as air-conditioning costs rise.

The experience with evaporative cooling in larger buildings was quite good, but is not appreciated by most architects or engineers today. The Walt Disney building and a medical complex used the successful Stockly plate system in the 1930s, providing up to 1.8 million BTUs of cooling at very low energy cost. A cooling shaft for direct or indirect evaporative cooling can extend the full height of a building and could be open or regenerative, with a system that recycles water. The administration building at the University of Arizona–Tucson was cooled with a very efficient system that ran from 1936 to 1952 and provided 500,000 BTUs of cooling with only 17.5 hp. The cooling shaft was 4 by 5 feet and extended from the basement to the attic. About 135 gpm of water were sprayed down the shaft as 16,000 cfm flowed up it. The cooled water was used in counterflow radiators providing 10,800 cfm to the conditioned space. The moist cool air was emptied into the attic, further reducing heat gain to the occupied space. The system was simple: two fans, a pump, and a 10 hp refrigeration system used during the infrequent hot moist monsoon weather in Arizona. It was totally concealed and had no exterior features that could weather or freeze. It maintained temperatures 15°F below exterior dry bulb.

Evaporation cooling systems using fabric tubes might prove very economical. These would use a counterflow system with an updraft of moist air and/or sprinklers in the center tube and a downdraft of cooling air in the outer tube. The same approach could also be taken with a pair of nested culverts. The center culvert might be wrapped with a weeping hose. The inner culvert would be used for downdraft makeup air.

Radiant Cooling for Comfort

Water chilled by evaporation can also be used in a radiant cooling mode. L. W. Neubauer at UC Davis demonstrated this use in a test trailer in the 1950s. Metal pans full of water in the ceiling were cooled by airflow through the attic, providing 15°F degrees of cooling in the room. Comfort increased from the reduced temperature and the impact of radiant cooling surfaces above the head.

Indirect radiant systems have also been developed using panels or coils chilled by water cooled by a cooling tower or other form of

---

INDIRECT EVAPORATIVE COOLERS RETURN

Arizona's hard (mineral laden) and corrosive water limited the use of indirect evaporative coolers there, but they remained in use in California until air-conditioning systems and energy became cheap. Fortunately they are coming back, with several new models on the market. Temperatures at or below wet bulb are possible with these new systems. Improved models use a more complex heat exchanger that involves multiple steps and are more powerful and efficient. The Climate Wizard can deliver significantly colder air than traditional evaporative cooling with air temperatures near, and at times below, those produced by refrigerated air-conditioning. The Coolerado Cooler uses a patented heat and mass exchanger (HMX) and cools the supply air in twenty stages. At each stage, the humidified air is exhausted and enhances the cooling effect of the supply air. The MasterCool 2-Stage Indirect Cooling Module can be added to any MasterCool evaporative cooler to provide even greater cooling power and energy/cost efficiency. Another version is also offered by OASys. These indirect evaporative coolers and their larger cousins are also well suited for commercial and industrial uses and may be integrated with a conventional AC system.

- **Coolerado** (residential). Coolerado Corporation, 4430 Glencoe Street, Denver, CO 80216. Phone: 303-375-0878. Email: CustomerService@Coolerado.com. Web site: www.coolerado.com.

- **Climate Wizard** (residential and commercial). Seeley International Americas Corporation, 1202 North 54th Avenue, Building 2, Suite 117, Phoenix, AZ 85043. Phone: 602-353-8066. Web site: www.climatewizard.com.au.

- **OASys** (residential). Speakman, PO Box 191, Wilmington, DE 19899. Web site: www.oasysairconditioner.com.

- **MasterCool** (residential & commercial). **Champion/Essick EPX** (commercial). Des Champs Technologies, 225 South Magnolia Avenue, Buena Vista, VA 24416. Phone: 540-291-1111. Web site: www.deschamps.com.

- **Stage II** (commercial). Spec-Air, 6850 McNutt Road, Anthony, NM 88021 Phone: 505-589-6200. Web site: www.specair.net.

A home system can be built by a skilled do-it-yourselfer. J. R. Watts tested a system built using a truck radiator for the heat exchanger with a ¼-horsepower 18-inch fan to move air into the house. The water was chilled in a redwood packed cooling tower of nominal 90,000 BTU capacity that was capable of cooling water to within 1°F of wet bulb temperature and circulated with a ½-horsepower pump. None of these was optimized, but the system was very effective. A plate-type system built by a grad student at the University of Texas provided 57,400 BTUs of sensible cooling per hour using less than 1 horsepower.

evaporation. R. R. Irwin at Oklahoma State University–Stillwater used water from a cooling tower to chill radiant serpentine copper coils in the ceilings and walls of student apartments. Temperatures never exceeded 82.5°F and varied only a degree over the day, despite outdoor air temperatures of 106°F. A similar system in an energy-efficient building shell would be much more effective.

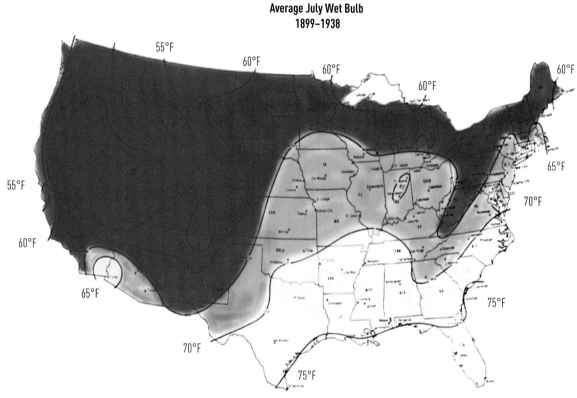

Average July Wet Bulb
1899–1938

Fig. 3.37. *How much cooling? July wet bulb is a good indicator of evaporative cooling potential. The Southeast has less cooling potential, but the comfort temperatures are higher and indirect evaporative cooling can still be very useful. In the arid Southwest, evaporative cooling is very effective, and indirect evaporative cooling is even better.*

Evaporative cooling is effective!

Ventilation is the key element in passive cooling systems 1 and 2, and is needed to meet the health requirements mentioned on page 51. It is also a large subject with many facets, so it deserves its own section. Air flow plays a key role in passive cooling and a major role in comfort and health.

Ventilation based on natural forces is quiet, requires no electricity, does not create global warming gases, and works even when the power is off. Passive ventilation can improve comfort, offer occupants more control over their comfort, and reduce operating costs. Building costs can be reduced even further when the HVAC system can be eliminated or reduced in size.

While a cooling breeze can be delightful, a hurricane is not. Most people find airspeeds up to 100 feet per minute (fpm) comfortable, while airspeeds between 100 and 200 fpm are often acceptable. Air movement on legs can be at higher speeds, but beyond 150 fpm, hair, loose paper, and light objects on desktops may start to blow around. Outside dust, pollen, and smog may also require special treatment, although most studies have shown outside air is often less polluted than inside air due to stagnation, molds, and concentrations of toxic materials, finishes, and household products in buildings. Noise can also be an issue. Building configurations and landscaping elements need to be designed to limit noise problems so that vents or windows can be open.

While ventilation can provide needed cooling in summer, ventilation in winter is needed to provide fresh air. This can be provided by trickle vents, makeup air vents for fireplaces and furnaces, and ventilation for bathrooms, kitchens, and other areas where moisture or pollution are concentrated. In a very efficient passive solar home, the performance is often good enough that windows can be opened as needed to let in more fresh air.

There are three general approaches for natural ventilation. Although they are often combined in various ways, we will cover each separately for clarification. The three approaches are:

1. Cross-ventilation.
2. Stack ventilation.
3. Various augmentation techniques.

Cross-Ventilation

Cross-ventilation techniques were highly developed in many traditional architectures and buildings. A visit to a plantation home in the Deep South offers a living textbook for natural ventilation. The large window openings, vents, tall ceilings, large doors, hallways, stairwells, cupolas, and orientation of these buildings were all refined to produce the greatest possible comfort without air-conditioning.

Planning for Cross-Ventilation

Where natural ventilation is sufficient to provide comfort, urban planning and subdivision design should protect or enhance natural wind flows. Streets and landscaping should be laid out to protect natural breezes for cooling. This is rarely done, but the wind flow around windmills in Holland is protected by "wind rights," and a similar concept can be considered in the layout of subdivisions and cities. Wind flow can be protected by running the streets at only a small angle to the wind and using trees and landscaping to channel the wind into the houses. Where strong winds occur regularly, landscaping and design can be used to block the unwanted gusts, yet still protect the cooling breezes.

Cross-ventilation will vary from hour to hour as the wind speed and direction change. It is best to develop a very flexible ventilation system that can adapt to changes in wind direction, changes in surrounding landscaping and structures, and changes in use within a building. The goal is always to provide occupants with the ability to adjust ventilation to meet their comfort requirements.

Cross-Ventilation Details

If there is only one opening into a room, breezes generally will not flow into it very far. These cave-type rooms may experience much less than half the ventilation of a comparable room with window openings on two sides. Cave-type rooms are prone to air stagnation and the buildup of indoor air pollution from furnishings, finishes, appliances, and mold. Although these nonventing rooms are most common in apartment buildings, motels, and office complexes, they can also be created by poor design choices in homes and commercial buildings.

Cross-ventilation should be a guiding element in design starting with the schematics. It is relatively easy to include by rethinking design, and reconsidering older design strategies that provided cross-ventilation. David has asthma and allergies that make modern hotels and motels with cave rooms a problem, but older motels almost always have cross-ventilation that allows clearing scents and reducing mold density to tolerable levels. So it can be done, often for free with good window placement.

Shown are average interior airspeeds as % of exterior wind speed

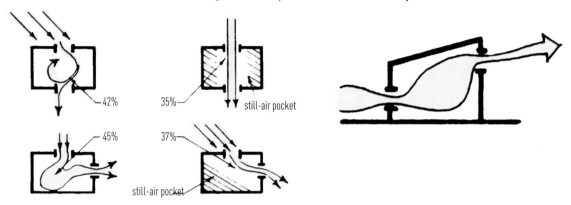

Fig. 3.38a. *Room and window orientation. If windows are on opposite sides, the room should be oriented askew to the wind direction. If the windows are on adjacent walls, the room should be oriented to face directly into the wind. Increasing height difference between inlet and outlet helps induce natural ventilation during still times.*

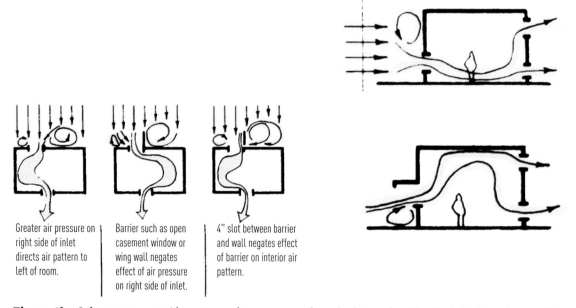

Greater air pressure on right side of inlet directs air pattern to left of room.

Barrier such as open casement window or wing wall negates effect of air pressure on right side of inlet.

4" slot between barrier and wall negates effect of barrier on interior air pattern.

Fig. 3.38b. *Inlet treatment. Air patterns in a room are largely determined by the inlet location and its relationship to the exterior surfaces of the building. It is important for night-vent cooling to wash thermal masses with cool night air via the technique shown. The same principles apply to the vertical dimension. Overhangs can have the same effect as wing walls and other barriers in the horizontal dimension.*

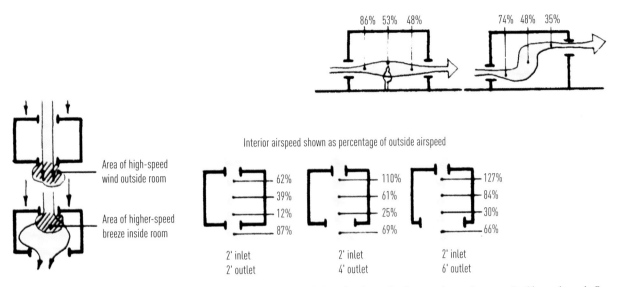

Interior airspeed shown as percentage of outside airspeed

Fig. 3.38c. *Outlet treatment. Outlet size in relation to inlet size largely determines the speed of interior airflow. Change in direction causes greater spread but less speed.*

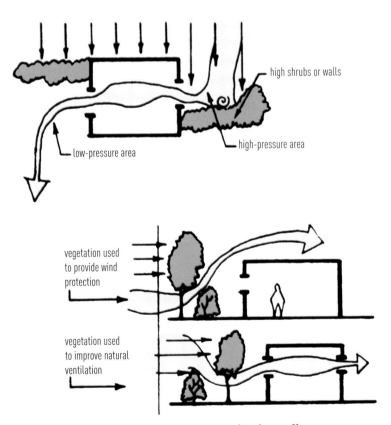

Fig. 3.38d. *Landscape elements. Trees, shrubs, walls, et cetera, can often be used to improve natural ventilation even if the building cannot be optimally oriented to the wind.*

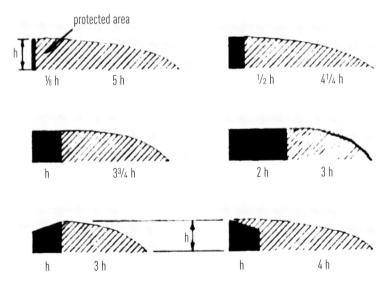

Fig. 3.38e. *Reducing unwanted ventilation in the heating season. For a typical house, heat loss by air infiltration can be two and a half times as great in a 5 mph wind versus no wind. Since infiltration may account for up to half of the building's heating load, protection from wind with a windbreak can reduce heating requirements.*

Predicting Cross-Ventilation Benefits

The pressure difference between the intake and exit points on the building, vent placement, screening materials, and interior arrangements all affect ventilation, but estimates can be made using simple formulas and rules of thumb. For more detailed predictions, we can use computational fluid dynamics, but this is costly and generally restricted to larger buildings.

To calculate the potential rate for cross-ventilation cooling when inlets and outlets are about the same size and the flow path is straightforward, the basic formula (adapted from the American Society of Heating, Refrigerating and Air-Conditioning Engineers, ASHRAE) is:

$Q_w = EA_f V_f S_f$ where

Q_w = volume flow rate, cubic feet minute

A_f = free area of inlet openings, square feet

V_f = wind velocity, feet per minute (miles per hour × 88)

E = effectiveness of openings (E = 0.5 for perpendicular winds and 0.3 for diagonal winds)

S_f = screen factor (see table 3.5)

For example, if the perpendicular wind speed is 5 mph and the room has one 2-by-4 foot casement window on each side with dirty fiberglass screens, the flow rate would be:

$Q_w = 0.5(E) \times 8\ ft^2 \times (5 \times 88) \times 0.5(S_f)$ or 880 cubic feet minute or 52,800 cubic feet hour

A slightly more generous estimate is developed using the equation:

$Q_h = IOR_c A_f V_m S_f$

IOR_c = inlet outlet ratio constant

Q_h = volume flow rate per hour

A_f = free area inlet, square feet

V_m = wind velocity, mph

S_f = screen factor

$Q_h = 3150 \times 8\ ft^2 \times 5\ mph \times 0.5(S_f)$ or 63,000 cubic feet per hour

In the more conservative calculation, a 10-by-14 foot room with 10-foot ceilings would still experience about forty air changes per hour. Other adjustment factors for the second equation include the effect of different inlet and outlet sizes.

Table 3.4. *Cross ventilation I-O ratio*

Inlet:Outlet Ratio	Constant
1:1	3150
2:1	4000
3:1	4250
4:1	5350
3:4	4400
1:2	2000
1:4	1000

For a cave-type room:

$Q_w = 53(A_f/10.8) \times (V_{mph}/2.2) \times (S_f)$

Using the same example, a 140-square-foot room with a 2-by-4 foot casement window on one side only, the flow rate would be:

$Q_w = 53(8/10.8) \times (5/2.2) \times (0.5) = 43$ cubic feet per minute

43 cfm × 60 minutes = 2,580 cfh   2,580 cfh/1,400 cf = 1.8 ACH

so it would provide only about two air changes per hour, and many pockets of stale air would be left.

The energy transfer at a given flow rate will depend on flow paths, vent configuration, interaction with wind flows, air moisture content, and temperature differences and will be influenced by thermal mass. At its simplest:

Energy transfer = airflow × specific heat of air × density of air × temperature difference °F.

See page 122 for an example.

The climate information needed for ventilation design is available for many locations around the world, from NOAA to climate-data centers, Department of Defense engineering design guides, and other local, regional, and state climate resources. The Internet has made this much more accessible, but some areas still lack easily accessible information. Even if you are able to find a nearby weather station, consider the possible microclimate differences if your site is on a hill, in a canyon or forest, or shaded or wind-blocked by trees or a building next door. It can be helpful to take notes on the wind flow and temperature on site and compare them with the nearest weather station data.

Table 3.5. *Screen effects: Insect screens are a necessity in most locations. They can greatly reduce airflow, particularly when they are dirty. Airflow calculations should take screen type and condition into consideration. And clean screens regularly. Aynsley, 2007.*

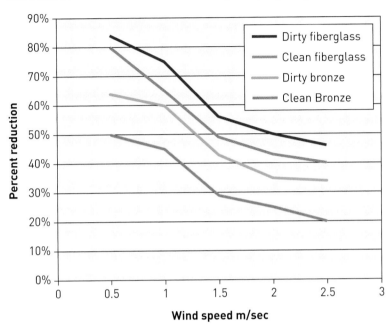

Stack Ventilation

This second type of natural ventilation utilizes the fact that hot air is less dense than cool air to generate air movement in a building with a low intake and high outlet. The intakes should be as low as possible and from an area with cooler air, perhaps a landscaped area or shaded courtyard with a fountain. Louvers can be used on intakes to help direct cooling air toward people. The outlet should be placed as high as possible.

Stack ventilation was used in many traditional building designs, and usually included very high ceilings, multiple floors, thin buildings, open stairwells, and roof monitors, dormers, or cupolas with operable windows. Usually the stack effect will supplement cross-ventilation. Stack-effect ventilation can also help remove pollutants from interior spaces as well as provide cooling. Performance can be estimated with simple formulas, calculated with software or computational fluid dynamics, or tested with models if well-developed design and climate data exist. For larger buildings, computational fluid dynamics programs allow for more accurate modeling.

The stack effect becomes more useful for larger and taller buildings and can augment or replace cross-ventilation. Taller ceilings help air stratification and airflow and also improve occupant satisfaction. Open plans are generally best. Cubicles and partitions can interrupt the flow of window-driven cross-ventilation and may limit natural ventilation benefits unless floor vents are used.

The stack effect works best when the exit air is warmer than the outside air. The interior air will be warmed by the people and equipment inside the building or by gains from artificial lights and sunlight.

Design Choices for Stack Ventilation

Taller buildings with atria, open stairwells, ventilation shafts, or courtyards are well suited for stack-effect cooling. Windows and vents are needed to provide flow paths for warmer, lighter air to escape and for cooler makeup air. The inlets and outlets should be as far apart as possible in height, with 5 to 6 feet as a minimum and 15 or 20 feet preferable. Multistory buildings offer even greater potential for stack-effect ventilation. The airflow induced by thermal force is proportional to the effective area of the apertures and the square root of the vent height difference and the inside–outside temperature differential. Bigger vents are better, although a combination of smaller automatic vents and user-controlled windows and doors can make a good combination.

Over-door transom windows or vents can help maintain ventilation flow between rooms while providing privacy and security.

To work effectively, the stack effect needs knowledgeable operators. Building users or owners should be trained and provided with a simple guide to proper operation. This should be printed, placed in a plastic sleeve, and mounted in a secure location where users can see it, perhaps in a hallway or on the inside of a closet door. Clear temperature guidelines can be provided with paired thermometers showing exit and intake temperatures to guide operators. The mechanisms for operable inlets and outlets should be well designed and maintained. Although a long pole with a hook can be used to open and close high windows and vents, a permanently mounted crank mechanism is better and cannot be misplaced.

Predicting Stack-Ventilation Benefits

The stack effect of simple, open buildings is relatively easy to estimate. More complex buildings are better studied with computational fluid dynamics to estimate the distribution of airflow in the many flow cells in a building and to integrate the effects of stack and cross-ventilation. Most passive buildings are designed to integrate stack and cross-ventilation effects, and the high outlets are often placed where wind will increase the exhaust rate.

The value of the stack effect with no wind (for example, on a clerestory house with operable windows) can be estimated from the following formula if inlet and outlets about the same size and the outdoor temperature is around 80°F (ASHRAE).

In English measurements

$$Q = 9.4 \sqrt{H(T_i - T_o)}$$

cubic feet/min

Q = airflow cubic feet per minute

A = free area of inlets or outlets (assumed equal) in square feet

H = height from inlet center to outlet center

T_i = average temperature of indoor air in height H °F

T_o = temperature of outdoor air °F

9.4 = constant of proportionality for 65 percent effective openings, use constant of 7.2 if 50 percent effective *(to take into account screens, grilles, et cetera, see table 3.5)*

For a sample home with a free area of inlets (equal to outlets) of 16 square feet, a height difference of 15 feet to a clerestory window, indoor air at 78°F, and outdoor air in the early evening at 74°F, the flow would be: = 1164 ft³min

Heat transfer = 1164 ft³min × 0.24 BTU/lb/°F × 0.075 lb/ft³ × 4°F = 84 BTU min, or 5,000 BTU/hr

This expression requires adjustment in cases when the area of outlets is appreciably different from the area of inlets according to the following ratios:

Table 3.6. *Outlet-inlet relations affect ventilation*

Outlet:Inlet Area	Value to be substituted for 9.4 in above expression:
5:1	12.4
2:1	11.3
1:2	5.6
1:4	3.1

Combining Cross-Ventilation and Stack Ventilation

Cross- and stack ventilation are commonly combined and can often provide full comfort. Special opportunities are offered in larger commercial buildings. And when these simple methods are not enough, ventilation cooling can be augmented with solar chimneys, cowls and ventilators, wind catchers, and mechanical systems. Thermal mass can be added to improve cooling performance.

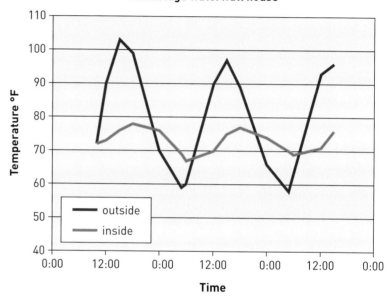

Fig. 3.39. *Davis experiences a cooling breeze most summer nights. This can provide very effective cooling with night ventilation.*

Fig. 3.40. *David leans on the first rectangular metal waterwall in his home in the Village Homes solar subdivision. We now know that this tank was taller and thicker than needed, but it worked well.*

Ventilation cooling can be particularly effective if the night air temperature drops significantly; simply open the windows and doors to let breezes cool the inside at night and store the coolness or coolth using the thermal mass of the house (sheetrock, tile floors, waterwalls, and so on). The potential for night ventilation can be estimated from the high and low temperatures, dry and wet bulb temperatures, prevailing wind patterns, and diurnal temperature patterns.

Ventilation for Large Buildings

Hybrid ventilation for larger buildings may include cross- and stack ventilation, a wind catcher or wind tower, roof monitors or cowls, a solar chimney, and a mechanical system. Costs may be comparable to those for a pure mechanical system, but energy savings, improved comfort, and reduced energy use have long-term payoffs. Current codes and standards often discourage use of natural ventilation, and a reworking of ASHRAE standard 62.1 is in order. Human comfort, health, and sustainability should be given greater attention.

Buildings work best if occupants understand how they work. In commercial buildings, passive ventilation may be automated to some extent, but occupants often play an important role in opening and closing windows and vents. Vents and openings can be adjusted with control logic based on temperature, moisture, airflow, and concentration of carbon dioxide.

It can be helpful to isolate major heat-generation sources from occupied space. Servers, laser printers, copiers, and other heat-generating equipment can be screened from occupied areas. This will also reduce noise problems. Computers and office equipment should be chosen for energy efficiency and low noise generation.

One of the most flexible approaches for ventilating larger buildings is under-floor ventilation, which can also be very effective for heating. This ventilation is often done with a fairly large separation so that the utilities can be run in the same space and be easily reached for repair and revision. Running, connecting, and revising IT systems is much easier. In some lab buildings, the space may grow to become a separate utility floor, but in a home it might be kept to air passages under a slab or sand-suspended stone, paver, or urbanite flooring.

Under-floor ventilation in larger buildings works best when it is an open system and vents can be easily placed or moved. This makes it possible to set the vents where they are needed to keep people comfortable and supplied with fresh air. When desks, tables, and cubicles are moved, the vents can be moved as well.

Computational fluid-dynamic modeling becomes more important for larger buildings where stack and cross-ventilation effects are more complex and where more accurate predictions may be needed for code approval.

The actual ventilation rate can also be determined for larger buildings after the building is built to provide more accurate estimates of ventilation performance and control issues. This is usually done with a study of the time decay for an introduced marker gas such as nitrous oxide, helium, or hydrogen. These tracer gases should be stable, not react with materials, and be easy to detect. Venting characteristics and leakage can also be evaluated with a blower door.

Building design should incorporate full solar control and good ventilation features to make use of ventilation cooling. Buildings should also be designed, commissioned, and operated with the users in mind. Educational materials or indicators may be needed to help occupants open and close windows, shutters, and vents in the appropriate pattern. Retrofitting buildings is also possible, and many successful projects have been undertaken. However, what is free or almost free in a new building can be more costly and challenging to apply to a poorly oriented and built older home or office.

Techniques for Enhancing Ventilation

Augmenting Airflow with a Wind Catcher

In areas where the wind almost always flows from the same direction, a fixed wind catcher or wind tower may be incorporated in the design of the building. These fixed wind catchers are used in many traditional designs. They usually extend above the buildings to reach into the stronger and more laminar flow winds and can be very effective. However, studies suggest they need not be as tall as traditional designs might suggest; a 12-foot tower might suffice. There is, however, less dust and debris farther off the ground. These towers can become effective rain catchers in storms, so design details must allow for rain entry or exclusion—perhaps as part of the rainwater harvesting system.

Wind catchers and wind towers were traditionally used to ventilate and cool buildings where winds are common. There are sophisticated designs throughout the Middle East, from Egypt to Iran. They may be big wind scoops in areas where the winds reliably come from the same direction, wind towers (which will work with winds from any direction), or wind sails. The wind sails used along the Persian Gulf and Gulf of Oman use four sailcloth vanes to deflect wind into the house. Although wind towers and fixed wind scoops like those in Isfahan and Hyderabad Sind, shown in figure 3.41a, might be most applicable in commercial buildings, they can also be included in residential structures when the cooling breezes blow consistently from one direction. Wind sails can also provide a delightful and effective ventilation boost.

Augmenting Airflow with a Cowl

Where wind direction is more variable, a roof-mounted cowl is effective, allowing winds from any direction to be used. If the roof vent is placed in the low-pressure area, ventilation will be improved.

Exhaust venting might also be done with an exhaust cowl or attic turbine ventilator on a roof monitor or near the peak of a cathedral ceiling. An exhaust cowl can be fixed or rotate with wind direction. Buckminster Fuller had a large cowl on his Dymaxion dwelling, figure 3.41b. Much larger rotating exhaust cowls have been used on some commercial buildings. Commercial exhaust cowls are also being developed and used in Europe, figure 3.41c. The Wind Jetter uses a wing profile to enhance exhaust.

Turbine ventilators were first commercialized in Australia and are now used around the world. These include a set of curved or straight vanes, with taller vents performing better than lower vents. Research suggests the straight vanes are more effective than the more commonly seen curved vanes. These are lightweight and with high-quality bearings will spin in even very light breezes. In an 18 mph wind, a 9-inch-diameter chimney cowl vent provided 3 cfs (87.5 l/s) of ventilation. These vents can be augmented with a PV-driven fan. These rotary vents can provide a reasonably weatherproof vent.

While seemingly simple, the airflows of cross wind, stack effect, vents, windows, doors, and wind catchers add up to a fairly complex problem of understanding and modeling ventilation flow.

The wind direction and wind speed information will also help determine the best way of venting a house, building, or simply an attic. Venting the attic of a building can help reduce unwanted heat gain, particularly in a building with poor ceiling insulation. A wide variety of vents are available, including gable vents, ridge vents, skylight vents, different types of roof vents, and turbine vents. Ridge vents are often desirable. Soffit vents should be kept unobstructed when insulation is installed. In wildfire-prone areas, venting should be carefully designed to prevent embers from entering the attic.

One of the greatest challenges in cross-ventilation is finding ways to retrofit existing sealed buildings. This is a problem at all levels, from single-level commercial buildings to apartment towers and high-rises. It is likely some clever solutions can be developed, even for double-facade buildings.

Fig. 3.41a. *Hyderabad Sind, Pakistan (1928).*

Fig. 3.41b. *Buckminster Fuller, Dymaxion house (1950).*

 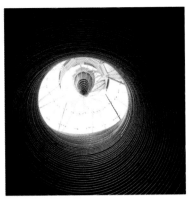

Fig. 3.41c,d. *Ventilation cowls, UK, from the exterior and looking up into a cowl (2000).*

Augmenting Airflow with a Solar Chimney

A solar chimney can be used to enhance the stack effect and drive ventilation. At its simplest, this can be just a pipe painted black, but more commonly is a more sophisticated solar air heater with glass face and black interior. A typical solar chimney has glazing on the sun side, an air channel, and thermal mass painted black to capture and store solar energy to enhance airflow. Insulation helps keep temperatures high, and the thermal mass enables the solar chimney to work for a while after the sun sets.

For maximum flow, the chimney should be very smooth with generous dimensions. The most basic solar chimney consists of a section of large-diameter black pipe (8-inch minimum) extending up the wall and a few feet up from the roof. These pipes are used on composting toilets to enhance ventilation. For better results, a rectangular chimney with east, west, and south glazing might be used, with an insulated high-thermal-mass back wall with selective surface or flat black paint. The chimney can be set at the roof pitch to reduce visual impact and reduce the angle of incidence of the solar radiation on the collector in midsummer when cooling is needed most.

A wind-powered turbine vent may be a suitable cap for the chimney top if the area is windy. You'll also want an insulated inside shutter to close it off in winter or a return vent to capture the warmed air. Again, remember to supply a cool air intake (basement, crawl space) along with a solar chimney. There will be little benefit in using the stack effect only to pull in hot outside air.

To be effective, the solar chimney has to have a clear flow path, good solar absorption, and good insulation and heat storage. The solar chimney may be incorporated in the wall of a building, typically facing the equator, or placed on the roof or in a separate stack that reaches above the roof. It can be vertical or inclined. Modeling and tests suggest an optimum airflow-rate value was achieved when the chimney inclination was between 45° and 70° for a latitude of 28.4°. This is a typical solar collector orientation in relation to latitude for good performance. Time-of-day ventilation needs may suggest a westerly or southwesterly orientation for optimum gain in the afternoon on the hottest summer days.

Considerable research has been done on solar chimneys, but no clear consensus has developed on the best shape or characteristics for them. More empirical studies are needed to support extensive modeling and simulation. The width of the chimney, the depth of the channel, the thermal-mass type and distribution, and the inlet and exit configurations all can be adjusted to fit the particular goals of the building design or engineering considerations. The width has been found to be important (the wider the better), and the channel depth should probably be in the range of 10 to 20 inches, although some have been only 4 inches and some air collectors were only 1 inch. Taller chimneys are much more powerful, but even models as small as a 12-foot-tall simple wall chimney in Athens, Greece, were able to generate a temperature difference of 9°F and airflow of up to 82 cfm on a summer day.

Architectural Configurations and Concerns

An aerodynamically efficient reversible ceiling fan may be incorporated in a tower or roof monitor to increase airflow. In summer, the fan would help exhaust hot air; in the winter it could return hot air from the thermal chimney down to the floor at its lowest setting. These fans use very little energy yet provide very good ventilation and can be PV-powered.

Air-conditioning systems should also be designed to work with natural ventilation. A displacement design can be used to help drive stack ventilation. Displacement ventilation is essentially a buoyancy-driven "displacement" process where "fresh" cool ventilation air is introduced at low velocity and at low level into the occupied space. The supply air spreads out across the floor, forming a reservoir of cool fresh air. Any heat source in the room, such as a person at a desk, generates a positively buoyant thermal plume rising upward. This plume draws air from the reservoir of cool fresh air at low level in the room. Heat and pollutants are transported up. The incoming air and thermal plumes help drive the stack ventilation.

Replacement air could also be passed through a cooling chamber that is cooled by evaporation, a solar-absorption chiller (using solar heat to power the cooler instead of mechanical energy), or seasonal storage. In traditional designs in very hot areas, the makeup air would come from yards, courtyards, or streets shaded with arbors or shades. In some cases these designs contain multiple layers, and may include thermal-stack ventilation to cool the lower-shade levels so the people on the street below are more comfortable. Shades, such as the courtyard *toldo* of Spain, may also be designed to enhance convective cooling.

The best configuration for a building with very high summer temperatures and consistent sun might include two vertical solar chimneys, one on the east wall for morning ventilation and one on the west for afternoon ventilation. Solar chimney performance might also be enhanced with a solar air collector below the chimney to preheat air. A quick early pop in temperature might also be provided with an internal black mesh or screens often used in solar air collectors.

Selective surfaces on the absorber plates or mass can be helpful as higher temperatures are desired. Double-wall or high-performance glazing may also be of value. Phase-change materials are very promising as a solar chimney thermal mass, offering higher temperature storage and good energy return.

Performance will depend on solar exposure, air temperature, wind, and the design and operation of the chimney. Solar-chimney performance can be further enhanced if the makeup air is drawn into the building from a cooling cavity with thermal mass, chilled by night ventilation, evaporation, or solar adsorption refrigeration. Modeling performance in an 8-foot-tall chimney and a solar adsorption unit of 53 square feet, 1.8 inches thick, using methanol and activated carbon suggested the solar chimney was more important, but the two worked well together. Ventilation rates at night were higher than during the day.

COURTYARDS AND ATRIA

Courtyards and atria (a courtyard with glazing) can be very helpful in facilitating cross-ventilation and are used in many traditional designs. The courtyard makes it easier to provide windows or vents on both sides of rooms. It can also eliminate hallways, substituting covered walkways around the courtyard. Airflow across the courtyard may provide extract ventilation, pulling air through all the rooms around the courtyard. Atria should have large operable vents and may need to be shaded in the summer.

ACOUSTICS

Acoustical aspects are a big part of natural ventilation. Ideally there should be cross-ventilation without losing acoustical privacy of major rooms. There are many clever design devices for doing this, such as large individual ceiling plenums, use of secondary spaces, and so forth. Vent placement can be used to minimize sound transmission. Landscaping, berms, and walls can also be used to reduce traffic noise.

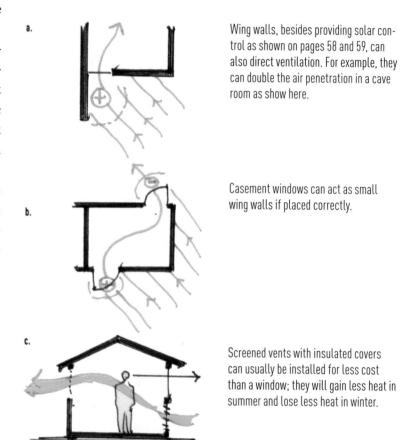

a. Wing walls, besides providing solar control as shown on pages 58 and 59, can also direct ventilation. For example, they can double the air penetration in a cave room as show here.

b. Casement windows can act as small wing walls if placed correctly.

c. Screened vents with insulated covers can usually be installed for less cost than a window; they will gain less heat in summer and lose less heat in winter.

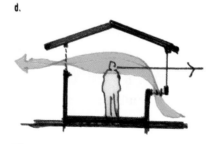

d. A sill vent like this one in a bay window allows ventilation while providing protection from driving rain and allowing an unscreened view. Sill vents can also limit noise.

Fig. 3.42a–d.

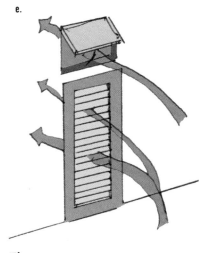

e.

Fig. 3.42e.

Interior walls and doors can impede or support ventilation depending on their placement and design. Louvered doors, vents, or transoms over doors can provide cross-ventilation while still maintaining privacy.

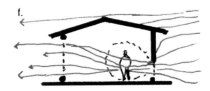

f.

Venturi effect. Providing a larger air exit than entrance will increase the airspeed in the room for ventilation cooling.

g.

Insect screening can reduce ventilation, as described on page 121. Therefore, large areas like screened porches can often be more effective than smaller screened windows for ventilation cooling.

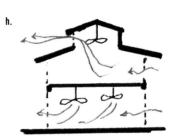

h.

Ceiling fans. Newer, more optimum ceiling fans such as the Windward II ($120) are quiet, reversible, and can be set to start at any temperature. They should be placed in every room in a hot humid climate. Ceiling fans can also be helpful outside on porches and patios (if weatherproofed).

Fig. 3.42f–h.

For smaller residential applications, stairwells can be extended to become a tower for stack ventilation (see fig. 3.45). Or a clerestory window can be placed in an open, full-height room (see fig. 3.42h).

The goal is to optimize the interaction of the many parts of a building—to get more and spend less.

Fig. 3.43. *Security can be maintained by installing stop locks and fixed or locked grilles, screens, and vents or by providing other security for open windows and vents. Grilles or louvered vents can be use to provide ventilation without a loss in privacy or security. The magnificent grilles in the Middle East, Spain, and Mexico are prime examples.*

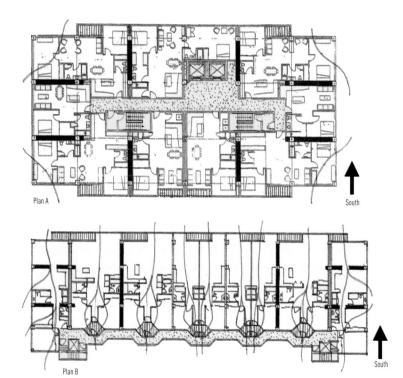

Fig. 3.44. *Plan A (top). Plan B (bottom). Statistics for related areas (below).*

Plan 'A'		Plan 'B'
10,145	< sq. ft. / floor area >	10,836
5-2 bedroom	< units / floor area >	5-2 bedroom
4-1 bedroom	< units / floor area >	4-1 bedroom
33%	< % units with solar access >	100%
44%	< % units with natural ventilation >	100%
78.50%	< % area in units >	81%
13.70%	< % area in circulation >	10%
4.70%	< % area in structure >	3%
3.10%	< % area in balcony >	6%
2 bays @ 20'		2 bays @ 20'
L 4 bays @ 25'	< structure >	4 bays @ 28' L
2 bays @ 20'		2 bays @ 12'
W 1 bay @ 25'		1 bay @ 20' W

A common impression is that providing solar access and natural ventilation is not applicable to buildings other than low-density custom homes. Fig. 3.44, Plan B illustrates that this is not true.

Plan A, Taylor Towers, is a fifteen-story apartment complex in San Jose, California. Several have been built. We suggested that it would be possible to provide solar access and natural ventilation equally for all units and still fit the site, building envelope, and budget. In San Jose's climate, this could save 100 percent of the cooling cost and 80 percent of the heating costs of the units. The developer was very skeptical of this, so he commissioned this design study.

The result is Plan B "Green Towers" and a comparison figure showing that limitations of passive applications are only limitations of thinking, not limitations of the passive approach.

Ventilation comfort is also affected by furniture choices. Wicker will be cooler than solid furniture.

Allergies might be created with the introduction of pollen, fungi spores, dust, or smog with ventilation. These can best be dealt with using large free-flowing filters. These need to be large, since they will reduce airflow. Allergies can also be minimized by careful landscaping choices using the Ogren Plant Allergy Scale (www.allergyfreegardening.com/opals.php).

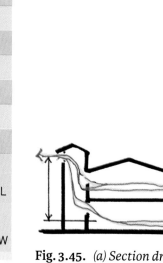

Fig. 3.45. *(a) Section drawing. (b) Stack effect with staircase.*

Where stack ventilation is important, increasing the height between incoming air and outgoing air increases its efficiency. Wonderful examples of doing this exist in historical architecture in the Middle East, especially Iran.

Fig. 3.46 *Wind catchers, called* badgirs, *are common in Yazd, Iran. These may draw cool makeup air from over reservoirs, fountains, or the underground stream channels called* qanats.

Fig. 3.47. *Modern use of ventilation cooling and traditional materials in Bali.*

Fig. 3.48. *BedZED (zero energy development), Beddington, London (2006), incorporates wind scoops for ventilation, translucent photovoltaics, gardens, rainwater harvesting, mixed-use occupancies of commercial and residential space, and an integrated wastewater treatment system.*

Example of Integrated Design for Passive Cooling

Many excellent examples of integrated design for passive cooling can be found in historic buildings. It is less common in modern buildings, but it can be done. It is often felt that assembly buildings are the most difficult to passively cool because of high internal loads and ventilation needs. To show how cooling such a space can be done, let's look at a passively conditioned assembly building that also integrates regional, environmental, and social considerations.

Planning Considerations

The 92-acre site for the synagogue at the edge of the city of San Luis Obispo is a beautiful locale with striking views of the entire sweep of volcanic peaks known as the Seven Sisters, stretching from San Luis Obispo to the coast. The proximity to the city and natural beauty were advantageous, but the site came with some challenging environmental considerations. It contains an ecologically important wetland, and the ocean winds that regularly blow down the valley are unusually cold. In addition, heavy traffic noise flows onto the site from the adjacent highway, accentuated by the wind direction. Thus the site is thermally uncomfortable and acoustically difficult almost all year. Bioregional planning was needed to respond to the challenging conditions. The construction area for the build-out of this 20,000-square-foot facility was minimized so that site disturbance involved only 9 of the 92 acres. Most of the remaining land was put into an open-space easement, protecting the extensive wetlands and visually adding to the city's developing greenbelt at one of its most publicly visible locations. In addition, a major component of the site-planning process was the development of a 10-foot-high earth berm in an arc from the southwest to the northwest of the building and parking area, creating a first layer of noise and wind protection as well as a planting area for native vegetation above the high water table. Public view of the building from the highway is greatly diminished by this berm, helping to protect the public viewshed.

Architectural Considerations

Assembly buildings can be a challenge to design for passive conditioning, but in this case this was accomplished without providing any centralized HVAC system. This saved $160,000, some of which was spent on passive solar components such as high-performance windows, light shelves, thermal mass, and automation of natural ventilation capability. Natural lighting is a critical part of any high-performance building. This synagogue is designed so that artificial lighting is not needed during daylight hours—the design utilizes daylight as an integral part of the whole passive solar strategy.

The final design concept that was chosen from four alternatives was given the nickname of "the onion bagel"—onion because both the site plan and floor plan of the building consist of a series of layers. The outer layers protect from the cold winds and the noise that dominate the site—the layers represent a sequential ordering from the busy outer world to a quieter, inner spiritual world. A "bagel" came to represent the final scheme because of the hole in the middle of the building, the courtyard.

Actually, upon phase-two construction, there will be two courtyards. The main one will allow south light into the social hall and aid in natural ventilation. A smaller one will serve the expanded school area—a kind of fractal self-similar-scale progression of older to newer, bigger to smaller, wisdom to regeneration, and so forth.

Thermal Analysis

The sanctuary area for the synagogue utilizes solar gains to replace heating by conventional means. South-facing glazing is used in the occupied space and in the overhead lantern area. The two spaces are separated by acoustical panels, or "clouds," that were included for acoustical, lighting, aesthetic, as well as thermal purposes. Initial thermal modeling of the space assumed solar heat gain from the lantern area could be effectively distributed to the lower occupied space when needed, and therefore the two areas were treated as a single zone. In order to ensure that thermal comfort was possible, a three-dimensional CFD model was used to test various designs for distributing the solar gains from the lantern in January. The final configuration uses a high-efficiency but inexpensive ceiling fan mounted just above the Bema (pulpit) to provide the destratification required. This fan can also be reversed to help with ventilation when necessary.

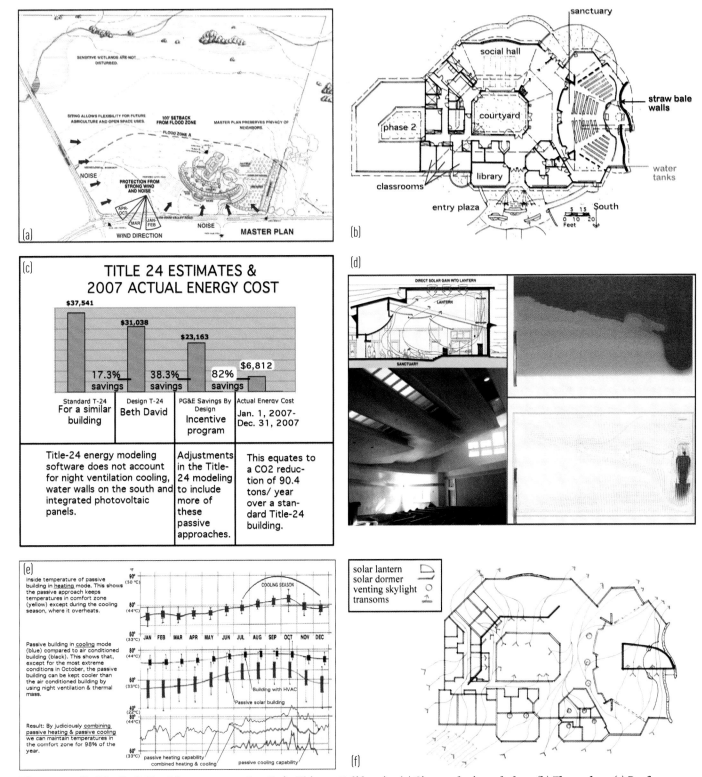

Fig. 3.49a–f. *The Beth David synagogue, San Luis Obispo, California. (a) Site analysis and plan. (b) Floor plan. (c) Performance chart. (d) Ventilation cross-section and computational fluid-dynamics model. (e) Chart of passive strategies and modeling. (f) Ventilation plan.*

(g)　　　　　　　　　　　　　　　　　　　　　　　　　(h)

Fig. 3.49g,h. *(g) South facade. (h) March of the Torah and congregation to their new home.*

Social Response

Paul Wolff, a member of the design committee, made the following comments regarding the social dimension of the building.

> *This facility has dramatically influenced our congregants and community in unexpected ways. The building provides an outstanding illustration of a major concept of environmental psychology—that architecture directly influences human behavior. Green architecture can have a very positive effect on the behavior of its users. Inspired by our new building, Congregation Beth David initiated the Green Shalom program, intended to bring into the daily behavior of our congregants the same principles that governed the building's sustainable design.*

> *We introduced monthly programs to promote activities, education and life styles that will increase awareness (with subsequent actions) of the need to protect our environment and conserve energy.*

> *These programs have included seminars on fair trade coffees, teas, chocolates, etc., recycling, green gardening, shopping with a conscience (anti sweatshops), green cleaning supplies, socially responsible investing, and compact fluorescent light bulbs. Through the local ministerial association, we have now widened the Green Shalom program to reach out to our whole community. Our relatively small congregation has long sought to make a more significant contribution to the local social fabric; the functionality, sustainability, and aesthetics of this building has allowed us to do just that in positive and unforeseen ways.*

Backup Cooling

The key to backup cooling is to acknowledge that we can provide the majority of the cooling needs by passive systems so that mechanical cooling is eliminated or reduced to a much more economical and manageable backup system. It is important to avoid the redundancy of having two complete cooling systems just because the passive system may need an occasional boost. This is even true in the hot humid climates considered so difficult by today's mechanical cooling mind-set (see page 97).

Once the majority of the cooling load is handled by passive design, several traditional cooling-augmentation approaches can be considered. Recent technological improvements in three of these allow them to fulfill this function efficiently and economically.

Ceiling Fans

Backup cooling can be provided by the traditional ceiling fan, which has been vastly improved by Paul McCready's group of aeronautical engineers (figure 3.50). If powered by photovoltaics, this mechanical device essentially becomes part of the building's passive system.

Fig. 3.50. *Aerodynamic design improved efficiency dramatically.*

Whole-House Fans

There has been recent improvement in large fans that can upgrade the traditional whole-building night-ventilation capability.

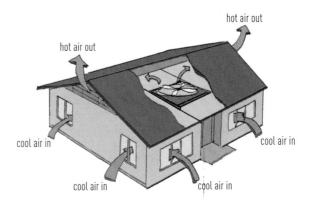

Whole-house fans can augment night ventilation cooling.

Fig. 3.51. *Whole-house fans enhance night ventilation cooling.*

Evaporative Cooling

Another old standby has been improved and is capable of providing cooling backup to passive systems (see page 115).

Radiant Cooling

Eventually radiant cooling systems may become well developed and commercialized for both new buildings and retrofits.

Ventilation for Health

In the 1970s, rising energy prices and demand for conservation led to a disastrous forty-year emphasis on sealed buildings with mechanical ventilation and air-conditioning. The code development process and regulations illustrate the problem of narrow focus and dominance by special-interest groups. The most active participants in the process were quite naturally those with a vested interest in selling mechanical equipment—and they succeeded. Sadly, the occupants and environment lost. Occupants suffered sick building syndrome from moldy and chemically contaminated air, with costs estimated at $58 billion a year in health-related expenditures and as much as $200 billion in lost productivity (Fisk, 2000). The focus on mechanical systems also helped increase building impact on global warming gas production to 40 percent of the US total. Many of these buildings will be hard to retrofit, but others will be easy to upgrade. In addition, many once naturally ventilated and cooled historic buildings were sealed up, and thereby ruined, in order to meet "modern" codes.

As a result, there is now a great deal of emphasis in green buildings on indoor air quality. Avoiding unhealthy materials, finishes, cleaning products, and behavior (like smoking indoors) is a first step. Careful fresh-air-supply management and venting of combustion appliances, including woodstoves, is also important. Material choices and detailing to avoid mold and rot are also important, and moisture from kitchens and bathrooms must be well managed. When groups of people are involved, the management of CO_2 and moisture is also critical. Finally, the ventilation system should be understandable and transparent to the user so that deferred maintenance or mechanical failure does not diminish effectiveness.

Fig. 3.52. *Radiant cooling study, Cortez, Colorado. We need to encourage more research on passive cooling techniques.*

Summary: Passive Cooling

Many passive systems are equally capable of providing heating, cooling, and ventilation as an integral part of architectural design. Too often, passive cooling is neglected or treated as the lesser twin of passive heating. In many parts of the United States and the world, however, more energy is used for cooling than heating. Passive cooling can improve comfort and save money.

We must also overcome the neglect of ventilation that remains an unfortunate legacy of the "energy conservation" approach of the 1970s. Sealed buildings should be opened, and windows should operate.

Knowledge of passive cooling principles and improved modeling techniques, including the availability of computational fluid dynamics for airflow performance predictions, can allow a majority of cooling and ventilation to be provided by passive systems in any climate.

FOUR NATURAL LIGHTING

COAUTHOR: RACHEL ALJILANI

Natural lighting provides a space with a sense of interest, warmth, and excitement besides saving energy and creating healthier interiors.

We were born of light. The seasons are felt through light. We only know the world as it is evoked by light. . . . To me natural light is the only light, because it has mood—it provides a ground of common agreement for man—it puts us in touch with the eternal. Natural light is the only light that makes architecture architecture.

—LOUIS I. KAHN

Natural lighting uses sunlight and diffuse radiation from the sky to provide light inside buildings. It should be considered essential for every new building. Natural light adds delight to our lives by providing movement, change, and connection to the outdoor environment. Global greenhouse gas emissions and the environmental impacts of mining, power production, and power distribution can be greatly reduced by integrating natural light; and unlike artificial light, natural light works when the power grid goes down.

Interest in natural light has increased in the last few years as the many benefits of natural light have become clearer. Studies have proven natural light can improve moods, spirit, performance, and health. Students in schools with natural light perform better, with marked improvements in both English and mathematics. Natural light in work settings tends to increase the productivity of workers and reduce absenteeism. Lockheed found productivity at one facility increased 15 percent when they moved from a conventional building into a naturally lit building, and days off work dropped by 15 percent. The Herman Miller Company found even higher productivity gains in its daylit furniture factory. In larger facilities, human resources are often 90 to 95 percent of the company's operating budget (far exceeding the initial cost of the building and energy costs of operation), so small investments in natural light up front will yield considerable savings over the long run. Surveys consistently show that people prefer natural light and desire a connection to it. In most cases, they want a view to the outside rather than a luminous panel. User control, flexibility, and adjustable controls are also preferred.

Visible Light

Measured in wavelengths, the typical human eye perceives a portion of the electromagnetic spectrum from violet to red light from about 380 to 750 nanometers. Different creatures can see variations of this range; for instance, ultraviolet light can be sensed by most

insects and some birds, while some snakes can see the infrared heat given off by warm-blooded bodies. For the most part, natural lighting is concerned with the visible spectrum—although studies have recently identified the number one cause of bird fatalities to be buildings due to the specular reflection from glass window and wall systems (see figure 4.1). These reflections, rather than the usual suspects—cats, vehicles, or pesticides—can be minimized with good design. Since birds can see the ultraviolet end of the spectrum, glass can also be coated with a UV pattern to allow them to see the glass while it remains transparent to humans.

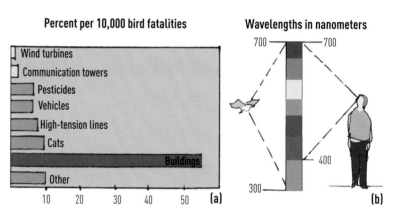

Fig. 4.1. *Since humans and birds can see different parts of the electromagnetic spectrum, glass can be coated with UV patterns to reduce bird fatalities from buildings. This chart shows annual bird fatalities by source as a percentage. Annual US bird fatalities are one hundred million and worldwide one billion from buildings. (a) Percent bird fatalities by cause. (b) Wavelengths in nanometers.*

Healthy Light

Natural light is necessary for humans. Physiologically, natural light sends a signal to the pineal gland to stop producing melatonin, which the body releases at night to help the body rest. In higher latitudes, short winter days are known to cause seasonal affective disorder (SAD), a depression characterized by lethargy. SAD can be treated with early-morning exposure to light levels of 2,000 to 12,000 lux, depending on the severity of symptoms. Buildings with poor natural light can cause SAD even in the summer, and lethargy is the number one symptom in the majority of sick building syndrome cases.

While exposure to excessive amounts of direct sunlight is not advised, there is a human need to absorb ultraviolet light for the body to produce vitamin D. Bone disease due to vitamin D deficiency has been linked to the lack of exposure to natural light. UVA (380 to 320 nm) and UVB (320 to 280 nm) are known to cause certain types of skin cancer, but this end of the spectrum is not often transmitted through glazed apertures. Most ultraviolet radiation is scattered by the ozone, so a minimal amount reaches the earth's surface. Changes in the atmosphere are likely to affect UV exposure levels, as has been the case in areas of Scandinavia where ozone depletion has begun to occur. In Canada, students under full-spectrum light attended school an average of three days more per year and had nine times less dental decay than students in rooms with average lighting conditions. The rapid rise in myopia over the past fifty years may also be driven by the increased dependence on artificial lighting systems.

Sources of Natural Light

The ultimate source of all natural light is the sun, yet only part of the light used for natural lighting is received as direct sunlight. The rest arrives as indirect or diffuse radiation reflected off dust or water particles in the atmosphere or reflected radiation bounced off other structures or features of the landscape. The proportion of each varies as a function of both building orientation and design, variation in ground surface, cloudiness and type of clouds, atmospheric clarity, and the sun's daily and seasonal path and position. The main factors influencing natural light available for use are microclimate and solar altitude (refer to pages 23–26 for a brief overview of how these affect a specific site). The same tools described on page 54 for solar geometry can be used to determine shading and solar obstructions. North and south light also vary (see figure 4.2), with diffuse and direct sunlight being influenced by the sky exposure angle (see figure 4.3).

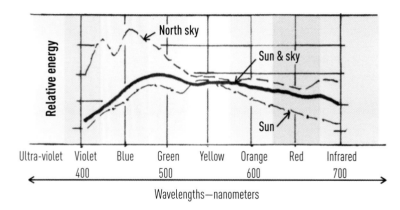

Fig. 4.2. *This spectral-energy-distribution diagram illustrates the color difference between light available for daylighting under different sky conditions.*

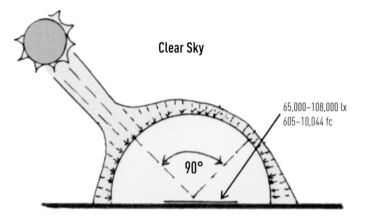

Fig. 4.3. *The brightness distribution is typically about ten times greater near the sun than at the darkest part of the sky, which is 90° in the other direction.*

Surprisingly, even at 46°N latitude, the average illumination level under overcast skies is 7,500 lux, fifteen times as much is needed for average indoor tasks. In the 1950s, electrical engineers increased the use of electric lighting in buildings dramatically to enhance visual performance and increase sales of light fixtures. Figure 4.4 illustrates the limits of only increasing the intensity level of light. *The abundance of natural light is not an availability problem, but a challenge of planning and geometric manipulation to capture the resource and use it effectively.* Once the resources are understood, it is possible to naturally light almost any application, from single-family homes to high-rises and industrial plants.

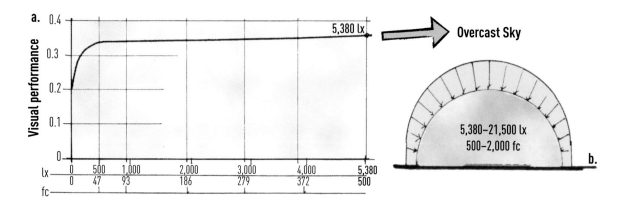

Fig. 4.4. *(a) Increased illuminance beyond 500 lux or 47 foot-candles yields minimal increases in visual performance. (b) The brightness distribution is typically about three times greater at the zenith than the horizon for an overcast sky.*

UNITS USED IN NATURAL LIGHTING

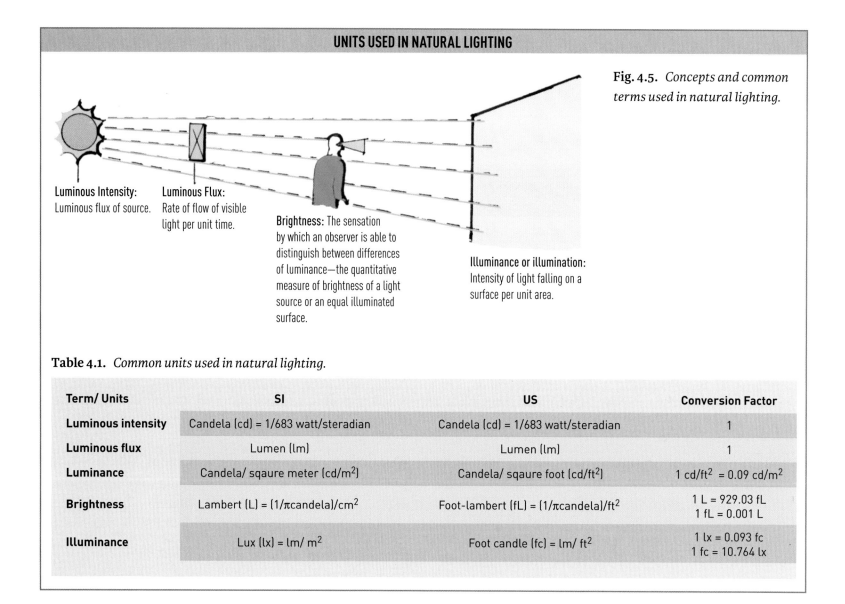

Fig. 4.5. *Concepts and common terms used in natural lighting.*

Luminous Intensity: Luminous flux of source.

Luminous Flux: Rate of flow of visible light per unit time.

Brightness: The sensation by which an observer is able to distinguish between differences of luminance—the quantitative measure of brightness of a light source or an equal illuminated surface.

Illuminance or illumination: Intensity of light falling on a surface per unit area.

Table 4.1. *Common units used in natural lighting.*

Term/ Units	SI	US	Conversion Factor
Luminous intensity	Candela (cd) = 1/683 watt/steradian	Candela (cd) = 1/683 watt/steradian	1
Luminous flux	Lumen (lm)	Lumen (lm)	1
Luminance	Candela/ sqaure meter (cd/m^2)	Candela/ sqaure foot (cd/ft^2)	1 cd/ft^2 = 0.09 cd/m^2
Brightness	Lambert (L) = (1/πcandela)/cm^2	Foot-lambert (fL) = (1/πcandela)/ft^2	1 L = 929.03 fL 1 fL = 0.001 L
Illuminance	Lux (lx) = lm/ m^2	Foot candle (fc) = lm/ ft^2	1 lx = 0.093 fc 1 fc = 10.764 lx

Terms Used in Natural Lighting

Many concepts are involved in lighting, as shown in figure 4.5 and table 4.1. The first is **luminous intensity,** a measurement of light in a certain direction, measured as candela. Luminous intensity is analogous to pressure in a hydraulic system and voltage in an electric system and represents the force that generates the light that we see. Since luminous intensity is characteristic of a light source, it is not affected by a viewer's perception.

Luminous flux is the rate of flow of visible light per unit time and is measured in lumen (lm). Analogous to flow in a hydraulic system and current in an electric system, luminous flux is a measure of photometric power. Unlike luminous intensity, the sensitivity of a viewer's eye will cause variation in perceived luminous flux.

Brightness is a factor of the level of illumination and the reflectance of the surface we are viewing. A white surface may have a reflectance of 90 percent, while a dark black surface may reflect less than 10 percent. Brightness is known as the sensation by which an observer distinguishes differences in **luminance** or the quantity of light emitted or reflected in a given direction measured in candela/m² or candela/ft².

Lighting is described in terms of **illuminance,** the density of luminous flux incident on a surface, measured in lux (lumens/m²) or foot-candles (lumens/ft²). Illuminance or illumination is the amount of light spread over a surface or the light output falling on a working area.

Color

Lighting **color** also matters. Most people prefer natural light color with diffuse skylight perceived as white, while direct-beam sunlight may seem warmer or redder. Lightbulbs also output light in different colors. The quality of the light color can affect the ability to see and understand colors. When objects are white, black, or any shade of gray, the objects are technically colorless. When objects appear colored, they are selectively absorbing pigmentation and reflecting or transmitting to the eye only the objects' hue. **Hue** can be defined as the attribute by which we describe colors such as red, blue, or green. When white is added to a color hue, it is a **tint;** adding black creates a **shade**.

Reaction to color will vary as much as temperament from one person to the next, so color must be used carefully. Typically, white sources of illumination are used unless a particular mood or atmosphere is desired. The eyes have an amazing ability to adapt to low levels of illumination and still be able to decipher color, even though shaded. On the other hand, high levels of illumination tend to wash out or tint colors, giving them a less saturated appearance.

Warm and cool colors also have a perceived temperature and can actually be used to perceptually heat and cool spaces. A cold climate would benefit from warm-colored surfaces, whereas a warm climate should use cool-colored surfaces to take advantage of this sensitivity. Cool colors are also known to be calming and can change the perception of time; dull, repetitive tasks may be more tolerable in a cool environment. Warm colors make people more alert and have been considered more appetizing than cool colors.

Color choice can be influenced by cultural meaning. For instance, white is appropriate for a funeral in China, while black is considered appropriate attire for a funeral in the United States, and a bride in India is likely to wear red rather than white, as is common the United States. Color choice depends on the activities, microclimate, and people's personal or cultural preference.

The color temperature scale shown in figure 4.6 was derived by heating a black body, called a light-absorbing body. When a black body is heated, the first color it turns is dark red, then cherry, then orange, and so on, until it glows bluish white. Using a black-body temperature scale, we can assign color

Fig. 4.6. *Color temperature in Kelvin of common light sources.*

temperatures in Kelvin, or K. Color temperature only applies to heated objects, so illumination sources such as fluorescent lamps are assigned a correlated color temperature (CCT). The quality of light can be measured and described with the color-rendering index (CRI), which is a two-part concept based on color temperature and a number that indicates how closely the illuminant approaches the standard (daylight at the same color temperature). Table 4.2 describes the various color characteristics of common illuminants.

Glare

Glare is a subjective response to excessive brightness and can be described as visual noise usually attributed to a contrast problem. Direct glare is caused by light sources that are bright enough to cause discomfort or loss in visual performance. There are both **disability glare,** which impedes performance, and **discomfort glare,** which produces physical discomfort. Bright windows or a bright light behind a computer user can create disabling glare on a computer screen.

Table 4.2. *CRI, CCT, and color effect of light sources.*

Lamp FLUORESCENT	CRI (approx.)	CCT (K)	Whiteness	Colors Enhanced	Grayed	Notes:
Warm white	52	3050	yellowish	orange, yellow	red, green, blue	
Cool white	62	4200	white	orange, yellow, blue	red	
Cool white delux	77	4050	white	orange, yellow, green	red	
Triphosphor	75	2800	yellowish	red, orange	deep red and blue	
	80	3000	pale yellowish	red, orange, green	deep red	
MERCURY						
Clear	20	7000	blue-green	green, blue	red, orange	Poor overall color rendereing
Deluxe	45	3700	pale-purplish	deep red & blue	green, blue	Shift over life to greenish
METAL-HALIDE						
Clear	65	4000	white	yellow, green, blue	red	May shift to pinkish over life
Phosphorcoated	80	4200	white	yellow, green, blue	none	Shifts to pinkish over life
HIGH PRESSURE SODIUM						
Standard	21	2100	yellowish	yellow, green	red, blue	
Color-corrected	60	2200	yellowish-white	red, yellow, green	blue	CRI decreases slightly w/ life
INCANDESCENT						
	99+	2900	yellowish	red, orange, yellow	green, blue	
LEDs (Light-emitting diode)	70	2500-6500	yellow-blue	varies	varies	CCT varies with viewing angle

Direct glare is also dependent on the proximity from the offending light source to the user's center of vision. For this reason, there has been considerable research and development of indirect lighting fixtures. Figure 4.7 illustrates direct glare caused by a window. Think of talking with someone when the sun is behind them; though you would like to be able to focus on the person, all you see is a dark silhouette.

Indirect glare is caused by reflections on glossy surfaces (figure 4.8). Specular reflections in particular appear as though someone has put a veil of light over the area you are focused on, and it is simply a mirror-like reflection of the light source. Matte and flat finishes can be used to reduce indirect glare, which diminishes the effectiveness of product displays, signs, and advertising. Placement of computers, registers, projector screens, and other equipment and fixtures should be designed to minimize glare, and then strategies to control glare should be utilized.

Peripheral glare is the most subtle and often overlooked type of glare that occurs from the physiological response of the human eye to various light levels (figure 4.9). The amount of opening of the iris is determined by peripheral light, not the object you are focusing on. A bright spot at the very edge of your vision can give you the wrong iris setting for the specific task at hand. This is why the ubiquitous "can" lights are generally problematic. This type of glare is a major cause of eyestrain and can trigger falling asleep at lectures and meetings in response to the excess stress on the eyes.

Control of Glare

Since glare is a contrast problem, it is usually reduced by introducing light from multiple directions, thereby reducing the contrast. Direct sunlight is constantly changing, and owing to its high intensity is difficult to use without being diffused.

Washing a surface with light is a great way to diffuse light. This can be done in the case of wall washing where a tall, thin strip of windows is used near a room corner, thus washing the adjacent wall with light. Several of the shading devices discussed in chapter 3 on pages 90–91 can be used to control glare, including louvered shades, shutters, light shelves, roller blinds, curtains, and many other options, by diffusing direct sunlight. The ceiling can also be washed with light.

Fig. 4.7. *Direct glare.*

Fig. 4.8. *Indirect glare.*

Fig. 4.9. *Peripheral glare.*

Fig. 4.10. *Light aperture with rounded splay.*

Elements of Natural Lighting

Apertures

Any opening in the building's envelope is considered an aperture. Some apertures are primarily for circulation, like doors, while windows and skylights are often associated with light and ventilation. The surrounding surfaces of an aperture affect the distribution of natural light in a space. The rounded window splay shown in figure 4.10 helps to reduce the contrast of light and dark areas near the aperture by creating larger areas of intermediate light. Angled apertures are more efficient at increasing the intermediate light areas because the entire angled surface is illuminated by light entering the aperture. They also can increase the acceptance angle.

Reflectance from roofing materials may be used to increase light gain through roof monitors and clerestory windows. Black roofs may reflect 6 percent or less, while white roofs may reflect 70 percent or more. The push toward white, cool roofs to reduce air-conditioning loads in summer is also helping to improve the capability for natural light. Outside ground conditions may also affect lighting. A field of bright fresh snow or a water body to the south may increase light gain dramatically, and the changing leaf patterns or plant canopies over the year may limit daylight and alter light quality.

Glazing

Natural light usually enters a space through a glazed aperture that may have several functions. An understanding of glazing properties is needed to be able to choose the appropriate glazing product. Both the **U-value** and **solar heat gain coefficient (SHGC)** are discussed on page 49. The **visible transmittance (T_{vis})** is of great concern when considering natural light. T_{vis} is a measure of the relative amount of sunlight passing through a glazing assembly, usually ranging from 0.3 to 0.8, with higher numbers representing larger values of light transmittance. Table 4.3 describes attributes of some common glazing assemblies. Choosing the proper glazing for natural light and passive heating and cooling is critical for integrated design. A one-size-fits-all glazing selection typically yields a trade-off between cooling and heating and is unlikely to perform optimally throughout the year.

Natural Lighting Goals

The basic goal of lighting design is to provide a comfortable, healthful, pleasant, productive, and safe visual environment for people. This is not as simple as it might seem because the human eye and brain are complex and adaptable, and personal preferences, visual capability, and task requirements vary widely. The typical human eye can see from around 0.0001 to 10,000 foot-candles, with sensitivity declining with age. Vision can also be affected by corrective lenses, allergies, disease, and injury. But our vision is very flexible, and we can adapt to a broad range of lighting intensities and frequencies. Research has repeatedly shown that low light levels will not cause eye damage, despite what our parents said, but may lead to tired eyes or errors in reading. Although we can adapt to almost

Table 4.3. *Properties of common glazing assemblies.*

Glazing assembly	U-value		SHGC	T_{vis}
	W/m²C	BTU/ft²F		
Single-glazed clear (alum. frame)	7.37	1.3	0.79	0.69
Double-glazed clear (alum. frame)	3.63	0.64	0.65	0.62
Double-glazed clear (wood or vinyl frame)	2.78	0.49	0.58	0.57
Double-glazed bronze (alum. frame)	3.63	0.64	0.55	0.47
Double-glazed bronze (wood or vinyl frame)	2.78	0.49	0.48	0.43
Double-glazed Low-E (low-emissivity 0.20, wood or vinyl frame)	1.87	0.33	0.55	0.52
Triple-glazed Low-E 0.08 w/ argon (wood or vinyl frame)	1.7	0.3	0.44	0.56
Double-glazed spectrally selective Low-E 0.04 w/ argon (wood or vinyl frame)	1.65	0.29	0.31	0.51
Double-glazed spectrally selective Low-E 0.01 w/ argon (wood or vinyl frame)	1.76	0.31	0.26	0.31
Triple-glazed Low-E 0.08 w/ krypton (insulated vinyl frame)	0.85	0.15	0.37	0.48
Triple-glazed clear w/ air (wood or vinyl frame)	1.93	0.34	0.52	0.53

anything, it is good to design with the following criteria in mind, knowing that trade-offs and priorities will help determine the final natural lighting solution. These criteria include:

- Visual comfort.

- Healthful levels and frequencies of light.

- Light for efficient task completion and productivity.

- Minimal glare.

- Varied light levels and patterns—connection to outdoors.

- Maximum use of daylighting.

- Integration with other building-systems goals: passive heating, cooling, and ventilation.

- Minimal life-cycle energy use and cost.

- Low initial cost.

- Reduced operating cost and environmental impact.

- Maximum flexibility and user control.

- Maximum desired heat gain in winter.

- Minimal undesired heat gain in summer.

- Minimal use of nonrenewable energy sources.

- Well-developed educational materials and guides for use.

- Automatic control of switching to adjust to varying natural light levels.

A naturally lit office space can operate without artificial light, as seen in figure 4.11. Utilizing many of the techniques described in the following pages, this office incorporates an equator-facing dormer placed over the ridge, light-colored surfaces to help reflect and distribute light, and light shelves on the interior and exterior to extend the reach of natural light into the building; in addition, operable, insulating, translucent blinds are available to reduce unwanted glare if necessary.

Fig. 4.11. *Naturally lit office space.*

Approaches to Natural Lighting

Natural light was an integral consideration in building design and influenced building orientation and fenestration until the 1950s, when a long decline began. Using natural light is not difficult, yet it has been widely ignored in the United States because of subsidized prices for electricity and the ease of specifying all-artificial lighting and nonrenewable fuel–based HVAC systems. Daylighting books, articles, and tools have often neglected the connections to heating, cooling, and ventilation.

History is full of wonderful architectural achievements where natural lighting was a major consideration. It had to be because artificial lighting was too primitive, expensive, and difficult to have much effect. Some examples are shown in figure 4.12.

400

Fig. 4.12a. *The upper clerestory with lower lit side aisles of the Roman basilica was adopted by the early Christian churches.*

538

Fig. 4.12b. *Large domes, vaults, and sumptuous surfaces with integrated lighting apertures characterize Hagia Sophia in Istanbul.*

1300

Fig. 4.12c. *Stained glass and stone curtain walls of Gothic architecture evolved as a way of maximizing natural lighting for low light conditions.*

1400

1600

Fig. 4.12d, e. *The integration of lighting apertures, structure, and modular vaulting allow exquisite light and scale at the Alhambra in Granada, Spain and the chapel in Palermo, Italy.*

Fig. 4.12f. *Movable translucent walls, grilles, and screens allowed classic Japanese architecture to have wonderful natural light as well as visual privacy.*

1650

1885

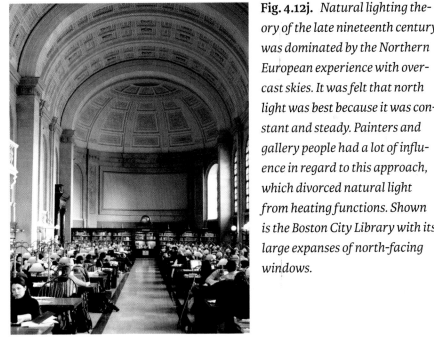

Fig. 4.12j. *Natural lighting theory of the late nineteenth century was dominated by the Northern European experience with overcast skies. It was felt that north light was best because it was constant and steady. Painters and gallery people had a lot of influence in regard to this approach, which divorced natural light from heating functions. Shown is the Boston City Library with its large expanses of north-facing windows.*

Fig. 4.12g, h. *Natural lighting in Isfahan, Iran, with modular lighting vaults covering the central bazaar. Tiled domes provide a cool but pleasantly lit space.*

Fig. 4.12i. *The Baroque architecture of seventeenth-century Southern Europe used carefully designed natural light to create highly dramatic spaces. This example is in Salzburg, Austria, where much of the Baroque architecture has been preserved.*

We're just now emerging from a period when natural lighting became a lost art, and artificial lighting became the norm. This inversion resulted in some really strange and perverse situations if we look at them objectively. Artificial lights burned night and day, indoors and out, whether needed or not and never questioned by anyone. Turning on electric lights became an automatic part of entering a space, regardless of any actual need. The use of a once useful tool, electric lights, became an unhealthy, uneconomical, unecological, and unconscious ritual act. How we got to this unfortunate state has a history as well, which is shown here.

1845

1920

Fig. 4.13a. *Natural lighting for large covered spaces was achieved by embracing construction techniques developed for use in large greenhouses. The train station in east Paris marks the change from architecture sensitive to natural light to architecture dependent on artificial light, as oil lamps, and then kerosene, gas, and then electric lights became more available.*

Fig. 4.13b. *The all-glass high-rise was proposed by Mies van der Rohe as a utopian concept. The simplicity and single-function implication of this concept became dogma in the 1950s.*

1950

managerial class   working class   managerial class

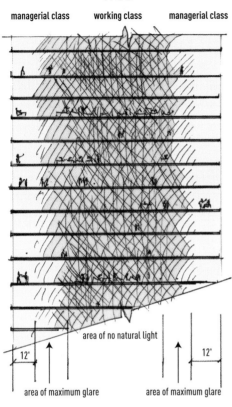

area of no natural light

12'   12'

area of maximum glare   area of maximum glare

Fig. 4.13c. *Section of a typical 1950s corporate tower showing social hierarchy of poor natural lighting.*

1950–2000

Fig. 4.13d. *The all-glass curtain-wall building created a city of all-glass cubes (New York City) that paid little attention to natural lighting and often had significant glare and overheating problems. Whether built with clear, tinted, dark, or reflective glass, this modernist approach turned out to be a simplistic formula that really only provided rentable square footage made possible by cheap fossil fuel. Ironically, although the original idea was natural light and view, the reality as shown in the section drawings (4.13c) was much different.*

1985

Summer

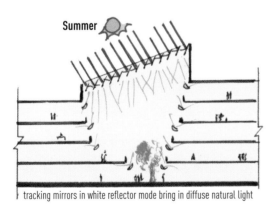

tracking mirrors in white reflector mode bring in diffuse natural light

Winter

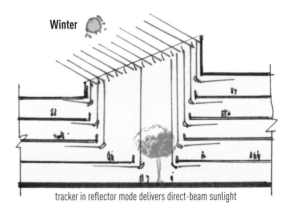

tracker in reflector mode delivers direct-beam sunlight

Fig. 4.13e, f. *The beginning of the return of natural lighting as an architectural consideration occurred in the work of William Lamm, Benjamin Evans, Mike Nicklas, and others. Techniques for extending natural lighting applications started to develop as energy prices started to rise after the oil crisis of 1979. South light was found to be superior to north light if it was related to passive heating and cooling needs. As interest grew, increased computer speed began to make prediction models better and more useful. Studies by William Lamm for the TVA building in Chattanooga, Tennessee.*

Since one of these fundamental needs is for access to daylight and to the sun, the architect, when considering the general form and character of building will have to bear in mind this requirement for daylight . . .

—R. G. HOPKINSON

Planning for Natural Light

Natural light most commonly enters a building through its envelope in the form of top-light and side-light. Since light can only penetrate a building so far, thin buildings and ones that integrate central spaces have been used to allow for natural light and ventilation. Figure 4.14 illustrates the relative daylight potential for buildings with thick versus thin footprints. Top-lighting can easily provide light to landlocked interiors on the top floors, and multistory buildings can use variations of central spaces and translucent floors to enhance natural lighting, as illustrated in figures 4.15 and 4.16.

There are two generic approaches to natural light: top-light at various scales (lithium, light well, and light tubes) and side-light.

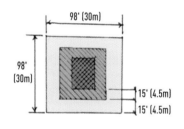

If we use the standard window arrangement for side-lighting on a 32,292-square-foot (3,000 m²) square building, available daylight is limited by its reach.

In this example:

51 percent of the area is in full daylight.

33 percent of the area is in partial daylight.

16 percent of the area has no daylight.

In this case, only half gets good light and only half of that light that has good orientation. This loss of daylighting is even worse for larger buildings.

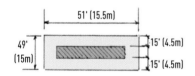

Longer, thinner buildings are better, especially if they run along an east–west axis.

In this example:

59 percent of the area is in full daylight.

41 percent of the area is in partial daylight.

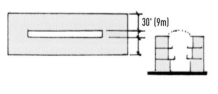

Further improvement could be made by adding a hall/light gallery down the center of the building.

In this example:

100 percent of the area can be daylit.

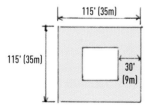

Adding a central open space to the square building would also give 100 percent full daylight. For this reason, we often see atria in large buildings.

Fig. 4.14.

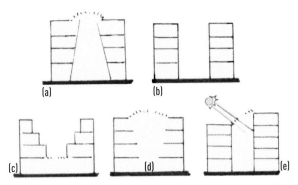

Fig. 4.15. *Variations of central spaces for natural lighting. An atrium shaped to optimize natural light is often referred to as a litrium. (a) Enclosed glazed atrium. (b) Courtyard. (c) Light court. (d) Atrium facing the sky. (e) Atrium facing the equator.*

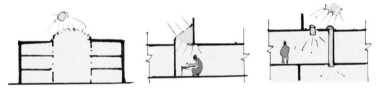

Fig. 4.16. *Various scales for top-lighting strategies.*

Top-Lighting

Top-lighting strategies vary depending on the scale of the space and structural systems. We will briefly discuss top-lighting systems and the best ways to control these systems for optimum lighting results.

Clerestory Windows

Windows on an upper part of a wall that light a central space are called clerestory windows. These can be integrated in most building designs

to provide light to the center or north side of a building. Clerestory windows can be relatively small for a single-story home with a loft, or substantial on a commercial building. They work best for one- or two-story buildings with relatively open floor plans. The clerestory placed in the middle of a typical pitched roof will make it possible for sunlight to reach directly into north rooms. It may be used to bring light into a hallway or open space, which provides indirect daylight to north rooms and the north side of deeper south-facing rooms.

A clerestory might typically be placed at two and a half to three times room height from the south wall. So for a 10-foot ceiling, the clerestory would be placed 25 to 30 feet in. South-facing windows with light shelves can provide excellent illumination up to that point. The clerestory window height might be at 12 to 15 feet for a simple one-story building, and can provide light up to 30 feet to the north. The increasing height difference between entry windows near floor level and the high clerestory window can also improve stack ventilation.

Roof Monitors and Washing Walls with Light

Roof monitors, dormers, and other bump-ups can be added to most roof patterns to provide benefits comparable to clerestory windows. A monitor with south-facing windows is often the best choice. Roof monitors can provide good quality light with minimal glare. They also allow warm air to rise further, and with operable windows or a reversible ceiling fan they can be very helpful for ventilation, heating, and cooling. A roof monitor over a corridor, stairwell, hallway, or central room can provide excellent ventilation flow paths as well as daylighting. Glare can be controlled with vertical baffles, curtains, or other diffusers. In dusty environments, provision should be made for dusting or cleaning these surfaces.

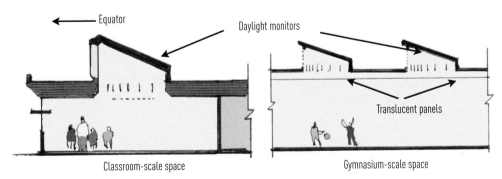

Fig. 4.17. *Roof monitors applied to spaces of various scales designed by Mike Nicklas of Innovative Design Architects.*

Table 4.4. *Aperture area expressed as a percent of floor area needed for natural light. Study by Mike Nicklas.*

Aperture area expressed as a percent of floor area needed for natural lighting	Small to mid-size space	Large volume Spaces
Equator-facing roof monitor	8-11%	5-8%
Equator-facing light shelf	8-11%	
Equator-facing light shelf w/ blinds between glazing	10-18%	
Opposite of equator-facing roof monitor	12-15%	7-10%
High, opposite of equator-facing transom glazing	15-20%	

Fig. 4.18. *Sawtooth apertures fashion the roof and tall vertical walls of the Tribune building in San Luis Obispo, California.*

For low-rise buildings or in conjunction with atria, top-lighting has many advantages. Table 4.4 expresses the amount of equator-facing aperture needed as a percent of floor area for various lighting strategies. The advantages of the orientation and configuration shown in figure 4.17 include:

- Greater natural light that is easily controlled.
- Cooling-load reduction (daylighting can produce lumens with half the heat of fluorescent fixtures).
- Maintenance cost of electric lighting is reduced.
- Solar gain for heating season.
- As effective as other strategies with less glazing.

One of the most effective approaches is the use of monitors facing the equator combined with side-lighting. Courtyards, light wells, and atria can move light to lower floors.

Sawtooth Roofs

Industrial buildings once commonly used sawtooth roofs to bring in light before air-conditioning and electricity subsidies made electric lighting appear more economical. They can still be used, with either south-facing vertical windows (added-advantage solar heating) or north-facing vertical or sloped windows (stable, very little glare). A 60° north-facing sawtooth provides fairly even light distribution, and is steep enough to make leaks less likely. The adaptive reuse of industrial facilities with extensive sawtooth roofs has become increasingly common.

Skylights

Although skylights are almost 100 percent efficient as the light enters, eventually that light is converted to heat, and added cooling might be required to offset the heat gain in summer. Likewise, infiltration and conduction of air through skylights may call for additional heating or cooling. However, skylights are better than electric lights, which give off more heat; even fluorescent lights require more cooling than properly used skylights.

Skylight efficiency can be increased with appropriate glazing and by using curbs with R-values comparable to roof insulation. Curbs should also be weather-tight with little or no infiltration. Flat, curved, or pyramid skylights can be used with recognition of their impact on summer cooling loads or with proper controls. Skylight size and spacing can be worked out with models. Curb and surround shapes, color, and detailing all affect light capture and contrast. If the ceiling height is low, then an angled aperture should be used to allow light to spread; otherwise glare can be a problem.

The standard rule is to start by placing the first skylights at one-half the height of the ceiling from walls that have no windows, and then adding another skylight at a distance equal to wall height (1/2H, H, H, H, H, 1/2H). Diffusers or glare busters are needed on most skylights. Figure 4.19 shows an existing building retrofit that incorporated a number of skylights with baffles to diffuse light and heat. Refer to chapter 3 for ways to control solar gain. Skylights are most commonly used to light large open spaces or arranged in a manner consistent with the ceiling module. They can also be placed to wash interior walls with light, which helps brighten the inner wall of a deeper room.

Light Tubes

Light tubes or light pipes include a clear acrylic dome at the roof surface and a circular aluminum duct with internal mirror finish and a diffusing-light emitter to channel light into a space below. Light tubes have been the most popular daylight solution in recent years. They have proven to be good lighting solutions for bathrooms, hallways, stairwells, garages, and shops. The small dome is relatively

Fig. 4.19. *This 1960s office building felt like a dungeon deprived of natural light until a major retrofit incorporated extensive natural lighting techniques including skylights with baffles to transform the interior into an inviting and pleasant place to be. Union-Locust building, Santa Cruz, California. Images courtesy of Swenson Technology.*

Fig. 4.20. *Light tubes incorporated into the retrofit of a 1960s office building in Santa Cruz, California, provide natural light while also maximizing roof area for solar electric production. Images courtesy of Swenson Technology.*

easy to install in sloped roofs, and leaks have not been a common problem.

Recently, a publicly owned facility successfully integrated natural light for 90 percent of its occupants with the addition of 101 light tubes. This facility achieved LEED Gold for existing buildings, and occupants have expressed their appreciation for the light tubes in particular. An unanticipated result of introducing natural light into this facility has been an increase in indoor plants, which love natural light and help take up indoor CO_2, thereby improving indoor air quality as well.

Another attractive quality of light tubes is that they can have adjustable joints, as seen in figure 4.20, so the roof penetration does not need to align with the interior ceiling surface. Flexible rather than rigid ducts with adjustable joints are available, but the corrugation in flexible ducts reduces light reflectance and transmittance. Operable light tubes are available and can be used for venting. Light tubes can have a fairly short payback period. In 2009, costs for a nonventing 13-inch light tube ranged from $200 to $500 per installation, with smaller-scale residential applications at the higher end.

Light Wells

Light wells differ from courtyards and atria because glazing is usually placed at the top of the aperture, but not present between the areas being served by the light well. Glazing typically reflects 15 percent of the light that falls upon its surface, so a light well can be more effective in some cases than atria. Generally, light wells are used at an intermediate scale between atria and light tubes. Figure 4.21 illustrates a light well used to introduce side-light on a lower level.

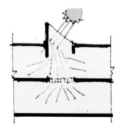

Fig. 4.21. *Light well serving multiple stories.*

Side-Lighting

Side-lighting is the most common method for integrating natural light, but it is severely limited by its depth of reach as shown in figure 4.22. Floor-to-ceiling height, light shelves, sloped ceilings

(sloping toward the back of the room), interior light apertures, and color can all be used to enhance the quality and quantity of side light.

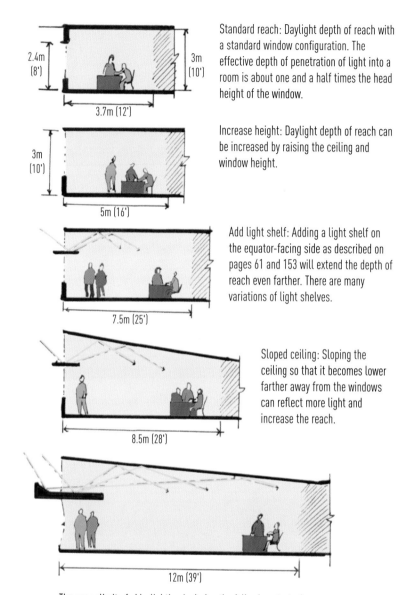

Standard reach: Daylight depth of reach with a standard window configuration. The effective depth of penetration of light into a room is about one and a half times the head height of the window.

Increase height: Daylight depth of reach can be increased by raising the ceiling and window height.

Add light shelf: Adding a light shelf on the equator-facing side as described on pages 61 and 153 will extend the depth of reach even farther. There are many variations of light shelves.

Sloped ceiling: Sloping the ceiling so that it becomes lower farther away from the windows can reflect more light and increase the reach.

The upper limit of side-lighting includes the following strategies:
High ceiling: 15 feet
Slope ceiling to rear: 13 feet
Deep light shelf: 13 feet with reflective sloped edge
This is why side-lighting is often used in conjunction with top-lighting.

Fig. 4.22. *Side-lighting enhancement techniques and their limits.*

Side-Lighting Details

Light Shelves

The light shelf reduces glare in the room and reflects light up onto the ceiling and farther back into the room. A bright white upper surface is usually preferred, as seen in figure 4.23. Light shelves provide fewer benefits on east- and west-facing windows and almost none on the north. In the future, there will likely be retrofit light-shelf systems that can be easily installed on existing windows. Even a few inches of window above a light shelf can make a big difference in light penetration and glare control.

The **interior light shelf** may be opaque or translucent and shaped to improve performance. Flat light shelves are the least costly, but curved, adjustable, or even shape-changing light shelves are in use today. The width of the shelf can be adjusted to provide glare protection over a longer period or all year. Internal light shelves have also been found to help with ventilation using high room fresh-air vents. The cooler fresh air spills off the light shelf and into the room better than it would in a room where it simply falls down the outer wall.

Construction of interior light shelves does not have to be very costly, as the materials can be lightweight. The windows used may be fixed, but operable sections may prove helpful for ventilation. Access for operation should be considered carefully, especially if room darkening is a consideration and shades or curtains will be installed.

Interior light shelves may be shaped to reflect light differentially. They can be solid with a diffuse reflective upper surface (semi-gloss for easy cleaning), translucent, or a grid or egg-crate-style baffle. Interior light shelves also work well with exterior light shelves to reduce glare and to increase light penetration into the room. Interior light shelves can be used when exterior light shelves cannot be easily integrated in a new or retrofit design. A set of blinds may be installed in the light shelf window, and interior shelves can double as light soffits to provide backup lighting. Some optimized applications even integrate mirrors to improve light penetration and quality.

Fig. 4.23. *Exterior and interior light shelves can take many forms, as shown here, but having a light-colored or reflective top surface is critical.*

Exterior light shelves should be sloped to direct water where desired. The angle can be selected to increase gain for specific periods of the year. The exterior light shelf not only provides light but also helps with solar control of the window below it and can reduce summer cooling loads. If the exterior light shelf tilts down toward the building, it can increase light penetration with the higher summer sun; if it tilts down to the outside, it can increase summer shading and light penetration in fall and spring. It can help to leave a small gap between the exterior light shelf and the wall for ventilation and drainage. A light shelf can also be louvered or adjustable. An adjustable awning with white canvas could be a very flexible, seasonally adjustable light shelf.

Exterior light shelves need to be robust. They must withstand the weather, wind, and rain. Louvered or slatted light shelves will catch less wind on walls exposed to very high winds. Light shelf supports must be well integrated in the wall system to avoid leaks.

Interior Light Apertures

Natural light from areas that enjoy a surplus can be shared with other spaces that have less, such as hallways and landlocked interiors. Interior windows can move light to the core of a building. These may be in doors, transoms, or walls. Figure 4.24 depicts light sharing with transoms and glass doors. For privacy these may be translucent, but if placed high on the walls, clear may be better. Operable windows in interior walls can also be used for ventilation; adjustable metal vents may be much cheaper, but they are typically thermally transparent.

Although heavy, glass has been used in walkways, floors, and sidewalk pavers to allow light penetration. Pavers and translucent panels have a lower light transmittance but can also be effective at diffusing direct radiation. Figure 4.25 illustrates a natural lighting scheme with a series of transparent walks and light wells for a structure in Saudi Arabia where 120°F temperatures demand the use of reflected light to avoid heat gain.

Color

Choice of interior surfaces and fixtures also matters, with brighter colors helping. In general, warm colors such as red, orange, and yellow are advancing colors that appear closer to the viewer. Cool colors such as green, blue, and violet are opposite in that they are receding and will appear to be farther from the viewer.

Fig. 4.24. *Glass doors can be used to share light through spaces and can be fashioned with translucent or dark curtains or blinds for privacy. Transoms in the wall above share light with the hallway on the other side. The hallway is full of natural light thanks to interior apertures in the surrounding walls and glass doors.*

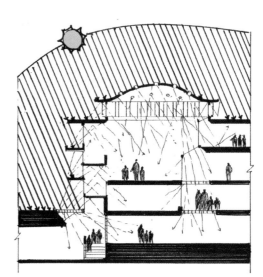

Fig. 4.25. *Natural light can be used in extremely hot-dry climates—but solar radiation must be diffused so light enters and heat does not. Interior light apertures are a primary design technique in this case.*

Windows

For small buildings, natural lighting with windows is the best place to start. The building will have windows in the walls, so why not make them work for daylighting, natural heating, cooling, and ventilation? The incremental cost may be zero, or even pay a bonus as mechanical backup systems are downsized or eliminated. Windows can provide many benefits: views, good lighting for work, ventilation, cooling in summer, and heating in winter—but only if they are designed and installed correctly. Make the wrong choice, and they will provide unwanted heating in summer and cooling in winter.

Effective use of windows begins with proper building orientation, facing the equator, and a building shape that maintains thin elements that make daylighting with windows possible. The finger plan schools, with a series of very narrow, long buildings, of the 1950s were a good response to daylighting demands. Increasing the building perimeter adds to the cost, but provides the best potential for daylighting and natural heating, cooling, and ventilation. Taller ceilings as shown in figure 4.26 enable windows to be higher, increasing light penetration and facilitating ventilation and summer cooling. They can also help reduce glare and lighting discomfort.

Windows offer one of the better methods for providing natural light because they are already included in a building, and their use for daylighting is free or almost free. Thoughtful design and careful analysis can maximize the value of light from windows. Orientation, placement, type, and solar control are essential to provide good natural lighting—without glare, excessive heat gain, or great variation in brightness. Good design can also ensure that the windows also provide needed opportunities for cross- and stack ventilation for fresh air and natural cooling—an added bonus.

Windows should have narrow glazing bars and frames. They should be shaded during the summer in hot areas and spring through fall in very hot areas. Translucent insulated shutters or shutters with light ports may be desirable to reduce unwanted heat gain, particularly on east- and west-facing windows.

Effective window placement can yield the best light for a given window area. Higher windows admit more light and are also good for venting hot air. Thin tall windows placed in walls next to wall intersections can wash the walls with light and provide good lighting without excessive contrast. Vertical windows are preferred. Tilted windows are difficult to shade in summer and are more likely to leak

Fig. 4.26. *A taller ceiling accommodates higher windows to allow more daylight to penetrate this office and library space.*

because water accumulates on the glazing during heavy downpours, and the seals tend to degrade faster with continuous exposure to solar radiation. Tilted windows are also vulnerable to damage from hail and accumulate dirt faster, so maintenance is necessary for optimum light transmittance. The placement of windows also depends on the intended use of the space and the interior design. More than one window on more than one wall can provide better lighting distribution. A strip of windows can give more balanced light than a series of discrete windows. Window placement may also be limited by the desire to reduce glare for a projector screen, monitors, or computer stations. A dark space may be provided for screens or TVs, and a bright spot for displays or whiteboards if control devices such as vertical blinds as shown in figure 4.27 are not enough.

Fig. 4.27. *Vertical blinds on windows are quite effective at controlling direct gain and glare while providing user operability.*

The distribution of light in a room is also affected by the glazing, the window covering, and the width of the window (wider is usually better on equator-facing walls). A translucent window or window covering may also improve the quality of light and distribution in the room. Alternatively, a view and ventilation window of clear glass may be included in a translucent window wall.

Seasonally adjustable exterior fins are often the best solution for difficult-to-control east- and west-facing windows (see the Olgyays'* book, listed in the reference section, for inspiration). Fixed awnings or roll-down shades, wing walls, and egg-crate devices can help. And exterior blinds, a shade screen, or a green wall of vines a few feet from the window can also be used.

Design and Prediction

Light Measurement

Hand calculations can help you explore the energy implications of natural lighting design, or you can use a more complex annual calculation or models, perhaps with an energy-simulation program. However, many of these are not very good at integrating natural light or considering night ventilation issues, and they may underestimate performance significantly. Using the schematic analysis described below is a good place to begin.

Physical models (figure 4.28) are particularly useful in lighting-design work because the scale model of a building is a true photometric analogue, and models are easier and more accurate to use than calculations or computer programs. Even larger models are relatively inexpensive to make and easy to construct. They can provide very useful information and are easy for clients to relate to and understand. These can be evaluated through the seasons using the sun-peg diagrams described on page 54 photographed with a digital camera. Options can be tested quickly and efficiently, especially if a light meter is used to take readings from the analog model.

A number of daylight design tools have also been developed, including Daylighting Nomographs (Environmental Energy Technologies Division, LBL); University of Washington Graphic Daylighting Design Method (Professor Marietta Millet; see the details in Stein et al., 2006*), and the *AAMA Skylight Handbook* (American Architectural Manufacturers Association). Computer models can also be used to evaluate daylighting, but this can be more costly. They may be required for some applications to satisfy code requirements and to assess energy implications for heating and cooling. Software options include Lumen-Micro (from Lighting Technologies), Superlite 2.0 (Environmental Energy Technologies Division, LBL), DOE-1 (Simulation Research Group, LBL), Radiance 3.4, Energy-10 (Sustainable Buildings Industry Council), and many others.

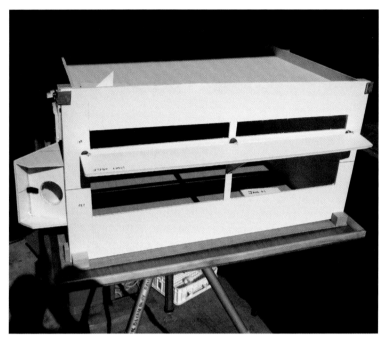

Fig. 4.28. *Tools for daylight analysis—a physical model. Walls and roof can be easily changed to test different daylighting solutions. Camera port on left.*

Understanding Light Availability

A number of effective and low-cost light meters are now sold. A good light meter can be found for under $100; a very good one for less than $200. Approximate values can also be checked with an older light meter designed for photographers, with the film speed set at ASA-100. The EV = 5 at 10 fc, EV = 7 at 30 fc, EV = 9 at 50 fc, EV = 10.5–11 at 70 fc, and EV = 12 at 200 fc. Readings are only approximate because the light meter is set to measure the spectrum that film responds to rather than the human eye.

Schematic Analysis—A Good First Step

Start the following process during schematic design. It may be recycled through many times as design trade-offs become more apparent. Each step will ask you to draw or compare—do it at the level you are designing—overall or space specific. Sketches of a typical situation provide general guidance:

1. Draw the general plan view of the area under consideration. Label compass directions with a big equator-facing arrow (south in the Northern Hemisphere and north in the Southern Hemisphere).

2. Where in the plan do you want natural light for stationary tasks, such as reading? Draw in the region with a 45° cross-hatch.

3. Where in the plan do you want natural light to illuminate circulation routes? Draw the region with a horizontal cross-hatch on an unmarked general plan. Don't redraw step 2.

4. Where in the plan do you desire general background lighting? Draw the region with a vertical cross-hatch on another unmarked plan. Again, don't redraw earlier steps.

5. Where in the plan do you want visual accent lighting? Draw this region with a dot pattern.

6. Now draw a composite sketch showing all lighting goals.

After you have completed these steps, look carefully at what you have. How realistic is it? Cut down all "excess" light requirements as much as possible. Remember, task lighting and lighting for circulation routes are brighter than general background or accent lighting. Therefore, light for those first requirements might be utilized for less demanding needs as well. After you have reexamined your lighting goals, draw a new composite diagram reflecting the changes. If you were working at the overall scheme level, later as you start dividing up the space you can meet more specific criteria by repeating this process. If you were already at a small-space level, now you can repeat the process for some other areas in your project.

Methods for natural lighting can be categorized as either top-lighting or side-lighting, but advances in interior lighting such as translucent walks and walls have proven useful for extending the distribution of natural light throughout a building. To achieve a good balance of natural light and to avoid unwanted glare, a mixture of top- and side-lighting should be incorporated into the design.

Iconic Buildings

The cathedral of Santa Maria del Fiore in Florence, Italy, started in 1296, stood for 140 years without any enclosure over its central altar. The task of enclosure was too difficult because of the large span involved, which didn't allow traditional wood centering, and also because of the rejection of flying buttresses by the building commission as too foreign (Northern European).

Fig. 4.29. *Basilica di Santa Maria del Fiore, Florence, Italy. The dome was engineered by Filippo Brunelleschi and completed in 1436. Today, it remains the largest brick dome ever constructed and marks the beginning of the Renaissance.*

The architect, Brunelleschi, solved the engineering problem of the span by using a double-shell dome and iron tension rings. This allowed construction of the dome that could use internal reinforcing to hold itself in place as it went up. Beyond its engineering innovation, however, the resultant context, scale, and form allowed this building to instantly became the symbol of the city-state of Florence and very quickly symbolize the confluence of new and old ideas now known as the Renaissance. Iconic buildings are those innovative enough and lucky enough in their timing to become symbolic of large changes in the social and cultural context in which these architectural expressions occur.

The Reichstag in Berlin

This building played a significant part in the turbulent twentieth century. Built in a severe Prussian Classic style in 1894, it was supposed to become the expression of a new democratic Germany. But it was shunned by Kaiser Wilhelm II (not inclined toward democracy) when he came to power. It was then used as a government building by the more progressive Weimar Republic from 1919 to 1933. It was badly damaged by arson in 1933, an event that was used as a pretext by the Nazis to begin an era of repression culminating in the catastrophic Third Reich. In historical context, it was a kind of a Twin Towers of its time. Further damage by Allied bombing and the Soviet capture of Berlin at the end of World War II added to its tragic history as well as its near destruction.

Fig. 4.30. *Reichstag, Berlin, Germany*

Although it was part of the western sector of Berlin during the Cold War, the Reichstag was cut off from access by the Berlin Wall. Some limited restoration work was done in the early 1960s, but it wasn't until the reunification of Germany and increased recognition—fueled in part by a Christo art wrap in 1995—that the building was slated for a return to its original function.

In 1999, it was the subject of an international design competition to restore it as a legislative building for the new democratically unified Germany. Norman Foster and Partners developed the winning design based on expressing the following goals:

- Providing a democratic focus.

- Emphasizing public accessibility.

- Expressing sensitivity to history.

- Fulfilling a rigorous environmental agenda.

The design uses passive lighting and ventilation utilizing the traditional dome form as a gigantic daylight chandelier and public walkway. It operates with hundreds of mirrors and a movable shading device. Electrical needs of the building are provided by photovoltaic panels and a generator powered by biofuel from vegetable oil. The design has reduced the carbon footprint of the building by 94 percent.

Fig. 4.31. *Reichstag, Berlin, Germany. Photo: Richard Beller.*

This building rose from the ashes like the phoenix and provides a refreshing vitality with the very strong contrast between the ponderous, heavy old building and its new airy dome, which emphasizes light, openness, and public participation. These characteristics give it power similar to that of Brunelleschi's dome in Florence, built 560 years earlier to mark a new cultural era. In this case the transition is from an industrially dominated era to a new cultural era of sustainability.

Fig. 4.32. *(a, b, c, d, e) Interior photos by Richard Beller. (f) Exterior photo. (g) Section drawing of Reichstag, Berlin, Germany.*

The typical illumination specialist has a background in electrical engineering: he is thus all too prone to rely upon artificial light sources exclusively, paying little or no attention to daylighting.

—J. M. FITCH, 1972

Supplemental Lighting

Although natural light can meet most of the lighting demand for many buildings on a good day, artificial lighting is needed to supplement daylighting at night or on dark, cloudy days. Natural lighting can typically meet about 75 percent of the annual lighting needs for a building used between 8 AM and 5 PM. Careful integration of design and controls are crucial to ensure comfort and economy of the combined daylight and artificial lighting systems.

As energy prices continue to rise, the cost of artificial lighting is also increasing, and this is encouraging more investment in daylight design and improved lighting systems and controls. Artificial lighting may be needed to meet the demand for both area and/or task lighting when natural light is insufficient. The design of artificial lighting should also focus on comfort and productivity. Glare avoidance is critical for the computer-screen, PDA-dominated world we live in today.

Light efficiency varies from about 10–20 lumens per watt for incandescent bulbs to 30–100 for fluorescents, and 25–100+ for LEDs. LEDs last much longer and are the most efficient, but their light is very directional. They are also the most expensive lights, and fewer types are available for 110V. In the future, buildings may have a 24-volt lighting circuit for LEDs.

Fluorescent lights are more efficient, economical, and cooler than incandescent. Light quality is good with some types of fixtures and bulbs, and dimmable ballasts are available for some types of fluorescent lamps. Full-daylight-spectrum fluorescents are available and should be considered in cases without natural light. Low-cost bulbs and ballasts can be noisy and provide poor light quality. Fluorescents' flicker and hum may also be troublesome to people. Ideally, much of the supplemental lighting will be reflected rather than direct light, to reduce glare.

Light placement should also be carefully considered when ceiling fans will be used for supplemental cooling. Downward-facing lights set above ceiling fans can create an irritating flutter from blade shadows. It can be better to wash the ceiling with light for indirect lighting or to use a ceiling-fan-integrated high-efficiency light that is mounted below the blades.

Controls

One of the primary challenges is developing an integrated control system that will take maximum advantage of natural light, provide user control and comfort, and function reliably for many years. Easy-to-understand-and-operate controls are critical. Lights can be photo-cell switched to turn off or dim when natural lighting levels are adequate. Savings of 50 percent or more may be achieved with automatic switching. Occupancy sensors can also be used to turn lights off when no one is in the room. Motion and even sound waves are being used to sense occupancy, so it is important to know which should override the other. Most often the photometric sensors will determine light levels sufficient for movement through spaces. Savings have varied from 20 to 76 percent in various studies. In general, the better the control system, the bigger the savings. However, lighting-control systems can slightly increase energy use for the detectors and controllers.

Lighting Manual

A **lighting manual** should also be prepared as part of each building's operating manual to ensure that staff are familiar with maintenance and operation of the lights, windows, blinds, curtains, and artificial lights. This will also help ensure that task and background lighting are properly set when rearrangements take place. This can improve comfort and productivity and will help minimize energy use.

Summary: Natural Lighting

Natural light should be an integral consideration in the design of every new building; it reduces heat gain from lighting to one-fourth of the heat from fluorescent lights and as little as one-sixth of the heat from incandescent lights. This can lead to a substantial reduction in air-conditioning load and substantial energy and financial savings as well as reduction in global greenhouse gases, because lighting adds 30 to 50 percent of the cooling load in many commercial buildings.

The health benefits of natural light are well documented. Businesses and schools are catching on as they realize workers are healthier, more positive, and more productive with natural light. These benefits far outweigh the benefit of lower utility bills. Students have demonstrated fewer behavioral problems under full-spectrum light, which makes the learning environment more pleasant and efficient for everyone, including the teachers.

Interior design must be developed and integrated with the natural lighting system. Office layout, including placement of desks, monitors, and other equipment, needs to consider lighting requirements and lighting opportunities and constraints. The planning should also consider where different activities and tasks will be undertaken. Good interior design can help a poorly developed light system function better, while poor interior design can cripple a brilliant daylight design. Lighting design influences color and material choices, the design of interior partitions and interior decoration, and choice and placement of fixtures and equipment. Everyone must be encouraged to understand and accept responsibility for his or her potential impacts on lighting. High reflectances are usually desirable for the ceiling and walls, partitions, and floors. However, desktops, storage, and partitions in workers' viewscapes should be chosen for moderate reflectance to reduce potential glare problems on computer screens and other monitors.

In 2007, about 526 billion kilowatt-hours of electricity were used for lighting by the residential and commercial sectors. This was equal to about 19 percent of the total electricity consumed by both of those sectors and 14 percent of total US electricity consumption (US Energy Information Administration). The use of natural light can not only reduce the pollution associated with electricity production, but also save quite a bit in terms of water resources, since 47 percent of US water use is for energy production.

Even with abundant natural light, people have been programmed to reach for the lights as they enter a room. It is time for everyone to think before automatically hitting the switch. After all, even though electricity is subsidized to make it affordable now, that will not be the case in the future. Natural light will play an increasing role in buildings in the future, just as it did before the fossil-fool era.

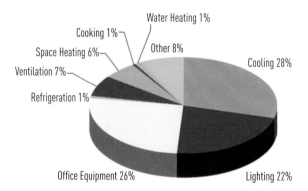

Fig. 4.33. *1999 US DOE-EIA electricity end use in office buildings.*

All sites are endowed with multiple flows of energy and resources that can be used as part of a sustainable design.

Basics of On-Site Resources

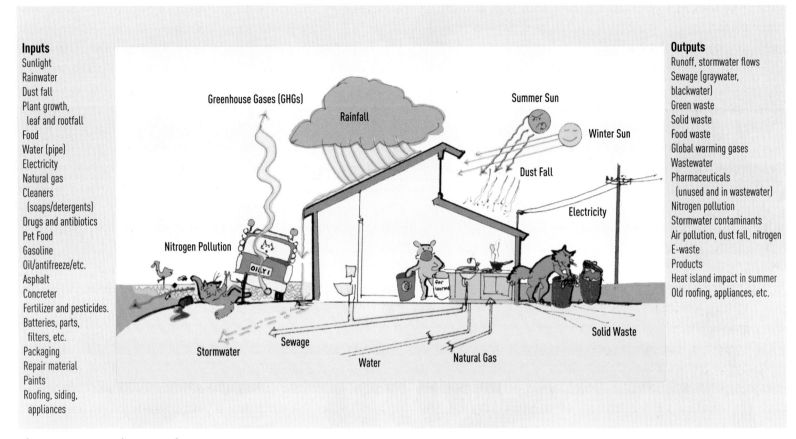

Inputs
Sunlight
Rainwater
Dust fall
Plant growth,
 leaf and rootfall
Food
Water (pipe)
Electricity
Natural gas
Cleaners
 (soaps/detergents)
Drugs and antibiotics
Pet Food
Gasoline
Oil/antifreeze/etc.
Asphalt
Concreter
Fertilizer and pesticides.
Batteries, parts,
 filters, etc.
Packaging
Repair material
Paints
Roofing, siding,
 appliances

Outputs
Runoff, stormwater flows
Sewage (graywater,
 blackwater)
Green waste
Solid waste
Food waste
Global warming gases
Wastewater
Pharmaceuticals
 (unused and in wastewater)
Nitrogen pollution
Stormwater contaminants
Air pollution, dust fall, nitrogen
E-waste
Products
Heat island impact in summer
Old roofing, appliances, etc.

Fig. 5.1. *Resource inputs and outputs.*

A sustainable building will optimize use of renewable resources and minimize waste. Integrated design makes it possible to harvest many on-site resources (sun, wind, rain) to reduce operating costs and to minimize the external costs of off-site waste disposal or releases. Harvesting on-site resources and using resources more wisely can help improve the quality of life for everyone and can rebuild ecosystem health. This section reviews the harvesting of available resources (water, energy, food scraps, yard clippings) and minimizing waste. There are two key concepts to remember:

1. A waste is an unrecognized resource (waste = food).

2. There is no "away" (where wastes will disappear to).

Resource flows can be understood by developing a better picture of their pathways through the home, neighborhood, and community. Very few studies have been done to understand these flows,

their costs, and the opportunities they provide. Many reports are based on largely incomplete and inaccurate information. The garbology research project at the University of Arizona (beginning in 1973) has provided some clear information on what is used and discarded and how it behaves after it is sealed in a "sanitary" landfill. What people say they do, and what they *really* do, was also revealed. The amount of food waste was found to be double US EPA estimates.

Positive Impact Development

Land development in the United States has historically been catastrophic for nature and ill suited for human health and well-being. As a result we are broke, fat, and unhappy. But development doesn't have to be evil. If we frame the question properly and count the costs and benefits carefully, we can create developments that are good for people and help protect and restore the function of natural ecosystems. Achieving this requires a very different approach to development, beginning with careful analysis of the ecological setting, the economic matrix, and the social structure, as well as an integrated, holistic vision for the future.

Although we depend on natural systems for the air we breathe, the food we eat, the water we drink, and the materials we use to build our homes, we have lost touch with this connection to nature. Water now comes from the faucet; food comes packaged and prepared; energy flows from the wall socket; and wastes are simply flushed or hauled away. But natural and managed ecosystems still provide us with the requirements for life, and every one of us has an impact on our planet. If we don't take more from the earth than it has to offer we can continue to prosper; but are we taking more than we can or should?

The growing awareness of serious problems with global and local ecosystem stability and resource availability is encouraging new consideration of the sustainability of our current lifeways and communities. This has been addressed with eco-footprint calculations and sustainability indicators. Both are of value, but both are challenging to do well. Eco-footprint calculations are particularly effective for awareness building, while sustainable area budgets (refer to chapter 6, R. Levine) and sustainability indicators can be more useful for management and monitoring. Most approaches have emphasized environmental concerns, but economic and social concerns may be equally important.

To develop appropriate and sustainable solutions, we need to understand the causes of these problems, not just the symptoms. As British economist A. C. Pigou (1920) noted early in the last century, the market will fail unless it includes all costs. The market today considers only a small fraction of the total transaction cost, leaving many "externalities" out of the picture. These externalities include the costs of pollution, disease, and damage to vital ecosystem services.

These externalities are integral costs of goods and services, often exceeding the current costs. In many cases we have not studied them, because we do not want to know the answer. For an excellent review of the issues involved in calculating the external costs of automobiles, see Bainbridge (2009*). Some critics suggest that users currently pay only 10 percent of the true costs for using automobiles in the United States. These enormous subsidies benefit the auto users, the automakers, oil companies, and highway builders; but taxpayers who do not use cars and future generations pay the price.

If true costs were known, many current market transactions would not occur, resources would be conserved, pollution would virtually vanish, and we would face a much more hopeful, secure, and sustainable future. To reduce consumption of nonrenewable resources and limit adverse environmental and social impacts, we need to understand the true cost of products throughout their full life, from the cradle to the grave (made, used, disposed) or cradle to the cradle (made, used, recycled, reused, or returned to nature). This is the goal of most sustainability reporting and environmental management systems, from the Eco-Management and Audit Scheme to the Global Reporting Initiative and ISO 14000 series.

For monitoring our community sustainability, we might start with a set of indicators that we will monitor. Choosing the appropriate number of indicators can be a challenge, for although we could perhaps reach four hundred, such a large number would become burdensome; for general application it appears that ten to twelve indicators for each sector (social, economic, environment and perhaps institutional) will suffice. This can yield a total of about thirty or forty indicators, which can be easily presented in graphic form to decision-makers and the public.

Despite the growing recognition of the problem, and recent efforts such as the Sustainable Sites Initiative and Low-Impact Development, the planning process has failed to create sustainable communities. With a few notable exceptions, such as Village Homes, the development process typically creates unsustainable homes, support systems, and ways of living while providing inadequate financial support for costly infrastructure services, destroying local ecosystems, and disrupting local hydrologic cycles. Starting earlier and working with a more complete land development model that includes human, economic, and ecological health as key criteria can shape a more humane and sustainable landscape.

What Would It Take?

Long-term sustainable development will require a new approach that embraces

- Understanding ecological communities, their structure, and their function. In most of the United States and the world, development will occur in degraded and destabilized ecosystems, and development offers the opportunity to restore endangered ecosystems and restore ecosystem function, particularly water flow.

- Understanding the community of people, their interaction, health, education, and economics. What subsidies and perverse incentives exist for unsustainable development? What health costs are related to development decisions? What government costs should be met with fees instead of taxes, and how would these be assessed and collected? And how can education be revised to provide a more comprehensive understanding of place, food, culture, ecosystems, and their relation to sustainability?

- Engineering and planning with a multidisciplinary team and community input. This type of planning can only begin once the basics of place are well understood and mapped. How can homes be clustered to provide ease of access to schools and interactions among people while retaining privacy, access to garden space and recreational areas, and easy commutes by bicycle or walking to work and essential services? What local building materials are most appropriate and sustainable?

- Schematic design and economic evaluation—resilience under global climate change. Plans for ecological restoration, food production, composting, water supply, waste management, water harvesting, and on-site energy capture.

- Detailed development plans and economic analysis.

- Construction done in a slow, phased way, with opportunities for workers to buy and live in the development.

- Development of food system and water harvesting and management facilities.

- Ecosystem restoration, with development of local and regional seed banks, along with propagation of endangered species.

SOME DEFINITIONS

How we manage resources depends on how we understand and define them. Here are some key issues and terms:

- **Discards:** Used resources that are disposed of at homes, businesses, or institutions.

- **Ecotoxicity:** The adverse impacts of discards on ecosystems. High risk discards include pesticides, herbicides, copper, zinc, cadmium, drugs, lead, nitrogen, phosphorus, and organic waste in wastewater.

- **E-waste:** Electronic waste.

- **Extended product responsibility:** When a manufacturer's responsibility does not end with the sale, but with the recovery at the end of a product's use cycle.

- **Energy life-cycle assessment:** Analysis of the true cost of energy over the life cycle of an asset.

- **Life-cycle assessment (LCA):** Analysis of total true cost of materials and energy over the life of an asset.

- **Life-cycle design:** A synthesis of analysis and design using life-cycle assessment that creates cradle-to-cradle resource cycles.

- **Materials life-cycle assessment:** Analysis of the true cost of materials, including environmental costs used over the life cycle of an asset (also called cradle-to-grave analysis).

- **Rainwater:** Any rain, snow, sleet, or other precipitation.

- **Recycling:** Collecting, sorting, processing, and converting discards into raw materials for production of "new" products or resources.

- **Return to nature:** Safely returning resources to ecosystems, gardens, or landscape.

- **Reuse:** Finding new homes for discards and/or refurbishing, repairing, washing, or dismantling for parts.

- **Stormwater:** Flow on or off a site from rainwater or snowmelt.

- **Waste:** When the residual value of discards is destroyed by burning, burying (landfill), or other means.

- **Zero waste:** The goal of eliminating waste: All resources are recovered.

- **14040 Standards for life-cycle assessments:** To help refine these approaches and give some semblance of order to the complexities of LCAs, the International Standards Organization (ISO) created publication 14040 for LCA standards.

- Commissioning of facilities and homes, with training and education about the area, ecosystems, and culture for all new residents. Homes and buildings come with operator manuals.

- Implementation of community-building activities, festivals, planting and restoration activities, community gardens, school–community interactions.

- Maintenance with careful assessment of cost and material requirements, vulnerable systems, correcting flawed designs.

- Monitoring begins with cooperation among scientists, engineers, and educators. Most monitoring will be done by schools and posted online. Home-monitoring systems will be easy to understand and use, and data on energy and water use will be relayed to community managers to assess the relation between planned function and actual function.

Context

The twenty-first century faces a series of resource crises as serious as our energy and climatic crises. The resources involved are all essential to agriculture and related to our consumption, settlement, and building patterns. Using passive design approaches that combine use, production, recycling, and efficiency at the scale of buildings and neighborhoods can help relieve these situations.

Energy and climate have been in a crisis state long enough to be widely understood; the problems of freshwater supplies are generally recognized as well. Resource crises 4 and 5 in figure 5.2 are less well known. Phosphorus and fixed nitrogen are essential to plant growth and therefore to agriculture. Phosphorus deposits that are easily exploitable are diminishing. As a result, phosphate costs have increased 500 percent during the last ten years. As with oil, many nations have depleted phosphate mines and now must rely on imports. One of the best sources of phosphate is human waste, and restoring a sustainable phosphorus cycle is important. One-half of that is available in urine, which is easy to recover if separated from solid waste. Modifying toilets and toilet habits to collect urine is a passive approach to tapping into a resource that is also rich in fixed nitrogen.

Advanced cultures have a remarkable history of sophisticated development of on-site resources, with periods of great success followed by periods of stress and collapse. We are not immune to the historical patterns illustrated in figures 5.4–5.7. Creativity cannot stop with the development of one aspect of infrastructure, because we live in a dynamic world that is becoming more dynamic with time, as illustrated by crises 1, 2, and 3.

Much of our present infrastructure has been developed in a reductionist state of mind that ignores connections between parts. However, in reality everything is intimately connected. The chart in figure 5.3 shows this connection between water use and energy in the United States. In California, 20 percent of energy use is water-related.

We must reconnect pieces that have to date been designed in isolation. This is why the passive approach to harvesting on-site resources is so important to our present situation and our continuance as an advanced culture.

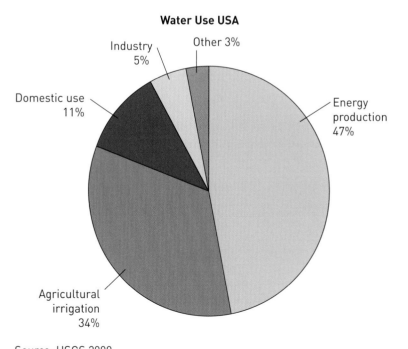

Source: USGS 2000

Fig. 5.3. *US water use.*

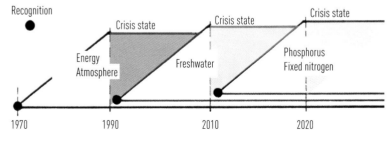

Fig. 5.2. *Resource crises of the twenty-first century.*

300–1200

Fig. 5.4. *Petra is located in what is now Jordan. The Nabatean people who lived in the Negev desert in Petra were probably the most sophisticated rainwater harvesters the world has ever known. They used rainwater catchments for drinking, washing, cooking, and farming. Petra prospered in an area with less than 5 inches of rainfall per year.*

800–1500

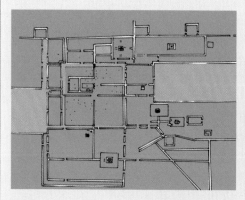

Fig. 5.5. *Angkor is located in what is now Cambodia and was the capital of the Khmer empire. It was the largest pre-industrial city in the world with a population of 1 million and an area similar in size to present-day Los Angeles (500 square miles). This was made possible by sophisticated technology and building for managing and harvesting water for use during the dry season in this tropical climate. (a) Plan; (b) Angkor Wat temple; photo: Chris Yip; (c) aerial photograph.*

1375–1521

1930–1985

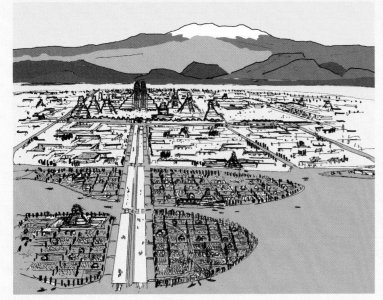

Fig. 5.6. *Tenochtitlán, now known as Mexico City, was the capital of the Aztec empire and built in the shallow part of Lake Tetzcoco, one of five interconnected lakes that occupied much of the valley of Mexico. The city was dependent upon an elaborate infrastructure of causeways, dams, sluice gates, canals, dikes, and* **chinampas***. The* **chinampas,** *a highly efficient system of marshland agriculture, provided more than half the food required for the city's 200,000-plus inhabitants.*

Fig. 5.7. *In the western United States, huge dams and related water projects created massive irrigation systems with inexpensive water and cheap electricity, resulting in conspicuous consumption. Las Vegas is the most extreme example. However, this unsustainability is becoming more and more obvious. Nevada leads the country in the rate of bankruptcy, and Las Vegas faces water scarcity. (a) Siltation is the main enemy of large dams and the reason, it is thought, that dams will outlive the lakes they create. In the first thirty-five years after the Hoover Dam was built, Lake Mead filled with more acre-feet of silt than 98 percent of the reservoirs in the United States are filled with acre-feet of water. (b) Las Vegas water extravagance in a hot desert environment.*

Solar Hot Water

Hot Water from the Sun

One of the most efficient and affordable solar applications is a solar water heater. These are three to four times more efficient than photovoltaic systems and cost from one-fifth to one-tenth as much to install. At the turn of the twentieth century (1900), solar hot water was in the ascendancy in the United States, and by the turn of the next century (2000) solar hot water was a fact of life in Cyprus, with 95 percent of homes heating water with the sun, and Israel, with 90 percent. But by 2000, solar water heaters had virtually disappeared in the United States, with less than 2 percent of homes so outfitted. Hawaii is leading the way by now requiring solar hot water for all new homes. China is installing seven million solar water heaters a year, while the United States is installing less than thirty thousand. Federal and state credits are once again available in some cases; still, the obstacles include not just cost but also ignorance, the pernicious effects of public/private regulation, and management of the utilities and subsidies for fossil fuels.

Hot water is a major energy demand in most homes, as much as 20 percent of total energy. Hot-water demand tends to have two peaks, a morning peak (7–10 AM) and an evening peak (5–9 PM).

A well-built, properly installed system can be very cost-effective. For example, a building-integrated integral-collector hot-water system installed in Village Homes in Davis, California, is now in its thirty-third year of service. One of the six tanks recently developed a small leak and was bypassed at very low cost. To date, this system has provided about 290 mBTU of solar energy for about a penny per kWh equivalent.

While a commercially built and installed system may cost $2,000 to $8,000, an integral-collector system can be built for less than $500 by a crafty homeowner. Even the more expensive systems make sense. Although payback in the simplest sense may require ten to twenty years for expensive systems, as we start to consider all the costs and benefits we will soon see solar water systems on most homes and many commercial buildings. In most areas the cost comparison with backup electricity is very positive, and even when compared with gas solar hot water is desirable.

Solar heating water typically costs only 1 to 8 cents per kWh equivalent, compared with fossil fuels at 6 to 20 cents per kWh. But to get more systems installed, we need to overcome the regulatory deadlocks that keep utilities from investing in solar hot water. We need to provide mechanisms that reward utilities for installing solar hot-water systems on a large scale. By installing a thousand at a time instead of one at a time, the cost can be reduced significantly. One Florida utility will install a solar water heater, and then charges for the hot water at standard prices as the solar energy is delivered. This has become much easier today thanks to improvements in telemetering. We also need to accelerate real-time metering and time-of-use-based costs; these make solar hot water look even better, because they help reduce demand during the critical August afternoon peak periods when energy from the grid is more costly.

Collector Options

Integral-Collector Systems (ICS)— Temperate and Warm Climates

In their simplest form, these solar heaters are little more than a black tank set in the sun in an insulated box with a double-glazed window. The cost is minimal and reliability is excellent. Service life is very long because temperatures are moderated by the mass of the tank. The relatively low temperature of the collector also improves efficiency because heat losses from re-radiation and conduction are reduced. An early study in California by the University of California (Brooks, 1936*) showed that an integral system outperformed flat-plate collectors. ICS systems are also called batch, bread box, and integral water heaters.

The mass of the water in the system helps protect it from freezing and the extreme high temperatures that can harm materials in other collectors. This leads to very long life for tanks and materials. An ICS system using a glass-lined steel tank may last thirty to fifty years, while a gas water heater averages only about seven. A solar water heater also reduces stress on the gas water heater and improves service life.

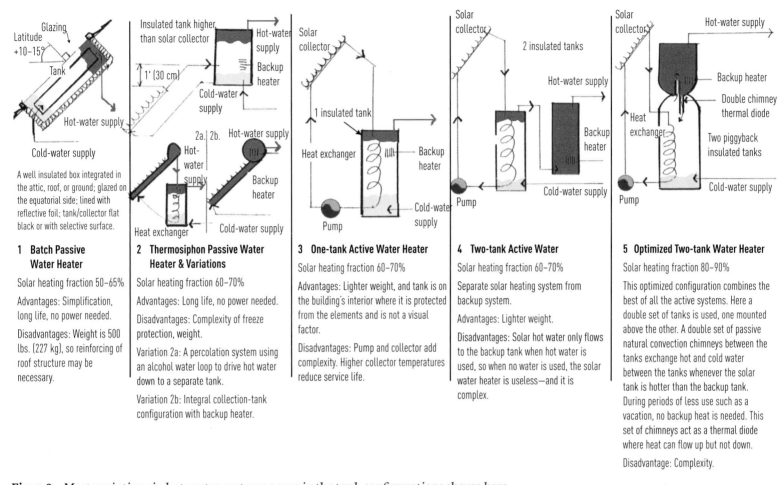

1 Batch Passive Water Heater

Solar heating fraction 50–65%

Advantages: Simplification, long life, no power needed.

Disadvantages: Weight is 500 lbs. (227 kg), so reinforcing of roof structure may be necessary.

2 Thermosiphon Passive Water Heater & Variations

Solar heating fraction 60–70%

Advantages: Long life, no power needed.

Disadvantages: Complexity of freeze protection, weight.

Variation 2a: A percolation system using an alcohol water loop to drive hot water down to a separate tank.

Variation 2b: Integral collection-tank configuration with backup heater.

3 One-tank Active Water Heater

Solar heating fraction 60–70%

Advantages: Lighter weight, and tank is on the building's interior where it is protected from the elements and is not a visual factor.

Disadvantages: Pump and collector add complexity. Higher collector temperatures reduce service life.

4 Two-tank Active Water

Solar heating fraction 60–70%

Separate solar heating system from backup system.

Advantages: Lighter weight.

Disadvantages: Solar hot water only flows to the backup tank when hot water is used, so when no water is used, the solar water heater is useless—and it is complex.

5 Optimized Two-tank Water Heater

Solar heating fraction 80–90%

This optimized configuration combines the best of all the active systems. Here a double set of tanks is used, one mounted above the other. A double set of passive natural convection chimneys between the tanks exchange hot and cold water between the tanks whenever the solar tank is hotter than the backup tank. During periods of less use such as a vacation, no backup heat is needed. This set of chimneys act as a thermal diode where heat can flow up but not down.

Disadvantage: Complexity.

Fig. 5.8. *Most variations in hot-water systems occur in the tank configurations shown here.*

The standard integral-collector solar water heater brings cold water into the solar heater tank through a side inlet near the bottom or through a dip tube that enters the tank at the top and discharges unheated water near the bottom, heats it, then moves it along to a backup heater—which can be fueled by gas, electricity, or wood—through an outlet near the top where the water will be warmest. An instantaneous gas water heater with thermostat controls works well as a backup.

During the summer months—or where it is warm and sunny year-round—the backup heater can often be turned off. David's three-tank integral solar water system provided full solar hot water for nine months of the year in Davis, California. A simple ICS in Germany provided 60 percent of the annual hot water (sometimes referred to as a solar fraction of 60 percent).

Integral systems lose energy at night even with selective surfaces (as you will recall from chapter 1, these have high absorptivity

and low emissivity) on the tank and good glazing systems. This makes them best for people who like to shower in the evening after work. It also reduces performance in cool seasons and increases risk of freezing in winter. Most integral systems should be drained in winter in cold climates. The pipes are often most vulnerable to freezing. Experiments in Europe suggest that collectors with less than 2 gallons of collector storage per square foot of glazing are more at risk of freezing. These recent studies suggest that up to 20 percent of the water in the collector can freeze without damaging the tank.

Building-integrated integral systems offer the lowest freeze risk and easiest long-term maintenance in new homes because they do not have exposed pipe runs and do not need to be pulled off the roof for reroofing. ICS solar heaters use waterline pressure for circulation, eliminating the need for expensive pumps and/or controls.

Fig. 5.9. *(a) Integral-collector system. (b) Harpiris Suncache integral-collector system (ICS). (c, d) Building-integrated integral-collector system.*

Flat-Plate Collectors—Warm or Cool Climates

A flat-plate solar thermal collector usually consists of copper tubes fitted to a flat absorber plate. Common setups include either a series of parallel tubes connected at each end by two pipes, the inlet and outlet manifolds, or a serpentine pipe. The pipe-collector assembly is contained within an insulated box and covered with low-iron tempered glass. These collectors may operate by thermosiphon action, with circulation provided by simple warm water rising to the collector tank, or with controllers and pumps. Simple thermosiphon systems with the water storage in an insulated tank above the collector are very common in many areas of the world. The pumped systems can be made more sustainable by using a solar panel to power the pump.

Systems that operate with water can freeze as a result of cold air and night sky radiant cooling. Freeze protection for these systems may be provided by draining the system in winter. In swing seasons, a drain-back design can reduce risk of freezing. With these collectors, the system is dry except when it is working. Drain-down control valves that would drain the collector when temperatures drop to dangerous levels have not proven very reliable. Flat plates can also use antifreeze solutions to move heat to a heat exchanger in the water heater or a solar tank that is connected to the solar water heater with a heat exchanger. When flat-plate collectors are empty, they get very hot, and service life can be limited. In some situations, flat plates may clear themselves of snow better than the highly insulated evacuated tube collectors, so check with local solar hot-water installers and users to see what will work best for you.

Thermosiphon systems are very simple and have a long service life, but active systems with controls and sensors are more likely to need maintenance. Although they may work twice as long as a gas-fired appliance, active systems have tended to fail after ten to fifteen years. Repairs are usually simple, but often not made. The quality of controls and pumps is improving thanks to European investment, regulations, and higher expectations, but systems with high-quality pumps, controls, and heat exchangers can be costly. The added complexity reduces energy performance over the lifetime of use as manufacturing and materials costs of pumps and controllers are added to operating cost, but these can be a good choice for many homeowners and businesses.

Evacuated-Tube Collectors— Any Climate, Best in Colder Climates

Evacuated-tube collectors (ETCs) were invented in the United States but first put into widespread use in China and Europe. An evacuated-tube collector includes a row of parallel transparent glass tubes that are evacuated like a vacuum bottle. They can be run in several different configurations, including single and double tube. In the double tube, the vacuum is in the area between the tubes. These can be set up in several different configurations, including heat pipe, U-pipe, and direct-flow systems. These collectors include an absorber and a working fluid that transfers the energy from the tube to the collector tank or a manifold with another fluid that transfers energy to the storage tank. Very high temperatures can be reached, so a tempering valve is essential. The high temperatures also make these a good backup for space heating using a fan coil or hydronic heating system, suitable for almost any climate.

The most common designs today use a "heat pipe" configuration to transfer energy to a manifold above, which then transfers the energy to the storage tank. These vacuum tubes are made with borosilicate glass and are expensive to manufacture. Borosilicate glass is tough and resists most impacts from hail and wind-driven debris. Many are modular, which makes it possible to assemble the collector on the roof. It also makes repairs easier; many can be repaired without draining the system.

These evacuated-tube systems perform well even in cold temperatures but may not provide an advantage in milder climates. Tests in Sydney, Australia, suggest the performance of water in an ETC system was about the same as a flat-plate collector (a flat plate may cost only a third as much per m²). The solar fraction in Sydney rose from 45 percent winter to 90 percent in summer, while it was 92 percent year-round in Darwin.

Costs are relatively low for Chinese models, but European systems can be pricey. Competition should increase quality and availability and reduce prices. In China, household hot-water demand is small and sizes are small. The cost is also low, as low as $100/m² with

Fig. 5.10. *Thermosiphon flat-plate collector and PV array.*

Fig. 5.11. *Evacuated-tube collector.*

an average cost about $235/m², while German systems were $700–$1,700/m². These systems, primarily evacuated tube, will often provide 100 percent of hot-water heating needs during the summer and about half in the winter.

Absorber Systems

A simple absorber system collects energy from the sun without glazing or an insulated box. These are the most commonly used systems in the United States, installed primarily for pool heating. These are often made of polypropylene and have performed well. We have also known people to develop a solar hot-water system using a food-grade dark-colored hose coiled on the roof. Not elegant, but inexpensive and effective.

What Kind?

The best system for a particular site will depend on the water-use pattern, the sun, the climate, and the user. Simple low-cost systems can have the best performance per dollar, but may require more participation and involvement. A home-built integral-collector system can be very effective and will last a long time if well made, but may have to be drained in winter. In a cooler climate, a high-quality commercial flat plate or an evacuated-tube collector installation should be trouble-free. Austria, with a fairly cold interior climate, for example, has very widespread use of solar hot-water systems, primarily flat-plate collectors. The ETC can perform well even in much colder climates.

How Big?

If you wish to develop a better understanding of sizing or plan to build and install your own system, you can develop a chart of daily use by looking at your gas-use pattern in summer (if you have a gas heater) or by maintaining a hot-water-use diary. Then refer to performance data for commercial systems from the Solar Rating and Certification Corporation and climate and sun data to fine-tune the sizing. Your supplier and installer can help you figure out the best type and size of collector and storage tanks for your use pattern and climate (see Gil and Parker, 2009*). Local experts can also help you determine the best kind of backup system, perhaps a gas-fired on-demand heater.

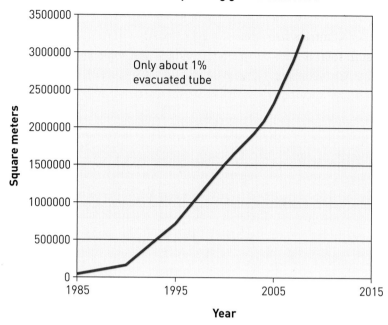

Fig. 5.12. *Installed collector area in Austria.*

Efficiency First

As with most other sustainable systems, the first step should always be improving efficiency and reducing use of hot water. Can you reduce hot-water demand by improving showerheads? Installing a horizontal-axis clothes washer that uses less water? Hand washing dishes with care instead of using a dishwasher? Using cold or warm water to wash most clothes?

Rules of Thumb

You can ask about the local "rules of thumb" to check on your calculations or commercial recommendations. In the Sunbelt, a recommendation might be for 1 square foot of collector for every 2 gallons of storage. In colder areas, it might be 1:1. In Davis, California, a good rule of thumb for integral-collector systems was for at least 30 gallons of collector capacity per person, with 2 to 3 gallons of tank per square foot of glazing. For Florida residences with a dishwasher and an automatic clothes washer, a rough rule of thumb is 10 square feet of flat-plate collector area per person, with 20 gallons of water storage per person.

A wide range of solar incentives and support programs are offered by states and the federal government in the United States. Other countries also offer very effective supports and assistance to install solar hot water. In Hawaii, Israel, and some areas in China, solar hot-water systems are required. DSIRE (www.dsireusa.org) is a comprehensive source of information on state, local, utility, and federal incentives and policies that promote renewable energy and energy efficiency. Established in 1995 and funded by the US Department of Energy, it is an ongoing project of the North Carolina Solar Center and the Interstate Renewable Energy Council.

Fig. 5.13. *Solar waters heaters in Athens, Greece. Greece leads the EU in solar water heater installations.*

Electricity Production BY STEVE HECKEROTH

We know that relying on coal, oil, and natural gas threatens our future with toxic pollution, global climate change, and social unrest caused by diminishing fuel supplies. Instead of relying on unsustainable fossil fuels, we must transform our economy and learn to thrive on the planet's abundant supply of renewable energy.

Our best and easiest option is solar energy, which is virtually inexhaustible. Most important, if we choose solar we don't have to wait for a new technology to save us. We already have the technology and energy resources we need to build a sustainable, solar electric economy that can cure our addiction to oil, stabilize the climate, and maintain our standard of living all at the same time. It is well past time to start seriously harnessing solar energy.

Fossil-Fueled Problems

Before you read on, take a moment to look at the two corresponding pie charts comparing the earth's estimated total reserves of nonrenewable energy resources with the annual renewable energy options. You'll see that the potential of solar energy dwarfs all other options, renewable or otherwise. To understand why a solar electric economy is our best option, let's look at the energy resources we currently depend on and compare them with the solar energy available to us.

- **Coal** is burned mainly to produce electricity, and coal-fired power plants produce more than half the electricity used in the United States. But burning coal has serious drawbacks. It

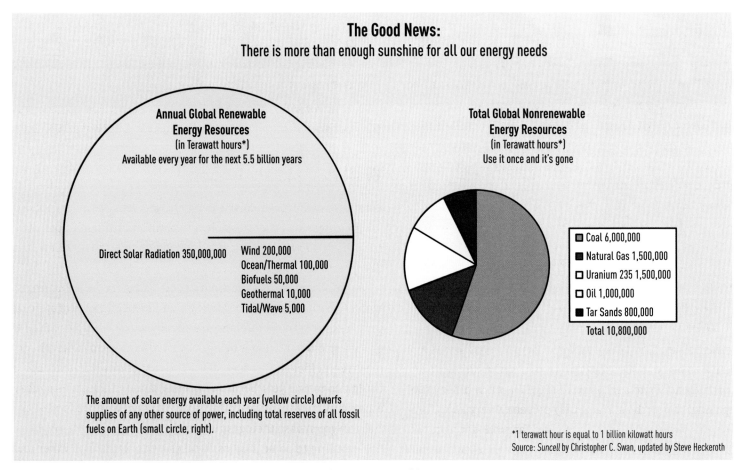

The Good News:
There is more than enough sunshine for all our energy needs

Annual Global Renewable Energy Resources
(in Terawatt hours*)
Available every year for the next 5.5 billion years

Direct Solar Radiation 350,000,000

Wind 200,000
Ocean/Thermal 100,000
Biofuels 50,000
Geothermal 10,000
Tidal/Wave 5,000

The amount of solar energy available each year (yellow circle) dwarfs supplies of any other source of power, including total reserves of all fossil fuels on Earth (small circle, right).

Total Global Nonrenewable Energy Resources
(in Terawatt hours*)
Use it once and it's gone

- Coal 6,000,000
- Natural Gas 1,500,000
- Uranium 235 1,500,000
- Oil 1,000,000
- Tar Sands 800,000

Total 10,800,000

*1 terawatt hour is equal to 1 billion kilowatt hours
Source: *Suncell* by Christopher C. Swan, updated by Steve Heckeroth

Fig. 5.14. *Available renewable energy resources compared to nonrenewable energy resources.*

releases carbon dioxide, nitrogen oxides, and sulfur dioxides that contribute to global warming. It also releases toxins such as mercury that were locked in the earth's crust over billions of years but are suddenly spewed into the atmosphere and degrade our air, water, and soil. The exhaust from burning coal contains more pollutants and global warming emissions per unit of energy produced than any other fossil fuel. The nitrogen oxides and sulfur dioxides also damage ecosystems in the form of nitrogen deposition and acid rain. In addition, the methods used to mine coal are destructive to the land and surrounding communities, and often dangerous for the miners.

To make things even worse, coal is very inefficient from a total energy perspective. It took billions of years of solar energy to form the coal we have today. And while coal is the most abundant fossil resource, the total amount of energy produced by burning all the coal on the planet would only be equal to the solar energy that strikes the earth in just six days.

- **Natural gas** supplies more than half the fuel used to heat buildings and about 15 percent of the electricity in the United States. Natural-gas-fired power plants only emit about half the pollutants produced by coal plants, as long as the fuel is extracted close to where it is burned. However, US natural gas extraction can no longer keep up with demand, so expensive and hazardous methods to liquefy and ship foreign natural gas are being devised. In the future, natural gas for the United States will have to be imported from countries such as Russia, Kazakhstan, Qatar, and Iran, which together have 60 percent of the world's reserves. When all the externalities, such as the cost and pollution caused by liquefying and transporting this fuel, are included, liquefied natural gas (LNG) is much more expensive than coal, and almost as dirty. Natural gas is the second most abundant fossil fuel, but its total potential energy is equivalent to only about a day and a half of sunshine striking the earth.

- **Nuclear** power plants fueled by radioactive isotopes of uranium produce 20 percent of the electricity used in the United States. When radioactive materials were sequestered and dispersed deep under the earth's surface, they presented very little threat to life. But we've made those materials far more dangerous by mining and concentrating them, with a very high cost to the mining communities in the American Southwest. The by-products

left over after a nuclear reaction are even more dangerous than the original isotopes. Nuclear power plants create hundreds of thousands of tons of radioactive waste that will continue to be a threat to life for longer than humans will walk the earth. As events in Japan have shown, nuclear power is very costly.

Even if the problem of radioactive waste could be solved, the recoverable world reserve of fissionable uranium is equivalent to less than one and a half days' worth of the energy striking the earth from the nuclear reaction of the sun.

- **Oil**-fired power plants have all but disappeared in the United States, but oil (diesel fuel and gasoline) powers nearly all our transportation. More than 60 percent of the oil consumed in the United States is now imported. Demand for petroleum will soon exceed world production capacity, and at that point the price of fuel will start to rise dramatically. We should be asking ourselves how we will cope with gas prices as they rise from $2.50 to $5 to $10 per gallon and keep rising. It's hard to imagine the hardship that will be faced by countries that remain addicted to oil, and even harder to imagine the suffering in countries that have oil, but do not have the strength to protect their resources or themselves.

Now consider that the entire recoverable world oil reserve is equivalent to the solar energy that strikes the earth in one day.

Biofuels and Hydrogen

Before we explore the solar electric future, let's consider biofuels and hydrogen as other possible alternatives. Although both have received good press lately, neither is a viable solution for our future energy needs.

Waste oil and biomass can make good transition fuels, but unless human population growth slows, we will need all existing agricultural land to grow food. There are already many examples of food-producing cropland that is being converted to crops to make ethanol to power inefficient flex-fuel SUVs. The cost of tortillas quadrupled in Mexico in one year because of rising demand for corn to make ethanol. Why should the world's poor struggle to afford food so the rich can greenwash their gas guzzlers?

According to some studies, it takes 1,000 gallons of water and more than a gallon equivalent of fossil fuel to produce 1 gallon of corn ethanol. And biofuels just aren't very efficient. When you do the math, the overall efficiency of biomass used as transportation fuel, from sun to wheel, is about 0.01 to 0.05 percent. In contrast, the overall efficiency of using solar panels to charge electric vehicles from sun to wheel is 3 to 10 percent. This means that solar-charged electric vehicles are from sixty to one thousand times more efficient than vehicles burning ethanol or biodiesel. Food should always trump fuel.

Hydrogen fuel-cell vehicles are no more efficient than biofuels. Hydrogen is much lighter than air, and it must be contained in order to keep it from escaping the earth's atmosphere, unless it is bound up in water or hydrocarbon molecules. The strong bonds that hold these molecules together take a significant amount of energy to break apart to extract hydrogen. Once the hydrogen is extracted, more energy is needed to compress it into a container that is small enough to store on a vehicle. In order for a fuel-cell vehicle to go 200 or 300 miles on a reasonably sized tank, the hydrogen must be stored in metal hydrates or at 10,000 psi in heavy containers.

Even after more than twenty years of development, fuel-cell vehicles still cost more than a million dollars each and don't last very long or go very far. And finally, it takes about four times more renewable energy to drive a fuel-cell vehicle than it does to charge the batteries in an electric vehicle to go the same distance. This is like the difference in fuel economy between a Hummer and a Prius. If you are wondering why hydrogen fuel-cell vehicles continue to receive billions of dollars in funding given all these barriers, the fact that 97 percent of all hydrogen is currently extracted from fossil fuels may give you a clue. There are powerful vested interests controlling our energy policy. Only informed citizens acting together can steer the best course.

Fig. 5.15. *Montara Elementary School lunchroom with building-integrated photovoltaics (BIPV) on the metal roof.*

A Bright Solar Electric Future

A solar electric economy is well within our reach. We're already generating solar electricity at the utility scale using powerful concentrating solar power technology. We're also generating electricity through wind energy, which is really an indirect form of solar energy because it's driven by temperature differences created as the earth rotates and is exposed to heat from the sun.

Simply incorporating the energy efficiency, conservation, and solar design strategies in this book can save up to 95 percent of the energy that is used in conventional buildings. With the addition of building-integrated photovoltaics, buildings can be turned into net energy producers.

The cost of conventional crystalline PV modules dropped more than 25 percent in 2009, and new thin-film technologies are pushing the manufacturing cost even lower. Crystalline PV modules are made by encapsulating wafers of highly refined silicon under rectangular sheets of glass framed with aluminum extrusions. Crystalline PV has dominated the industry since the discovery that sunlight could be turned into electricity. For more than fifty years, incremental improvements in conversion efficiency and manufacturing competence have resulted in glass-covered aluminum-framed modules capable of converting 12 to 18 percent of the solar radiation that strikes them into electricity. Crystalline modules still dominate in PV sales, but in the last few years most of the new development work has been focused on thin-film PV technologies.

Large-area thin-film PV modules and laminates have been commercially available since the 1990s, and the products now on the market have conversion efficiencies of between 6 and 11 percent. The higher the efficiency, the less area and support structure is required to produce the same amount of electricity. But the cost of manufacturing some thin-film PV technologies is much lower, and some thin films have much better high-heat and low-light performance than crystalline PV cells.

In 2005, more than 95 percent of the PV market was served by crystalline modules. Since then there has been a steady rise in the market share of thin-film PV. Hundreds of thin-film PV companies have entered various stages of product development or production. For every thin-film company having some measure of success, there are a dozen or more that are struggling with lack of adequate funding, development delays, or cost overruns. The vast

1. Amorphous silicon (a-Si), first developed in the 1970s by Stan Ovshinsky, the founder of Energy Conversion Devices (ECD), became the material of choice for charging consumer products such as watches and pocket calculators. ECD's solar division, Uni-Solar MI, produces a-Si, flexible thin film with a real-life conversion efficiency of 8.5 percent and a maximum lab efficiency of 13 percent. They offer a twenty-five-year warranty on their laminates when they are bonded to specified roofing products like standing-seam metal or flexible-membrane roofing. Despite relatively low efficiency and high manufactured cost (around $2/W), the unique ability of their laminates to be adhered to roofing products has made Uni-Solar the undisputed leader in flexible thin film for more than a decade. This dominance will probably soon be challenged by manufacturers that use less expensive deposition and encapsulation techniques or develop products that do not require roofing as a substrate. There are many companies attempting to compete in the rigid PV module market with a-Si deposited on glass, but none will likely survive unless they can challenge the low cost records set by First Solar with CdTe (see below).

2. Copper indium gallium diselenide (CIGS) was developed in the 1980s as a high-efficiency (11 percent real life, 20 percent lab) alternative to a-Si. The fact that CIGS degrades rapidly in the presence of moisture has led several well-funded companies including MiaSolé, Nanosolar, and SoloPower, all of California, to encapsulate their flexible cells under glass. This method of encapsulation squanders the lightweight flexible advantage of thin film and puts these companies in direct competition with every other PV module manufacturer in a race based only on cost. Global Solar in Arizona, HelioVolt in Texas, and Ascent Solar in Colorado are the leaders in flexible encapsulation but do not yet have commercially available products. Solyndra is the only CIGS manufacturer that

has a product ready for the building industry. To solve the moisture-degradation problem, Solyndra deposits CIGS on the inside of small glass cylinders and hermetically seals the ends. They have developed a method of fast installation of their finished modules on large flat roofs that does not require the roof penetrations or the heavy ballast needed for the installation of most glass PV modules. If the moisture-degradation issue can be solved, CIGS, with the highest potential efficiency of any thin film, will probably be the flexible thin-film material of choice.

3. Cadmium telluride (CdTe) was developed in the 1990s and has a real-life efficiency of about 11 percent and a maximum lab efficiency of 16 percent. First Solar in Ohio has recently overcome concerns about the toxicity of cadmium and is now the low-cost leader for large-scale ground-mount installations. The Swiss Federal Laboratories for Materials Testing and Research in Dubendorf, Switzerland, announced in August 2009 that it has improved the efficiency of flexible CdTe thin-film solar cells to 12.4 percent. This development has the potential to make CdTe the low-cost leader for flexible thin-film applications.

4. Organic thin films currently are low efficiency (less than 6 percent) and have a short life expectancy (under six years), so they are far from having a viable product for the building industry or to compete in the PV module market. G24 Innovations, a manufacturer of dye-sensitized solar cells, made the first-ever commercial shipment of PV modules in October 2009 to Hong Kong for use on bags and backpacks. Konarka in Massachusetts, another organic thin-film manufacturer, has purchased a Polaroid printing facility capable of producing 1 GW of flexible plastic PV per year. This manufacturing output is predicated on the company's goal to raise efficiency to 10 percent and the life of its product to twenty years by 2011.

majority of these companies are encapsulating their thin-film cells under glass. The glass PV module market is almost entirely driven by installed cost, so there will ultimately only be a few low-cost survivors.

Fig. 5.16. *Photovoltaic systems integrated into roofs.*

Utility-Scale Ground Mount

In 2009, First Solar was the undisputed leader in PV-module price reduction. They overcame concerns about the toxic cadmium used in their modules with a cradle-to-cradle recycling program and produced more than 1 GW (1 million kW) of cadmium telluride (CdTe) on glass modules with an average of 10.9 percent efficiency and excellent high-heat performance in 2009. First Solar's revenues have grown from $14 million in 2004 to $2 billion in 2009 as they have lowered their manufactured cost from $3/W to $0.93/W. This is close to half the manufactured cost of crystalline modules and most other thin-film PV products on the market. They also dramatically reduced the balance of system (BOS) costs to $1.20/W. The BOS includes wiring, inverters, and mounting structures, essentially everything but the PV modules.

Their winning cost-cutting approach also includes reducing the permitting and installation time from years to months on utility-scale projects. Initial side-by-side comparisons done by Fat Spaniel show a 10 to 15 percent savings in installed cost with First Solar modules and about 10 percent greater output than crystalline modules with the same rated capacity. In August 2009, Southern California Edison signed a contract for 500 MW of First Solar modules for a desert installation capable of powering 170,000 homes. Then in September, First Solar announced plans for a 2 GW installation in China. By 2014, First Solar is committed to increasing

the efficiency of their modules to 15 percent, decreasing their manufactured cost to $0.52/W, and decreasing their BOS cost to $0.95/W. If First Solar is successful in meeting these goals, sometime early in the next decade utility-scale thin-film PV will take a place alongside wind and concentrating solar power (CSP) to make the construction of new fossil or nuclear power plants a thing of the past.

A future with utility-scale solar power plants is a step in the right direction, but it still leaves control of power production in the hands of relatively few large corporate and municipal utilities. In addition, getting the power from areas that have the best solar resource, like the Southwest, to the heavily populated areas of the country that have less sunshine would require a vast new network of transmission and distribution lines along with a huge buffering infrastructure to store excess power when demand is low and release power when it is needed. The monetary and environmental cost of this scale of new infrastructure will be a significant obstacle to centralized power production.

Roof-Mount Distributed Generation

The alternative to centralized power production is distributed generation (DG). DG can make the existing grid operate more efficiently and limit the need for a huge expense in installing new transmission and buffering infrastructure by producing power where it is used. There is enough existing sunbathed roof and parking-lot area that could be covered with PV arrays to provide all the electricity used in buildings and to charge a national fleet of plug-in vehicles. The same mass adoption that made room-size mainframe computers give way to laptop PCs will make huge central power plants give way to rooftop PVs.

Fig. 5.17. *(a) DG on the Google headquarters. (b) DG on residential roofs in Japan.*

Net Metering

Net-metering laws that allow the energy produced by residential and commercial PV installations to be fed into the grid are now in place in almost every state. Net metering is a win–win–win for the utility, building owners, and all life on the planet. The utility adds more clean power to its network from a power source located close to demand centers, reducing not only the need to build new plants to meet peak demands but also the load on distribution lines. The process is a win for the building owner, who doesn't need a bank of batteries to store electricity to power the household at night or during overcast days. Instead the system uses the utility grid as a storage battery. And with every PV installation there are less CO_2 emissions, and we all breathe a little easier.

Here's how net metering works: When a solar electric rooftop produces more electricity than the household needs (at midday when the family is away at work and school), electricity is sent to the utility grid, and the home's meter runs backward. When the household needs more electricity than the rooftop system produces (at night), it is drawn from the utility grid and the electrical meter runs forward. The net difference between electricity exported to the grid and grid electricity used forms the basis for the homeowner's electric bill. In many states, net metering is annualized: The utility credits solar electricity produced by the rooftop system during the summer against electricity needed from the grid during the winter. Some states like California have Time of Use (TOU) net metering that allows PV owners to be compensated at a much higher summer afternoon rate when their array is at peak performance. It is time to make the advantages of net metering available to everyone with a national standard that would incorporate the best from the individual state programs.

Incentive Programs

Many states also have incentive programs for installing solar power and hot water, and there is currently a 30 percent federal tax credit to offset the cost of PV installations that will expire in 2016 unless it is renewed. There is a very helpful Web site (www.dsireusa.org) that lists all the incentives, programs, and laws that pertain to renewable energy in every part of the country. States such as New Jersey and Pennsylvania have programs that can make PV installations cash-positive from day one.

Not so long ago, the United States led the world in PV installations, but today places like Japan, Germany, and Spain are well ahead of the United States in installed capacity. Many countries in Europe have encouraged solar installations by offering low- or no-interest loan programs that can be paid off with premiums paid for electricity from clean renewable sources like the sun. These payments for energy produced from renewables, called feed-in tariffs (FITs), have been so successful that solar roofs are common in some countries. One in five roofs are covered with PV in the state of Bavaria, Germany, and 15 percent of Bavarians' electricity comes from solar energy. By comparison, California, with over 60 percent of the PV installations in the United States, gets less than 1 percent of its electricity from the sun.

To date, most of the federal stimulus money earmarked for renewables, is going to utility-scale projects. It will take citizen action to convince Washington that these funds should be redirected to revolving low- or no-interest loans and FITs. These programs would cost the taxpayers less money and promote true solar independence.

Many of the countries that have used FITs to stimulate renewable-energy installations have acknowledged the benefits of DG by offering a higher payment for PV that is installed on buildings. Germany was the first to establish a FIT and started with a program that paid $0.74/kWh for electricity for DG installed on buildings and $0.52/kWh for electricity from ground-mount installations. Ontario, Canada, now has one of North America's first FITs, which pays up to $0.80/kWh for roof-mount PV and only $0.44/kWh for PV mounted on the ground. France recently introduced a FIT that pays $0.38/kWh for ground mount and $0.57/kWh for PV mounted on commercial buildings. The higher payment for PV mounted on buildings is intended to help businesses, factories, and farmers take profitable advantage of their large rooftops. France also has a new category that pays $0.70/kWh for building-integrated photovoltaics (BIPV) to recognize and promote the synergies and cost savings available when PV materials are used to replace conventional building materials in parts of the building envelope such as the roofing, skylights, awnings, or facades. Finally, the advantages of using the sunbathed portions of a building's skin to generate energy are starting to be understood and supported.

Fig. 5.18. *Habitat for Humanity/Uni-Solar project in Sacramento, California.*

Building-Integrated Photovoltaics (BIPV)

The idea of BIPV is not new. Architects like Steven Strong and Richard Schoen have been using PV modules as roofing since the early 1980s, but using the glass modules that were available at that time was both challenging and expensive. Glass is transparent, weatherproof, and long lasting, but it can shatter, and it is not an ideal roofing material.

There are applications where glass PV modules can replace existing architectural elements such as awnings and facades. A few companies produce thin-film modules that can be used as windows with various degrees of transparency. These modules, like their crystalline cousins, come at a fairly high cost, but in urban areas at high latitudes the walls of multistory buildings receive more solar radiation than their roofs, so glass modules will continue to be used for a few applications. Having products for their high-end BIPV applications is important, but imagine the potential of being able to cover the solar-exposed surface of any building with low-cost roofing or siding that generates electricity at competitive costs.

Uni-Solar's amorphous silicon (a-Si) thin-film laminates have been demonstrating the advantages of lightweight flexible solar cells on rooftop applications since 1997 with hundreds of megawatts of installations bonded to roofing substrates. In the late 1990s, Uni-Solar started the transition from framed modules to BIPV with flexible laminates bonded to metal roofing and strips of thin-film cells that mimicked asphalt shingles. Uni-Solar's shingles were difficult to install and the traditional adhesives used in the PV industry were flammable, so the product never got into mass production and was

eventually discontinued. In 2001, Southern California Roofing spun off Solar Integrated Technologies (SIT) and developed a process for bonding Uni-Solar laminates to membrane roofing. SIT became the first of many roofing companies to work with PV manufacturers to make products that serve the dual function of weather-tight surface and power generation.

Fig. 5.19. *A Solar Integrated Technologies project in Los Angeles, California.*

Fig. 5.20. *SRS Energy's Solé Power Tile, which incorporates Uni-Solar cells.*

In January 2009, Carlisle Energy Services, a newly formed division of Carlisle Construction Materials, a leading manufacturer of energy-efficient single-ply commercial roofing systems, announced a multi-year agreement to purchase Uni-Solar laminates. In July 2009, Johns Manville, a leading global manufacturer of single-ply, built-up, and modified bitumen roofing-membrane systems, announced the formation of a new business entity called E3 Company and a multiyear agreement to purchase Uni-Solar laminates. In August 2009, Uni-Solar announced a merger with SIT and in October 2009, the merged company announced the sale of 4.8 MW of PV laminates to be installed on eight large commercial rooftops in Barcelona, Spain. Also in October, CertainTeed, a leading North American manufacturer of asphalt shingles, announced a joint agreement with Uni-Solar to develop roof-integrated PV products for the residential market. *The New York Times* ran an article in October 2009 on SRS Energy's Solé Power Tile, which incorporates Uni-Solar cells into a curved Spanish tile roof.

In addition to alliances between roofing companies and PV manufacturers, major chemical companies such as BASF, DuPont, 3M, and Dow have all formed solar divisions to improve the transparency, durability, and fire resistance of the materials used to encapsulate PV cells. In September 2009, Dow Building Solutions announced that they are working with Global Solar, a leading manufacturer of CIGS flexible thin-film cells, to develop 15.5 percent efficient solar roofing shingles.

Electric Vehicles and Plug-In Hybrids

The other development that will bring solar energy to the mainstream is the plug-in vehicles that are now available on showroom floors. Given the choice between paying 10 cents or more a mile for fuel in a polluting, fossil-fuel combustion car and 1 to 3 cents to go the same distance in a clean EV, people should promptly start adopting plug-ins and plug-in hybrids. BIPV installations will follow as a popular way to achieve energy independence and to provide clean electricity for battery charging.

Most people don't realize how much energy they use in their cars. A gallon of gasoline is 30 kWh of concentrated solar energy that was hundreds of millions of years in the making. About 30 kWh is consumed each day in the average US home. So if you burn more than a gallon of gasoline a day, you could be using more energy in your car than you are in your home.

Fortunately, electric-vehicle drivetrains are inherently five to ten times more efficient than internal combustion engines, so switching to EVs will require far less energy than fossil-fueled transportation. Even if the electricity to power EVs comes from fossil-fueled power plants, emissions are much lower per mile traveled than with internal combustion engines, and they produce no greenhouse gases at the tailpipe. In addition, electric vehicles can be charged directly from renewable sources, eliminating emissions altogether.

One of the main excuses the auto industry offers for the lack of electric vehicles is that "the batteries are not developed yet." But consider how quickly cell phone batteries developed, transforming mobile phones from heavy, bulky, short-lived nuisances to amazingly light, small, and long-lasting necessities. The oil companies are doing a good job of protecting the American consumer from "dangerous" batteries, but in parts of the world where oil companies have less control, large-format battery development is progressing very rapidly. The collapse of the American auto companies is at least partially the result of the petroleum industry's ability to stifle clean technology development. As affordable EVs come on the market, despite Big Oil's best efforts, and word gets out that you can do your commute with the same comfort and convenience for 2 cents a mile instead of 10 cents, even billions of dollars in advertising won't stop the revolution. Don't wait, or you'll be on a waiting list. Electric scooters and trucks are also on the way. China now has 120 million electric scooters in use. Urban trucks and transfer vehicles are well suited for electric power, with clean, low-cost, and high-torque motors well suited for short trips. Flywheels may also prove valuable in some applications.

Fig. 5.21. *Toyota RAV4 EV and solar-charging shed on the Heckeroth Homestead, Albion, California.*

Agriculture and Electric Tractors

Experts have estimated that it takes eight to ten units of fossil energy to put one unit of food energy on American tables, and that it takes the annual equivalent of 10 barrels of oil to feed each person in the United States. It is frightening to imagine what will happen as oil supplies dwindle and prices rise. Farm machinery, like almost all modes of transportation, is totally dependent on oil.

The good news is that not only can tractors run on electricity, they make even more sense than other EVs because they can use battery weight for increased traction, and they operate at slower speeds. A solar-charged electric tractor can quietly accomplish all the tasks necessary to maintain productivity on a farm.

Dealing with the rising cost of mobility and energy are huge challenges, but the biggest challenge facing humanity may be maintaining an affordable and nourishing food supply. We can have fresher and more nourishing food without fossil fuels. What it will take is public support for a switch to local food production on small organic farms using solar irrigation pumps and solar-charged electric tractors.

We Have the Power

It's easy to feel confused, cynical, and even hopeless about the state of the planet these days. But we are excited and optimistic because we know the technology now exists that will allow us to wean ourselves from fossil fuels and move to a renewable solar electric energy system.

Fig. 5.22. *SolTrac and solar-charging shed on the Heckeroth Homestead.*

Yes, solar panels are still too expensive for many. But ten years ago, nobody gave hybrid cars a chance of succeeding. Today, the Toyota Prius is the hottest thing going. Plug-in hybrids and a wide range of all-electric options are now available. For every new development that has been announced in the press, there are dozens more in the works that will make future generations wonder why people ever burned fossil fuels to make energy.

If we work together and demand that our government set a wise energy policy and use taxes to support the right renewable energy options, we can put the brakes on climate change and enjoy clean, truly green energy sources and a healthy planet.

Your Solar Electric System

The design and detailing of a solar electric system is not difficult, but it is important to get it right for safety and performance. Working with an experienced contractor is often a good idea. The general steps include:

1. Minimizing energy demand. It is cheaper to conserve than to generate electricity. Smaller, more efficient appliances and minimal parasitic losses are essential to reduce demand. Develop a load profile of your current use as a starter, then rethink and revise to fit a solar electric lifestyle. This is less important if you are doing a grid-tied system—but essential for a stand-alone system. Time for that Sun Frost refrigerator! Many off-grid rural residents do just fine with a 1 kW PV array that might produce only 5 kWh a day (one-quarter to one-tenth the energy use in many new homes).

2. Understanding sun availability and microclimate. When and where does the sun reach your home or site? Solar-site evaluation is not difficult once you understand the sun paths through the year. A solar-site selector or other tool can help. Full sun is best, but partial shading can be managed by choosing a more flexible inverter or different wiring configuration. Roof, ground, and, more rarely, wall mounting may make sense. Understanding the site microclimate, wind speeds, snow loads, highest and lowest temperatures, frequency of lightning strikes, cloudiness, and sun availability can help guide the design process. Could you add microhydro or wind? For more details on step 1 and 2, see "Getting Started with Renewable Energy: Professional Load Analysis and Site

Survey" from *Home Power* magazine, www.homepower.com /webextras.

3. Developing, with this information, a plan for your home solar electric system. Will it be stand-alone, grid-tied, or grid-tied with batteries? Will it be minimalist ($3,000) or full capability ($30,000)? Stand-alone usually makes sense primarily where the building is far from a power line and where power line installation costs would equal or exceed the cost of a solar system. What kind of PV panels will be used? Tracking or fixed? Thin film on metal roofing, crystalline glass, or some other option? Will the system be 12, 24, or 48 volts? Wire size? Battery bank size? AC or DC? Inverters? Controllers? Monitoring system? Lightning protection?

4. Doing a full economic analysis and exploring the availability of rebates and incentives comes next. Can you afford the system? What is the current cost? Maintenance cost? Future cost? What are the steps to qualify for rebates?

5. Determining whether you will be self-installing, hiring a contractor, or working with a contractor. What are the code requirements, incentive requirements (some require certified systems), skill and time constraints? Make sure all information needed for incentives is collected and maintained. Pull permits, construct, manage inspections, and complete.

6. Testing and refining the operation of the system. Some tuning is often needed to improve efficiency and performance.

7. Enjoying, monitoring, and maintaining your energy independence.

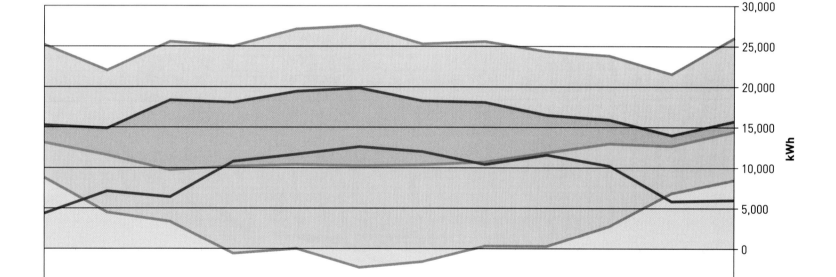

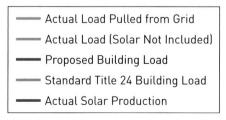

Fig. 5.23. *Electricity consumption analysis for on-site generation with rooftop PVs.*

Rainwater and Water-Use Management for Low-Impact Development

Low-impact development (LID) is characterized by having a high percentage of pervious surfaces; regenerative, native, or edible landscaping; water filtration and filtration of on-site pollutants; and surface drainage that recharges the local aquifer or is harvested for use.

High-impact development (HID) is characterized by having high percentages of impervious surfaces, landscaping that is mostly decorative, stormwater issues and pollution that have typically been handled by concrete curbs, pipes, and canals.

Rainwater Harvesting and Use

Rainwater or snowfall is often an important on-site resource. Ideally a building and site will be designed to live with the precipitation that falls on-site—without imports. Building and site-design choices determine how efficiently these resources are captured for use. Water may be captured and stored for landscaping use by site-development choices, or captured for use in the home or garden from the built surfaces. This salt-free and generally fairly pure water is a

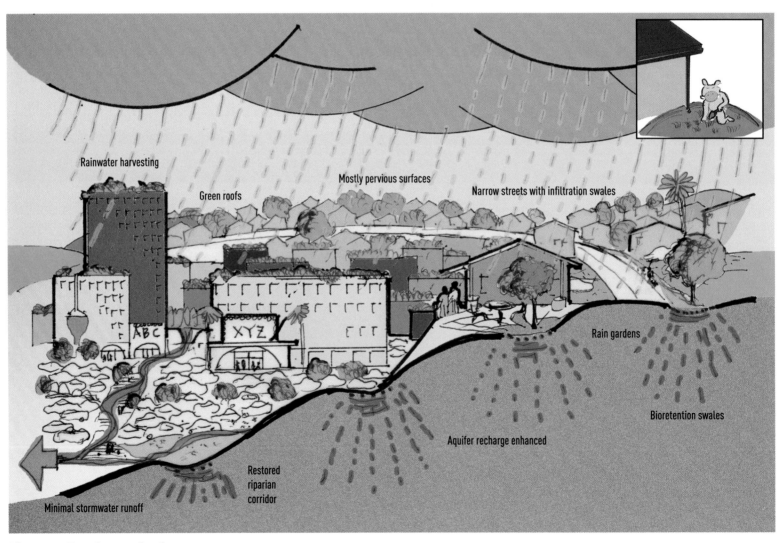

Fig. 5.24. *Low-impact development.*

tremendous resource that is often neglected and wasted. Capturing rainwater for use on-site reduces the adverse impact of impervious surfaces on stormwater runoff and flooding.

Materials don't matter much if the water is intended for landscaping use, but if water is collected for drinking, the choice of catchment materials is important. Some cities and counties, like Tucson and Santa Fe, now require rainwater collection for some types of development. Texas was the first state in the United States to embrace rainwater harvesting, but Hawaii, North Carolina, and many other states are now catching up. North Carolina and the Florida Keys now have rebate programs. Parts of Australia have relied on rainwater harvesting for many decades, and many building codes now require catchment and storage systems, with tanks up to 800 gallons required on the Gold Coast. Europe and the UK have also become much more interested in rainwater harvesting after recent droughts. Rebates or tax credits are being offered in more areas every year. As interest grows, contractors emerge to provide turnkey rainwater harvesting solutions. Communities that charge a stormwater runoff fee can also encourage rainwater harvesting if the runoff reduction is recognized in lower fees. Sadly, in many areas of the United States and other developed countries, building officials may obstruct use of this important resource; the stormwater problem is rarely seen as a rainwater harvesting opportunity, and in some areas rainwater harvesting has been deemed illegal.

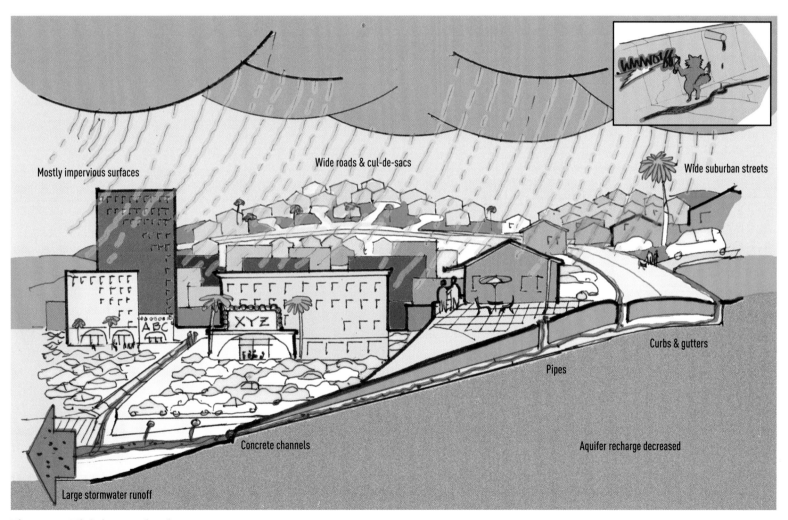

Fig. 5.25. *High-impact development.*

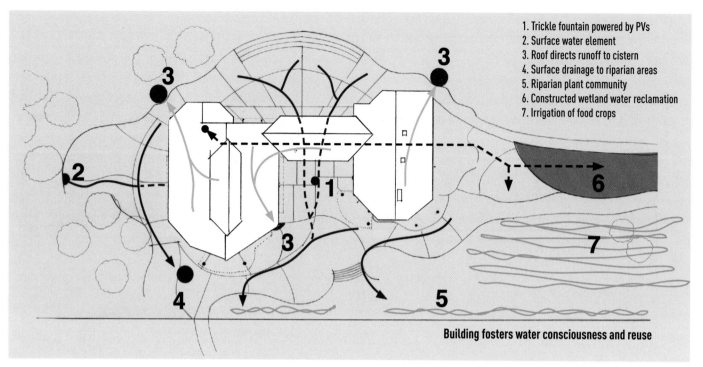

1. Trickle fountain powered by PVs
2. Surface water element
3. Roof directs runoff to cistern
4. Surface drainage to riparian areas
5. Riparian plant community
6. Constructed wetland water reclamation
7. Irrigation of food crops

Building fosters water consciousness and reuse

Fig. 5.26. *San Luis Obispo Botanical Garden Education Center fosters water consciousness and reuse.*

Landscape Design for Rainwater Capture

Landscape design for rainwater capture and use can include use of permeable (pervious) pavement or cement for driveways, patios, and sidewalks, living roofs, and ground shaping to hold rainwater so it can infiltrate into the soil. Permeable pavements are made by reducing the amount of fine material in the mix of concrete or asphalt. Once contractors become familiar with the process, the costs are comparable. In Europe, these materials are sometimes used even on freeways and major highways. Rectangular stone paving (setts), pavers, and bricks with porous fill in the spaces between pieces can also help retain and capture rainwater.

Rainwater capture on the development or city scale is often more effective using aboveground drainage systems. Swales, berms, check dams, infiltration basins, and depressions can be used to slow or capture runoff. Gravel infiltration beds under parking lots or impermeable surfaces can also be created. Streets, sidewalks, and natural rock outcrops can also be used to collect and channel water to landscaping areas. Landscaping plant choices can also improve rainwater capture and use. These natural rainwater management approaches are typically less costly than stormwater pipe systems and should be a first priority in drier areas where water is in short supply. A living roof can be used to capture and hold rainwater on a building's roof.

Buildings

Building design for rainwater capture and use typically includes a catchment area (usually the roof), conveyance systems (gutters, downspouts, and piping), possibly a filter or two, storage (tanks or cisterns), and some method for redistributing the water for use. The best roof materials are coated steel or aluminum (to reduce zinc or aluminum leaching), slate, clay, or cement tile, or other durable materials. Asphalt shingles are less than ideal, as they can contribute grit and chemical compounds to the system, but they have been used. Copper and lead flashing should be eliminated to reduce leaching. Catchments of metal roofing material or concrete can also be created specifically to capture water.

Rainwater Collection

Gutters are commonly used to collect water from the roof. Gutters must be sloped for good drainage (often suggested as minimum 1/16-inch drop per foot of run). Gutters should be well mounted and durable. Gutter screens can help keep debris out of the water.

Fig. 5.27. *Rainwater harvesting, Village Homes in Davis, California. The city resisted aboveground drainage—but was finally convinced to try it. After the first flooding rainfall, only Village Homes experienced no problems and the city revised its policies.*

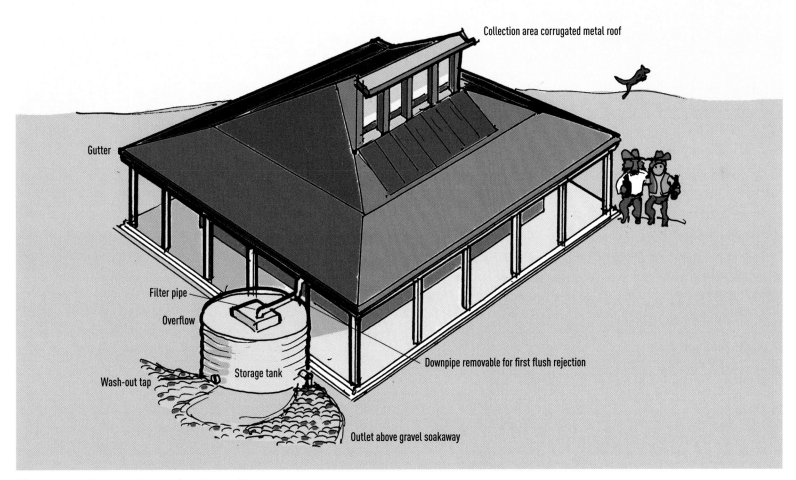

Fig. 5.28. *Rainwater harvesting, Australia.*

Downspouts should be sized for typical rain intensity, often 1 square inch of downspout opening for every 100 square feet of roof area. Rough filtering can be done at the gutter-to-pipe transition with a sloped screen. The WISY company in Germany has developed a clever filtering system for rainwater using a fine-mesh filter that is widely used in Europe.

First-flush filtering is desirable to eliminate dirt, bird droppings, and other deposition on the roof. A wide range of first-flush filters have been developed. One common type runs water into a chamber that must fill before the water can run into the cistern or tank. In some cases a floating ball rises and seals the chamber so the water from the now clean roof runs by. The first-flush chamber usually has a slow drip or outlet so that it will be empty by the time of the next rainfall. A manual switch can be used in areas with pronounced seasonal rainfall. The first rainfall of the season might all be diverted to wash off months of dust and deposits.

Pipe Runs

Pipe runs to the tank or cistern should be sloped sufficiently and run without complex turns or drops that can lead to clogs. Use large pipe diameters to reduce overflow and blockage. Provide cleanouts as needed. Screen or mesh should be in place to prevent mosquitoes from breeding in pipes or tanks. A variety of system configurations can be used to suit aboveground or belowground storage and pressurization needs. An aboveground tank can be more challenging to reach from gutters and may lead to a collector pipe array that is not attractive. A belowground tank is easier to fill from a buried collector system and more attractive, but it's harder to clean and repair. A larger home might have a belowground tank in front, and an aboveground tank in the back or a side yard. A belowground tank can be pumped through a filter system up to a use tank to provide a gravity head.

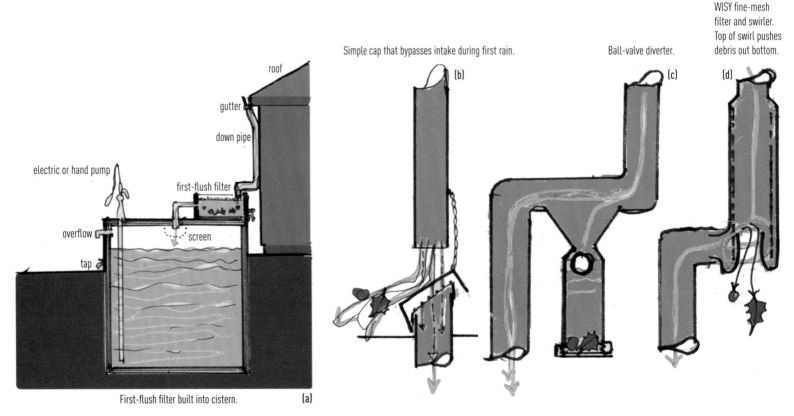

Fig. 5.29. *(a) First-flush filtering. (b) Metal cap serves as first-flush diverter (seasonal). (c) Ball-valve diverter. (d) Commercial filter system.*

Fig. 5.30. *Storage tanks in Sweden, Australia, and the UK.*

Fig. 5.31. *Access hatch. A childproof lock should be installed.*

The storage tank or cistern is sized to fit the rainfall and use patterns. Tanks can be located above- or belowground, made of concrete, steel, polypropylene, food-grade polyethylene, or other materials. They can be incorporated in the house as thermal mass,

or installed in an insulated shelter and used as a heating or cooling source. A cistern or tank can be installed in the backyard or under a patio or courtyard. In a retrofit situation, a small swimming pool can be converted into a cistern by adding an appropriate cover.

Storage should be durable and watertight with a clean, smooth interior surface. It should be fully accessible through a manhole for cleaning and silt removal. The cistern should be covered to keep children and critters out and prevent mosquito breeding and algal growth. A lock should be installed to keep children out. Two or more cisterns can be used to improve water quality and to allow servicing one of the units without losing the operation of the system.

WATER TERMS

- 1 cubic foot = 7.48 gallons or 28.3 liters.
- 1 acre foot = 325,829 gallons, or 1,233 cubic meters, or 1,233,000 liters.
- 1 gallon = 3.785 liters.
- 1 cubic meter = 1,000 liters or 264.2 gallons.
- 1 inch of rain delivers about 0.62 gallon per square foot; 10 inches of rain on a 2,000-square-foot roof will provide about 12,000 gallons.

Maintenance

A rainwater system requires maintenance and care. It is a living system, and to operate efficiently, it needs to be cleaned and cared for properly. The gutters will need to be cleaned, roughing filters will need to be cleaned, and silt may need to be removed from the cistern periodically. Careful maintenance is particularly important if rainwater will be used for drinking water. Approved water-quality testing may be required for home systems that use the water for drinking water, and will almost certainly be required for community systems.

Cistern Sizing

Storage sizing depends on the patterns of use and rainfall. The more even the rainfall pattern is, the smaller the tanks can be, particularly if use is regular as well. Storage for just a couple of weeks of use may be sufficient if it rains almost every day (1,000 gallons). A 4-foot-deep cistern built under a 200-square-foot patio will hold about 6,000 gallons.

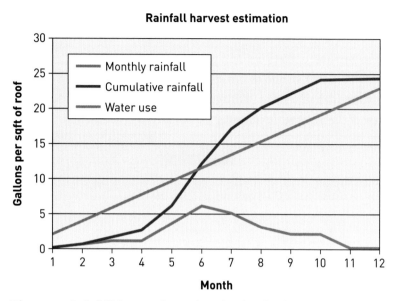

Fig. 5.32. *Rainfall-harvesting estimation by plotting use and collection.*

Table 5.1. *Water use in the home and outside varies widely locally and globally. Understanding water resources and uses is necessary for designing a sustainable water supply system that may entail rainwater, gray-water, and perhaps black-water use.*

Location	gallons/day/capita
Kenya drylands	<2 gallons
Beijing	40
Bainbridge house (SD)	51
Mexico City	96
Tucson, AZ	100
Lakeside water district (SD)	110
San Diego	157
Phoenix, AZ	260
Rancho Santa Fe (SD)	571

In areas with strong seasonal rainfall patterns (dry winter or dry summer) and recurrent droughts, bigger tanks are needed. In San Diego, some early homes had 35,000 gallons of storage. For more detailed procedures on estimating size, see Gould and Nissen-Petersen (2003*).

You can estimate the potential for rainfall harvesting and the cistern size needed by plotting average likely rainfall harvest per month and contrasting this with water demand. Figure 5.32 shows a strong seasonal rainfall pattern. A large cistern would be needed to carry this house through the dry months and a drier-than-average year. For a home with a 1,200-square-foot roof, the 5-gallon-per-square-foot deficit would suggest at least a 6,000-gallon tank, but a tank twice as large would be even better to allow for a drier-than-average year.

Gray-Water Harvesting and Use

Following the material flows through a house or building offers many opportunities for turning perceived wastes into resources. Water that has been made dirty or "gray" by use in a sink, shower, or laundry is a good example. Reuse of some types of gray water is technically simple, but may be restricted by public policy. The types of gray water produced by a building include a wide range of physical, chemical, and biological loading—as we can imagine by comparing the shower, sink, and laundry water of a retired couple that buys only "organic and readily biodegradable soaps and cleaners" with a young family with three children in cloth diapers and little time, money, or inclination to seek out safe cleaners and soaps. These differences contribute to the regulatory pressure from health departments for "Cadillac systems," but growing water shortages and improved understanding of the best gray-water practices are encouraging many jurisdictions and states to encourage gray-water use and to support personal initiatives to reduce environmental impacts of living.

The water flows out of a home include clean water, gray water, black water, and yellow water. Clean water and gray water will be discussed in this section.

Clean Water

Water run while warming water for a shower or cleaning dishes, drip from a refrigerator compressor, and reverse-osmosis drain water is often completely clean. This should be captured for reuse in toilet flushing or landscaping. Return pipe systems are available to avoid losing water during warm-up. Hot-water recirculation systems are popular for delivering hot water in a timely and water-conserving fashion, but they do require a pump and additional energy to recirculate the water. Locating the water heater near major uses can reduce water waste.

Gray Water

Gray water may be used for landscape irrigation and toilet flushing depending on local regulations. Some areas will even allow kitchen-sink water to feed into the gray-water system, but this usually only occurs when there is treatment of the gray water before it is reused or sent into irrigation pipes.

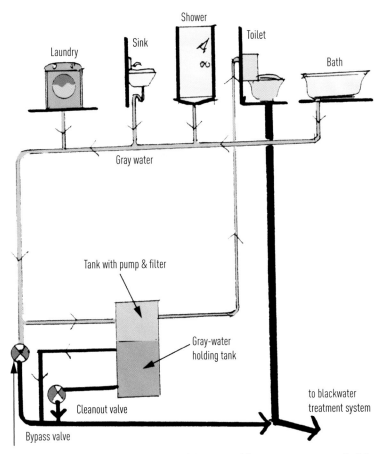

Fig. 5.33. *The gray-water system illustrated here uses a pump, holding tank, and filtration to reuse large quantities of gray water for toilet flushing. Excess gray water must be able to be directed to the septic or sewer system via a bypass valve. Plumbers are usually able to deal with gray-water plumbing inside a building, and landscape installers are able to distribute the gray water into the landscape.*

Fig. 5.34. *Available in Japan are dual flush, gray-water-integrated toilets that provide water for hand washing via a faucet and washbasin. Rinse water then fills the toilet tank and is used for the next flush. Dual plumbing is not required for this integrated system.*

Gray water has been integrated into some innovative toilets that utilize a faucet and washbasin on the top of the toilet's holding tank. When the toilet is flushed, the water used to refill the tank prior to the next flush is directed through the faucet for hand washing, then it drains via the washbasin into the toilet's holding tank. This type of integrated gray-water system is popular in Japan and is one of the only systems that does not require dual plumbing.

Water from a washing machine using minimal amounts of a safe detergent to clean lightly soiled clothes is relatively clean in the wash cycle and even cleaner in the rinse cycle. My parents used this water for landscape watering for more than fifty years without a problem. Water from a shower or bath can also be fairly clean if safe soaps and shampoos are used. A pre-wash, following Japanese practice before entering the *furo,* would further reduce loading in the water. However, when users are sick, the load of viruses, bacteria, or parasites may increase.

If gray water is used for irrigation, it should be distributed subsurface and not sprayed overhead. It is also not recommended for use on certain edible plants, but this will vary depending on local code and risk factors.

Health Risks and Challenges from Gray-Water Use

Gray water is typically not regulated by the building, water, or stormwater departments, but by the health department. The health department is generally not interested in the problem of water supply or cost, but narrowly focused on eliminating or reducing the risk of disease. The health risks of using gray water are minimal—this is, after all, the water you just bathed in, or the residue from clothes you were wearing. A recent study of simple gray-water reuse systems in Jordan found no increase in infection.

There is no question that gray water can end up containing some infectious organisms, but so can city drinking water systems (David's parents both got giardiasis from their city water system) and rainwater harvesting systems. It is possible to virtually eliminate pathways for infecting people from gray water by preventing human contact with gray water before purification and purifying gray water with healthy topsoil or other treatments.

If a flush toilet is required by law, it may be possible to use gray water for the toilet (some areas allow it; most do not at the moment). Gray water is best suited for subsurface irrigation of nonedible landscape plants or trees and shrubs where fruit will never contact the soil surface. Gray water can play a major role in watering landscapes even in very arid environments if salt, chloride, and boron levels in source water are not too high. Harvested rainwater can be used to dilute gray-water salt concentrations.

The amount of gray, black, and clean water a house will produce will depend on the occupants, their behavior, and the design of the house or building. The demand will also depend on the landscaping and gardening choices made. Average uses within a home vary nationally, regionally, and locally depending on the price of water,

the attitude of the occupants, and the style of development. *Note:* Figure 5.36 and table 5.2 neglect the clean-water flow that can be significant (perhaps 5 percent) with home designs where the point of hot-water use is a long way from the water heater.

A single-family household in Southern California coastal areas uses 38 percent of its total water budget outside, but in desert cities and neighborhoods with larger lots this can rise to 80 percent or more. Multifamily units have less outside landscaping, and use drops to 20 percent or less. Institution and commercial use is extremely variable.

Advantages of Gray-Water Use

The most obvious advantage of domestic gray-water use is that it replaces cleaner potable water that may have been shipped hundreds of miles at a very high economic and ecological cost. In places like San Diego, water from reclamation has the lowest energy cost, see figure 5.35. By storing winter gray water for use during the hot-dry summer months, sufficient gray water was captured to meet the full Casa del Agua landscape irrigation demand. Cohen (2009) suggests that a simpler system using light gray water (Tiers 1 and 2, see table 5.2) could meet about 84 percent of outdoor residential water use without the need for treatment under current California regulations. Recycling all Tier 1 and 2 gray water would be sufficient to meet the full demand of outdoor water use in coastal Southern California.

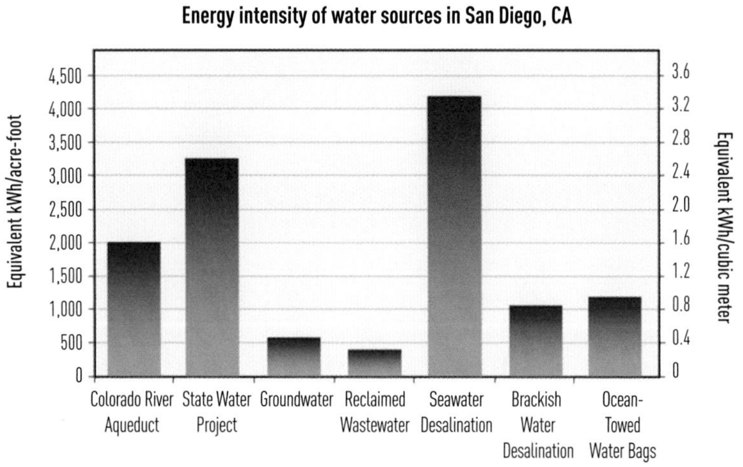

Fig. 5.35. *Energy intensity of water sources in San Diego, California. Source: Pacific Institute, Wolff et al., 2004.*

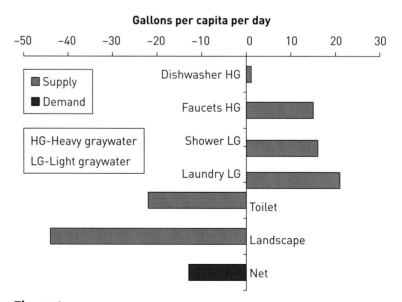

Fig. 5.36.

Table 5.2. *How big is the resource?*

Use within the home	EPA %	Southern CA %	Category	Tier
Toilet	26.7	25.0	Blackwater	
Clothes washer	21.7	24.0	Light gray	1
Shower and bath	17.6	18.0	Light to heavy gray	2
Sinks	16.7	17.0	Light to heavy gray	3
Dishwasher	1.4	1.3	Heavier gray	3
Other domestic	2.2	15.0	Variable	

Adding heavy gray water would meet up to 41 percent of toilet-water use, provided this heavy gray water undergoes treatment before use. The estimated residential per-capita potable-water savings range from 16 to 40 percent for Tiers 1–3. It works at the scale of a home, but what if more homes got involved? With a participation rate of only 10 percent, the potable-water savings for the South Coast Hydrologic Region would range from about 40 to 100 million gallons per day (Cohen, 2009). This is equivalent to a modern large seawater desalination plant now proposed for California at cost of several hundred million dollars plus the ongoing energy cost of operation. The reuse of gray water at the point of use has the advantage of much lower cost and environmental impact.

With water costs rising, water, even gray water, will be considered a resource of greater value. This is leading homeowners and policy makers to view gray water as a valuable domestic water resource.

Gray-Water Systems

Typical gray-water systems include a collection system, surge capacity, filtration, a distribution system, and an end use. Storing large quantities of gray water is not recommended because it can turn into black water if it is not treated before storage. Treatment can take the form of sand filters, or chemical, UV, or ozone disinfection for gray water that will be held for toilet flushing.

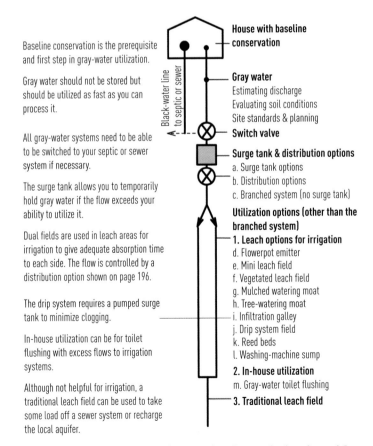

Fig. 5.37. *Five typical gray-water system components.*

Fig. 5.38. *Distribution options for landscape irrigation with gray water.*

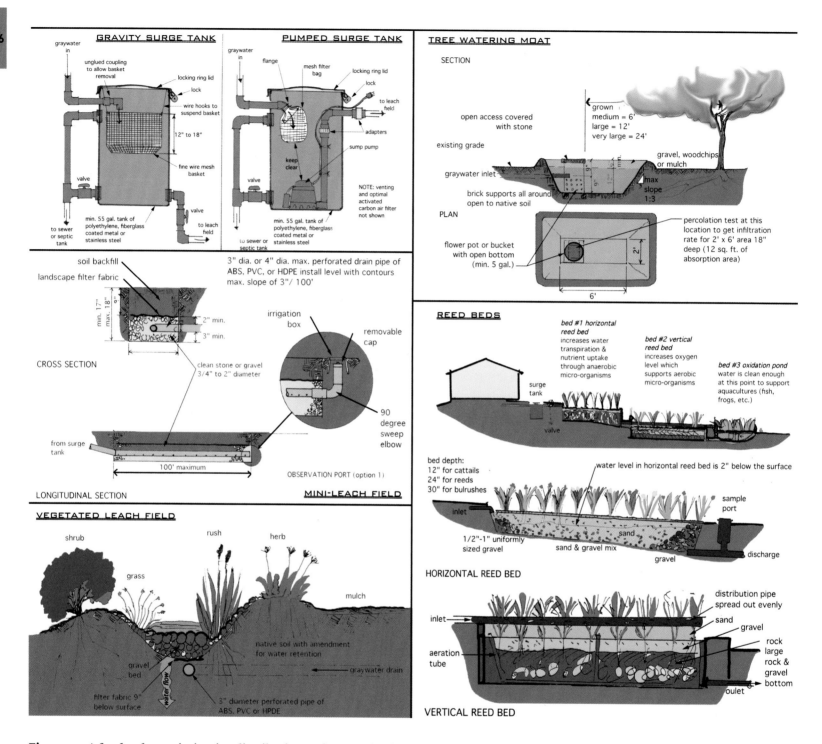

Fig. 5.39. *A few landscape irrigation distribution options are detailed below, but each site is different, and designing the right system for your site will be based on local codes, soils, et cetera. (a) Surge tanks. (b) Mini leach field. (c) Vegetated leach field. (d) Tree watering moat. (e) Reed beds.*

The development of a gray-water system depends on the home or building, occupant, use, and goals. These installations range from very simple low-cost systems to highly complex and costly systems. A simple diversion pipe for the laundry might cost less than $10. A bucket to catch the clean water as the shower heats up may cost only $5. A gray-water use system designed to recycle washing-machine rinse water back into the washer for use in the wash cycle of the next load will cost more, but is easily constructed using a 32-gallon trash container placed adjacent to the washing machine, at a slight elevation. After the wash cycle has drained, the drain hose from the washing machine is removed from the sewer standpipe and positioned to drain the rinse water into the container. The rinse water later is run back into the washing machine for use in the next wash cycle.

Often a valve-and-drain system can be added to make it possible to divert gray water for reuse, but to return flows to the sewer or septic system if there is a backup or surface flow. More sophisticated gray-water retrofit systems with settling tanks, pumps, controls, filters, and treatment devices can cost several thousand dollars. Designing gray-water plumbing systems for new homes is easier and reduces the cost. Even if a gray-water system is not installed, the stub outs and layout of the pipes can be made in a manner that facilitates retrofitting.

The system installed at Casa del Agua in Tucson is fairly simple. It drains gray water from the household's water-using appliances into a 55-gallon sump surge tank with a filter fitted over the gray-water drain to remove lint and hair before the water is pumped to other components of the recycling system. As the sump fills, it activates a float switch and then pumps gray water into various treatment systems. The gray water is then pumped through an underground drip irrigation system to the landscape or for use in the toilet. The cost was about $1,500 (Gelt, 2009*). The gray-water storage tanks hold winter flows for use in the summer. Municipal water use was reduced 47 percent; gray water met 20 percent of total demand, rainwater 10 percent (Karpiscak et al., 2001*).

Rules and Regulations

The various states and counties can develop more sustainable water programs by increasing gray-water recycling as Australia has done. This effort will require public education and participation, certified and properly managed distributed gray-water recycling systems, centralized recycling plants where applicable, and incentives for gray-water recycling efforts.

Arizona has an approach that seems to work, based on size. Systems for less than 400 gallons per day that meet a list of reasonable requirements (thirteen best management practices, or BMPs) are covered under a general permit without the builder having to apply for anything. With this one stroke, Arizona has raised its compliance rate from near zero to perhaps 50 percent. Homeowners are more likely to work toward compliance for the informal systems that still fall short of current requirements. This simple code also opens the door for professionals to install simple and cost-effective systems. Systems that process more than 400 gallons a day or don't meet the list of requirements, as well as commercial, multifamily, and institutional systems, require a standard permit. Systems that are larger than 3,000 gallons a day are considered on an individual basis. The Arizona law does not prescribe design specifics but requires that systems meet performance goals. This creates a favorable climate for innovation while technical progress is likely to eclipse prescriptive laws—but the manual and BMPs can easily be updated because they deal with performance.

Black Water, Dark Gray Water, Yellow Water

Your shit is gold.

—F. HUNDERTWASSER, 1976

What is normally demeaned as human waste is usually transported by water that is then demeaned by calling it black water. One of the strangest things our society does is transport water hundreds of miles, clean it at great cost, then contaminate it in a toilet and ship it again for high-cost treatment. This is expensive not only in terms of water but in terms of energy and the loss of a valuable agricultural resource. It is estimated that 20 percent of the energy used in California is used for pumping water.

Besides using valuable water and expensive energy, the infrastructure involved has become very expensive. The federal government no longer pays such a large percent of sewer and water treatment plant costs, and the hidden subsidies have declined. As a result, water scarcity and sewer system expenses have begun to limit growth.

A case in point is Los Osos, California, a moderate-income community on the coast, under a twenty-five-year-old building moratorium resulting from the failure to build a traditional sewer system. This would be so expensive to homeowners that many on fixed incomes would probably have to leave. The politics of this situation has been very intense and divisive to the whole community. Los Osos is just the harbinger of things to come for many communities as high energy cost and water shortages are exacerbated by rising sea levels, drought, and erratic weather from global warming.

Black Water

Black water can be treated at the home or building scale with a biological treatment system (just as nature does it); but this treatment is more complex, requires more care, and is likely to be resisted by building and health authorities. Reed beds and engineered wetlands have been developed and successfully operated at the home and building level and will one day be common, but are best at the neighborhood scale.

Composting and other waterless toilets are another alternative but can pose a challenge in retrofits. It's best to plan for them before construction. These cost less than adding equal capacity to a sewer system and treatment plant. Regulatory conditions are also a factor. Many state and national parks use waterless toilet systems, and composting toilets are legal in some areas like the state of Arizona.

Dark Gray and Medium Gray Water

Dark gray laundry water from washing a big load of dirty diapers can be close to black water. Water from a kitchen sink with a heavily used garbage grinder or disposal unit can be fairly rich in biological material and might be called medium gray. It's better to have a compost or vermicompost (worm bin) for kitchen scraps so that sink water can be used in a gray-water system as discussed on pages 195–196.

Yellow Water

Water from a toilet flushed with just urine is relatively safe. The challenge is separating it, perhaps with a urinal for men. A more complex arrangement of an in-toilet urine diverter has been developed for women—but would face strict health-code scrutiny.

Urine is close to sterile as it leaves the kidneys but may be contaminated on the way out of the body. The Inuit used to use urine to brush their teeth, and soldiers are advised to use urine to clean wounds if no water is available. A waterless urinal can be installed in a home or commercial or industrial space. These are good for water conservation, but not so good for resource recovery.

Urine as a resource is beginning to gather attention because of the looming phosphorus and fixed-nitrogen crisis mentioned on page 167. As time goes by, perhaps the term for urine will progress to *yellow water* and then to *gold water*.

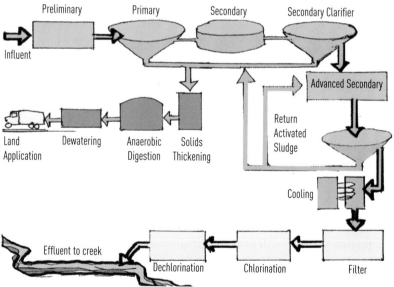

Fig. 5.40. *(a) Conventional wastewater treatment plant, San Luis Obispo, California. (b) Diagram of the wastewater treatment process.*

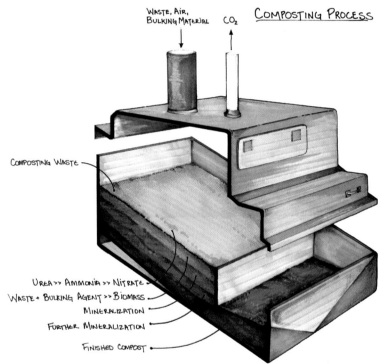

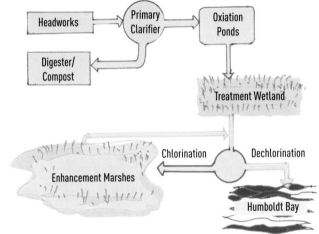

Fig. 5.41. *C. K. Choi Building, University of British Columbia, incorporates composting toilets. (a) Exterior of building. (b) Maintenance chamber. (c) Diagram of Clivus Multrum composting toilet.*

Fig. 5.42. *(a) Arcata, California, constructed wetlands waste-treatment facility. Photo: Poppendieck. (b) Diagram of wastewater treatment process.*

Good-Bye to Black Water, Hello Gold Water!

Waterless toilets are readily available and can be installed in many situations without a great deal of difficulty. In rural areas a simple pit privy or long-fall toilet may suffice. Composting toilets of many kinds are sold and approvable in most jurisdictions, but if you are the first in your area, be patient. An electric-assisted compost toilet can be used even in retrofits with restricted space, but adds a global warming burden. A solar-assisted composter might be the best solution in many homes.

Composting toilets have been used on multifamily and commercial buildings in Europe. In Canada, there are five Clivus Multrum Model M28 composters at the C. K. Choi Building at the University of British Columbia. These serve ten flushless toilets and several flushless, trapless ventilated urinals. Each of these Clivus composters has an annual user capacity rated at 45,000 visits with a total annual capacity of 225,000 visits for the building.

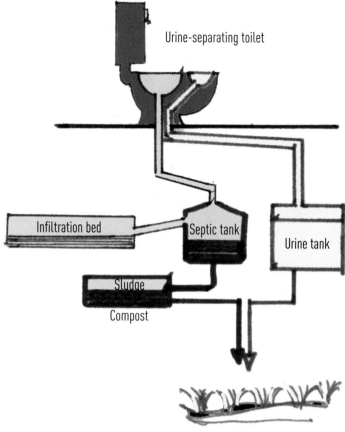

Urine-separating toilet

Infiltration bed

Septic tank

Urine tank

Sludge

Compost

Fig. 5.43. *Urine is valuable. Once separated, a passive building can be thought of as a collector of urine as well as sunlight. Residents of a housing project in Sweden and Svanholm Gods collective and organic farm in Denmark are recovering nutrients in this way. (a) NoMix, "the bowl of the future," © 2007. (b) Diagram of wastewater process for a urine-separating toilet.*

WOOOOOOO

sewer bill

composting toilet bill

Los Osos, CA, sewer cost $12,333/property

Los Osos, CA, composting toilet cost $1,000/property

Converting	tax-gobbling, growth-inhibiting, energy-intensive infrastructure
to	a pleasant, profitable, public amenity
replacing	diminishing environmental resource mining
with	naturally occurring renewable resources.

Starts with three conceptual shifts:

❶ Redefining waste as resource.

❷ Recognizing the superior efficiency of synergy.

❸ Applying the passive concept of integrating production and use at the scale of building and community.

Fig. 5.44. *Converting and replacing existing systems. (a) The Los Osos, California, sewer would cost $12,333 per property. (b) A Los Osos composting toilet would cost $1,000 per property.*

Green Materials

Sustainable buildings should be built with materials that are readily available, inexpensive, renewable, enhance biodiversity, resilient, with local control (to harvest or collect, build, maintain, fix, dispose of safely), community building, efficient of energy and resources, soft, safe, fun, healthful, asset building, equitable, pleasing, and empowering. They should improve access to healthful housing, improve quality of life, and increase ownership, and at the end of use they should be easily dismantled, separated, and returned to nature or returned to the eco-industrial cycle. The pueblos of the Southwest, the oldest occupied buildings in North America, are a good example. They are simply made of earth, wood, and stone. If abandoned, they would gradually return to the earth.

To understand the sustainability of materials, we need to consider their life cycle from their creation to their death or recovery. We should also consider the rarer, but still common events of buildings—flood, fire, and earthquake.

Material Life Cycles

Collection, transportation

Processing, transportation

Manufacturing elements and components

Transportation to site

Site erection and construction

Maintenance

Repairs

Refurbishment/remodeling

Demolition or dismantling of the structure at the end of its life

Transportation

Processing required for reuse, recycling, return to nature or disposal

How do the building materials respond? These can become the basis of the cradle-to-cradle life-cycle design described on pages 208 and 211.

Most analyses of building materials have neglected several of these steps. Sadly, the interesting and important challenge of developing more sustainable building materials has largely been ignored. The focus has typically been placed on low first cost, without considering life-cycle value, end-of-life issues, and external costs and risks. Material choices are complicated by larger systemic problems, including centuries of unsustainable forest management that have led to the growing use of less durable materials such as oriented strand board (OSB) in place of solid wood or plywood.

In the US construction industry, the materials choices and finishes have often become cheaper and less durable to reduce first costs. Even expensive homes often emphasize high-cost finishes such as granite countertops, while neglecting quality and longevity of basic home components and building materials. The failure of thousands of expensive homes with high-sulfur Chinese drywall is a perfect example. Seven million sheets of drywall were imported during a drywall shortage, and the high sulfur content has led to health and electrical problems. Although only a few thousand complaints had been registered with the Consumer Product Safety

Icons related to the 6 steps of life-cycle balancing

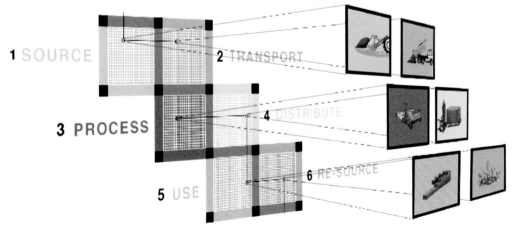

Fig. 5.45. *Six steps of life-cycle balancing. Source: Center for Maximum Potential Building Systems.*

Commission as of 2009, as many as sixty thousand homes may be involved.

Building size and related ecological impacts are often neglected in green building magazines. A 5,000-square-foot home for a childless couple is not very sustainable, even if it has a high-efficiency furnace and energy-conserving high-quality windows. Green materials can be used to build a very inefficient building if sustainable design principles are ignored.

Green building has often focused rather narrowly on energy, and more recently on carbon footprint—rather than looking at the broader picture of sustainability and ecological and health effects. Plastic insulating foams, for example, are very good for improving thermal performance and structural integrity, but are virtually unrecyclable and make dismantling a structure very difficult.

A More Sustainable Approach

It doesn't have to be this way. We can find many marvelous examples of local, site-adapted building technology from almost every country, climate, and region—yet they are often little studied and little known. Many superb books can introduce you to sustainable traditional designs, including *Japan's Folk Architecture; Just Enough; Architecture Without Architects; Architecture for the Poor; Built by Hand; Spectacular Vernacular;* and *Traditional Buildings,* to list just a few (see references and further reading for more suggestions).

Fig. 5.46. *This birch-bark and green roof building in Sweden has been used for six hundred years.*

Many traditional designs were limited by understanding of engineering and energy principles. This led to reduced performance at climate extremes and high risk during earthquakes. Sadly, despite new understanding and new materials, risk has remained high in many areas as concrete slab or block buildings with inadequate reinforcing or poor build quality have replaced equally dangerous stone or earth homes. More needs to be done to explore and improve the sustainability of traditional materials and to develop new building systems that take advantage of modern, but still sustainable, building materials that offer improved performance and safety. These include such things as straw bale building, flax insulation (now available in Europe), and straw panels. To choose green materials, we need to know their impacts, life cycle, and toxicity. Ideally they will be local and renewable, recyclable at the end of life, and safe for people and the environment.

Material Impacts

Peter van Dresser addressed the sustainability issue well in *Home Grown Sundwellings,* emphasizing the use of locally available materials even when performance would not be as good as the best available nonlocal alternatives. The straw bale building movement has stimulated discussion of many of these questions, but more detailed life-cycle cost analysis remains to be done. The comparison of materials can benefit from the careful use of the materials' comparison technique developed by "Bio" Schmidt Bleek* and colleagues at the Wuppertal Institute in Germany. Their rating system for material (including energy) intensity per unit service (MIPS) is a useful method for estimating the ecological stress potential of materials, goods, and services.

MIPS is the "ecological rucksack" or ecological footprint of materials, including abiotic and biotic material costs, air, water, land,

Fig. 5.47. *Mud, stone, and wood, Taos Pueblo is one of the oldest continuously occupied buildings in the United States.*

and energy. MIPS is computed in material input per total unit of services delivered by the material or product over its entire useful life span (resource extraction, manufacturing, transport, packaging, operating, reuse recycling, and remanufacturing are accounted for, and so is final waste disposal). MIPS can help us account for the sustainability of materials at local, regional, national, and global levels.

Industrial products typically carry nonrenewable ecological footprints about thirty times their own weight. This means that less than 5 percent of the nonrenewable natural material disturbed in the ecosphere ends up in a technically useful form. For electronics it is worse, with ecological footprints of a personal computer often two hundred times their weight.

At the Wuppertal Institute in Germany, MI values were calculated for a number of materials including many used in building construction, as shown in table 5.3. Construction was found to account for almost 40 percent of the material flows in Germany.

As with all products, there can be good sources and bad sources—for example, an efficient cement factory versus a polluting factory, or a sustainably managed forest or a looted one. Most conventional buildings and building materials come with a high life-cycle cost today, particularly when plastics are an important part of so many products. Many building products are environmentally damaging, may be unhealthful as is or when wetted or burned, and may require potentially harmful glues and finishes.

Reducing transportation costs is also important. Importing granite countertops from Europe is made possible by subsidies for fossil fuels and ignores external costs. Plundering tropical forests to make more durable decks is as foolish as cutting the giant redwoods to build fences was in the United States.

Some building materials are easy to recycle (steel, copper), but many are very hard or costly to recycle (PVC pipe, asphalt shingles). Many have environmental effects that were not appreciated until recently—these include lead, galvanized steel, and copper. We

Table 5.3. *MIPS for specific materials (tons/ton).*

Material	Abiotic material	Biotic matl	Air pollution	Water	Energy kwh/t
Aluminum, primary	37.0	–	10.9	1047.0	16,000
Aluminum, recycled	0.85	–	0.9	30.7	na
Copper, primary	348.5	–	1.6	367.2	3,000
Steel, rebar (Blast)	1.5	–	0.5	63.7	441
Polyethylene, LD	2.5	–	1.6	122.2	na
Polyurethane foam	7.5	–	3.4	532.4	na
PVC	3.5	–	1.7	305.3	1,153
Sheet glass	3.0	–	0.7	11.6	157
Fiberglass	4.7	–	1.8	46.0	4,538
Portland cement	3.2	–	0.3	16.9	253
Plywood	2.0	9.1	0.5	23.6	na
Pine wood	0.9	5.5	0.1	10.0	113
Linoleum	2.0	0.4	2.0	6.7	4

Not including transport impacts

Wuppertal Institute

haven't used lead pipes for a long time (for human health reasons) and are replacing lead solders, but many countries still use lead flashing on roofs. Water analysis in urban areas has found that lead, copper, and zinc from galvanized roofs are also very common eco-toxic pollutants in water.

Improving the service life of materials is also important. The desire for lowest possible first cost has led builders and developers to embrace cheap materials and low-quality windows, sinks, and electrical fixtures. Many have a lifetime of twenty years or less. Life-cycle costs are high because the labor and material costs to replace low-quality products are high. A high-quality stainless-steel kitchen sink should last a hundred years or more; a low-quality steel sink with poor enamel or porcelain may last only five. A cheap window may last ten years, a good one hundreds of years.

The challenge of sustainable buildings is to use materials that have low MI costs and a long service life. A well-detailed earth or lime-plastered straw building with recycled stainless-steel sinks and a recycled metal roof would have very low MIPS. In northern New Mexico, these metal roofs often work well for forty years or more, and they also facilitate rainwater harvesting.

Material Flows

The flows of materials through the world should be mapped carefully so we know where they end up in terms of people and the environment. Even in developed countries we often have very little information. At best we are tracking the most toxic materials, such as the heavy metals cadmium, lead, chromium, and arsenic, and a few of the more than one hundred thousand chemical compounds now in use. However, most of the effort has been expended on understanding human health risks, and the more complex and challenging understanding of the toxicology of materials on ecosystems remains in its infancy.

To understand both human and ecosystem effects from building materials and supplies for maintenance, we need to know several things:

1. What is the spatial distribution? How much is there? Where does it come from? Where does it go? Does it move in air, water, food, dust? Is it local or global? Concentrated or diffuse? Are materials biomagnified?

2. What secondary effects or pathways are there? Are metabolites or breakdown products more hazardous? Even if materials are nontoxic to humans, do they lead to ecosystem catastrophes (ecotoxicity)?

3. Are effects cumulative or instantaneous? Lethal? Mutagenic? Teratogenic? Can we and/or ecosystems shed materials if exposures are infrequent or do they build up?

4. How persistent are the materials in the environment? Do they break down in hours? Days? Years? Millennia? Can they be collected and destroyed or recycled?

Some materials are relatively easy to recycle, but PVC pipe, urethane foam, composite plastic wood (TREX), and others are end-of-life products. Most of the products used in building and maintenance have not been studied in detail.

Energy Cost

The energy cost of building materials has been studied more carefully than the environmental or health impacts and costs of materials. This is important because as much as 10 percent of all energy use in the United States may be for building construction and maintenance. Transportations adds quite a bit of energy cost to most materials. Few are locally produced, and many are shipped internationally. Preliminary studies suggest the energy costs for typical construction materials and labor, shown in table 5.4.

Table 5.4. *Energy cost BTU/unit.*

Material	Unit	Before Delivery To Job Site	After Delivery
Rough softwood lumber	Board foot	5,229	7,661
Finished softwood lumber	Board foot	5,399	7,859
Softwood exterior plywood	Square foot	4,393	5,779
Shakes and shingles	Square foot	4,682	7,315
Roll roofing, mineral	Square foot	10,673	11,012
Asphalt strip shingles	Square foot	24,553	25,334
Galvanized steel sheet	Square foot	26,458	27,836

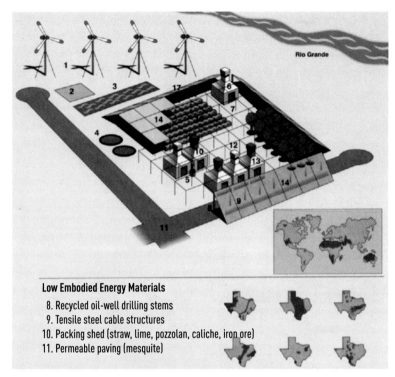

Low Embodied Energy Materials

8. Recycled oil-well drilling stems
9. Tensile steel cable structures
10. Packing shed (straw, lime, pozzolan, caliche, iron ore)
11. Permeable paving (mesquite)

Fig. 5.48. *Plotting low-embodied energy materials in Texas by Center for Maximum Potential Building Systems.*

If we add up the material energy cost and construction cost we can estimate energy intensity by building type. This has not been done very often, but table 5.5 shows how one study mapped the energy intensity.

To give a sense of perspective on the quantities of material and energy used, a 2,000-square-foot wood-framed house might use about 16,000 board feet of lumber and 6,000 square feet of structural panels. These weigh about 24 tons, and the impact for these wood products alone might be 100 tons of abiotic impact (waste, erosion), 7 tons of air pollution (accounting for transportation would

Table 5.5. *Energy intensity.*

Building Type	Energy Intensity BTU $	Total Energy BTU, 1967	BTU/Sq.ft
Single family housing	55,500	781 trillion	700,000
Remodels	51,600	262 trillion	n.a.
High-rise apts.	60,000	118 trillion	740,000

Bainbridge 1980

increase this dramatically), and 360 tons of water (again, accounting for transportation would increase this dramatically). The energy cost might exceed 35,000 kWh of energy just for the lumber.

However, when we look at life-cycle costs, it becomes clear that operation and maintenance are much more important than material cost for buildings. This same house might directly use 3,600 kWh of electricity a year, so within twenty years the building energy cost will probably be matched. The lifetime may well be one to five hundred years, although repairs and replacements will be needed.

We Can Do Much Better

The energy cost of constructing a passive solar straw bale or adobe house may be only a tenth or a twentieth as much as a conventional building, as shown in table 5.6. If we use energy-conserving design the house will have an oiled mud floor, vigas (round rather than

Table 5.6. *Energy intensity of a 1,000-square-foot straw bale home with locally cut roof beams, puddled adobe floor, and metal roofing.*

Content	Energy form	Calories /day	BTU
Foundation	Labor		4,000
Floor	Labor		4,000
Linseed oil	6 gallons		200,000
Walls	Labor		4,000
	Baler		500,000
Wood beams/ headers Saw, truck			600,000
	Labor		4,000
Insulation, R-11			624,000
Glass	200 sq.ft.		2,687,400
Metal roofing, recycled steel			15,000,000
	Labor		4,000
Total materials			19,611,400
Total labor	12 man months	960,000	4,000,000
Total Energy			23,611,400
Renewable			4,200,000
Total non-renewable			19,411,400
Energy Cost, BTU/sq. foot			23,611
% of conventional construction		<5%	

sawn beams), wood-bond beams, rubble trench foundation, and a willow roof deck. Almost the entire structure can be built using local materials. The exceptions are the window glass, insulation for the roof (although cattail fuzz or bagged straw could be used), and metal roofing. The vigas may have to be hauled in as well, but require no other energy. The energy cost of this structure is shown in table 5.6.

We may not all be able to do this well, of course, but we can do much better than we do today. Consider lifetime energy cost and environmental and health impacts as well as energy savings. The initial energy cost of a good passive structure built with energy-intensive materials may equal the energy use for space heating and cooling over eighty years, while for a typical house it only represents about fifteen years. By using energy-efficient materials in a passive solar house, as in the adobe example above, this factor can be reduced dramatically and the life-cycle energy cost will be very low indeed. When true energy costs (including health and environmental impacts of energy production) are counted, then all buildings will start to include these sustainable materials and design choices.

Local Control

Peter van Dresser was one of the first to fully understand this issue, and he described local development in an ecological context in northern New Mexico in *A Landscape for Humans* (1976*). The Center for Maximum Potential Building Systems (CMPBS) in Austin, Texas, has done extensive local resource mapping and developed appropriate material solutions that fit the local bioregion; they encourage others to study these issues. The key is to understand what you have, and to use it well. In some cases the availability of materials will influence choices of natural heating, cooling, and ventilation designs.

Community Building

In addition to using local material resources, we also need to assess local human resources and capability for using and repairing them. One of the great advantages and joys of the straw bale building movement has been the ease of participation for people and children of all skill levels.

Toxicity Reduction

Some building materials are potentially harmful to people during construction; many more are harmful if they get moldy or burn in a fire. Many materials have environmental effects that are often still

ignored—and the ecotoxic effects of most building materials have not been studied.

Fig. 5.49. *A good test of a building material: How do you feel about your child playing with it or eating it?*

Fig. 5.50. *Straw bales for wall and ceiling insulation.*

Fig. 5.51. *Building community by working together in straw bale building.*

Building Materials and Systems with Green Advantages

Adobe (see page 17)	
Bamboo	
Cob	Cob construction uses lumps of soil mixed with straw or other fibers. Cob walls are assembled without forms. Cob construction is common in parts of England where soils were suitable and timber was short. Typically the mix is 5 to 6 percent clay, sandy subsoil, and straw. Cob was traditionally mixed by hand and then shoveled onto the walls to make lifts of 18 inches on 20- to 36-inch-thick walls. The lift was allowed to dry before the next lift was applied. Perhaps twenty thousand are still in use in Devon, England, and a few modern buildings are being constructed in the United States, the UK, and France. The correct mixtures of earth and fibers and compaction are important for strength. Built well, they will last for centuries and are easily recycled. These high-mass walls have very low material costs, but are labor-intensive and typically need exterior insulation. They can also be used as an interior thermal-mass wall.
Earth bag	
Earthen Finish	
Earthen Floors	
Earth rammed tires	
Ferrocement	Ferrocement was developed by L. Nervi in Italy in the 1930s as a response to expensive materials and inexpensive skilled labor. It consists of a composite material of thin light-gauge steel wire and light-gauge thin concrete to allow the construction of very thin but strong elements. After the 1950s, this economic condition reversed to cheap material and expensive labor, so ferrocement fell out of favor. However, as triple-bottom-line economics becomes more common, this economic equation will reverse once again— especially when we consider the environmental costs of cement production, with its high embodied energy and large contribution to greenhouse gases.
Light Clay Straw	Light straw clay construction is a traditional German method (Leichtlehmbau) of building. The straw is well mixed with a light clay slip (cream consistency) using pitchforks or hands (it is like tossing a salad to get dressing on all the lettuce). The straw with clay is then put into forms (24 to 48 inches tall) and packed evenly. The forms are then moved up and the next layer is laid. After the wall is finished, it dries to an open lattice with clay protection against fire. It doesn't have as much insulation as straw bales, but it is relatively quick, light, and durable. The light straw clay is usually incorporated in a timber- or pole-framed building. Exterior walls are typically 10 to 15 inches thick, but interior walls can be thinner. The feathery surface is ideal for plastering.
Rammed Earth (see page 17)	
Recycled Aluminum	
Recycled Concrete	
Recycled Houses	In many respects, the house built of recycled materials may be best. Rather than letting energy-expensive materials (5,600 gallons of gas equivalent per house) be consigned to the "sanitary" landfill, we should recycle them whenever feasible. David's parents' home was built almost entirely from recycled materials saved from an existing ramshackle house on their property. We took this apart very carefully and managed to save probably 90 percent of the wood, as well as many of the windows, fixtures, and wire; most of the nails were straightened in the evening and polished in the cement mixer. By cleaning boards carefully before stacking them by size and length, it was possible to minimize handling and increase efficiency. Using this method, pieces could often be used without cutting during construction. The quality of wood used in the first part of the house (circa 1890) was amazing. Vancouver, British Columbia, has done a particularly good job of encouraging reuse of building materials, which is often complicated by codes and regulations.
Recycled Steel	
Salvage Materials	
Straw Bale (see pages 9, 13, 14, 18, 22, 23, 36, 131)	
Stone	
Water and Plastic (see pages 103, 105)	
Wood	Wood remains an excellent material for building and can become a sustainable resource if we manage our forestlands better. Certification programs for sustainable forestry make it possible to use wood that has less impact. In many cases, it is also possible to mill your own lumber. Wood can be a renewable and sustainable resource for building, and wood buildings can be taken apart and almost completely reused and repurposed. Solid wood cabinets, panels, and interiors are much more resistant to mold and rot than pressed wood, chipboard, and fiberboard. Wooden buildings with simple wood or birch-bark and earth roofs have remained in use for more than six hundred years in Scandinavia.

Fig. 5.52. *The top nineteen green building materials (for more detail, see the reference section).*

Sustainable Materials in a Sustainable Design

The goals in design and building-material choices should be joy in use, health, durability, minimal environmental impact in manufacturing and maintenance, ease of recycling, and low life-cycle cost.

Wood, mud, clay, straw, stainless steel, stone, glass, and ceramics are excellent. Gypsum plaster is better than wallboard, and mold-proof wallboard is better than conventional. Insulation that can be removed and reused (cotton batt, polyester batt, fiberglass, mineral wool, cellulose) is preferred over insulation such as foil-faced or sprayed plastic foams that are very difficult to reuse or recycle.

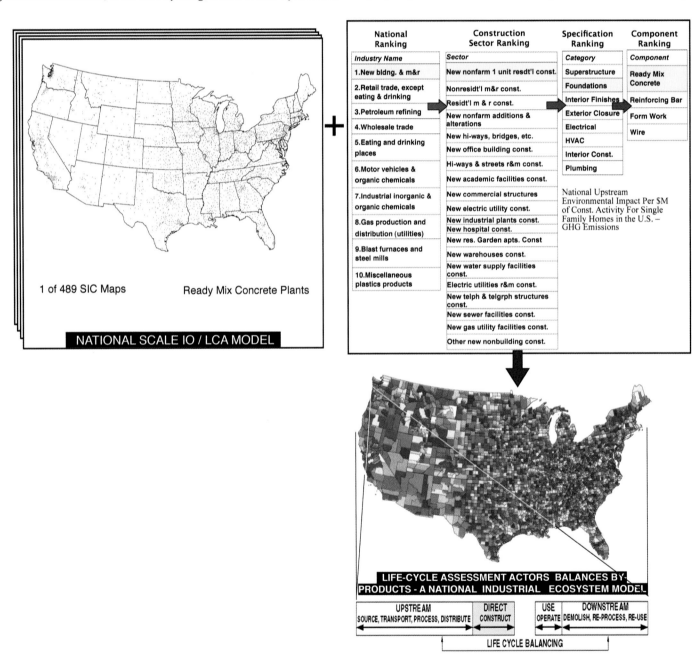

Fig. 5.53. *To allow development of real costs via the life-cycle assessment and the potential of cradle-to-cradle life-cycle design, we need to quantify potential "waste" to resource connections.*

More natural materials will be used once we start counting these costs. Even the simplest materials, like adobe, can last a very long time—as the buildings of the Middle East and the pueblos of the Southwest have shown. And these materials can be used to build structures that delight the senses, and are healthy, economical, and durable.

This type of quantification has started. An example is the Baseline Green Study done by G. Norris, P. Fisk III, R. MacMath, B. Bavinger, and J. McClennan along with the staff at the Center for Maximum Potential Building Systems, which was funded by the US Environmental Protection Agency (EPA) see fig. 5.53.

Fig. 5.54. *Construction waste. (a) Typical discards. (b) Salvage material sorted for reuse—often without cutting.*

It consists of cellular tracking of the life-cycle of products for 12,500,000 businesses and industries in 52,480 spatial cells tracked by the US Bureau of Economic Analysis with environmental data from the US EPA, including greenhouse gases, criteria air pollutants, and toxic releases. It allows analysis at global, state, regional, and community scales. This includes material sourcing, processing, transportation, distribution, use, and resource product footprints.

The manner in which we design and engineer buildings throughout their life cycle determines 40 percent of our environmental impact as a country and can increase our local and regional job multiplier from two- to sixfold. Tools like this can have immense effects on our triple-bottom-line economic condition.

The designer, builder, occupant, and community leaders can take many steps to reduce waste and improve reuse. These include specifying sustainable and recycled materials and making it easier to reuse salvaged materials. Vancouver, BC, has walked the walk: The material reuse research facility was built with reused materials. The EPA has started funding reuse research and educational materials, including a deconstruction handbook for residential construction. Associations and groups are also working to develop reuse solutions for common construction and demolition (C&D) materials, including asphalt shingles, drywall, and concrete (www.cdrecycling .org). Habitat for Humanity, cities, private firms, and other nonprofit groups have also set up and manage construction recycling centers. Many cities now maintain a directory of certified and uncertified recyclers to assist builders in providing outlets for C&D discards.

Construction Discards

About a third of the discards in the US waste stream are estimated to be from construction, demolition, and remodeling. This amounted to about 170 million tons in 2003. C&D waste for new construction can be virtually eliminated by careful design and management of materials when constructing a new home or building. Wastes can also be minimized when renovating and/or undertaking a full-scale demolition and removal, though this is sometimes complicated by previous choices and materials that have been found not to be safe after all (lead, asbestos, PCBs, CFCs, and so on). A recent study in California showed that even with current recycling/reuse technology, more than half of the discards from C&D could be reused. With more advanced treatment, recovery rates can reach 90 percent. For example, painted wood, considered nonreusable in the California study, can be safely field-cleaned as demonstrated at Fort Ord (Chartwell School, 2006*). For new nonresidential construction in California, the potential recovery was 86 percent, see chart (Cascadia, 2006*).

Design for deconstruction can play a critical role in minimizing future wastes. This includes keeping components and materials separable and safe and providing future occupants and deconstructors with a building plan and as-built photographs. A deconstruction plan may one day be included in the building-commissioning package. Design for reuse can be more effective than design for recycling, though both are important. In the future, building materials should be bar-coded to make source separation more efficient and less costly. Sprayed foam, glues, and binders can all make deconstruction very difficult. Screws, nails, and other fasteners can often be recovered or removed in ways that allow for reuse or recycling.

Reducing or eliminating the ecological impacts of building-material sourcing, processing, and manufacturing is also important. Straw bale buildings are a good example of a local, renewable, and low-impact material that is easy to recycle. Waste from trimming and cutting is easily returned to the earth. Durability of straw bale buildings is excellent with good detailing—straw bale buildings in Nebraska and Alabama remain in excellent condition after more

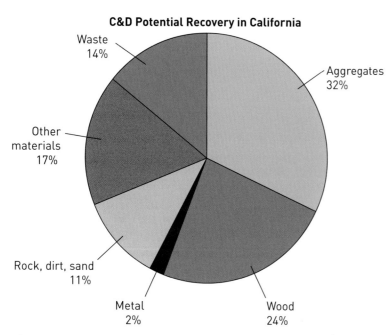

Fig. 5.55. *Potential C&D recovery in California nonresidential construction.*

than seventy years—but when deconstructed the bales could easily be broken down and composted.

Green Discards

More than 30 million tons of green resources are discarded by homeowners and businesses every year. Most of this could be eliminated by better design choices and changes in maintenance. An increasing quantity of green discards is collected separately and composted by cities every year. However, most would be better recycled and reused at home or at the business.

Compost is one of the better uses. Compost is simply the biological degradation and transformation of organic solid waste by aerobic decomposition. By providing the ideal blend of nitrogen (greens), carbon (browns), and decomposition organisms, the appropriate moisture level, and turning or fluffing regularly, compost will heat up. The high temperatures help kill weed seeds and pathogens and speed up the decomposition process. A temperature of 150°F is often considered desirable for pathogen control. More casual compost piles also work, since compost will "happen" even if you just pile on yard and food waste, water sporadically, and wait. Neighbors may be less forgiving of casual composting. Chipping and shredding can reduce the volume and speed decomposition. A cooperatively owned or neighborhood shredder/chipper can make composting more attractive.

Compost can play a critical role in reducing water consumption by trees, shrubs, and gardens. It can also reduce stormwater runoff and erosion. Home sheet composting, compost piles, bins, and tumblers, and vermicomposting can all play a role. The heat from composting has also been used to warm greenhouses, heat water, and heat homes.

Larger materials such as tree trunks can be milled into lumber, as is done at the Green Waste Recycle Yard in Berkeley, California, and comparable programs in other cities. Many older trees have valuable wood. Large planks of walnut, oak, maple, and other species favored by woodworkers are collected, milled, and sold.

Sheet composting is very effective but underappreciated (promoted in permaculture and other management systems). Sheet composting can be as simple as leaving lawn clippings on lawns or spreading leaves, clippings, and cuttings under trees and shrubs; or it can involve chopping weeds, watering, and adding soil amendments and then a layer of cardboard or multiple layers of wet paper under a deep layer of mulch or compost. Many homeowners feel clippings are bad for lawns, but a reeducation effort on the value of clippings for lawn health reduced annual disposal by 94,000 tons a year in Montgomery County, Maryland. Many university extension programs and environmental groups offer composting instructions and training geared to local conditions. Many areas now offer training to become a certified master composter.

Compost bins and tumblers also work and may be more appropriate for town houses or multifamily units. Many communities have encouraged the use of composting bins and/or provided them at reduced cost to minimize the cost of green waste handling. Contra Costa County in California, for example, offers composters at about half price. Homeowners are also eligible for a composting discount of $1.50 a month on their garbage collection fee. This would offset the cost of the bins within three to five years.

Closing the Cycles

The developer, building designer, and builder profoundly affect the amount of waste and impacts of waste of a home, neighborhood, or city. They can make it easy or hard for the occupant to make sustainable choices. While it is possible to live a more sustainable lifestyle even in a poorly designed and built home, it is much easier in a sustainable home. Very few studies have been done to understand the resource flows through the home, neighborhood, and community, their costs and impacts, and the opportunities they provide for recovery or reuse. The health and ecological impacts of waste are significant, including water pollution, disease, and ecosystem impacts.

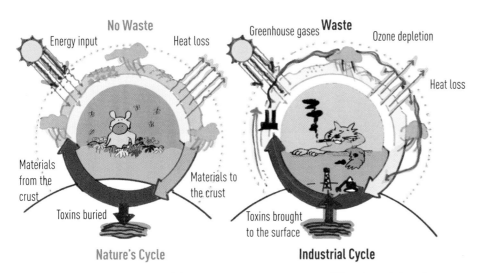

Fig. 5.56. *Closing the cycle. (a) Nature's cycle = no waste. (b) Industrial cycle = waste.*

Measure to Manage

As we often say, "What isn't measured, isn't managed." The garbology research project at the University of Arizona (beginning in 1973) has provided some very clear information on what is used and discarded and how it behaves after it is sealed in a landfill. The resource waste is appalling. In the United States, for example, the average American discards almost 5 pounds a day. This adds up, and every year we throw away 250 million tons of municipal "solid waste."

Many of these discards can be reused, recovered, or recycled. They include 77.5 million tons of paper, 33 million tons of green waste, 70 million tons of food waste, 3 million tons of e-waste, hundreds of thousands of often ecotoxic cleansers and disinfectants, and 5,000 tons of pharmaceuticals and personal care products.

The overall US recycling rate is about 30 percent, but many communities, including Seattle (near 50 percent overall and 87 percent for single-family residential curbside materials), have done much better. San Francisco passed a mandatory source-separation ordinance in June 2009, which came into effect in October. The first of its kind in the United States, the ordinance requires residents and businesses to separate organics and recyclables from the garbage. "This ordinance essentially makes sure that no matter where you go in San Francisco, you'll have opportunities to recycle and compost through the city's curbside programs," says Robert Reed, city recycling director.

Waste minimization has received less attention. This is particularly important for hazardous materials that sicken or kill people and ecotoxic materials that sicken or destroy ecosystems. These include a wide range of hazardous materials in cleaners, paints and solvents, batteries, electronics, and biocides. Use in the home is a problem, but use in home landscaping is also critical. Lawns and landscaping use not only much of the increasingly scarce water, but also more than 1 million tons of fertilizer and 67 million pounds of pesticide every year. These materials cause problems for public health and local and global ecosystems.

A single home or business can make many steps toward zero waste, but it is much easier in a community that has adopted a zero-waste program. Some resources are hard to recycle or repurpose at the individual level, but can more easily be managed at the neighborhood, city, state, or national level. In many cases, the imposition of impact fees will help change behavior. After instituting per-bag fees for trash, per-household trash generation in Dover, New Hampshire, dropped from 6.2 pounds per day to only 4.7, and the city's residential recycling rate increased from 3 to 52 percent (Platt and Seldman). Neat and clean home and neighborhood recycling centers can make it easier to keep material separated, and easy to recycle or repurpose.

Zero-Waste Communities

Education and supporting facilities can also be effective. The goal is increasingly to reach zero waste, something several communities, including Del Norte (California), Boulder (Colorado), Austin (Texas), Palo Alto (California), and others have embraced as a goal. Nantucket Island has perhaps come closest, with 92 percent recovery. Education is essential to help homeowners and businesses understand what can be reused and recycled, what goes together, and what must be separated.

This section can provide only a short introduction to this book-size topic. It includes a short review of several key issues that are easily changed by design and behavior to reach for the zero-waste home and development. It is important to begin by rethinking the nature of the things we throw away: Are they really waste, or are they potentially reusable or recyclable discards that we no longer want? In most cases, they are potentially repairable, reusable, or recyclable. These include construction discards, green discards, food discards, e-waste, product discards, packaging discards, hazardous materials, and ecotoxic materials.

Always remember: There is no "away," and waste = food. Waste minimization is all about optimizing resource flows.

Return to Nature

One of the most important aspects of sustainable development is returning to systems that facilitate the return of organic wastes to nature and technical materials to the industrial cycle. This is not as hard as it might appear to be. Too often we simply have not tried to complete the cycles and to return materials to use. Organic materials are easily captured and recycled at the neighborhood or city level. Technical or industrial materials often must be captured and repurposed at the regional or national scale.

The neighborhood scale is ideal for composting. Compost can be prepared, maintained, and distributed by the landscaping service. It is easier to keep neighborhood green waste clean and safe than it is to manage a citywide program. It also reduces the travel cost of shipping the compost around and can complete the nutrient cycle if it is used to grow food in neighborhood farms, gardens, or edible landscaping. Village Homes, in Davis, California, with its own vineyard, orchard, and gardens/farm, shows what can be done.

Battery Park City Conservancy in Manhattan developed an innovative organic lawn maintenance program using compost teas that has been operating successfully for more than fifteen years. Although many people are afraid the compost piles will smell, the BPCC compost manager has the experience to prove that composting, when managed well, doesn't produce any unpleasant aromas. "We're composting 20 yards from the Ritz-Carlton Hotel," T. Fleisher explained. "We never have complaints about the odor coming from our site—we have complaints about starting work too early." Harvard University's FMO Landscape Services recently tested this system and found that the compost tea makes an excellent fertilizer providing high-quality, readily available nutrients and helping to close the nutrient cycle. The health of lawns and landscaping improved, water use decreased (30 percent), and costs for chemical fertilizer and biocides dropped. Home or neighborhood level use of compost tea will play an important role in reducing the health and ecological impacts of lawns and landscaping.

Although home, institution, or neighborhood use is best, city programs can also be effective. More than half the cities in California now have green waste collection programs. These are often well run and provide compost for sale or free. These collection programs can have a harder time keeping compost clean and free of biocides. Concerns over air emissions from composting are leading to calls for covers and filters in affected areas.

Methane emission avoidance can be used for carbon credits in some areas. Eosta in the Netherlands is developing this option, third-party verified, with its SMR subsidiary in Cape Town, South Africa, with a goal of recovering 95 percent of green waste. Organics can also be used to produce bio-gas. Sweden has been a leader in this effort and now has bio-gas-powered cars, buses, and trains. Palo Alto is trying a bio-gas production facility as well.

It is important to keep compost clean of hazardous or ecotoxic materials. These include common contaminants such as herbicides, fungicides, and insecticides from lawn "care" products. Educating the public about the need to keep green waste clean is often essential. Native and edible landscaping that can be maintained without toxic chemicals should be favored. Use of toxins should entail impact fees to support monitoring and education efforts.

Food Discards

Food discards are the third-largest component of generated waste by weight, and they can also be recovered at home or at the neighborhood scale. The garbology group's research suggests that each American throws away 1.3 pounds of food a day, or about 500 pounds a year. This is more than double the previous US Environmental Protection Agency estimate. This includes trimmings, leftovers, spoiled, out-of-date, overripe, and simply unwanted food. There is also a great deal of waste throughout the food supply chain from the farm to the wholesaler to the market to home. Most of this is not recycled or reclaimed. The current recovery rate for food waste in the United States is estimated at below 5 percent, but research is limited and very incomplete.

Home recycling by composting, feeding to chickens, pigs, guinea pigs, or other animals, or burial in the garden is not uncommon in rural areas, but little studied. The impact of food waste on the environment has also not been well studied, but we do know that when food waste decomposes in an anaerobic environment it releases methane, a greenhouse gas twenty-one times more powerful than carbon dioxide. Thirty-four percent of US methane emissions are from landfills.

Organic kitchen waste poses a problem in the liquid waste stream as well if it is ground up and flushed down the sewer. The food waste adds problem materials such as suspended solids, oils, and grease to wastewater treatment plants. It also increases the levels of biochemical oxygen demand (BOD), and chemical oxygen demand (COD), using up the available oxygen in water, resulting in oxygen levels that are too low to support aquatic life. Garbage grinders (disposals, disposer, garbarators, or garbagerators) should not be included in new homes unless a significant fee is added for use.

The neighborhood scale is excellent for food-discard recovery. A piggery, chicken coop, and guinea pigs could be managed alongside the neighborhood compost treatment center. Peruvian families often feed guinea pigs kitchen wastes, and later eat them as a source of protein. Animals can also make good use of food waste from dropped fruit in the community orchards and excess produce from the neighborhood gardens.

Fig. 5.57. *(a) Happy piggy. (b) Guinea pig condo, Peru.*

Aerobic Food-Discard Processing

Most of the relatively small amount of food waste that is collected is composted or treated using aerobic decomposition. BioCycle reported ninety food discard recycling programs in 2009, up from just forty in 2007 (Yepsen, 2009*). "Alameda County finally has 100 percent saturation, with organics collection offered to all 403,000 households," says Brian Matthews, senior program manager for StopWaste.org. Wayzata, Minnesota, has collected green waste and food waste separately since 2005. This reduces hauling efficiency, but makes it easier to balance the mix for the right C:N ratio and to keep it clean.

Seattle and other cities have emulated the more common European practice of co-composting green and food waste. Single-family homes are required to participate in either curbside food and yard waste or home composting. All wastes including meat and dairy are collected. More than 90 percent of homes now participate.

Institutional food waste can also be collected and composted. In many cases, these single sources generate large enough volumes to be worth pursuing. Food waste may account for more than a third of school waste, but with an active waste management plan it can be reduced and recycled by co-composting with green waste. One elementary school in Kings County, Washington, composted almost a ton of food waste in one year. Five high schools in San Francisco were diverting almost as much every week. How food is served also matters. The Davis Joint Unified School District realized a net savings of $4,695 in one year by implementing "offer versus serve" in three schools, separating food scraps for vermicomposting, and using recyclable trays. The Berkeley, California, and Pittsburgh, Pennsylvania, school districts' organic food programs both encourage on-site use of food waste for compost and return to the gardens.

Anaerobic Food-Waste Processing

Waste processing without oxygen results in fermentation, which causes organic compounds to break down by the action of living anaerobic organisms. As in the aerobic process, these organisms use nitrogen, phosphorus, and other nutrients in developing cell protoplasm. However, unlike aerobic decomposition, the anaerobic process reduces organic nitrogen to organic acids and ammonia. Carbon from organic compounds is released mainly as methane gas (CH_4). A small portion of carbon may be respired as CO_2.

The bio-gas from landfills is often partially collected and used to run landfill operations, but capturing it all is difficult. It is easier if the food waste is treated in a closed reactor vessel managed to produce bio-gas. Food waste may also be digested with sewage and some green waste. In Oakland, California, the East Bay Municipal Utility District's (EBMUD) Main Wastewater Treatment Plant co-digests food waste with primary and secondary municipal wastewater solids and other high-strength wastes. Anaerobic digestion

Fig. 5.58. *Stackable vermicompost bins. Food scraps go in the top. The worms digest lower layers then crawl up to the fresh layers, leaving a superb soil amendment behind. Worm tea can be harvested as a super-fertilizer from a drain valve on the bottom bin level. Wire mesh is suggested to keep dogs and other critters out of the tea.*

of pulp from the EBMUD food-waste process provides 730 to 1,300 kWh per dry ton of food waste applied.

The City of San Jose is working with three private partners to produce 900,000 gallons of bio-gas using German technology and 150,000 metric tons of organic waste generated by San Jose residents (Lorinc, 2009*). The city estimates that the project will reduce its greenhouse gas emissions by the equivalent of 1,800 vehicles a year.

Sweden leads the way with 7,000 bio-gas cars on the road and 779 bio-gas buses. Linköping has been using bio-gas since 1997, and the city buses and vehicles have used nothing else since 2002. Twelve public bio-gas filling stations were set up in 2005. A bio-gas train with a 600-kilometer range runs from Linköping to Västervik. It was much cheaper than converting the diesel line to electric, which had been considered to reduce emissions.

Vermicomposting

Worms can also be used to process food waste. Even if you don't have access to, or permission to use, a backyard or side yard, you can compost indoors with a worm bin. Like any urban composting option, worm bins do require some time and attention; they're not trouble-free—nor is worm-bin composting for everyone. The best materials to add to a worm bin are washed fruit and vegetable scraps, coffee grounds and filters, tea bags (remove the staples—they harm the worms' stomachs!), eggshells, paper napkins and towels, and dead plants and flowers. Remember to feed worms a varied diet and don't overload the bin with fruit, or you'll attract fruit flies. Do not feed your worms meat, fish, or dairy products. These items will produce odors and attract flies as they decompose. Interestingly enough, vermicomposting has proved to be very useful in treating medical wastes—but this requires much more sophisticated management.

Recovery of Industrial Discards

E-waste

E-waste is among the most hazardous wastes in our homes. Older computers and electronics often include materials like mercury, lead, and cadmium that are harmful for people and the environment. In 2007, the United States generated more than 3 million tons of e-waste, but only 13.6 percent was recycled according to the EPA. Most was buried, some was burned in incinerators, some was dumped in the countryside, and a bit of it burned in home or commercial building fires.

Table 5.7. *E-waste in millions.*

Products	Total disposed**	Trashed	Recycled	Recycling (by weight)
Televisions	26.9	20.6	6.3	18%
Computer Products*	205.5	157.3	48.2	18%
Cell Phones	140.3	126.3	14.0	10%

* Computer products include CPUs, monitors, notebooks, keyboards, mice, and "hard copy peripherals", printers, copiers, multi-function printer/scanner/fax and fax machines.

** These totals don't include products that are no longer used, but stored—the large reservoir of outdated products stored in the nation's closets and garages.

Where e-products are still functional, the best solution is to find someone who wants them. This can be facilitated by non-profit groups or government exchange programs (www.mncfs.org /donate-your-technology; www.epa.gov/osw/conserve/materials /ecycling/donate.htm). Cell phones and computers often can find new uses in the United States or abroad. Half of the cell phones collected by recyclers can be reused after personal data is removed and new software is installed. The recovery rate could be dramatically increased with government incentives for reuse and support for computer disk scrubbing, reformatting, and distribution. Design guidelines based to the cradle-to-cradle approach could also facilitate recycling.

Although the recovery of e-waste should be a national program, states and local governments have made some efforts to improve recovery. Landfilling some types of e-waste, particularly monitors, has been outlawed in many states. In 2008, California, New York, and Maine had rules outlawing disposal of cell phones in the trash. Other states, like California, now charge a disposal fee when new e-products are sold. This helps fund recovery efforts and e-waste recycling days. Companies like HP, Apple, Dell, Toshiba, Sony, and others are also making greener, cleaner computers with much less harmful ingredients. In January 2009, Toshiba had the highest-rated such laptop. Look for a gold ranking and high EPEAT score. The best solution in the long term is extended product responsibility, where the manufacturer has to take back any products made. This can be an effective marketing opportunity, not simply a burden.

Fig. 5.59.
EPEAT label.

Product Discards

Many of the other products people throw away can also be reused, recycled, or returned to nature. A wide range of products, from clothing to furniture and appliances, are thrown away when new items are purchased. Often they are in good condition but no longer serve the needs or desires of the owner. The challenge is to make it convenient to recover these discards. Reuse used to be a common option before sanitary landfills were created. Products would be dropped off at the dump and picked up and used or resold by someone else. Today the alternatives are to donate the material to a group like Goodwill, to freecycle it, or to drop it at a free exchange site. The Nantucket Island waste reduction effort includes an exchange site.

Charitable organizations will often pick up materials at the home, or offer convenient drop-off sites. One of the more impressive recovery efforts is the Goodwill program in Portland, Oregon. The sale sites are modern, clean, and efficient, looking like an upscale store not a thrift shop. Goodwill Industries of the Columbia Willamette currently operates thirty-six retail stores, four outlets, two online retail locations, and nearly sixty attended donation centers. Their retail business turned more than 143 million pounds of used clothing and household goods into $88.8 million in sales revenues in 2008. And this money provided services for twenty-three thousand people with disabilities.

Freecycle is a growing movement that started in 2003 with about forty people in Tucson, Arizona. Freecycle now has almost five thousand participating organizations and seven million members in eighty-five countries. Freecycle.org uses the power of the Internet to help find new homes for usable products.

Reducing your product impact is easy. Buy well-made, durable products made with green materials. Take good care of them and they will last many years, decades, or lifetimes. A good example is a cast-iron frying pan in place of a plastic-coated steel frying pan. The cast-iron pan is nonstick if it is maintained properly and has a lifetime measured in hundreds of years. The plastic-coated frying pan has a lifetime of three to five years, and if overheated on the stove or in recycling produces a gas that is deadly to birds and not good for other living creatures. Buy cotton, bamboo, wool, or linen clothes. When they wear out, use them as cleaning rags and then toss them on the compost pile.

You can also help by asking your decision makers and political representatives to embrace extended product responsibility for all products. If a manufacturer knows it may have to take a product back, it becomes adept at making it easier to take apart, repair, refurbish, or recycle. Industry is already getting on board with zero waste and research into greener materials and industrial ecologies that mimic natural systems. One of the first was established in Kalundborg, Denmark, more than thirty years ago. Considerable research on developing these types of systems has now been done, but implementation is lagging. Improved consideration of true costs of materials and emissions will drive conversion to these more complete industrial systems.

Packaging Discards

About a third of the waste stream in the United States is packaging, but US government policies and laws generally have not addressed packaging wastes, per se, as a distinct class. These wastes include cardboard, paper, steel, aluminum, and a range of plastics and other materials. The metals, paper, and cardboard are relatively easy to recycle, but the plastics are not. Plastic-coated papers and boxes, often used for food, also pose problems. The growing use of multi-layer metal, plastic, and paper containers is also a problem.

You can reduce packaging to some extent by buying in bulk at the grocery store, using cloth or recycled plastic shopping bags, and by buying products that are not overpackaged. Buying at bricks-and-mortar stores or looking for used or recycled products can help reduce packaging at your home but may not reduce packaging waste overall very much. Clothes, for example, often come to the stores overpackaged in small boxes with paper, pins, and cardboard. Retailers could encourage much less wasteful packaging using reusable containers.

The best solution for packaging would be a national law similar to the German Packaging Ordinance (passed in 1991). This requires industry to take back, reuse, and/or recycle packaging material. Germany targeted packaging material because it accounted for about 50 percent of the volume and 30 percent of the weight of municipal solid waste. The German approach allows industry to determine the specific implementation mechanisms, rather than have the government oversee or micromanage the system. The German government has imposed no taxes or fees and is not

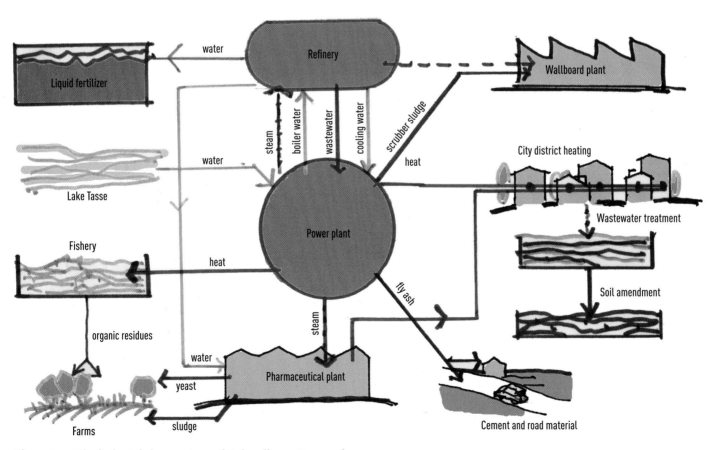

Fig. 5.60. *The industrial ecosystem of Kalundborg, Denmark.*

involved in creating markets for recyclable materials. This strategy has allowed industry to create an alternative take-back packaging system, the Duales System Deutschland (DSD), provided that the system meets specified collecting, sorting, and refilling quotas. The DSD is a privately operated public limited company. Consumers can unpack products and leave the packaging in the store so they can avoid the waste fee at home. This encouraged much more efficient packaging systems. The European Union followed this up with the 1994 Directive on Packaging and Packaging Waste. For all materials other than plastics, most EU member states achieved or surpassed the 1994 directive's minimum recycling and recovery targets well ahead of the June 2001 deadline.

Hazardous Material Discards

A surprising number of hazardous materials can be found in almost every home. An inventory of the garage, kitchen, bathroom (under the sink and in the cabinets), and workshop will usually include a wide range of hazardous materials. These include corrosive, toxic, ignitable, or reactive ingredients. Household hazardous wastes include certain paints, cleaners, oils, batteries, and electronics. Pesticides, rodenticides, chemical fertilizers, motor oil, antifreeze, batteries, paint thinners, solvents, fluorescent lightbulbs (mercury), computer and TV monitors, printer ink and toner, drugs and antibiotics, medical/biohazard waste, compressed gases (propane), and other highly toxic items should always be treated as hazardous waste. Improper disposal of household hazardous poses a threat to human health and the environment.

PROPER DISPOSAL

Many communities offer options for safely discarding household hazardous waste. These may include free disposal days at schools or at a waste site for paints, oil, et cetera. Check your government Web site for local programs. In some cases, these collected materials are recycled or reused. Paints, for example, can often be resold or combined by type and resold. Finding a proper outlet for disposal of unneeded drugs and antibiotics is more difficult, but it is clear that flushing them down the drain (once recommended) is inappropriate. Federal laws should be amended and improved to ensure control of prescription and nonprescription drugs and antibiotics. Guidelines for safer wrapping before disposal in landfills are provided online. California maintains a list of facilities that can accept drugs and is

developing a comprehensive plan. Ultimately a product take-back rule with free mailing may be required.

USE GREENER, CLEANER MATERIALS AND METHODS

The many products used around the home are increasingly recognized as a source risk. You can take a quick look at these at the National Institute of Health page, http://hpd.nlm.nih.gov. Soaps, surfactants, disinfectants, and cleaners are very helpful around the home, but they can be harmful for human health and ecosystems. The foams that are frequently seen in many urban creeks are an indication of how much soap and detergent is entering the environment. Soaps tend to be very well tolerated by mammals but can be toxic to insects, both the harmful ones (controlled by soap sprays) and beneficial or harmless insects in aquatic ecosystems.

Antimicrobial compounds are even more of a concern. Widely used materials such as triclosan have been approved by the EPA for use on more than 140 products without adequate testing. Triclosan persists in the environment, breaks down into substances highly toxic to wildlife, pollutes the human body, and poses health risks that are barely studied and poorly understood. This might make sense if it worked well, but a review of studies on the efficacy of triclosan in soap revealed that it did not reduce bacterial counts on hands significantly more than plain soap unless used repeatedly and in relatively high concentrations (greater than 1 percent, compared

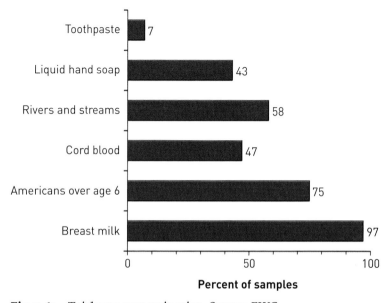

Fig. 5.61. *Triclosan contamination. Source: EWG.*

with the 0.1 to 0.45 percent in consumer antibacterial soaps; Aiello et al., 2007*).

Norway's national consumer council and food safety authority called for a ban on products containing the antibacterial compound triclosan in 2005. The Environmental Working Group has been working for a ban on triclosan in personal care products and any other products used at home for the United States. This is in line with the conclusion of the Canadian and American Medical Association's belief that common antimicrobials for which resistance has been demonstrated should "be discontinued in consumer products unless data emerge that conclusively show that such resistance has no effect on public health and that such products are effective at preventing infection."

Be Informed

Read labels carefully and try greener alternatives around the home. Many books are now available with a wide range of green cleaning techniques using readily available and safe materials such as vinegar and lemon juice. A wide range of cleaner, greener paints are now available as well. You can use compost or compost tea on lawns and gardens instead of chemical fertilizers. Cedar chips or cedar cupboards can replace mothballs. Biocontrols and organic treatments can be used in the garden. And boric acid can replace commercial ant and roach killers.

Ecotoxic Materials

Ecotoxic materials are a special concern for sustainable buildings. Many materials are not harmful to people, but can be very disruptive for ecosystems. These include materials that can be leached from roof materials or paints, such as copper, zinc, and lead, biocides and fertilizers from landscaping, biological wastes, drugs and personal care products in sewage (which is still often dumped in rivers untreated during high storm flows in communities with combined storm and sewage systems), and biocides and cleaners from around the house and garage. Cars and driveways also leak oils, gasoline, antifreeze, and other ecotoxic materials. Most families discard cleaners, solvents, paints, pharmaceuticals, and personal care products (PPCPs) that make their way to our local lakes and streams from landfills and sewage.

In 2000, the US Geological Survey sampled downstream from wastewater treatment plants in thirty states and found at least one pharmaceutical in 80 percent of 139 streams. In some streams, hormones and hormone mimics have led to unisex fish populations that do not reproduce. Triclosan was one of the most frequently detected compounds. Even more worrisome was that fact that when researchers added triclosan to river water and shined ultraviolet light on the water, they found that between 1 and 12 percent of the triclosan was converted to dioxin in the water, leading to fears that sunlight could be transforming triclosan to extremely dangerous dioxin in the environment.

Zero Waste

The sustainable home or building is a building that minimizes discards and facilitates reuse and recycling. Materials should be clean, green, and durable, requiring little or no maintenance. When maintenance is required, it should be with safe materials and processes. The design of the building and landscape should also minimize stormwater contamination and stormwater runoff and would include space and support for recycling, repair, reuse, and return to nature with composting. Neighborhood, community, and state-level support can make it easier and more attractive to minimize discards, ensuring that discards are reused, repaired, recycled, or returned to nature. Minimizing the discard stream is desirable and can be advantageous to the pocketbook as well as to health and the environment. Nature provides the best examples of zero waste.

Zero waste can be difficult to achieve, but 90 percent reduction is possible and proven. Industry has led the way with many facilities now seeking, and sometimes achieving, close to zero waste on-site. These include production of cars (Subaru, Indiana), tea (Lipton, Virginia), electronics (Xerox, New York), and wines (Fetzer, California). David's parents came close, reducing their trips to the landfill to one garbage can a year.

Acute Effects Of Overexposure:

Ingestion: Ingestion Can Cause Abdominal Pain, Nausea, Vomiting And Collapse, Along With Tissue Destruction In The Gastrointestinal Tract. Skin Contact: Corrosive To Skin On Contact. Skin Contact Can Produce Inflammation, Reddening And Blistering. Inhalation: Inhalation Of Spray Mist Or Vapors May Produce Irritation, Burning Or Destruction Of Tissues In The Respiratory Tract, Characterized By Coughing, Choking, Pain, Or Shortness Of Breath. Severe Overexposure May Lead To Fatal Lung Damage.

Eye Contact: Corrosive To Eyes On Contact. Eye Contact Can Produce Corneal Damage Or Blindness.

Fig. 5.62. *Choose wisely: a toilet bowl cleaner warning label.*

Landscape Regeneration

Regenerative Design of Places

In his book *Regenerative Design for Sustainable Development,* John Lyle describes most environmental design as being either part of a degenerative process that degrades the environment or part of a regenerative process that helps maintain our environment. Sustainable design is, by definition, regenerative design as well. Our impacts have been so great that a significant design effort must be made to regenerate degraded environments and landscapes while simultaneously providing for human activities and needs. This is similar to

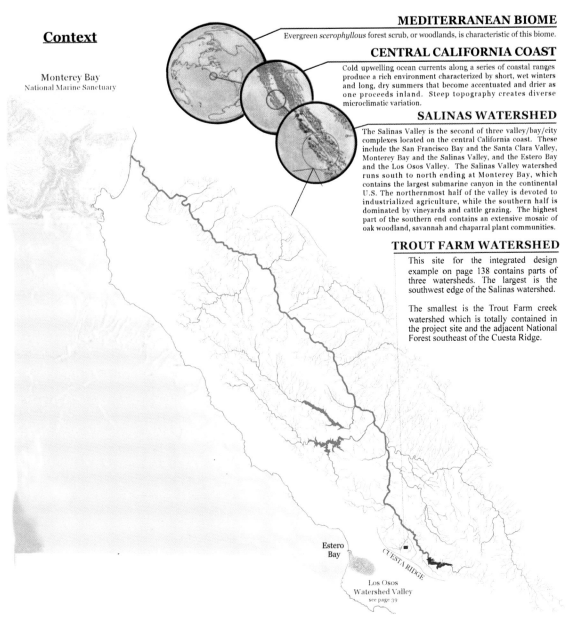

Context

Monterey Bay
National Marine Sanctuary

MEDITERRANEAN BIOME

Evergreen *scerophyllous* forest scrub, or woodlands, is characteristic of this biome.

CENTRAL CALIFORNIA COAST

Cold upwelling ocean currents along a series of coastal ranges produce a rich environment characterized by short, wet winters and long, dry summers that become accentuated and drier as one proceeds inland. Steep topography creates diverse microclimatic variation.

SALINAS WATERSHED

The Salinas Valley is the second of three valley/bay/city complexes located on the central California coast. These include the San Francisco Bay and the Santa Clara Valley, Monterey Bay and the Salinas Valley, and the Estero Bay and the Los Osos Valley. The Salinas Valley watershed runs south to north ending at Monterey Bay, which contains the largest submarine canyon in the continental U.S. The northernmost half of the valley is devoted to industrialized agriculture, while the southern half is dominated by vineyards and cattle grazing. The highest part of the southern end contains an extensive mosaic of oak woodland, savannah and chaparral plant communities.

TROUT FARM WATERSHED

This site for the integrated design example on page 138 contains parts of three watersheds. The largest is the southwest edge of the Salinas watershed.

The smallest is the Trout Farm creek watershed which is totally contained in the project site and the adjacent National Forest southeast of the Cuesta Ridge.

Estero
Bay

CUESTA RIDGE

Los Osos
Watershed Valley
see page 39

Fig. 5.63. *The landscape context of each building project should be analyzed in regard to the scales of place as described on pages 20 and 21. This is to determine how each project can be a working part that enhances the whole.*

the relationship between life-cycle assessment and life-cycle optimization where the goal of doing "less harm" is expanded to doing "more good."

To allow landscape regeneration to become part of our design processes, we need to once again acknowledge how dynamic natural environments really are. This is important in facilitating the modification of two mind-sets that get in the way of a successful practice of regenerative design.

The first of these mind-sets is the tendency to think of natural landscape as being in equilibrium outside of human effect. Accordingly, protection and continued stability are viewed as the goal. Federal policies in the United States with regard to fire prevention and flood protection have been large-scale examples of this mind-set, since flood and fire are assumed to be destructive natural disasters. But fire and flood control have created new, more costly extreme wildfires and floods. We have recently discovered that some non-equilibrium is a critical aspect of the health of many ecosystems. Thus, these federal policies are slowly being modified to create "controlled burns" in some national forests and "controlled floods" in areas downstream from some large dams. We are slowly coming to realize that the occasional disturbances we call "natural disasters" are an important part of the maintenance and operation of ecosystems and landscapes.

Life-cycle and regenerative design as applied to site is necessary in many settings, including regional, urban, town, suburban, and rural. Some argue that sustainable design, particularly architecture, should be strictly concentrated in existing built-up areas, leaving more rural areas intact. It is true that more urban areas need a great deal of attention, and the distinction between urban and rural places should be maintained and strengthened. We need to recognize, however, that very few rural areas are pristine, intact, and healthy; and that the urban edge is the area of most extensive impact. Industrialized mining, agriculture, and recreation practices have affected all our places except, perhaps, a few we designate as wilderness. Even these have been affected by climate change, nitrogen deposition, acid rain, and other pollutants. Therefore, sustainable design using life-cycle and regenerative principles needs to be applied almost everywhere. The differences are only in the specifics of landscape, relationship to density, and infrastructure.

This does not mean the continuous disturbances accomplished by existing degenerative design are desirable. Instead, it means that occasional disturbances are often an essential part of the system. There can be fires, earthquakes, and landslides in Mediterranean biomes; fires, floods, and intense grazing by hoofed animals in grassland biomes; floods, droughts, and tornadoes in the midwestern United States; ice storms in the Northeast; hurricanes and typhoons in coastal subtropical and tropical areas. Disturbance and regenerative processes are occurring constantly at multiple scales. We, too, in fact, must become a part of this dynamic process. All we have to do is tune in to the specificity of place to understand some part of it, and then design can be a regenerative, rather than degenerative force. We can't ever know everything that is involved and we can't control nature. It is far more important to hear the music and start to dance. With familiarity and practice, the steps will improve.

Example of Integrated Design for On-Site Resources

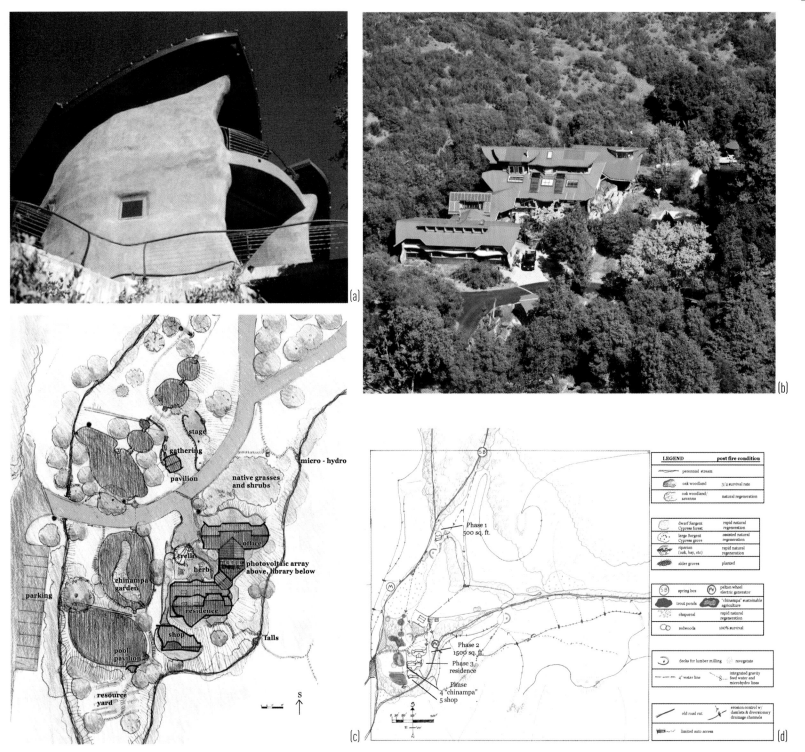

Fig. 5.64. *The Trout Farm, 1995–1997. (a) North facade straw bale wall. (b) Aerial photo. (c) Site plan. (d) Facility plan.*

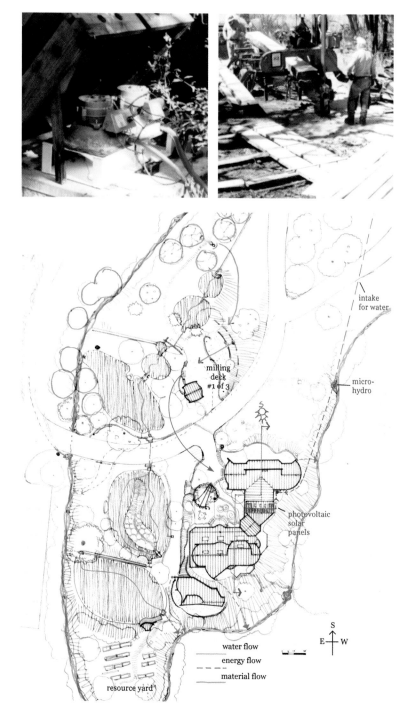

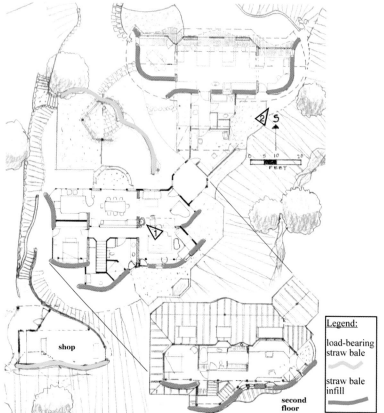

Fig. 5.65. *(a) Micro-hydro power unit. (b) Milling lumber from trees killed by the fire. (c) Infrastructure and material flow plan.*

Fig. 5.66. *(a) West facade. (b) Structure, finishes, and furniture made from milled trees. (c) Straw bale wall plan.*

Our final example of integrated design for these topics is a multi-use complex near Santa Margarita, California. This design in figures 5.64–5.66 responds to the requirements of providing a home and office, healing the site after a severe wildfire, and addressing some of the problems found in the greater Trout Creek watershed from damage done from 1910 to 1979 by mining, grading, and motorcycle racing. Sporadic wildfires are also a major design factor in this location. Healing the watershed required controlling erosion caused by all these factors to the point where water flows are regenerative rather than degenerative. In addition, infrastructure, energy production, and materials used for construction were drawn from the existing conditions.

The dead trees from the wildfire in 1994 were milled on-site, yielding more than 20,000 board-feet of high-quality custom lumber at a reasonable price. Regeneration of the landscape occurred in waves, starting with specialized fire-following plants like fire poppies, progressing through herbs and low shrubs to larger shrubs and brush to regeneration of the forests. In seven years, the landscape took on much of its previous character.

The architectural program for this site is for a mixed-use complex of offices, research, and residential facilities. The complex is designed to draw most of its energy for heating, cooling, lighting, and electrical generation from the site by passive means. In addition, 80 percent of the wood used in construction was obtained from the site.

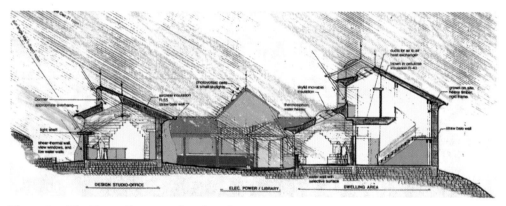

Fig. 5.67. *The Trout Farm section drawing.*

Summary: Harvesting On-Site Resources

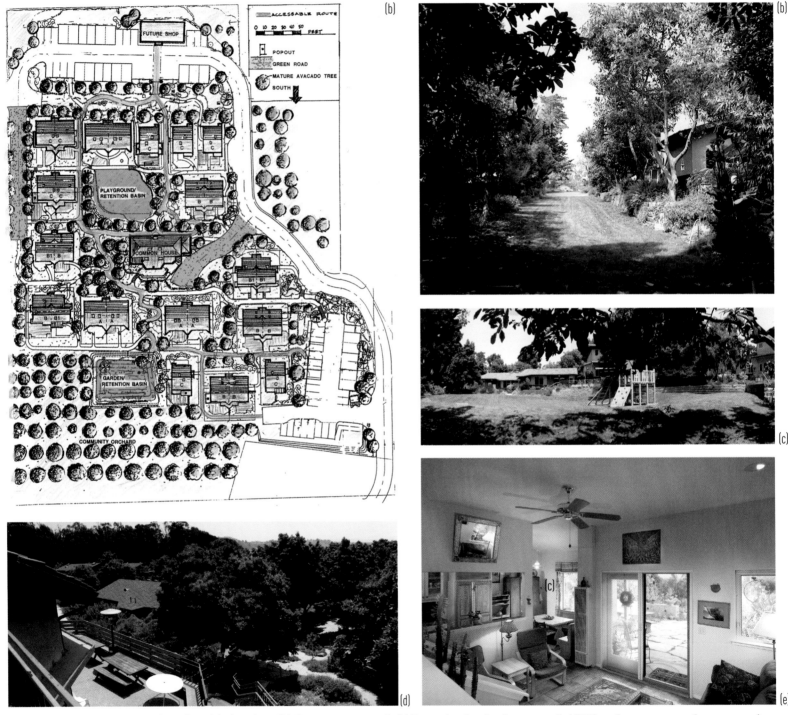

Fig. 5.68. *Tierra Nueva Cohousing. (a) Site plan. (b) Green access road. (c) Retention basin playground. (d) View from common house to units below. (e) Interior of residential unit.*

As has been stressed throughout this book, the passive approach to green building and sustainability is an integrative approach. Historically, the passive approach dealt just with thermal issues such as heating and cooling; then environmental issues such as ventilation and natural lighting were included, as well as materials and construction processes. But today, this approach to design is also dealing with resource use and production issues such as water, food, waste, and much more. The more expansive considerations include the responsibility of the building to landscape, ecosystem, and planet. In addition to these are the social dimensions and issues of sustainability.

All of these concerns are exemplified in the Tierra Nueva Cohousing community in Oceano, California. This twenty-seven-unit community utilizes many of the techniques described in this chapter—passive heating, cooling, natural ventilation, natural drainage, separate automobile areas, green roads, multiple community facilities, open space, a community solar photovoltaic array, and a mature sustained landscape. Beyond incorporating all these are the social aspects that enliven living there. In the words of Jim Leech, co-housing developer, "Community is the hidden dimension of sustainability."

Village Homes Community on the left in this photo still has not been equaled in thoughtful sustainable planning and passive solar design in the United States.

Introduction to Synergistic Design

Integrated design involves bringing together all the factors discussed largely in isolation in the previous chapters to create a workable whole. As the examples of designs and built projects at the end of each of chapter have shown, integrated design often involves having single components perform multiple functions. The goal is to remove redundancies that exist in the strictly additive assemblages used in most modern buildings in order to reduce cost and to achieve greater performance and efficiency.

The key to success with this integrated approach to environmental design is achieving synergy. Synergy happens where and when the whole becomes greater than the sum of its parts, and the parts become optimized in relationship to the whole. The concept of synergy is not difficult, but it is overlooked in most design. There are common examples of dynamic synergy all around us:

- In metallurgy, when an alloy of two metals is stronger than each component.

- In plant and animal breeding, when hybrid vigor can improve offspring of the parent stock.

- In team organization, when a collection of individual specialties fit together so well as to become invincible.

- In a good marriage, where each partner adds to the union in a way that the two can do much more together than apart.

- In aesthetic compositions, where color, form, and proportion interact to achieve that level of transcendence so common in great architecture throughout history.

Sadly, our industrial-era mind-set is obsessed with efficiency based on parts and narrowness of view rather than integration, systems, and synergies. The efficiency of a synergetic whole, once achieved, will always be greater than its components.

In this concluding chapter, we have invited two of our colleagues, Pliny Fisk III and Richard Levine, to join us in presenting longer-range views of how we can achieve a level of integration in architecture and planning where the whole exceeds the sum of its parts

and becomes synergetic design. Our complementary approaches for exploring this new design frontier all have the same goal—sustainability—but each takes a different tack based on its author's training and experience.

Fisk is well known for his intricate and sometimes difficult graphics (some of which illustrate his essay), but he is nonetheless on the cutting edge of graphically modeling the complexity of scales—from the planetary to the microbial—involved in any attempt to illustrate the interdependence and interactivity of ecological structures and issues, cultural and social concerns, and material and economic conditions. His work represents the beginnings of a new working language of sustainable design.

Levine's essay on city-regions quite succinctly critiques certain ideas about sustainability that are in themselves unsustainable. His advice is "Don't pick the low-hanging fruit." In other words, we need major changes, not just a few compact fluorescent lightbulbs.

Together, these four views illustrate the complexity and diversity that is inherent in synergetic design for our time and place. Use the one or a combination of approaches that best suits your interests and fits the challenges you face.

	EMPHASIS:	IMPLIES:	ACHIEVED BY:
1	Sustainable Community	Healthy and happy people	Living in a healthy ecosystem
2	Prototypes for a Living Future	Structuring decision making in a continuity of scales	Participation, feedback, and optimization
3	Sustainable City-Regions	Living in balance with a fair share of resources	Don't pick the low-hanging fruit
4	Cultural Transformation	Changing perceptions regarding history, geometry, and aesthetics	New conceptual tools

Fig. 6.1. *Topics of essays.*

Essay 1: Sustainable Communities

David Bainbridge, Associate Professor, Marshall Goldsmith School of Management, Alliant International University, San Diego, California

Community Matters

The growing awareness of very serious problems with global and local ecosystem stability and resource availability is encouraging new consideration of the sustainability of our current lifeways and communities. The World Commission on Environment and Development (1987), chaired by Norwegian Gro Harlem Brundtland, defined *sustainability* as "development that meets the needs of the present generation without compromising the ability of future generations to meet their own needs." This definition, the best that could be agreed upon from a diverse group with very different worldviews, emphasized environmental constraints; but I believe the social and cultural factors may be more important.

To be fully sustainable, a community must not only understand its dependence on nature's provisioning services (air, water, flood control, food) and natural capital while also meeting the psychological and social needs of its residents. This is not a new challenge; the Greek writer Alcaeus, writing in the seventh century BC, commented, "not houses finely roofed nor the stones of walls well built, nor canals or dockyards make the city, but men [and today of course women —eds.] able to seize their opportunities." This overview of social and environmental issues involved in sustainable, integrated design *is just a start* (refer to the references and further reading list for more detail). There is a spectrum of needs that must be met, beginning with physical needs for food and shelter and moving to more complex emotional needs. Most of these have direct implications for resource use and sustainability.

Physical Needs

Although we all depend on natural systems for the air we breathe, the food we eat, the water we drink, and the materials we use to build our homes, we have lost touch with this connection. Water now comes from the faucet or in a bottle; food comes packaged, prepared, and free of dirt; energy flows from the wall socket from distant power plants; and wastes are simply flushed away. But natural and managed ecosystems still provide us with the requirements for life, and every one of us has an impact on our planet. We need to rebuild a cultural awareness of our relation to and dependence on nature. Ernest Callenbach's *Ecotopia* (1975*) provides an entertaining fictional account to help people understand this connection and is a good book to introduce the concept to students in high school and college. As he commented in a more recent article, "It is just as important for all of us to grasp an ecological vocabulary as it is for us to understand arithmetic" (Callenbach, 1999*). His work also illustrates the slow change in culture, with Portland, Oregon, adopting many of the ideas he suggested after twenty or thirty years (Timberg, 2008*).

In chapters 1–5, we showed that it is possible to utilize renewable resources and dramatically reduce ecological impacts, often at little or no additional cost. In many cases, the individual building is an appropriate scale at which to work, but in other cases the subdivision scale or neighborhood or city will be more appropriate. Simply ensuring that new housing and buildings will be sustainable will not suffice; we need to rebuild our wasteful, unhealthy, and very inefficient neighborhoods and cities as well.

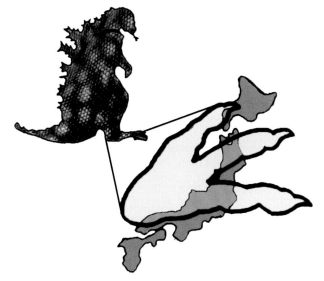

Fig. 6.2. *The eco-footprint of Tokyo illustrates the challenge we face.*

A Big Challenge

How big is the challenge? We can begin to explore the problem by calculating our ecological footprint to see how much productive land, water, and resources are needed to support our current lifestyles. Examine your own lifestyle with an ecological footprint quiz at http://ecofoot.org. The average American in 2006 required 24 acres. This seems plausible and even possible in a rural setting, but when we examine the ecological footprints of cities and countries, we begin to realize the enormous challenge we face. London's ecological footprint, for example takes up almost the entire country (Srinivas, 2006). Tokyo's footprint is three times the size of the entire country of Japan, and the Netherlands' ecological footprint is five times the land area of the country.

Improving the physical sustainability of communities and cities will not be easy, because we generally haven't studied these issues much, the flow pathways and impacts can be complicated, and they often have difficult-to-predict long-term consequences. However, the issues of buildings, energy, water, waste disposal, and air quality are generally well understood, and technical standards and solutions are known. The most basic goal was well stated by Aldo Leopold (1949*): "A thing is right when it tends to preserve the integrity, stability and beauty of the biotic community. It is wrong when it does otherwise." But the second goal is to protect, enhance, and maintain the culture and community.

Cultural and Psychological Needs and Health

To be sustainable, a community must have a healthy economy and a culture that provides support for interconnection and cooperation, safety, cohesion, education, opportunity, health, and equity. These issues are complex, interrelated, and often very difficult to change. We have spent too little time thinking about what a community should or might provide and what our goals for the future should be. Too often the greatest investment has been in programs and polices that are driven by special-interest groups that have disastrous health and environmental costs, such as "making commuting by automobile from distant bedroom communities easy and inexpensive" and "producing electricity by burning coal."

Everyone would perhaps define his or her ideal community a bit differently, based on his or her own experience, philosophy, and education, but consensus can emerge about the priorities for a sustainable community. Is it creativity, health, support for the disadvantaged, satisfaction, love, education, opportunity, income, identity, participation, safety, friends, volunteers, freedom, privacy, recreation, health, religion, lack of crime, affordable housing?

A number of cities in the United States, Europe, and Asia have now started sustainability programs, with an emphasis on environmental considerations. Amsterdam, Copenhagen, Freiburg, Munster, London and other European cities have made it clear that developed countries can make changes that improve sustainability. Curitiba, Brazil, has proved that even a growing city in a developing country can do a great deal as well. The United States has generally lagged, although Davis (California), Seattle, Portland, Scottsdale (Arizona), Boulder (Colorado), Santa Monica, and San Francisco have made a concerted effort to improve their sustainability.

Sustainability Across Time

Sustainability evaluation and assessment require a view across time. Oregon has perhaps done the most work in evaluating community sustainability over time, with some data series going back to 1990–1991 (Schlossberg and Zimmerman, 2003*). Surveys in person

Fig. 6.3. *Community markets bring people together and support local enterprise; this one is located in Davis, California.*

and online can help refine the community indicators and increase public participation in the process. Ultimately it is not what the data say, but what people feel that matters. Bhutan's use of Gross National Happiness (GNH) instead of Gross National Product (GNP) may be a more tenable approach for measuring community progress. This approach may seem idealistic and removed from hardheaded conservative administration, but as a few examples will show, it has clear and important cost implications.

Health

Health may be one of the most important criteria because it carries such large cost burdens if it is missing. Toronto, Canada, helped start the healthy cities movement with a meeting in 1984. This program overcame early objections in Toronto and has now spread to many other cities around the world. City restrictions on smoking have gained ground, adding immense health benefits to people and reducing health care costs, but other equally important factors, like obesity, have been largely ignored.

One of the results of the current disconnection between design choices and health has been the rapid rise in obesity. By 2014, the obesity and overweight rates in the auto-dominated countries are predicted to reach 70 percent in the United States, 65 percent in the United Kingdom, and 50 percent in Australia (Sassi et al., 2009*). In 2000–2001, the obesity rates in these countries were 31 percent US, 22 percent UK, and 21 percent Australia.

In contrast, countries with better bicycle and pedestrian planning and mass transit are less fat, but obesity is still cause for concern with Denmark at 10 percent, the Netherlands 9 percent, France 9 percent, and Japan 3 percent (OECD Health Data, 2003). Building our communities and cities for cars has made them distinctly unhealthy for people, with enormous long-term costs for medical care. Investing in bicycle and pedestrian facilities pays immediate health dividends and has a very high benefit-to-cost ratio. Amsterdam's excellent bicycle infrastructure was built and is being improved with an investment of millions of dollars—the cost of a short section of freeway or one freeway interchange. Forty percent of the commute traffic is now by bike in Amsterdam!

States and communities can also play a key role in getting people out and active (www.cdc.gov/obesity/data/trends.html). Only

Colorado was below 20 percent obese in 2008. Although Colorado still holds the title of "leanest state in America," the percentage of overweight and obese citizens in the state is on the rise. LiveWell is an NGO committed to fighting the obesity epidemic through consumer education and policy and environmental changes. The investment of money for health instead of professional sports would provide great returns.

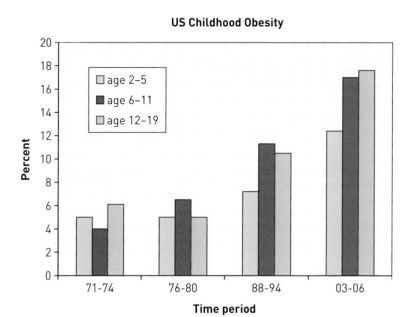

Fig. 6.4. *Childhood obesity rate.*

Fig. 6.5. *Bicycles are good for people and the planet.*

Education

The most critical challenge for sustainability in the long term is education. This includes developing ecological literacy and a near-universal understanding of sustainability, and providing the quality of education needed to remain globally competitive. Reductions in education spending in many areas as a result of the recent financial meltdown have reinforced a growing divide between rich and poor and have priced bright and hardworking minority and working-class children out of the educational systems. Opportunity for all should be the priority, with more full scholarships for outstanding students and more opportunities for students to work on paid community sustainability projects.

Sustainability issues may provide the compelling topic needed to reengage students in learning, combining hands-on work in food production, energy and water management (helping improve efficiency and comfort), and waste handling at every school. More than a third of students in the United States considered "school a place they do not want to go" in 2000 (Lyne, 2001*), and with the growing emphasis on teaching to the test this number has probably increased. One of David's best students looked back on his years at a San Diego high school as being "just like prison." Sustainability as a comprehensive theme for learning across the curriculum can help reengage the full student body from Advanced Placement science to auto shop. Education, engagement, and hope are also the best tools to fight gangs and crime.

Fig. 6.6. *Solar building class project, AIU.*

Interaction

The design of neighborhoods for automobiles instead of people limits interaction and community. Judy and Michael Corbett designed interaction into their innovative solar subdivision, Village Homes (see page 227). They created common spaces that were shared by several homes so that neighbors would have to meet and vineyards, fruit orchards, and gardens for people to work together. They also made the development for people instead of cars. A survey showed that residents of Village Homes knew forty of their neighbors, while residents in surrounding developments knew less than half as many (Bainbridge et al., 1979*; Corbett and Corbett, 2000*). In Village Homes, children play safely outside as part of a known community. These intertwined factors improve health, cohesion, equity, and quality of life.

Urban streetscapes in Europe and a growing number of American cities create spaces that bring people together. Music, art, food, festivals, and community-action projects can help create community among strangers and can solidify and support neighborhoods.

Fig. 6.7. *Michael Corbett, developer of Village Homes.*

Participation

Community involvement is also essential, but difficult to measure and rarely used as an indicator by politicians or decision makers. In general, community participation has gone down in the United States, particularly for the important thirty-through-fifty-nine age group (Putnam, 2000*). The increasingly long work hours, the necessity for double or triple incomes to support a family, and longer commutes (a design decision) are making volunteer work and community participation more difficult. The loss of these key players represents a loss of billions of dollars once contributed to these communities. Policies and programs can identify and encourage participation. Starting the search for community assets instead of focusing on community needs is helpful (Kretzmann and McKnight, 1993*).

Economy

A sustainable economy should generate good jobs, provide sufficient funding to maintain and upgrade infrastructure, education, and health, and offer opportunities for advancement and security. Innovation is increasingly important in the face of national and global competition.

New jobs should be at wages above the living wage, with opportunity for advancement and satisfying careers. Income should be sufficient to allow for saving, and hours worked should allow time for volunteerism and community involvement. Income inequality should be declining, because increasing inequity can lead to conflict and long-term instability. Income inequality and unequal access to medical care can also lead to a wide range of problems.

The health of the economy is also measured in government accountability and fiscal health. Sustainability requires well-funded and -maintained infrastructure and capital improvements made in a timely manner. Income should be balanced with expenditures, and costs should be paid by users from current accounts, not by bonded indebtedness of future generations. Broader measures of economic health, such as the Genuine Progress Indicator (GPI), should be used to measure the progress of communities, states, and nations. GPI integrates health, education, environment, and economics and more accurately reflects how people feel they are doing.

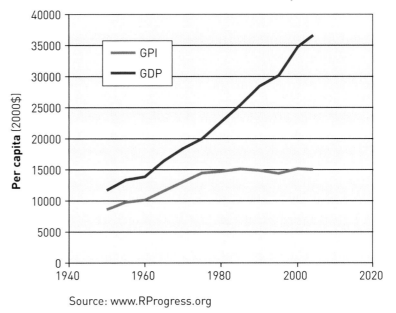

USA Genuine Progress Indicator v/s Gross Domestic Product Per Capita

Source: www.RProgress.org

Fig. 6.8. *GDP versus Genuine Progress Indicator.*

Eliminating the Drivers of Unsustainability

Awareness of sustainability issues is growing, but understanding does not change behavior very readily. Economic signals do. Uncounted and incorrectly attributed costs lead the market to perform very poorly. Consumers make unsustainable choices because prices reflect only a small fraction of the total transaction cost, leaving many "externalities" out of the picture. These externalities include the costs of social disruption, pollution, disease, and damage to vital ecosystem services (such as the impact of the Gulf oil spill on fisheries and tourism). These externalities are integral costs of goods and services and often exceed the current "price." Three examples will show how these costs can be incorporated in products, and the impact this would have on communities.

Autos

A conservative estimate suggests that Americans currently pay only one-third to one-half the true cost of driving (Bainbridge,

2009*). Others suggest it is closer to one-tenth, if a broader range of environmental and societal costs were factored in and if the true cost of infrastructure were more carefully costed out. The highway current infrastructure repair backlog in the United States is estimated to be almost half a trillion dollars and continues to increase daily.

Imagine what people would do differently if they had to pay the true cost of using an automobile. They would walk and ride bicycles more often, and they would change where they live in relation to work. Denmark recently committed $400 million for bicycle system upgrades; this would be $22 billion if we spent the same amount per capita in the United States. This might seem high, but it represents the estimated health costs for obesity in this country for less than one month in 2018.

Stormwater

Making the polluter pay impact fees is usually the most effective manner of addressing environmental problems, and stormwater is a perfect example. It is relatively easy to charge fees for both stormwater pollutants and stormwater runoff. For the pollutants found in stormwater, a pollution charge should be added at point of sale for nonrecyclables, and a deposit fee should be instituted for materials such as motor oil, pesticides, and fertilizer that show up in stormwater.

Stormwater-runoff-related flooding can be minimized by charging for runoff exceeding natural rates in undisturbed ecosystems. In the United States, a few cities have adopted stormwater fees, but rates are usually nominal. Denver collects a fee based on the impervious surface area for each property estimated using digital global satellite mapping.

Table 6.1. *The Denver Stormwater Fee Structure in 2007.*

Impervious Area (sq ft)	Fee
100 –2,000	$45
2,100 –2,900	$60
2,901 –3,900	$78
3,901 –7,500	$105
7,501 –50,000	$228

In Germany, fees more realistically reflect costs, with cost per square meter of impervious surface (McCann, 2008*) running about five times Denver rates. Rainwater harvesting and green roofs have been booming in Germany because they can minimize stormwater fees. These green solutions are also supported by codes and incentives. These types of incentives are also appearing in the United States. In Boulder, Colorado, systems that meet hundred-year storm requirements are eligible for an 80 percent fee reduction. Stormwater fees can reduce taxpayers' traditional general fund subsidies for developers and builders and support education, restoration, and repair of waterways and natural areas as well.

Food

Student food programs have traditionally emphasized lowest cost instead of best value. Low-quality, high-fat, and high-sugar convenience foods have contributed to the growing problem of diabetes in the United States. One in three children in this country is now expected to be diabetic by the time he or she graduates from high school. For African American children, it is likely to be one in two. These problems carry enormous costs to society in lost productivity, suffering, and medical care. Medical care costs alone for diabetes are now estimated at $45 billion a year. Berkeley's innovative school food program with curriculum and activities that embrace organic gardening, healthy and tasty food preparation, and sustainability has demonstrated what can be done (Waters, 2008*). The cost is not insignificant—almost $400,000 a year for a gardener, garden supplies, chef, and teaching support. But if just one student each year does not develop diabetes, the lifetime savings fully cover the added cost.

Fig. 6.9. *Stormwater costs paid by taxpayers, caused by developers.*

The Goal

Improving sustainability is a long-term goal and process. It will take inspiration, action, research, and monitoring. Monitoring and reporting are essential, because what isn't measured, isn't managed. Recycling of waste is a modest success in a sea of environmental failures, in large part because it is measured and carries penalties if diversion levels are not achieved. True-cost accounting is an essential element of sustainable management. This should include a careful review and dismantling of subsidies and perverse incentives for nonrenewable uses and waste and special-interest domination of the political process.

Sustainability reporting and labeling can help investors and consumers make wise choices. Development doesn't have to be a dirty word—if it is done well!

The ultimate goal of development should be a healthy, happy, and productive human community in a stable, rich, and productive environment. This is possible and perhaps essential; but it will not happen with current development focus on short-term profit based on exorbitant subsidies. In most cases, we can improve both function and structure rapidly by managing organic matter and water more wisely and limiting ecotoxicity impacts.

Descriptor	Characteristics
Boundaries	Physical, biological and artificial Relationship of development boundaries and ecosystem boundaries, watersheds, airsheds, communities Permeability of boundaries to fluxes of materials, energy, and organisms (local, regional and global impacts)
Energy balance	Forms of energy (solar, renewable, sustainable, fossil) Energy inputs as subsidies or stressors
Material flow	Inputs and outputs from site Expected magnitudes for development Local conditions of geology, soils, topography, rainfall, etc., that may produce extreme, and therefore limiting, rates of input or output Retention of important nutrients and/or pollutants on site Anticipated retention/loss characteristics of target ecosystem Creation, dispersal and retention of ecotoxic materials Mechanism of retention available on-site Likelihood that retention mechanisms can be restored
Ecosystem Components	Definition of components (e.g., herbivores, fungivores, primary consumers, etc.) Biodiversity, species richness, and resilience Food web structure Feedback loops among components
Intra-System Cycling	
Decomposition	Rates for different types of plant material, different micro-habitats; effects of soil, terrestrial and aquatic food web on rates
Nutrient Uptake	Rates for different nutrients, different plant species
Deposition in Litter	Rates for different nutrients, plant species, plant tissues
Turnover; Mean Residence	Relative importance of soil organic matter, litter
Efficiency of Transfers	Recycling, resorption or retention of nutrients
Dynamics	
Disturbance Regime	Characteristic types of disturbance; frequency, intensity, duration, spatial extent
Resilience	Temporal and spatial response to disturbances, rate of recovery
Resistance Trajectories	Temporal changes in other ecosystem descriptors during succession

Fig. 6.10. *Ecosystem descriptors useful for designing sustainable development.*

Development type and sustainability

Legend:
- solar based
- nutrient cycling
- %native plants
- rain capture

Categories (top to bottom): Sustainable development, Industrial, Urban, Industrial agriculture, Suburban, Rural, Ecoagriculture, Wilderness

X-axis: Sustainability (0, 20, 40, 60, 80, 100)

Fig. 6.11. *Development impacts by land use type.*

Time scale bubbles: 500–100,000 years; 15–200 years; 10–30 years; next product cycle; next election; next quarter; one season; one day

Characters: Hunter-Gatherer, Farmer, Business Manager, Politician, Industrialist, Plant Breeder, Forester, Ecologist

Fig. 6.12. *Time scales of concern.*

Fig. 6.13a. *The edible schoolyard, Pittsburgh. www.growpittsburgh .org/growpittsburgh/Projects.*

Fig. 6.13b. *The edible schoolyard, Berkeley, Alice Waters. Photo by Thomas Heinser.*

The important ecosystem-level issues that need to be addressed in sustainable development include ecosystem structure and function. The regulation of ecosystem processes, the relationship of ecosystem structure to function, the control of ecosystem dynamics over time, and the interchange of materials and energy with the surrounding landscape are all important parts of the puzzle. These are often explored in studies of landscape ecology (Naveh and Lieberman, 1994*), ecosystem restoration (Ehrenfeld and Toth, 1997*; Bainbridge, 2007*), and sustainable development (Mollison and Slay, 1997*; Termorshuizen and Opdam, 2009*).

The key to planning a sustainable development is understanding the ecological and cultural histories of the site. The tools of environmental history are better than ever before and can help us understand the ecosystem conditions we see today, by better understanding what was there before. These critical insights can help us plan a development that restores ecosystem structure and function and improves the quality of life today and for future generations.

Fig. 6.14. *Wolken Environmental Education Center at Hidden Villa in Los Altos, California, integrates straw bale construction, passive heating, passive cooling, natural light, and solar electricity production for a net zero energy building. It was among the first projects to integrate FSC-certified wood for the trusses, and even though regulations have not allowed gray-water or rainwater harvesting, the building was pre-plumbed to utilize these on-site water resources.*

Essay 2: Prototypes for a Living Future

Pliny Fisk III, Co-Director, Center for Maximum Potential Building Systems, Austin, Texas

The key to understanding and regenerating the ecology of place such as a city is establishing a framework to understand the conditions that influence how decisions are made and how the altered ecology of the city-region is evolving.

This realization grew out of our Center for Maximum Potential Building Systems (CMPBS) National Input–Output/Life Cycle Assessment/Geographic Information Systems model (page 208). Correlation of dollar equivalency and human impact revealed by a cell-by-cell accounting showed the greatest impact located along the urban edges. The pattern was consistent: Urban areas of higher population tended to mediate impacts, while rural environments took on the brunt of the pollution. If we are to "save our planet," a very different planning paradigm is needed that uses the city, combined with its rural partners, to trigger systemic planetary health and well-being.

A recent experience from Austin illustrates the need to understand the city as a system of public-, nonprofit-, and private-sector actors and the use of creative intervention to move toward a regenerative mode. CMPBS and associated activists recognized the land-use environmental challenge posed by the ubiquitous big-box-warehouse typology as an opportunity for Austin to continue its steps toward becoming a model green city. The plan that emerged involved retrofitting big-box buildings with rooftop systems for rainwater harvesting, ecological wastewater treatment, high-yield organic food production, high-efficiency organic fertilizer production, solar photovoltaic panels, and algal-based liquid fuel systems—all existing technologies. The plan incorporated the guiding principles of previous work by balancing needs with local life-cycle procedures that involved prioritizing local sourcing, transport, processing, and re-sourcing of needed materials and components. Without adding a single residential photovoltaic panel or LEED-certified building, this system as proposed was estimated to supply almost 20 percent of Austin's electric needs, more than 15 percent of Austin's water needs, exceed Austin's fresh-vegetable food demand, and meet close to 20 percent of Austin's biofuel needs. The plan illustrates the potential productivity and efficiency of synergistic design.

Our previous experience with developing Austin's award-winning Green Building Program, the first in the nation, shows what must be done to achieve a project of this magnitude even in a location with great advantages. The Green Building Program was a result of a progressive mayor and city council, forty-two supportive citizen commissions, and many activist renewable-energy groups. Furthermore, we established a very futuristic, "maximum potential" model as a goal to strive for. Our success was the process itself, one that capitalized on existing checks and balances within Austin's urban

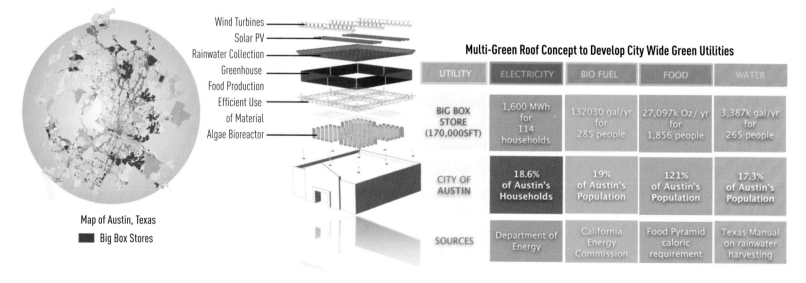

Multi-Green Roof Concept to Develop City Wide Green Utilities

UTILITY	ELECTRICITY	BIO FUEL	FOOD	WATER
BIG BOX STORE (170,000SFT)	1,600 MWh for 114 households	132030 gal/yr for 285 people	27,097k Oz/ yr for 1,856 people	3,387k gal/yr for 265 people
CITY OF AUSTIN	18.6% of Austin's Households	19% of Austin's Population	121% of Austin's Population	17.3% of Austin's Population
SOURCES	Department of Energy	California Energy Commission	Food Pyramid caloric requirement	Texas Manual on rainwater harvesting

Map of Austin, Texas
■ Big Box Stores

Wind Turbines
Solar PV
Rainwater Collection
Greenhouse
Food Production
Efficient Use of Material
Algae Bioreactor

Fig. 6.15. *Austin's Multi-Green Roof Concept to Develop City Wide Green Utilities.*

system, resulting in a program that used a fiscal and environmental accounting and balances system. The green building program required the following steps, and the Multi-Green Roof City Wide Green Utility will have to be even more rigorous.

- A city/region planning framework must be identified and put into practice so that all stakeholders (the public, private, and nonprofit sectors, citizen commissions, the mayor, and city council) understand their interrelated responsibilities with a system for monitoring and measuring.

- An understanding of the four essential flows (information, currency, energy, material) and how they organize society and resources in general.

- How best to strategically affect these flows. For example, if currency is not available for the support of venture capital applied to eco-technologies, action needs to be taken. The media and information regarding the regionalized flow of energy and materials will play a key role in finding new sources of funding.

- The need to identify the state of systems accounts (air balance, water balance, food balance, energy balance, and material balance).

- The need to find and apply appropriate information regarding place—for example, the project area's climate, hydrology, soils, and ecosystem with monitoring to track trends of improvement or decline.

- The need to identify influential and effective partners in the private, public, and nonprofit sectors to facilitate the process and to engage the community.

- Work within a national/international worknet to help keep us abreast of developments in other similar programs around the world so we can benefit from lessons learned and new strategies and technology.

- Integrate an information-dissemination network to reach practitioners, stakeholders, and the general public simultaneously.

Two conceptualization tools—one contextual and the other operational—have helped us understand how Austin, or other city-regions, could learn from and build on lessons to shape future programs. The contextual tool is the Development Ladder; it addresses the city-region's state of development at varying stages of its evolution. The operational tool, ProtoScope, provides a systemic representation of how the city could potentially function and has evolved from our experiences with a range of cultures around the world. This idealized, systemic view of the city-region became what now call a ProtoCity, or an idealized place-based prototype city of the future.

Development Ladder

The Development Ladder establishes the current status of a place and identifies effective action steps. It is structured around four basic stages: surviving, maturing, anticipatory, and worldly. The first step in effecting positive development at any scale is by determining the city-region's position on the Development Ladder. The goal is not to state that any of these stages are superior or inferior, but simply to help identify and recognize key attributes. The Development Ladder can apply to the city-region as a whole or can assess a city-region's position in terms of specific issues such as public health, education, governance, employment, environmental sustainability, or superstructure.

Four essential flows determine a city-region's position on and movement along the development ladder:

1. **Information:** The most fluid and most useful as well as the most easily disrupted of all the flows. We use it in several ways such as locating global partners who have had success dealing with similar issues in similar conditions. Embedding measurement and feedback mechanisms is essential (information progress improves feedback, such as the smart grid, where home energy meters and systems are interlinked and communicate with the utility).

2. **Currency:** The strategic flow of money through the city-region. This flow includes the strategic placement of available dollars to improve specific triggers for change. Innovation financing that ultimately accounts for ecosystem services is particularly important.

3. **Energy:** The energy flow, like the material flow, needs to be understood from an EcoBalancing standpoint with an emphasis on localized sourcing, processing, use, and re-sourcing. Energy flow must be worked with at every level of society so that codes, investment, design, and engineering become fail-safe owing to scalar life-cycle redundancy from home to neighborhood to region.

4. **Materials:** Similar to the flow of energy, material becomes a significant area of a localized creativity of use, so that it is not only sourced within the region but is low in embodied energy, efficient in the amount of material used, and is sophisticated relative to reuse through either shape or constituents.

Development of the ProtoCity

In 1990 while developing Austin's Green Building Program, CMPBS adapted Ashby's conceptual model of the brain as a tool to understand the interaction of the city's public and private sectors. The model that evolved placed public bodies in the role of the environment (better described as the keepers of the commons) and the private sector as the organism trying to respond to the environment but also effecting and helping to develop policy. Monitoring occurred via the commissions that kept close ties with the city, reporting to them if, and when, environmental problems arose.

The original model considers the city-region in homeostasis without accounting for change; we have since determined that a dynamic representation is required. For example, urban vegetation may increase in extent and diversity with increased urbanization, just as locally produced, organic food may become more available. Additionally, a damaged ecosystem needs to be repaired and restructured not only so it is self-healing but even more, so that it can be revitalizing and regenerating at a system level. A further adaptation

of Ashby's diagram provides opportunity to create dynamism in the limits of a system. This is accomplished with ProtoScope.

ProtoScope

ProtoScope provides the ingredients for triggering a city-region to move through the Development Ladder by creating the context for change. One may enter at any stage recognizing that every community is in one of four stages of development.

The initial steps in ProtoScope establish the biophysical metrics of how your location relates to global ecological, hydrological, climatic, and soil trends. This locates ProtoSpace (patterns of place on earth like your own), helping the citizenry to connect to relevant issues in other cities with similar biophysical conditions.

ProtoPartners are peer groups within these city-regions that can be linked by topic and location. These are our new global network partners that have been successful in helping bring these places to their next step in the development described in the Development Ladder.

In short, ProtoScope is a tool that helps identify systems for planetary revival. It helps search the world for solutions using pattern-finding algorithms that will soon be available to mine within eight different global databases.

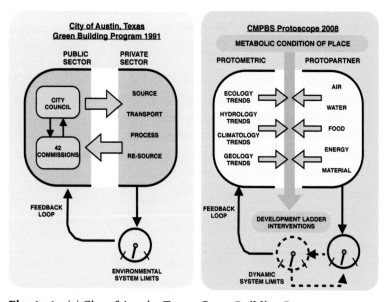

Fig. 6.16. *(a) City of Austin, Texas, Green Building Program 1991. (b) CMPBS ProtoScope 2008.*

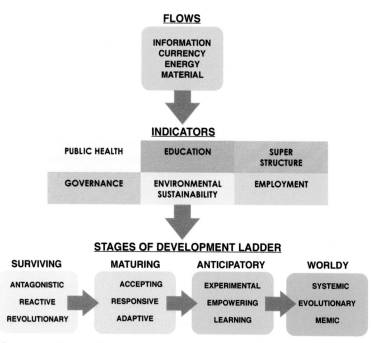

Fig. 6.17. *The Development Ladder helps assess the current status of a community and its potential for development by tracking four essential flows in one or more indicator categories.*

PROTOSCOPE

Protoscope provides a process for a city-region to move through the development ladder shown on page 240. The initial steps in Protoscope establish the metrics of how your location relates to global trends. This includes Protospace (i.e. patterns of places like your own) helping the citizenry connect to important issues of other cities with similar biophysical conditions.

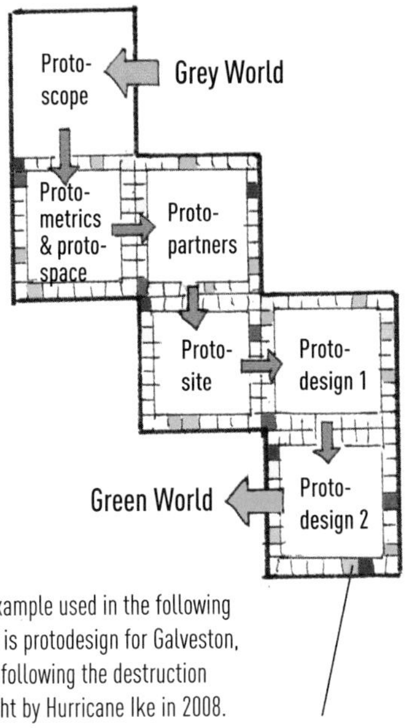

Proto-scope ← Grey World

Proto-metrics & proto-space → Proto-partners

Proto-site — Proto-design 1

Green World ← Proto-design 2

The example used in the following pages is protodesign for Galveston, Texas following the destruction wrought by Hurricane Ike in 2008.

icons to database

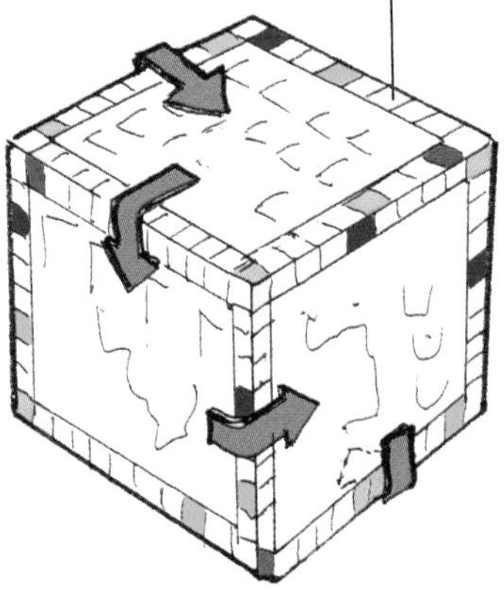

Protoscope searches for design solutions using pattern finding algorithms and feedback from rapidly developing databases.

PROTOMETRICS: A process for quantifying Greyworld and Greenworld TRENDS at all scales

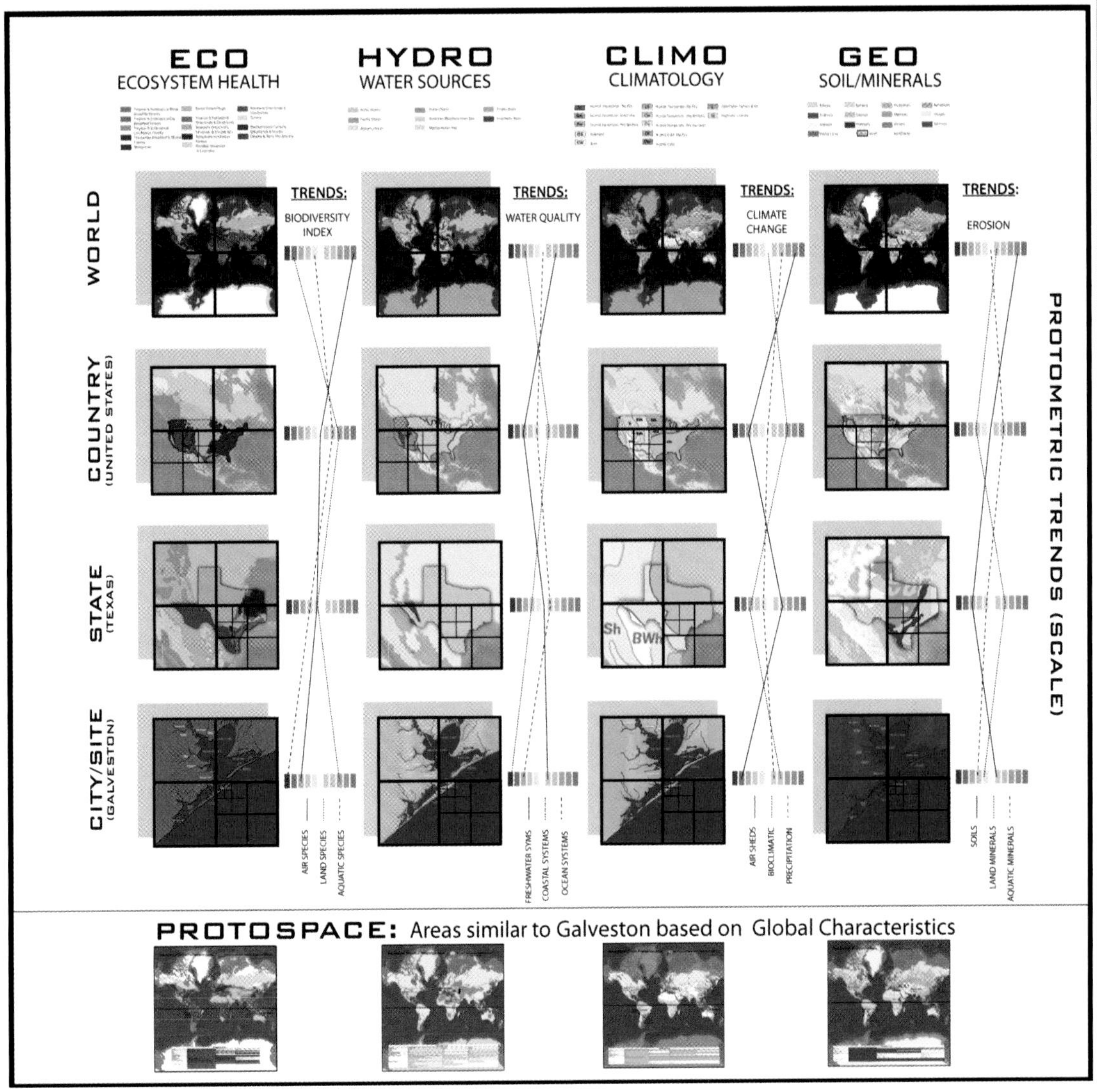

ECO ECOSYSTEM HEALTH

HYDRO WATER SOURCES

CLIMO CLIMATOLOGY

GEO SOIL/MINERALS

WORLD

COUNTRY (UNITED STATES)

STATE (TEXAS)

CITY/SITE (GALVESTON)

TRENDS: BIODIVERSITY INDEX

TRENDS: WATER QUALITY

TRENDS: CLIMATE CHANGE

TRENDS: EROSION

AIR SPECIES / LAND SPECIES / AQUATIC SPECIES

FRESHWATER SYSTEMS / COASTAL SYSTEMS / OCEAN SYSTEMS

AIR SHEDS / BIOCLIMATIC / PRECIPITATION

SOILS / LAND MINERALS / AQUATIC MINERALS

PROTOMETRIC TRENDS (SCALE)

PROTOSPACE: Areas similar to Galveston based on Global Characteristics

Fig. 6.18. *ProtoScope, ProtoMetrics, and ProtoSpace for Galveston, Texas.*

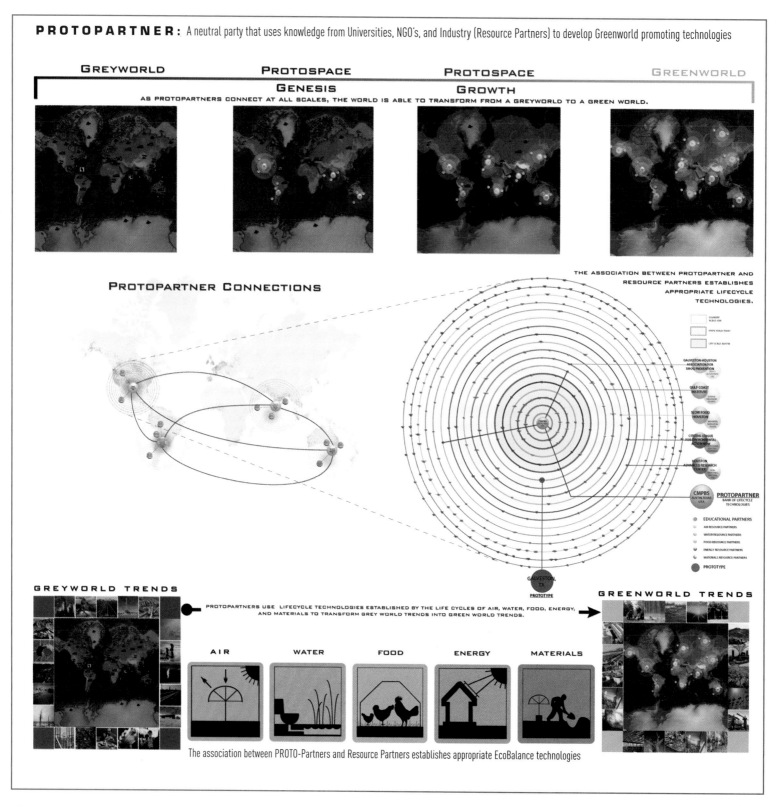

PROTOPARTNER: A neutral party that uses knowledge from Universities, NGO's, and Industry (Resource Partners) to develop Greenworld promoting technologies

GREYWORLD · PROTOSPACE · PROTOSPACE · GREENWORLD

GENESIS · GROWTH

AS PROTOPARTNERS CONNECT AT ALL SCALES, THE WORLD IS ABLE TO TRANSFORM FROM A GREYWORLD TO A GREEN WORLD.

PROTOPARTNER CONNECTIONS

THE ASSOCIATION BETWEEN PROTOPARTNER AND RESOURCE PARTNERS ESTABLISHES APPROPRIATE LIFECYCLE TECHNOLOGIES.

GREYWORLD TRENDS

GREENWORLD TRENDS

PROTOPARTNERS USE LIFECYCLE TECHNOLOGIES ESTABLISHED BY THE LIFE CYCLES OF AIR, WATER, FOOD, ENERGY, AND MATERIALS TO TRANSFORM GREY WORLD TRENDS INTO GREEN WORLD TRENDS.

AIR · WATER · FOOD · ENERGY · MATERIALS

The association between PROTO-Partners and Resource Partners establishes appropriate EcoBalance technologies

Fig. 6.19. *ProtoPartners example for Galveston, Texas.*

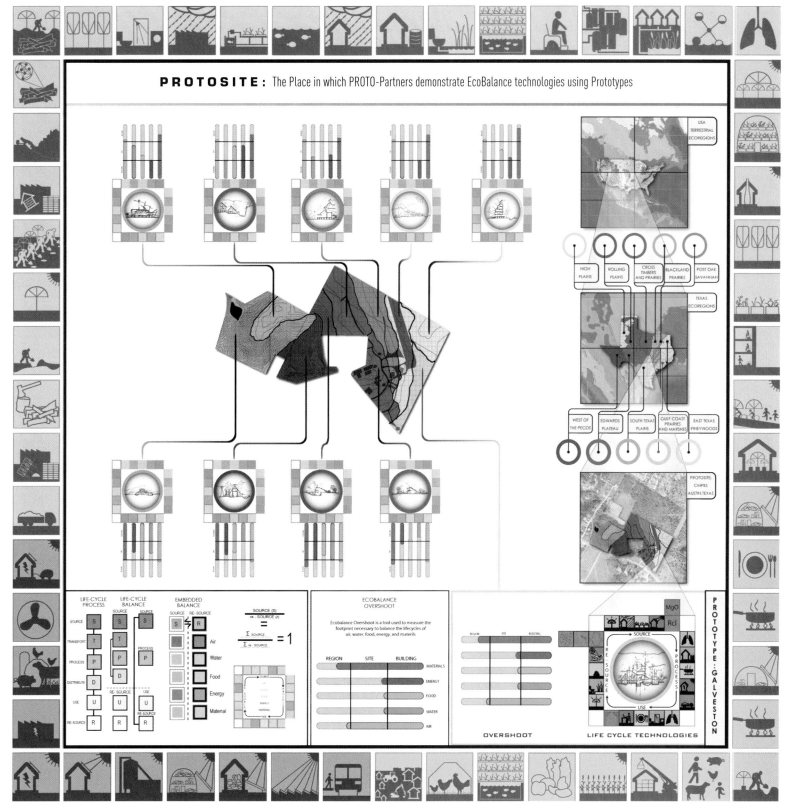

Fig. 6.20. *ProtoScope applied to development in Galveston, Texas.*

GREY WORLD: Galveston: post natural disaster—Hurricane Ike 2008

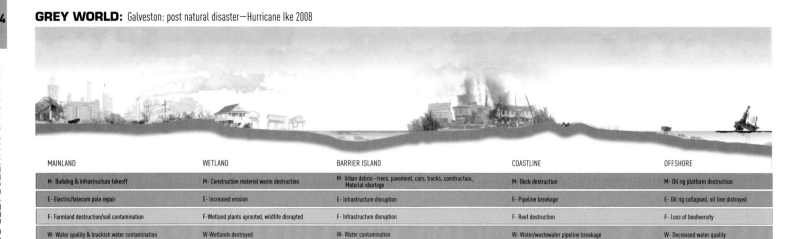

MAINLAND	WETLAND	BARRIER ISLAND	COASTLINE	OFFSHORE
M- Building & infrastructure takeoff	M- Construction material waste destruction	M- Urban debris—trees, pavement, cars, trucks, construction, Material shortage	M- Dock destruction	M- Oil rig platform destruction
E- Electric/telecom pole repair	E- Increased erosion	E- Infrastructure disruption	E- Pipeline breakage	E- Oil rig collapsed, oil line distroyed
F- Farmland destruction/soil contamination	F-Wetland plants uprooted, wildlife disrupted	F- Infrastructure disruption	F- Reef destruction	F- Loss of biodiversity
W- Water quality & brackish water contamination	W-Wetlands destroyed	W- Water contamination	W- Water/wastewater pipeline breakage	W- Decreased water quality
A-Reforestation needs	A- Carbon sink distruption	A- Loss of vegetation	A- Increased climate change	A- Increased climate change

GREY/GREEN WORLD: Rehabilitation of the Barrier Island Ecology

-Bridge/Road repair with fast setting S-cement, -Sulfur collection from stacks used for building and road construction	-Construction material waste destruction	-Reuse plan industries: remanufacturing economic development -Building demolition: wood, gypsum, asphalt, concrete, metals, plastics, clean organics, toxic waste	-Dock repair using micro electrolysis -Brine separation analysis at reverse osmosis	-Assessment relative to quantity and content -Oil Rig Rehabilitation
-Gasifier energy demo using recycled wood	-Decreased erosion	-Solar thermal and photovoltaics demonstration	-Sun wind wave cafe	-Energy conservation demonstration: Wind, Wave, Geothermal
-Reduced soil toxins with charcoal demo	-Fish food chain increase takeoff	-Greenhouses and vertical farming	-Coral reef demonstration	-Improved biodiversity
-Clean dredge water using microbial enzyme treatment	-Bio-remediation using phragmites -Disrupted spartina (replant)	-Municipal wastewater: brine removal, quantity, quality	-Toxic cleanup	-Toxic cleanup, improve water quality
-Forest rehabilitation with biochar	-Increase carbon sink takeoff -Increase migratory bird habitat	-Increase biodiversity		-Air improvement due to less oil use

GREEN WORLD: Galveston: post fossil fuel dependency, using green technologies

-Biochar megaflora plantation -Multi use brine processing	-High strength monocoque building system manufacturing	-MgO cement foam with monocoque prefab -High wind tension construction -Mimics float/swim adaptation, crestation structure, cable structure	-Transform oil rig technologies to wind/wave/geothermal	-Remineralize coastal areas
-Megaflora	-Carbon Sink	-Wind Powered Infrustructure	-Renewable based infrastructure	-Oil industry components (oil rig) retrofitted for renewable energy production: Wind, Wave, Hydrogen, Geothermal
-Increase food production due to micronutrient /compost biochar mix -Large scale remineralization of soil using processed sea brine	-Food Chain to Sea	-Obtained from local sources	-Dune Stabilization with biochar and micro nutrient organic furtilizer	-Revitilized ocean habitat
-Reduced Extraction	-Aquatic species diversity improvement	-Renewably purified	-Reverse osmosis / and solar desalination of sea water to make brine -Biochar/ash production to neutralize acidification of return water to seas	-Mineral and biodiversity balance improvement and carbon sink
-Increase carbon sink due to heavy forest	-Diverse habitat	-Reduced smog due to renewable energy	-Renewable based infrustructure with bird-friendly wind turbines	-Decreased CO_2 saturation

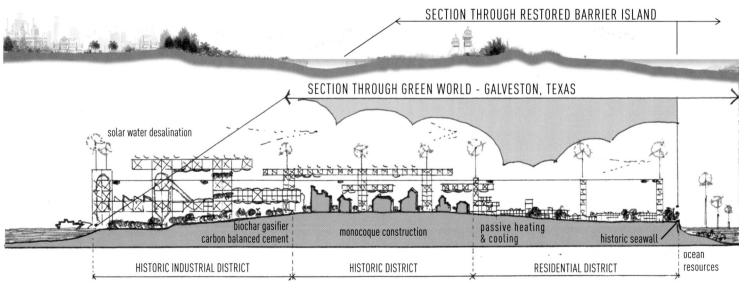

Fig. 6.21. *An open-building system for disaster recovery in Galveston, Texas.*

Richard Levine, Architect, CSC Design Studio, Director of the Center for Sustainable Cities, University of Kentucky, Lexington

Sustainability: Living within our fair share of the earth's resources on a renewable, regenerative basis is the great challenge of our generation. While it would be difficult to argue with the goal of sustainability in the abstract, the means to achieve it, and indeed the effective meaning of sustainability, is highly contested. Analytical approaches to sustainability are typically couched as wish lists of what you might find if you happened to stumble upon some future sustainable city. Though it makes for easy proposals, this approach is highly problematic.

The many dimensions of unsustainability are understood as a global problem, but the earth is far too large a scale to analyze the dynamics of unsustainability or to create programs to confront it. While many aspects of what is understood as the sustainability crisis—excessive consumption, resource depletion, water shortages, climate change, the energy crisis, peak oil, financial meltdown, and so on—are described in global terms, all contributions to unsustainability arise in a particular local place. It is also true that, although there are many actions we can choose at the scale of our homes and individual lifestyles to marginally lower our personal load on the environment, this is far too small a scale to make any real difference. In considering the many possible scales at which to tackle the question of sustainability—from local to global—the city and its supply region stands out as a scale that is both large and systemic enough to make the difference, yet small enough to be manageable.

It is at this city scale where sustainability becomes possible. Historically, ecological balances were negotiated within the scale of the city-region. We have called this historic balance-seeking process "proto-sustainability." It is achieved and maintained through a negotiated long-term balance between the needs of a town and the ability of its agricultural and natural countryside to provide for those needs on a continuing basis.

The passive solar movement, along with the environmental movement at large, has moved ahead in small incremental steps. Since the birth of the passive solar movement in the mid-1970s, each succeeding year brought the question: "What's the next step?"

and each year saw new emerging trends and innovations: from active solar calculation methods, to passive solar test structures, electronic-network-analysis-derived passive-calculation methods, roof ponds, super-insulation, and many other small and sometimes significant breakthroughs and changes in emphasis. In the earliest years, scientists and engineers formed the backbone of the solar movement in the United States. Their forays into developing solar hot-water collectors were backed up with extensive technical analysis and testing.

By 1978, the passive movement had demonstrated the efficacy of passive applications through both instrumented test cells and thermal network analysis pioneered by Phil Niles and popularized by Doug Balcomb. It was a very exciting time; each year a different approach reached ascendancy, and experimentation proceeded at a rapid pace. Many innovations stemmed from solid theoretical principles, but their actual levels of performance were initially unknown. As innovations developed in parallel with one another, there was an inevitable, if usually friendly, competition—active versus passive, passive versus super-insulation, Trombe wall versus direct gain, water-based systems versus air-based systems, et cetera. Both discussion and construction were largely limited to a building type that is not particularly sustainability oriented—the single-family house. These solar houses were built in diverse climates, with few being monitored and all being vulnerable to the vagaries of greatly differing usage patterns. Because of the additional difficulty of comparing relative costs and economics, it was not easy to draw any real conclusions. With the sheer volume of projects built, some applications inevitably proved much more effective than others, while still others revealed unforeseen negative consequences. It somehow came as a surprise to solar scientists working from an analytical perspective that an excellent, optimized solar collector might not necessarily work so well in a given system, and even an effective system might not perform as desired in an actual building. It is important to note that a given sustainability-oriented building might not necessarily fit well into the system of a particular sustainable city-region.

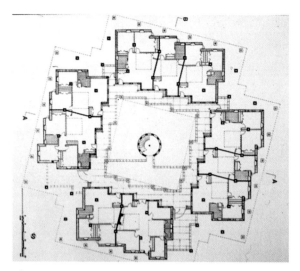

Fig. 6.22. *New Hope II, Berea, Kentucky, 1985–1986.Using an economical out-of-season heat-collection system that stores summer heat below the village with an appropriate thermal lag so that the temperature beneath the dwelling's floor slabs is hottest in midwinter—along with passive solar, super-insulation, and PV strategies—this retirement community would be food and energy self-sufficient. (a) Plan. (b) Model.*

These were the days before we had an integrated theory of sustainability to work with. There was no clear idea of any overarching goal as to just what it was that we were trying to achieve. And then there was the question of use and appearance. Should a passive solar home be designed differently and look different (and possibly weird?), or should it look like any other home, but with better performance? In the funk of the decades that followed after funding and support for research evaporated, the passive solar movement languished in the United States, but important progress and implementation continued to be made in Europe. With a renewed interest here, some of that European progress, particularly its emphasis on integrative systems, is returning to the United States. The passive house (*Passivhaus*) movement originating in Germany, which builds superbly well-insulated, tight houses and buildings of the sort that were first built here more than twenty-five years ago, is particularly noteworthy. It has now been well developed by the Germans in a formalized system of analysis and building standards. With its emphasis on extremely low energy usage, the age of economical zero net energy houses and carbon-neutral buildings is upon us.

The solar movement has gone through a series of names—solar homes, active solar, passive solar, energy-conscious design, sustainable architecture, and so on. It has finally landed on the most nondescript and indefinite name of all: green building, which tells us little, and promises even less than any previous description. Green quickly becomes "greenish," which can mean anything anyone wants it to mean. "Green" is still applied only at the scale of the building, with arbitrary measures of performance parading as standards. The long trajectory of passive innovation points most of all to a need, not for required prescriptive or performance standards, but rather for an overarching goal linked to tangible evidence of "sustainability." The list of certification schemes is a long one, with the dominant standard in the United States currently being LEED, an aggregated checklist approach that awards different medals—Certified, Silver, Gold, or Platinum—depending upon the total points amassed in many different, unrelated categories. All this is done in the interest of making better buildings, and seems a desirable goal, but ultimately does not guarantee any particular level of performance and has little to do with sustainability. Although most point categories in the LEED system are composed of positive, sustainability-oriented contributions, there is nothing that holds it all together. A LEED Platinum building is not a "sustainable" building, because as we now understand the concept of sustainability cannot be properly applied at the scale of buildings. In terms of certain aspects of performance, LEED buildings are better buildings, but in German there is the expression: "Better is the enemy of good." In this time of gathering crisis, better just isn't good enough.

For all the contributions made through passive solar design, its ultimate value will lie in its unique capability for supporting the sustainability of the human project on Planet Earth. Through passive solar methods, we understand that the importance or emphasis of any given idea or application cannot be known in isolation. Its quality can only be known through the balanced ways in which it may be integrated into a building seen as a larger system, and ultimately to support the sustainability of an even more encompassing system. When pioneering the operational definition of sustainability, we observed early on that the pursuit of small-scale efficiency gains and innovations can have the tendency of limiting the possibilities for systemic change on a more meaningful scale. Our frequent rejoinder has thus been, "Don't pick the low-hanging fruit." No farmer would choose a strategy of picking the low-hanging fruit, as each succeeding layer of fruit represents a succession of diminishing returns, becoming more difficult and more expensive to pick until finally, the fruit at the top of the tree is too expensive to pick at all. There are many small actions that make sense in our individual lives, like changing lightbulbs or installing low-flush toilets, but these things can only be done once. The next levels of performance are gained at increasingly greater costs. When the easy, affordable moves have been exhausted, we still find ourselves far from where we would need to be to approach a model that supports true sustainability. In this sense, ecological actions are "nonrenewable resources." You can only upgrade to a compact fluorescent or an LED once and then you have to look for something that is more difficult to do. Moreover, this response fosters the habit of doing the small easy things and avoiding the more significant, larger-scaled, systemic changes necessary to create a sustainability-driven culture. Fixing small problems does not develop the integrated solutions that make a difference.

So the quality of a particular application—in "passive" terms, a direct gain, a Trombe wall, or a super-insulation approach—starts with its contribution to the balanced performance of a particular system or a particular building in a particular climate or application. We cannot stop there. We must ask the question that finally is unavoidable: "How good is good enough?" As well as the question: "What scale is large enough?" Unless we are content with pursuing medals (silver, gold, platinum) with no particular meaning, we cannot be comfortable with any given level of performance. We must demonstrate how given achievements relate to building performance within a sustainability-balancing process in its neighborhood, within its city-region. In the incremental worldview, you can't

argue with changing lightbulbs, but success at this scale requires the investment of time and resources that tend to divert investment in larger-scale patterns of development. If we reject picking the low-hanging fruit, how then do we proceed with a plan of both action and substance? The question becomes, "What is the first action or the smallest activity that we can take toward sustainability such that each subsequent action is rendered easier and not, as with the more common, but unfruitful approach, more difficult?" This question requires that we both define sustainability in a more concrete way and identify a scale at which it can become operational. We maintain that the most appropriate larger scale is the sustainable city-region, the smallest scale at which human and environmental ecosystems can negotiate material and energy balances.

We can confidently say that what is good enough is sustainability at the scale of the city-region. "Sustainable architecture" is an oxymoron—a building is too small a scale at which to design or to negotiate sustainability. Conversely, no one can think globally, much less have any illusion to effect any sort of global change. These truths are borne out in important lessons from history. Towns and cities, whose origins go back thousands of years, have been the cradle of our civilization and its progress. One thing they all seem to have had in common until modern times is that they operated as what we would now call "proto-sustainable" settlements. That is to say that from a food, energy, and material-flow standpoint, they all had to develop a long-term balance-seeking relationship within the carrying capacity of the immediate environment that supplied them with almost all the resources they needed to maintain their way of life. Though we live in a time of unprecedented material wealth and technological innovation, today there is no city on the face of the planet that is able to do this.

Historically, in most locations, living within a city's carrying capacity was not a matter of choice. A town that started to live beyond its means or began to deplete its resource base would quickly be faced with the ecological signals of resource depletion and population decline. If these patterns of unsustainable consumption or inadequate production persisted, the town soon disappeared. Feedback as to the state of balance with resources was local and swift, so local communities quickly learned what their lands could provide. In the continual quest to improve individual and social well-being, these communities developed within the boundaries of innovations that worked. These living experiments happened in the continual spirit of experimentation and betterment that is the nature of our species. As we no longer live in a local or self-sufficient world, the boundaries that once made it possible to understand and react to the metabolic stresses of a locale as a largely autonomous system no longer exist. No feedback leads to no control. A system without effective boundaries cannot be maintained in balance. But if a local, resilient system has strong internal balance-seeking capabilities, it can actually thrive with changing conditions at its system boundaries even when those boundaries are rather porous. This is a fundamental characteristic of living systems.

The sustainable city is to become the unit through which the human experiment will not only survive but also thrive. This is really our only choice. The future sustainable city will conform to the following operational definition:

"Sustainability is a Local, Informed, Participatory, Balance-Seeking Process, Operating within its Sustainable Area Budget (SAB), and in doing so exporting no harmful imbalances beyond its Territory or into the Future, thus opening Spaces of Opportunity and Possibility" (Levine, Dumreicher, Yanarella*).

Despite the proliferation of abstract and even poetic definitions of sustainability, this is the only operational definition of sustainability currently in use. There is reason to believe that any alternative operational definitions of sustainability will cover much the same territory. Much has been written explaining the meaning of this definition. It may be enough in this overview to briefly explain the sustainable area budget, or SAB. Many readers will be familiar with the ecological footprint concept, which is a powerful analytical tool that aggregates many different factors to reveal to us just how badly we are doing. But the ecological footprint cannot accomplish an essential task. It does not instruct us in what we should be doing except to say that we should be doing several times less than we do in our current grossly unsustainable living patterns. The sustainable area budget is the design side of the analytical ecological footprint. The SAB tells us that each one of us as 1/6.4 billionth of the earth's population is entitled to the use of 1/6.4 billionth of the earth's resources on a renewable, regenerative basis—resources that are interpreted as biologically active land area (further information at www.centerforsustainablecities.com). Because we are a social species whose civilization can only exist through the emergent properties of aggregation, each community or city is then entitled

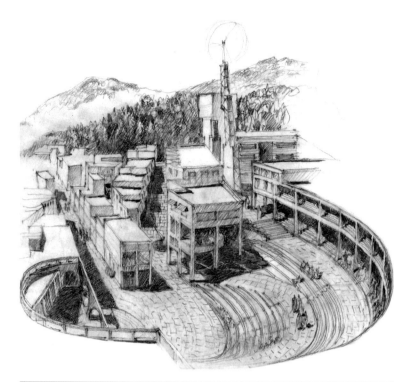

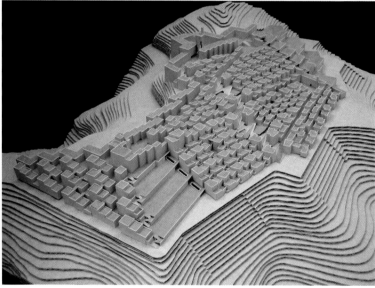

Fig. 6.23. *Sustainable Urban Implantation, Whitesburg, Kentucky, 2001–2007. Remediating the toxic characteristics of an unreclaimed strip-mine site with an inexpensive out-of-season solar collection system that also puts summer heat into mining bore holes for winter retrieval, while using the mining high wall as a backstop for the proposed Sustainable City. (a) Perspective sketch. (b) Model.*

to aggregate the SABs of its residents. This is their fair share of the earth's resources as well as their land and resource budget. Creating a way of life within the limits of this natural budget then becomes a question of negotiation and design. These design negotiations are conducted in a game-like construct of bottom-up participation in a multiple-scenario building process conducted by local stakeholders with a range of experts. Communities play this sustainability game with the assistance of the Sustainability Engine, a computer-aided design (CAD) or building-information-modeling-like tool (BIM) we also call the SCIM (Sustainable Cities Information Modeling) utility. We have kept the system boundaries both tight but highly flexible so that this process is able to function as a system while maintaining a great amount of variability in order to accommodate the many goals and interests of the various stakeholders as they build their competing city models and scenarios. Through several iterations of the Sustainable City Game, different competing scenarios come closer to balance, and begin to converge with one another, incorporating the better features of their counterparts and responding to the critiques of competing stakeholders.

At this moment in history, the SAB-based sustainability gaming process will have difficulty transforming the existing city, whose fabric and processes are deeply rooted in unsustainable principles and habits. What is needed is a new urban form whose structure is well suited as a supporting framework for the above-described principles and processes. The Sustainable City-as-a-Hill, sometimes called the Sustainable Urban Implantation, is such a new urban form.

The form of the Sustainable City-as-a-Hill is inspired by many historic towns around the world, but the primary inspiration comes from the medieval Italian hill town. These settlements, many of which have histories that pre-date the Roman Empire, bear the record of millennia of use and reuse—responsiveness to topography, climate, agriculture, the need for defense, but primarily the changing patterns of human culture and human use. Their organic, responsive character gives them an overwhelmingly human scale and a sense that they are good places to live at a high quality of life even though, as historic structures, they lack some amenities found in modern cities.

The City-as-a-Hill is designed to support the sorts of life patterns and metabolic requirements of a sustainable city as well as the

process by which the participatory aspects of the Sustainable City Game facilitates the design and evolution of the city. Rather than starting with the form and structure of the existing modern city with all its problems and trying, one by one, to resolve them, the new model has evolved over time as a city form where these seemingly intractable problems don't exist in the first place.

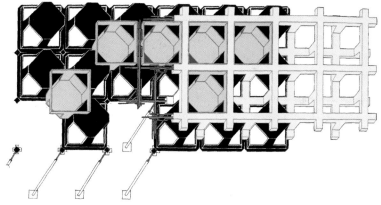

Fig. 6.24. *Coupled Pan Space Frame (CPSF), 1960–present. Spanning large spaces (up to 60 × 60 feet) lightweight (100 psf), moderate space frame depth (3 feet), with high live load capacities (130 psf), and having the capacity for running all service systems within its own depth, using a simple, repetitive forming system, the cast-in-place, concrete, CPSF offers the flexibility of being the underlying structural framework for Sustainable Urban Implantations. (a) Model. (b) Isometric.*

Over many years, we have evolved a family of modern urban forms that mirror many of the humane characteristics of these towns, but that are capable of supporting a modern, sustainable infrastructure and way of life. To do this, we have transformed the original concept. Instead of the medieval city on a hill, we project a city *as* a hill—a city as a single building, a compact pedestrian town that places those functions that in the modern city can be a blight on the visual and social landscape below the new ground surface of a constructed hill, yet organized along three-story-tall gallerias daylit through courtyards above. In this way, all large-scale commercial, institutional, and industrial facilities, most service functions, parking, and other activities and infrastructure that create often unsafe dead zones in a conventional town, are located within the hill. The "upper town" is supported by the Coupled Pan Space Frame (CPSF)—an innovative, economical, cast-in-place concrete structural system capable of large two-way spans that creates the space of the inner hill as well. All the service systems needed for city are housed within the systems space of the CPSF.

The sustainable City-as-a-Hill is composed of a network of level streets, crossed by sloped streets that wind their way to the top of the hill. In addition, there is a system of main streets sloping at a gentle 6 percent grade that create small parks or squares as they pass by each level path of the constructed hill. Like its historic predecessors, the town generates a rich diversity of public spaces; from narrow lanes to grand plazas and from commercial streets to monumental stairs, public amphitheaters, parks and greens—all supportive of a rich civic life. There are also elevators that connect the inner hill with the levels above. This pattern assures an unprecedented level of handicapped accessibility, as each building entrance and every level is accessed without having to negotiate any stairs or segregated spaces and machinery. The City-as-a-Hill is a much denser yet smaller town than would otherwise be possible: large enough to provide a full range of urban services and life opportunities, yet small enough to be manageable as an intelligent balance-seeking system, in partnership with an agricultural hinterland. Such a walkable town would typically be too small to contain the necessary variety and diversity of services, while maintaining the human scale essential for convivial living, but the vertical layering of different functions in the City-as-a-Hill combines the complexity and dynamism of a small city with the intimacy of a human-scaled town. This sustainable urban implantation also makes more land available for

agriculture and recreation while facilitating the reclamation of land back to wild nature, which is also valued for its unique ability to balance greenhouse emissions and become the supply area for energy, food, and materials (on a net basis) as the town's SAB.

The Sustainable City-as-a-Hill is a new urban form with a number of levels of structure, collectively managed by a sustainable city information management system (SCIM), which is derived from recently developed building information management software. The underlying structure is the coupled pan space frame (CPSF), which—although it is actually a continuous structure—for planning and modeling purposes is divided into three-story-tall, 100-foot-square building modules. These modules are seen as families of stackable building blocks, housed in the SCIM library. These blocks start out as being identical, but are developed into many different building forms and types with searchable characteristics that can be quickly assembled to form a primitive model of a new City-as-a-Hill. As the participatory scenario-building process proceeds, it is paralleled by the construction of three-dimensional urban models using the increasingly sophisticated, intelligent building modules that become part of an interchangeable "intelligent" module library. As these module-based city constructs are assembled, the stakeholders receive feedback as to the state of balance of their emerging cities within their given sustainable area budgets. As they develop their competing scenarios, the stakeholders playing the Sustainable

Fig. 6.25. *Obidos, Portugal, city on a hill.*

City Game can receive both qualitative and quantitative feedback as to the consequences of their emerging proposals both as sustainability-driven systems and as visual images of the cities being developed.

Summary

The Sustainable City Game is a safe place for conflict—a safe place to make mistakes. It is the sort of trial-and-error process that was played out over many generations in the medieval hill town: Decisions were made; over time the unworkable ones would fall away to be replaced with new experiments, while the workable ones would be incorporated within the traditions, crafts, and social patterns of the town. Any city that over the course of hundreds of years culls the negative influences in architecture, culture, and agriculture, and preserves and enhances the experiments that succeed, can't help but become a robust, supportive society as well as a wonderful place to live. Today we don't have the luxury of that sort of time span, but we do have computer-enhanced methods for setting up an interactive environment where the numerous mistakes as well as conflicts become the very source of emergent creativity in developing robust, beautiful, sustainable cities.

In a postmodern world there is little likelihood that a consensus will emerge among large groups of diverse people that pulls together the many disparate solutions of the different problems society faces. People may agree on the existence of these problems, but are unlikely to agree on any given list of specific proposed solutions, much less a singular overarching strategy or concept for their realization. People no longer believe in the pronouncements of experts, especially as there are no specialist experts in the category of the "whole." But they may believe in a process that is able to marshal the expertise of stakeholders and specialists alike, particularly if they can see and understand the quality of cities that emerge as the products of such a process. There is only one objection that can be raised against the emergence of sustainable cities, and that is the belief that one cannot be accomplished within a reasonable economic framework. Once the first sustainable city is built through these methods, it will be seen as an affordable and good place to live. This moment will instantly represent a paradigm shift. At the point that the viability of such a city is validated, no other sort of city or economic model could be seen to be viable, and every city, each in its own way through its own sustainability game, will be obliged to come up with its own model and process for the future within its own sustainable area budget.

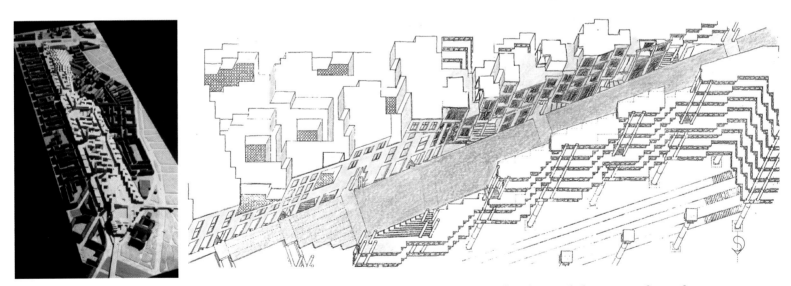

Fig. 6.26. *Westbahnhof Sustainable Urban Implantation, Vienna, Austria, 1994–1999. Using the coupled pan space frame for spans across a large existing rail yard, this sustainable urban implantation heals the wound in the existing city created by the railroad and creates a dense human-scaled, walkable City-as-a-Hill with all large-scale facilities—commercial, institutional, industrial, infrastructure, and parking—tucked neatly inside the constructed hill, giving the new ground surface above to people-oriented urban space, which combined with its rural "partnerland" balances its metabolism within the natural limits of its combined sustainable area budget. (a) Model. (b) Isometric plan sketch.*

Through the analytical approaches that dominate our science, technology, and economy as well as our very thinking processes, we are able to pinpoint the many increasingly threatening problems that challenge the continuation of anything like our current trajectory of progress and material comfort. The design-based approach outlined here depends not so much upon the skills of good designers, but rather on the collective genius that lies among the competing interests of different actors and sectors of society through the dynamics of multiple alternative scenario-building processes, where competition and conflict drive emerging scenarios toward greater quality. If we are to survive, it will be through the creation of such sustainable cities of the future.

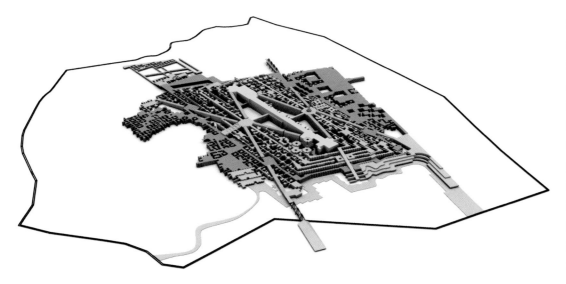

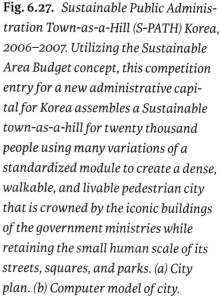

Fig. 6.27. *Sustainable Public Administration Town-as-a-Hill (S-PATH) Korea, 2006–2007. Utilizing the Sustainable Area Budget concept, this competition entry for a new administrative capital for Korea assembles a Sustainable town-as-a-hill for twenty thousand people using many variations of a standardized module to create a dense, walkable, and livable pedestrian city that is crowned by the iconic buildings of the government ministries while retaining the small human scale of its streets, squares, and parks. (a) City plan. (b) Computer model of city.*

Kenneth Haggard, Architect, San Luis Sustainability Group

Saying we are in the middle of a cultural transformation may sound like a stretch but becomes convincing once we look at patterns revealed in plots of human population growth over the last million years.

This type of analysis reveals cyclic patterns, each different, but similar in form. The three cultural eras indicated by these patterns are obvious, an era of hunting and gathering followed by agriculture and husbandry and now science and industry. The chart also shows

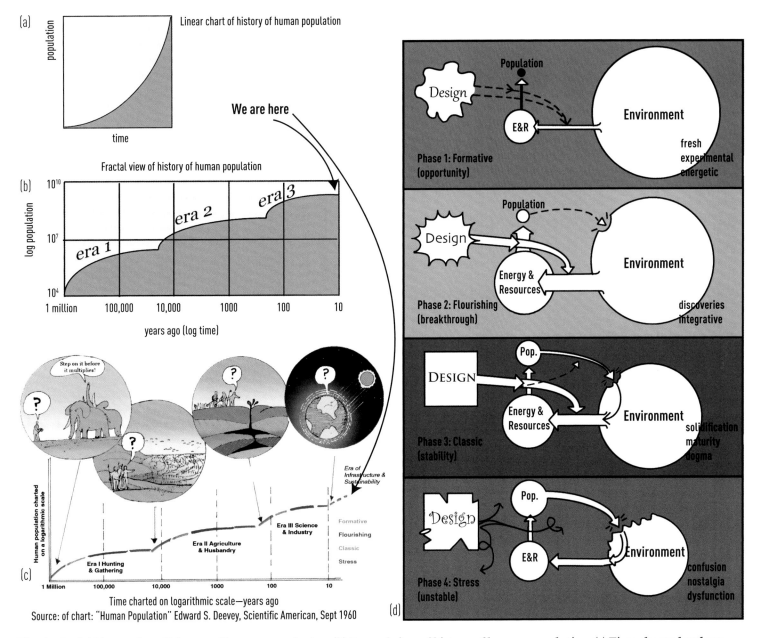

Fig. 6.28. *(a) Linear plot of history of human population. (b) Fractal view of history of human population. (c) Time charted on logarithmic scale. (d) Repetitive pattern that has occurred in each cultural era.*

that the life span of each era consists of a formative, flourishing, classic, and stressful period indicated by the slope of each point in the curve. This chart was first published over fifty years ago and has been accurate in predicting the stress occurring at the beginning of the twenty-first century we are now experiencing.

A highly simplified picture of the basic relationships among population, resources, and environment is shown in figure 6.28. Energy and resources are drawn from the environment and utilized by the human population. Design decisions including the invention of technical devices, establishment of social organization, and development of communication enhance the ability to extract energy and resources and determine how the population as a whole will utilize them.

These relationships can be visualized as a dynamic living system. At the beginning of a successful design development (one that provides more energy and resources than were previously available), times are good. Relatively large amounts of energy and resources are available to a relatively small population. There is usually a period of experimentation where trial and error are needed to develop the

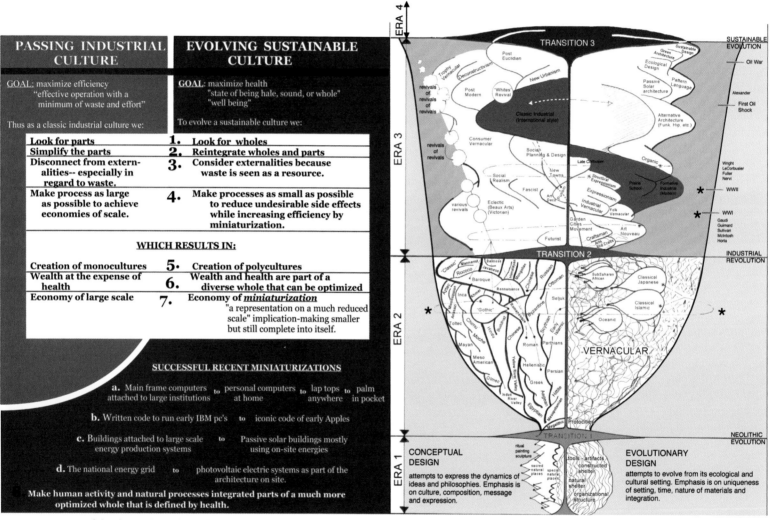

Cultural comparisons of the definition of efficiency.

History of architecture as related to four cultural eras.

Fig. 6.29. *(a) Cultural comparisons of the definition of efficiency. (b) History of architecture as related to four cultural eras. All this indicates that in terms of design, we are not just dealing with modern (industrial era) architecture in green clothing, but a whole new direction that has its own philosophy, techniques, and expression. Therefore, the traditional core design concerns of history, geometry, and aesthetics are drastically changing.*

designs that provide these advantages, but once successfully synthesized, the system's success can be dynamic; it may result in relatively rapid population growth. We can call such a period in history a formative period evolving to boom and expansion.

As design techniques are formalized and the population expands, systems tend to become comfortable and relatively static. This can be referred to as the classic period. At this point, however, the population is now large enough that pressure on the environment has increased, causing changes that affect the available resources. If a society is to maintain itself, some design efforts must moderate this pressure on the environment and social organization. Techniques for achieving energy and resources are then fixed into relatively static patterns, and social and cultural patterns are adapted to try to moderate population growth and more obviously destructive behaviors.

As the population continues to grow, resource consumption increases pressure on the environment, leading to inevitable chaotic changes in climate and society that further stress the environment, the source of available energy, water, food, and materials. As this continues, the entire system enters the period of stress.

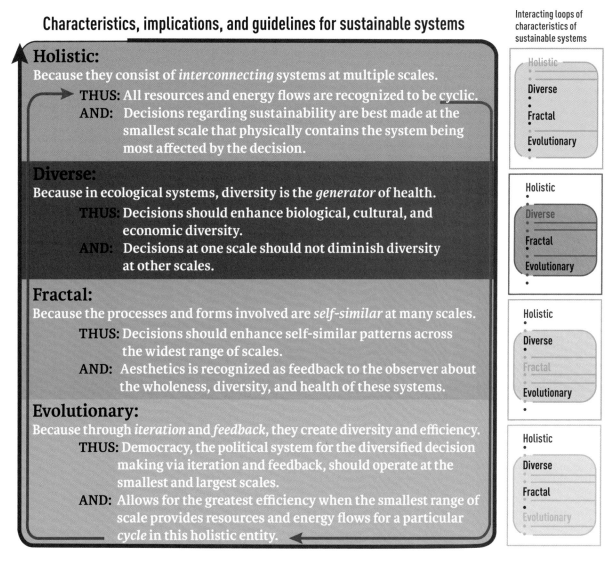

Characteristics, implications, and guidelines for sustainable systems

Holistic:
Because they consist of *interconnecting* systems at multiple scales.

THUS: All resources and energy flows are recognized to be cyclic.

AND: Decisions regarding sustainability are best made at the smallest scale that physically contains the system being most affected by the decision.

Diverse:
Because in ecological systems, diversity is the *generator* of health.

THUS: Decisions should enhance biological, cultural, and economic diversity.

AND: Decisions at one scale should not diminish diversity at other scales.

Fractal:
Because the processes and forms involved are *self-similar* at many scales.

THUS: Decisions should enhance self-similar patterns across the widest range of scales.

AND: Aesthetics is recognized as feedback to the observer about the wholeness, diversity, and health of these systems.

Evolutionary:
Because through *iteration* and *feedback*, they create diversity and efficiency.

THUS: Democracy, the political system for the diversified decision making via iteration and feedback, should operate at the smallest and largest scales.

AND: Allows for the greatest efficiency when the smallest range of scale provides resources and energy flows for a particular *cycle* in this holistic entity.

Interacting loops of characteristics of sustainable systems

Holistic
Diverse
Fractal
Evolutionary

Holistic
Diverse
Fractal
Evolutionary

Holistic
Diverse
Fractal
Evolutionary

Holistic
Diverse
Fractal
Evolutionary

Fig. 6.30. *(a) Characteristics, implications, and guidelines for sustainable systems. (b) Interacting loops of characteristics of sustainable systems.*

Societal and cultural dysfunction becomes more common. Anthropologists have traditionally called this a decadent phase. If enough stress occurs, the whole system will collapse or be replaced by a new cultural era. History is littered with examples. The only difference today is this is not isolated to one particular geographic area, but is worldwide.

A cultural shift of such great magnitude will change goals and perceptions as well as design and construction; see figure 6.29a.

At the beginning, most architecture movements start on the right side of figure 6.29b. As the culture enters the classic phase, it moves to the left side, where it eventually stagnates in the stressful phase.

To make the transition to the era of sustainability, we need to adopt a new approach that is holistic and evolutionary, figure 6.30. This will change the perception and practice of planning. Development will be understood in its place in the biome, as will the cycle of decay and renewal, figure 6.31.

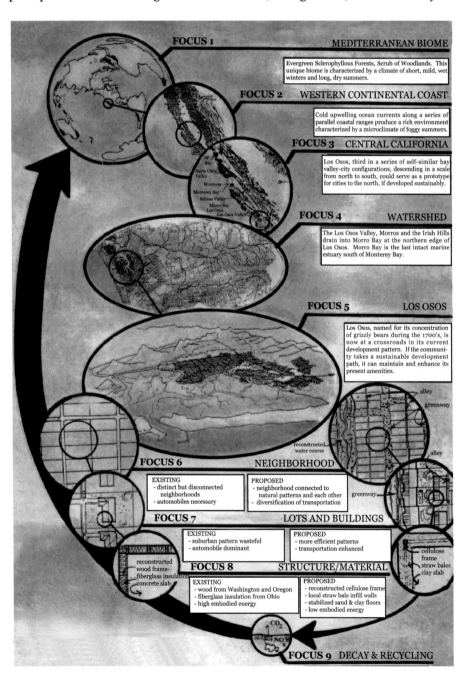

Fig. 6.31. *The characteristics and guidelines for sustainable development were used for the redesign of Los Osos, California, from a bedroom community to the nearby county seat to a sustainable community. This prizewinning entry in an international competition offers a clear view to the future. This fractal scan served three functions in the sustainable design process: (1) creating a framework that gave order and aided the information-gathering process; (2) digesting information into a concise graphic package directly usable in the design process; and (3) illustrating some comparable patterns with regard to existing elements and proposed elements. In this way, connections between different scales can be easily visualized. This holistic perspective allowed the development of a design theme, which evolved as the regeneration of the health of the watershed of Los Osos valley. Once this theme was determined, certain design decisions were relatively easy to make.*

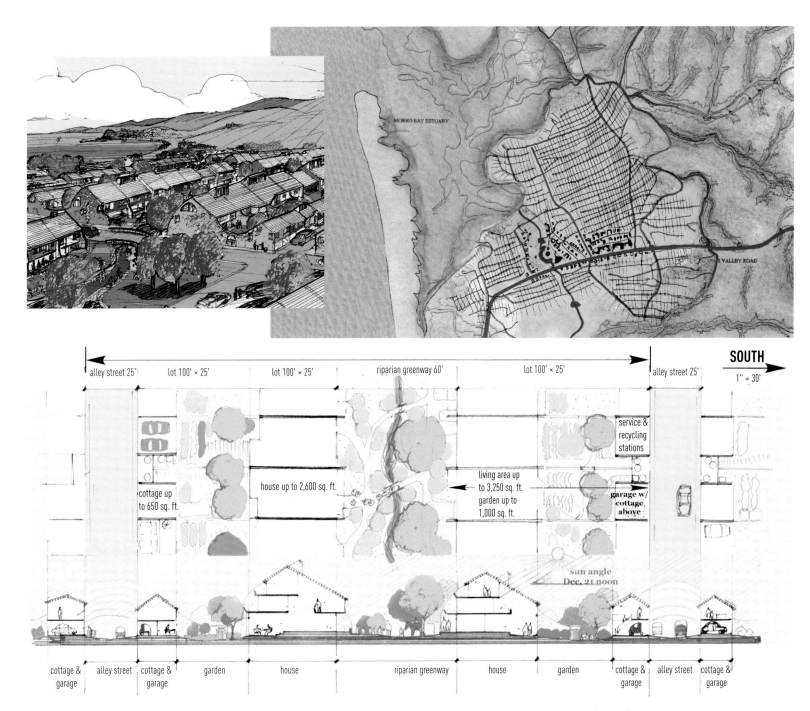

SOUTH

1" = 30'

alley street 25' | lot 100' × 25' | lot 100' × 25' | riparian greenway 60' | lot 100' × 25' | alley street 25'

MORRO BAY ESTUARY

VALLEY ROAD

cottage up to 650 sq. ft.

house up to 2,600 sq. ft.

service & recycling stations

living area up to 3,250 sq. ft. garden up to 1,000 sq. ft.

garage w/ cottage above

sun angle Dec. 21 noon

cottage & garage | alley street | cottage & garage | garden | house | riparian greenway | house | garden | cottage & garage | alley street | cottage & garage

Fig. 6.32. *Los Osos was platted in the nineteenth century with small 30-foot lots meant to serve the standard nineteenth-century row house. In the twentieth century, this evolved into typical suburban housing by requiring two lots per unit. This twenty-first-century hybrid goes back to narrow lots but with a new urbanist pattern and optimized passive design for each unit. This allows twice the density of the existing suburban pattern while also allowing twice the potential interior square footage than the typical suburban house in Los Osos, if desired. The new urbanist arrangement of riparian greenways, enclosed garden/courts, and alleys provides more spatial and social flexibility. (a) Perspective sketch of community. (b) Area plan. (c) Section sketch through community.*

Architecture in the Era of Sustainability will:

1. Embrace Complexity

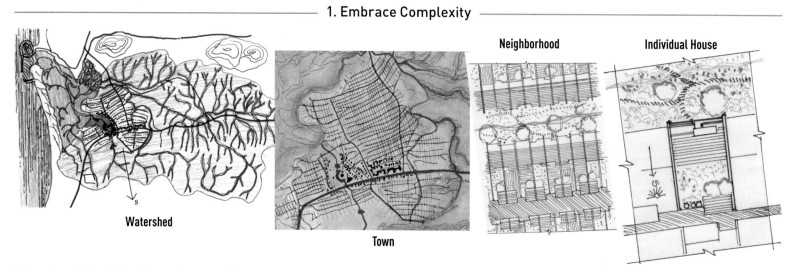

Watershed

Town

Neighborhood

Individual House

The value of simplicity in "modern" architecture has in this period of stress evolved to merely a simplistic response to complex conditions: "just change the size of the air conditioner and heater." Design must once again embrace complexity and natural flows. The geometrical basis of architecture will shift from harshly Euclidian to incorporate fractal forms.

2. Optimize Building Metabolism

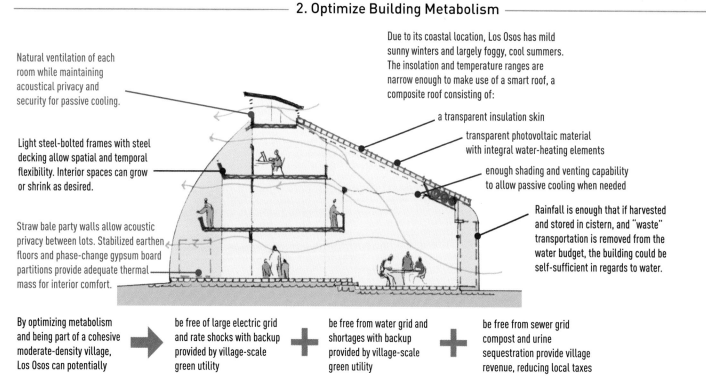

Natural ventilation of each room while maintaining acoustical privacy and security for passive cooling.

Light steel-bolted frames with steel decking allow spatial and temporal flexibility. Interior spaces can grow or shrink as desired.

Straw bale party walls allow acoustic privacy between lots. Stabilized earthen floors and phase-change gypsum board partitions provide adequate thermal mass for interior comfort.

Due to its coastal location, Los Osos has mild sunny winters and largely foggy, cool summers. The insolation and temperature ranges are narrow enough to make use of a smart roof, a composite roof consisting of:

a transparent insulation skin

transparent photovoltaic material with integral water-heating elements

enough shading and venting capability to allow passive cooling when needed

Rainfall is enough that if harvested and stored in cistern, and "waste" transportation is removed from the water budget, the building could be self-sufficient in regards to water.

By optimizing metabolism and being part of a cohesive moderate-density village, Los Osos can potentially → be free of large electric grid and rate shocks with backup provided by village-scale green utility **+** be free from water grid and shortages with backup provided by village-scale green utility **+** be free from sewer grid compost and urine sequestration provide village revenue, reducing local taxes

All buildings have a metabolism that can be either parasitic or symbiotic. A symbiotic building can produce scarce and costly resources—including energy, water, and more—rather than just consuming them.

Design will use universal architectural elements to create more fluid compositions to convey the emotion of peaceful connectivity to site, society, and the planet.

History: *Our past will be looked at more as a process, a worldwide process as indicated in figure 6.29.* **Geometry:** *Fractal geometry will be as important as Euclidean geometry.* **Aesthetics:** *An expression of connection, continuity, and fluidity will replace the aesthetic of reductionism, compartmentalization, and isolation characteristics of industrial-era architecture.*

Forty-year-old passive solar building in Davis, California, still operating and performing as designed.

Proposal for the International Brotherhood of Electrical Workers in San Jose, California, utilizing a translucent photovoltaic roof for passive heating and electricity production and cooled by night ventilation over distributed thermal mass.

Summary: Buildings for Comfort and Joy

We wrote this book because we wish to share the discoveries we have made about creating buildings that use the sun and microclimate resources to provide heating, cooling, ventilation, and lighting. These strategies are not new; some have been well understood for more than two thousand years. But they are not well known in the architecture and development industry today. We have had the opportunity to help many of our clients discover the comfortable and health-giving qualities of these buildings. In most cases these buildings can be built for the same cost or perhaps just a little less or more than a conventional building that is on mechanical life support.

These buildings may be built with cement siding in traditional styles that look like all the other homes nearby. Or they may include plastered straw bale walls to get the desired super-insulation at a more competitive cost. They may rely on added thermal mass from counter-height waterwalls in front of operable south-facing windows to provide winter heating and night ventilation cooling in the summer; or a roof pond to provide powerful cooling in the hottest desert. Daylighting may be enhanced with south-facing light shelves or a roof monitor. Visit or stay in one of these delightful buildings and you will want one of your own—at home and at work.

As we hope we have shown, these buildings are not hard to design or build; but to make these even more sustainable, they should be built using local resources that are adapted from and local to the bioregion. These locally adapted designs and materials return the beauty of place to design. A courtyard-oriented building made with local earth materials for a California climate will look very different from a compact two-story solar Cape for a snowy site in Maine. But both utilize the same principles and can provide the same level of comfort and security.

And while having a comfortable home made with local materials to fit the local bioregion is a great beginning, most of us do not live well in isolation. Ideally this building, whether home or office, will be an integral part of a vibrant and sustainable community. Using the concepts and strategies we suggest here, it is possible to build sustainable buildings in sustainable communities. How nice it is to walk or bike to work in a daylit sustainable workplace, rather than driving on crowded freeways from a delightful home to a sick, sealed office building. And this sense of place, community, connection, and security enables us to experience improved health and joy.

The supporters of the fossil-fool industry have tried to characterize conservation and solar as inefficient, uncomfortable, costly, and unproven. We will "shiver in the dark" if we follow this path, they argue, but they are the ones who are headed for trouble. When the price of oil rises, the power lines go down in an ice storm, or allergies and asthma from sick buildings lay you low, remember that there is an alternative. We can be dancing in the sunlight instead! And in buildings that will remain comfortable and secure even without electricity or heating oil; buildings where the daylight plays across surfaces and brings connection to the outside, where the air is fresh and clean, and where comfort is the norm instead of a fleeting feeling. Choose health and sustainability!

The end.

APPENDIX A EASY TO DO AND HARDER TO DO

Some sustainable design options are simply harder to implement well than others, or carry more risk going forward. They may still be the best solution for the problem, but must be approached with care. The difficulty of doing things well declines with experience and in some cases with improved technology; but often the limitations are related to microclimate, biological, or environmental stresses or complications.

With an excellent craftsman and the best materials, almost anything can be done in a way that works and will function well for many years. But if the workmanship or materials are not as good, things can go wrong sooner than expected.

Easy to Do Well

- Pitched roofs, greater than 4:12 (will often work long after shingles are worn out). Steeper pitch also appears less vulnerable to hurricane damage.
- Wood-framed buildings (but regional problems with termites).
- Vertical windows.
- Overhangs.
- Interior shutters.
- Interior blinds.
- Adobe, rammed earth, water tank thermal mass.
- Passive solar water heaters.
- Clotheslines.

- Microhydro (although intake grates can be problematic).
- Grid-tied photovoltaic systems.
- Basic rainwater harvesting (for garden).
- Simple gray-water recycling (washing-machine water, shower).
- Hot-air collectors and simple air circulation.
- Pit toilets.
- Septic tanks and leach fields.

Harder to Do Well

- Sloped windows and shallow-angled greenhouse roofs.
- Arbors and trellises (seemingly simple, but usually too massive and not designed to last).
- Sunspaces and solar greenhouses (overheating issues in summer, distribution of heat to house in winter).
- Roof ponds.
- Flat and low-angled roofs (shorter lifetime, leaks almost inevitable with poor maintenance or extending use past expected life).
- Subterranean houses (potential for leaks and mold; leaks very hard to find and repair).

- Living roofs (potential for leaks, leaks very hard to find and repair).
- Sawtooth roofs (potential for leaks).
- Exterior shutters and blinds (although more costly systems have a better track record).
- Exterior foam wall insulation and covering (but materials getting better).
- Earth and clay plasters on exterior straw bale walls (challenging to get it right).
- Skylights (overheating in summer, leaks, seal or glazing failures).

- Active solar water heating systems (controls, materials overheat when system is dry).

- Partially shaded photovoltaic systems (critical to get design right if some modules are shaded at times).

- Flush toilets (low cost, often faulty flush valves).

- Compost toilets (design and operation must be done well).

- More complete gray-water recycling (design and operation must be done with care).

- Biofilters and living sewage treatment systems (challenging design issues and operation).

- Off-grid electric systems (design, equipment choices, and battery maintenance and care are critical).

- Wind machines (getting better all the time, but they still work in a very hostile environment).

- Rainwater harvesting systems for drinking water.

- Hot-air collectors and gravel bed thermal storage.

- Cool tubes (design challenges with moisture and mold, maintenance).

APPENDIX B TOOL KIT FOR BUILDING EVALUATION

It is possible to put together a pretty good tool kit for a few hundred dollars. The key tools include a light meter, sound meter, windspeed meter, radiant and air temperature readers, and humidity gauge. A simple indoor/outdoor thermometer with max/min recording can be very useful, but recording thermometers like the HOBOs from Onset are even better and don't cost much. A thermal imaging camera can also be very informative, but can cost $5,000 or more. Rentals are a good compromise, but not cheap. A blower door ($2,000-plus) and other tools can also be helpful, but are expensive and require more practice and training. A sensitive portable carbon monoxide monitor, perhaps $300, is also useful.

Simple and not very expensive meters and test equipment can provide more insight into energy flows and sustainable building design.

Airflow

One of the most challenging tasks is understanding airflow. Airflow through a building or yard is complex and often changing, depending on wind direction and intensity, which doors and windows or open, and where furniture is placed. Understanding airflow better can help you improve the performance of your building. Tools can range from a windspeed meter (best at higher airspeeds) to helium-filled balloons on strings to soap bubbles. Incense or smoke pencils are also helpful.

Balloons

Bright-colored helium-filled balloons with bright-colored ribbon and a weight for each balloon can demonstrate airflow patterns clearly. You can use different lengths of ribbon to contrast flows at different heights. They gradually lose gas, so plan on testing while they are fresh. Try different combinations of open windows and fan placements to find the best ventilation pattern.

Bubbles

Bubbles are also informative, especially for outside flows. Indoors, little bubbles are good, but outdoors bigger bubbles are easier to follow. Here are a couple of recipes for bubbles. Karo syrup should only be used outside. With the right mix, the bubbles will last quite a while; you can even identify and follow very low-speed airflows, such as cold-air drainage. You can buy glycerine at many drugstores.

Indoor Bubbles

¾ cup cold distilled water

¼ cup dishwashing soap (Joy Ultra, Ivory, or Dawn)

5 drops glycerine

Big Outdoor Bubbles

3 cups distilled water

1 cup liquid detergent or no-tears shampoo

1 cup glycerine or light corn syrup

Smoke Pencils

Nontoxic smoke is preferred. A wide range of smoke puffers and pencils are available. The Chimney Balloon offers a nontoxic version for $25 (www.chimneyballoon.us/smokepencilstick.html). Some people prefer incense.

Blower Doors

Blower doors allow you to pressurize a building and explore airflows, leaks, and performance. Blower doors are often used for retrofit exploration and design, but also useful for commissioning new buildings. Blower doors, flow hoods, and duct blasters can be used to evaluate duct systems. For more information, see Keefe's "Introduction to Blower Doors" in *Home Energy Magazine* (www.homeenergy.org/archive/hem.dis.anl.gov/eehem/94/940110.html).

Training

To better understand how to monitor and evaluate a building, attend a training workshop with Vital Signs, an outstanding program coordinated through the Center for Environmental Design Research at the University of California–Berkeley, with great support from members of the Society of Building Science Educators (http://arch.ced.berkeley.edu/vitalsigns).

If you are an educator or will teach workshops, please join the Society of Building Science Educators (SBSE). SBSE (www.sbse.org) is an association of university educators and practitioners in architecture and related disciplines who support excellence in the teaching of environmental science and building technologies.

It is better to be crudely right than precisely wrong.
—L. W. "TOD" NEUBAUER

Computer Simulation and Building-Performance Modeling

The increasing speed of computers has led to a growing dependence on computer simulations and modeling in building design, engineering, and performance prediction. While computer models and software can be useful, the value of even the more complex models is often limited by the less-than-perfect understanding of the fundamental aspects of building materials, building systems and energy performance, site microclimate (particularly the difference from nearby stations with comprehensive weather data), and occupant behavior and preferences. Models tend to be special focus rather than holistic and rarely offer good integration of heating, cooling, lighting, and ventilation, let along microclimate and occupant behavior. The users may also use the models in ways that limit their value, lead to mistakes, or are otherwise inappropriate. Input mistakes are also easy to miss, but can lead to impacts that may be comparable to significant differences in design details.

Even so, building-performance estimates can be very useful in both design development and building evaluation for new construction and retrofits. They should, however, be treated with sufficient skepticism rather than accepted as gospel truth. This is sometimes hard to do with a complex and comprehensive model with multiple pages of slick colorful output based on "full"-year weather tapes. Most performance-model developers will admit that their models are limited in some or many respects. Most have not been well tested or validated in a variety of microclimates by running against the performance of existing buildings.

The American Society of Heating, Refrigerating and Air-Conditioning Engineers conducted a pair of shoot-outs a number of years ago to compare performance models. In Shoot-out 1, electricity, hot-water, and chilled-water use during a test period were provided, but no description of the building or other specific details about the data were provided. Twenty-one contestants submitted data, with wide variance in results. The winner, given the odd design of the study,

was probably just lucky. In Shoot-out 2, contestants were given pre-retrofit and post-retrofit energy data, and asked to predict some pre-retrofit data that were withheld. Only four contestants entered, again with a very high variance in prediction.

A new series of shoot-outs would be helpful, perhaps like the Defense Advanced Research Projects Agency (DARPA) projects with a large financial prize. In this case, architectural offices would be given building specifications and location and asked to predict thermal performance and energy use. How close could they come to several years of actual performance? This would help identify problems not only with the models but also with the interfaces.

After the first run, an evaluation and revision period would be offered. Most modelers can tweak the model to better match local performance—this is not wrong or cheating, but it suggests imperfections in the models. More recently, the International Energy Agency has sponsored some more detailed evaluations of specific issues in performance models; these have highlighted both the improvements in models and remaining challenges.

Prescriptive and performance models are sometimes confused. Prescriptive-based models are often used to check compliance to a set of predetermined prescriptions. A good example is the prescriptive model commonly used to pass California Title 24 Energy Code. Prescriptive standards are usually based on conservation standards, and passive design techniques are rarely considered. For example, the present Title 24 prescriptive standards do not take into account night ventilation cooling or high-mass interiors in California, even though cooling is the largest thermal load in much of the state. Prescriptive standards and their compliance models often lock people into bureaucratically developed standards constrained by history and lobbying efforts from special interests rather than encouraging innovative, integrated solutions. While they may offer a performance-based option, this option may rarely be used because it adds to first cost, and developers often seek the lowest first cost rather than good or outstanding life-cycle performance and savings.

Performance modeling is a much better analytical tool for creative passive design. Performance models attempt to predict the real performance of a specific building rather than just comparing it with some more abstract standard. Performance modeling with a good model and experienced analyst can be a wonderful tool for integrated passive design. We've found that good performance modeling usually allows us to increase the performance of a design by about 30 percent. Our approach is to develop schematic design by experience and rules of thumb and then analyze this design with performance modeling as it progresses into design development. A good performance model can allow an iterative development of a design and optimization of the design based on a series of prediction runs and design modifications at progressively greater detail.

For all its advantages, however, the golden era of performance modeling is yet to arrive. Most performance models are opaque with weak interfaces for users and limited integration of the complex interactions between heating, cooling, ventilation, lighting, and occupant behavior. Most models leave many critical questions unanswered: What algorithms or models are behind the fill-in box or tick on a checklist? Do the tools really have the capabilities indicated? What level of effort and knowledge is required to use them? What is missing? There are some things to look for that are often not included: night ventilation cooling, cross- and stack ventilation, lighting/daylighting interaction and loads, increased solar radiation gain in winter from south windows from snow reflection (30 percent or more in many cases), impact of occupant use on ventilation cooling and comfort during the day, impact of occupant use of insulated shutters or shades in winter and exterior or interior blinds in summer, and—perhaps most important—site microclimate differences compared with the nearest weather station.

Despite many advances over the years, a wide range of problems still exist with understanding building performance, and the garbage-in, garbage-out problem common in all computing remains. Much more empirical research is needed to provide better input data for modeling and simulation. Unfortunately, field studies are neither as easy nor as inexpensive as computer simulations, and as time commitments and budgets have tightened these have become increasingly rare among academics and practicing architects and engineers. Improved instruments and data logging have made field and lab studies easier to do well, but they remain woefully underfunded and underappreciated in research appropriations and faculty tenure considerations, particularly in the United States. Using a group of HOBO temperature and humidity data loggers is so much easier than the 12-point paper pin recorders we used to use that there really is no excuse for not including at least limited post-occupancy performance monitoring in all new buildings. The Vital Signs Project suggests how much can be done even with limited funding, a simple took kit, and limited time (arch.ced.berkeley.edu/vitalsigns).

Anyone considering building-performance simulations will benefit from reading James Waltz's *Computerized Building Energy Simulation Handbook*. He starts with a good introduction to the myths of simulation and offers an approach for using simulations wisely. As he notes, "Every program that's out there is flawed." But they can still be used to improve building design and performance if the user understands the building, the site, the occupants, and the program's limitations and strengths.

Models may also be flawed because of systems interactions. Improved performance from synergism is an important element of passive design, but combining models of subsystems does not always lead to a good prediction of integrated system performance. Computer models will also not work well without a better understanding of occupant behavior. This will require much more comprehensive surveys of behavior and preferences to develop improved algorithms for occupant comfort and behavior and the use of lighting, window blinds, window opening, supplemental heating, cooling, and ventilation, and equipment use with internal heat gain.

Using Models

Computer simulation and modeling can be very helpful in both the programming and schematic stage and in the more nitty-gritty design development and specification stage. It may be necessary to meet building-code requirements. And it can also be very helpful in evaluating building performance and post-occupancy management. The needs for these three different stages are quite different, but related.

Programming and Schematics

Ideally, at the programming schematic state a simple easy-to-use tool could be brought to bear to suggest the most likely solutions for passive solar heating, microclimate-based cooling, daylighting, and natural ventilation. In the future, we can imagine a time when we could simply type in "1,400-square-foot two-story office complex for Duluth, Minnesota," say, and the software would suggest three or four of the most promising passive solar options showing building configurations, window area and orientation (including window solar heat gain coefficient by orientation), daylighting options, wall and ceiling insulation, thermal-mass placement, ventilation options, and backup heating. It would also provide a passive survivability review for the worst week possible summer and winter.

We are far from this level of sophistication today, but with increased investment and testing it would be possible. Most of the existing tools for this level of work are specifically for one function—for example, daylighting—or limited in consideration of key factors such as night vent cooling, radiant sky cooling, or occupant use of windows for comfort ventilation.

The evolution of building-simulation tools that can work with simple graphic tools such as Google SketchUp is an encouraging

sign. For this stage, some simple rules of thumb may be enough to get started, but these simple models can then help refine window-area/thermal-mass and building shell efficiency choices.

Design Development and Specification

As the design moves forward, more complex simulation models may be desirable, particularly for more complicated commercial, institutional, and industrial buildings. The bigger, more complex models like Energy-10, DOE-2, and TRNSYS can be used to develop simulation models that can help refine designs and improve specification choices. But this is not simple or easy. It takes experience and practice to apply these tools well. And in many cases they will have to be supplemented with other, more specialized programs such as FloVENT (CFD for ventilation) and Radiance (daylighting). What is needed is an easy-to-use, relatively foolproof tool that any architectural design firm or builder could employ with some confidence, but we are not even close to that yet. A fairly sophisticated engineering group or energy analyst with considerable experience in passive

A SHORT HISTORY OF THERMAL-PERFORMANCE MODELS IN BUILDINGS

The challenges of improving building-performance simulations are linked to the history of their development. A more complete history would be helpful, but here is how it appears to us.

After a start looking at survival in nuclear shelters at the National Bureau of Standards in the early 1960s, building simulation made a number of advances in the 1970s, and the first international conference on building simulation was convened in 1971. Interest and funding grew after the oil crises in 1973 and 1979 and the resulting spikes in interest in renewable energy. This led to a range of private and public simulation models, including programs such as CalPas, Micropas, and Cal-ERDA. But with the collapse of federal research funding in 1980, the evolution of building-performance models slowed. Many were and still are based on simplifications and algorithms developed for very slow computers in the 1970s. These have simply rolled along from iteration to iteration and may limit accuracy and validity of program results. As Phil Niles, PE, has so wisely noted, rebuilding from the ground up is needed.

With renewed funding from governments (here and abroad), private firms and universities have created a wide variety of building-energy-simulation programs. In 2005, a comparison of the features and capabilities of twenty such programs was published by EERE, including well-known programs such as BLAST, DOE-2.1E, ECOTECT, Energy-10, EnergyPlus, HEED, SUNREL, TRACE, and TRNSYS. The EERE report provides a short introduction to each program and tables comparing the approach or inclusion of factors such as general modeling features; zone loads; building envelope, daylighting and solar; infiltration, ventilation, and multizone airflow; renewable energy systems; electrical systems and equipment; HVAC systems; HVAC equipment; environmental emissions; economic evaluation; climate data availability; results reporting; validation; and user interfaces, links to other programs, and availability. Many other programs have been developed and are in use around the world. The Energy Efficiency and Renewable Energy program maintains a list of Building Energy Software Tools at http://apps1.eere.energy.gov/buildings/tools_directory/tools_new.cfm. Several hundred are now on file, with new ones trickling in regularly.

solar architectural design and evaluation is still needed. When less skilled performance simulations are done, the results are often less than inspiring. As a recent review of LEED buildings showed, the performance was often far from predicted values, and it was rarely better.

Building Evaluation and Performance Improvement

More complex models are often needed to improve building management and to improve performance. Here the design details are known, the site is better understood (monitoring may still be useful), and occupants are known. Occupancy behavior is critical and should be monitored to improve simulation accuracy. Simple surveys can help identify occupant management issues. In one house in Village Homes, we found that the owners were opening the skylight insulated shutters at night during the winter. They weren't sure why they started, but somehow thought it was part of the solar system operation. In the Kitsun solar apartments in Vancouver, very heavy use of heating in one apartment suggested a flaw in the building envelope or heating system, but was simply the result of a family from the Caribbean trying to stay comfortable (78° to 80°F).

Recent growing interest in improving building performance to reduce global climate impacts has led to renewed investment, but no clear winners have emerged. Limitations in understanding of building science continue to limit a model's performance. Cooling factors have been particularly weak. As Givoni noted in 1991, there were significant problems with DOE-2 cooling simulations, with convective cooling coefficient values perhaps only one-fourth of actual, and with a need for a convective coefficient in relation to air change still lacking. Night ventilation and cross- and stack ventilation have also been missing from many models.

Limited experience with full-scale roof pond and cool-pool buildings has also limited modeling accuracy. Many more demonstration buildings with optimized passive solar architecture are needed to provide sufficient detail for more accurate models and simulation programs. And much more testing and comparison of products is needed to determine which work best for specific problems and climate challenges.

The renewed interest in simulation led to the creation of the International Building Performance Simulation Association, and they have been holding conferences since 1985. More recently they started publishing the *Journal of Building Performance Simulation*. The *IBPSA News* is also worth reading and is available free online, at www.ibpsa.org.

Specialized Tools

Building-simulation programs are often weak on ventilation and daylighting, but there are a growing number of specialized programs that can improve understanding of these factors.

Ventilation: Computational Fluid Dynamics (CFD)

CFD makes wind-flow and ventilation studies possible in great detail. Two of the leaders are FloVENT (www.mentor.com/products/mechanical/products/flovent) and FLUENT (www.fluent.com). They continue to improve and have been helpful in building design and evaluation, but they remain approximations, not reality. A retrospective analysis of B. Givoni's wing wall ventilation study found that CFD provided reasonably good concurrence with observed wind tunnel data, but differed by significant amounts in many respects. The CFD model used did not respond to angle of incidence in the same manner as the physical model, predicting about 30 percent less turbulence at 45° angle of incidence. The mean indoor airspeed was underestimated with a 3-D model and overestimated by a 2-D model.

Lighting

Daylight modeling appears to be the most useful of current computer simulations, but there has been little convergence on a preferred model. A recent survey found more than forty-two different daylight simulation programs were being used. More than half were based on the Radiance simulation engine. Daylight models also need more background research on user preference and behavior, ranging from preferred illuminance to control behavior using lights and blinds.

Occupants often prefer illuminance below code requirements as aspects of the lighting-manufacturer-driven codes of the 1970s linger on. As Galasiu and Veitch (2006) note, preferred levels were often only 50 percent of the British code, and in other field studies some people were comfortable with about 10 to 20 percent of standards and codes. The impact of occupant behavior on daylight use is also poorly understood. Very few well-designed buildings exist, so data on behavior in best-case buildings are largely lacking. Few buildings have offered good control systems, but when made available in one building 74 percent of occupants used their dimmers. Predicting the various types of glare is also not well understood and is complex, because it depends on furniture, equipment and fixture placement, and use.

Integrating Lighting, Ventilation and Thermal Performance Models, and Occupant Behavior

Ideally, the simulation and modeling programs would integrate lighting, heating, cooling, air quality, and ventilation with algorithms of expected occupant behavior and preferences. This has become more feasible as computer computational speeds increase, but it is limited by lack of understanding. Ultimately the goal would be to have a very simple, intuitive system that combines these features with a simple sketch-up-type design tools so that comprehensive estimates of performance can be easily tested at the schematic stage. And perhaps all buildings should be required to have a life-cycle energy-use label.

Best Choices Today

We have had some experience with these tools, but not enough to make any detailed recommendations, so we offer the results of a recent survey by Attia et al., 2009. HEED, IES VE, and eQUEST were considered most architect-friendly. Ecotect, DB, E10, and GBS were also widely used but much less easy to relate to design. The performance of these has not been compared on a range of passive solar buildings, so approach with caution.

Building-performance modeling and simulation is getting better, but limitations are still clear, and error accumulation can be significant. As Waltz noted in 2000, a 50 percent difference in performance prediction was not unlikely. In 2008, the BESTEST slab on grade study found a 9 to 55 percent disagreement among models. Why? Flaws in models, errors in entry, and errors in use may all be important. These can be compounded when we get to actual building by a poor understanding of site microclimate (±20 percent) and occupant response (±20 percent). Some of these errors may cancel out, but if we consider only a 20 percent error in the model and comparable errors for microclimate and occupant use, then an overall estimate is (80% × 80% × 80%), or 51 percent accuracy. We have a great deal to learn, but a good modeler should be able to get within 10 percent and perhaps 5 percent for a well-understood building system in a well-characterized microclimate and conventional occupant use.

Funding for building science must be increased from the current abysmally low level. A National Institute of Building Science (NIBS) with funding comparable to National Institute of Health ($30 billion a year) would be desirable and should have been created in 1970. Instead, funding for building science research dropped to the low millions per year. Testing and validation at full scale are needed for systems, building components, and whole buildings. And both CFD and building thermal-performance software need to be tested against known buildings and systems in a wide range of climates to improve confidence in their value. Simpler design tools and rules of thumb can also be validated to provide improved design skills for the rest of the world.

For more information on the most architect-friendly programs:

- Integrated Environmental Solutions: www.iesve.com/Software/Model-Building
- Home Energy Efficient Design: www.aud.ucla.edu/heed
- eQUEST: www.doe2.com/equest

Passive Performance Modeling Specialists

A specialist with considerable experience is needed to undertake serious performance modeling for a building. There are a number of firms capable of performing passive solar building simulations using the more complex simulation tools. Check in your local area for references and recommendations. Ask about their ability to integrate heating, cooling, lighting, and ventilation.

Special thanks to Phil Niles, who kindly offered us his views on modeling history, limitations, and opportunities.

Further Reading for Building-Performance Simulation and Modeling

California Energy Commission. 2008. HERS Technical Manual, California Energy Commission, High Performance Buildings and Standards Development Office. CEC-400-2008-012 (includes program requirements).

Clarke, J. 2001. *Energy Simulation in Building Design.* Butterworth, Heinemann. Oxford, UK.

Crawley, D. B., L. K. Lawrie, F. C. Winkelmann, W. F. Buhl, Y. J. Huang, C. O. Pedersen, R. K. Strand, Richard J. Liesen, Daniel E. Fisher, M. J. Witte, and J. Glazer. 2001. EnergyPlus: creating a new-generation building energy simulation program. *Energy and Buildings* 33(4):319–331.

Galasiu, A. D., and J. A. Veitch. 2006. Occupant preferences and satisfaction with the luminous environment and control systems in daylit offices: a literature review. *Energy and Buildings* 38:728–742.

Givoni, B. 1991. Performance and applicability of passive and low-energy cooling systems. *Energy and Buildings* 17:177–199.

Haberl, J. S., and S. Thamilseran. 1998. The great Energy Predictor Shootout II: measuring retrofit savings. *ASHRAE Journal* 40(1):49–56.

Haves, P., T. Salsbury, D. Claridge, and M. Liu. 2001. Use of whole building simulation in on-line performance assessment: modeling and implementation issues. Lawrence Berkeley National Laboratory Paper LBNL-48284. www.escholarship.org/uc/item/4g7923xn.

Hensen, J. L. M. and R. Lamberts. 2011. *Building Performance Simulation for Design and Operation.* Spon Press, London.

Hong, T., S. K. Chou, and T. Y. Bong. 2000. Building simulation: an overview of developments and information sources. *Building and Environment* 35(4):347–361.

Kosny, J., and S. A. Mohiuddin. 2004. Interactive Internet-based building envelope materials database for whole-building energy simulation programs. ASHRAE Thermal IX Conference, Clearwater, FL.

Kreider, J., and J. Haberl. 1994. Predicting hourly building energy usage: The Great Energy Predictor Shootout: overview and discussion of results. *ASHRAE Transactions* Technical Paper, v100, pt. 2.

Kusuda, T. 2001. Building environment simulation before desktop computers in the USA through a personal memory. *Energy and Buildings* 33(4):291–302.

Mak, C.M., J. L. Niu, C. T. Lee, and K. F. Chan. 2007. A numerical simulation of wing walls using computational fluid dynamics. *Energy and Buildings* 39:995–1002.

Neymark, J., and R. Judkoff. 2002. *International Energy Agency Building Energy Simulation Test and Diagnostic Method for Heating, Ventilating, and Air-Conditioning Equipment Models (HVAC BESTTEST).* Volume 1: *Cases E100-E200.* NREL Technical Report. National Renewable Energy Laboratory, Golden, CO.

Neymark, J., R. Judkoff, I. Beausoleil-Morrison, A. Ben-Nakhi, M. Crowley, M. Deru, R. Henninger, H. Ribberink, J. Thornton, A. Wijsman, and M. Witte. 2008. *International Energy Agency Building Energy Simulation Test and Diagnostic Method (IEA BESTEST): In-Depth Diagnostic Cases for Ground Coupled Heat Transfer Related to Slab-on-Grade Construction.* National Renewable Energy Laboratory, Golden, CO.

Reinhart, C., and A. Fitz. 2006. Findings from a survey on the current use of daylight simulations in building design. *Energy and Buildings* 38(7):824–835.

Ubbelohde, M. S., and C. Humann. 1998. Comparative evaluation of four daylighting software programs. *Proceedings of the 1998 Summer Study on Energy Efficiency in Buildings, ACEEE* 3:325–340. www.coolshadow.com/downloads/ACEE%20daylighting.pdf.

Waltz, J. 2000. *Computerized Building Energy Simulation Handbook.* Fairmont Press, Lilburn, GA.

Zhai, Z. J., and Q. Y. Chen. 2006. Sensitivity analysis and application guides for integrated building energy and CFD simulation. *Energy and Buildings* 38:1060–1068.

Znouda, E., N. Ghrab-Morcos, and A. Hadj-Alouane. 2007. Optimization of Mediterranean building design using genetic algorithms. *Energy and Buildings* 39:148–153.

Each chapter of this book, and sometimes each page, could be a book in itself. Listed here are the references and suggestions for additional reading on the key topics of the book. Many offer useful information or insights, but they are rarely comprehensive or well integrated. For example, daylighting books may pay little attention to space conditioning, and books on solar heating may pay little attention to daylighting, ventilation, and cooling.

Precomputer articles of interest are included, because too often work before the mid-1980s is not well indexed or considered. The papers from the time before "cheap" air-conditioning and sealed buildings are particularly relevant. The many Passive Solar Conference proceedings (US and UK) and Passive and Low Energy Architecture organization proceedings are also worth reviewing.

Preface and Chapter 1. Sustainable Buildings

Alexander, C. 1977. *A Pattern Language.* Oxford University Press, Oxford, UK.

Ali-Toudert, F., and H. Mayer. 2007. Thermal comfort in an east–west oriented street canyon in Freiburg (Germany) under hot summer conditions. *Theoretical and Applied Climatology* 87:223–237.

American Society of Heating, Refrigerating and Air-Conditioning Engineers. VD. *Handbook of Fundamentals.* Many editions.

ASTM. 2007. *International Standards for Sustainability in Building,* 3rd edition. CD-ROM.

Bainbridge, D. A. 1982. Microclimate. *Fine Homebuilding* June–July:14–16.

Bainbridge, D. A. 2004. Sustainable building as appropriate technology. Pp. 55–67, 75–77. In J. Kennedy, ed. *Building Without Borders: Sustainable Construction for the Global Village.* Island Press, Washington, DC.

Bainbridge, D. A. 2004. The price falls short. *Solar Today* 18(5):62, 59.

Balaras, C. A., K. Droutsa, E. Dascakaki, and S. Kontoyiannidis. 2005. Deterioration of European apartment buildings. *Energy and Buildings* 37:515–527.

Barnett, D. L., and W. D. Browning. 1995. *A Primer on Sustainable Building.* Rocky Mountain Institute, Snowmass, CO.

Behling, S., and S. Behling. 2000. *Solar Power: The Evolution of Sustainable Architecture.* Prestel Verlag, Munich, London, New York.

Benyus, J. 1997. *Biomimicry: Innovation Inspired by Nature.* William Morrow and Co., New York.

Brady, G. S., H. R. Clauser, and J. A. Vaccari. 1997. *Materials Handbook,* 14th edition. McGraw-Hill, New York.

Brager, G. S., and R. de Dear. 2001. *A Field-Based Thermal Comfort Standard for Naturally Ventilated Buildings.* Collaborative for High Performance Schools (CHPS) Best Practices Manual, Appendix C (Eley Associates, 2001). www.chps.net.

Brager, G. S., and R. J. de Dear. 1998. Thermal comfort in the built environment: a literature review. *Energy and Buildings* 27:83–96.

Bringezu, S., H. Schütz, and S. Moll. 2002. Towards sustainable resource management in the European Union. Wuppertal Papers 121. Wuppertal Institute, Wuppertal, Germany.

Brooks, F. A. 1959. *An Introduction to Physical Micrometeorology.* University of California Press, Davis.

Brunckhorst, D. 2001. Building capital through bioregional planning and biosphere reserves. *Ethics in Science and Environmental Politics* 1:19–32.

Butti, K., and J. Perlin. 1980. *A Golden Thread: 2500 Years of Solar Architecture and Technology.* Van Nostrand Reinhold, New York.

CEC (Secretariat of the Commission for Environmental Cooperation). 2008. *Green Building in North America.* www.cec.org/greenbuilding.

David and Lucille Packard Foundation. 2002. *Building for Sustainability: Sustainability Matrix.* www.softfirmstudios.net/webimage/projects/packard/2002-Matrix.pdf.

Department of Defense. VD. *Engineering Weather Data.* Various editions and online.

Edinger, J. 1967. *Watching for the Wind.* Doubleday-Anchor, New York.

Edwards, B., ed. 2003 [1998]. *Green Buildings Pay.* Spon Press, New York.

Fanger, P. O. 1972. *Thermal Comfort: Analysis and Applications in Environmental Engineering.* McGraw-Hill, New York.

Fisk, W. J. 2000. Health and productivity gains from better indoor environments and their relationship with building energy efficiency. *Annual Review of Energy and the Environment* 25(1): 537–566.

Fisk III, P., and G. Vittori. Vd. Bioregional design materials. Center for Maximum Potential Building Systems, Austin, TX. www.cmpbs.org.

Geiger, R., R. H. Aaron, and P. Todhunter. 2009 [1950]. *The Climate Near the Ground,* 7th edition. Rowman and Littlefield, New York.

Givoni, B. 1969. *Man, Climate and Architecture.* Elsevier, New York.

Guertin, M. 2009. Attic insulation upgrade. *Fine Homebuilding* 200:68–73.

Haggard, K., and P. Niles. 1980. *Passive Solar Handbook for California.* California Energy Commission, Sacramento.

Haggard, K., P. Cooper, and C. Gyovai. 2006. *Fractal Architecture: Design for Sustainability.* San Luis Obispo Sustainability Group, Santa Margarita, CA.

Haggard, K., P. Cooper, J. Rennick, and P. Niles. 2000. Natural conditioning of buildings. Pp. 37–69. In L. Elizabeth and C. Adams. *Alternative Construction: Contemporary Building Methods.* John Wiley and Sons, New York.

Han, J., W. Yang, J. Zhou, G. Zhang, Q. Zhang, and D. J. Moschandreas. 2009. A comparative analysis of urban and rural residential comfort under natural ventilation environment. *Energy and Buildings* 41:139–145. http://atmos.es.mq.edu.au. Thermal comfort index calculator.

Kats, D. E., L. Alevantis, A. Berman, E. Mills, and J. Perlman. 2003. *The Costs and Financial Benefits of Green Buildings.* Report to California's Sustainable Building Task Force. Capital E. www.usgbc.org/Docs/News/News477.pdf.

Kennedy, J., M. Smith, and C. Wanek. 2002. *The Art of Natural Building.* New Society Publishers, Gabriola Island, BC.

Kern, K. 1975. *The Owner-Built Home.* Charles Scribner's Sons, New York.

Kutscher, C. 2006. Confronting the climate change crisis. *Solar Today* 20(4):28–33.

Leopold, A. 1987 [1949]. The land ethic. Pp. 201–226. In *A Sand County Almanac and Sketches from Here and There.* Oxford University Press, New York.

Lstiburek, J. 2008. Some old lessons distilled. *ASHRAE Journal* September:82–86.

Marshall, B., and R. Argue. 1981. *The Super-Insulated Retrofit Book.* Renewable Energy in Canada, Toronto, Canada.

Mazria, E. 1979. *The Passive Solar Energy Book.* Rodale Press, Emmaus, PA.

McDonough, W., and M. Braungart. 2002. *Cradle to Cradle: Remaking the Way We Make Things.* North Point Press, New York.

McHarg, I. L. 1995 [1969]. *Design with Nature.* Wiley, New York.

Mendell, M. J., Q. Lei-Gomez, A. G. Mirer, O. Seppänen, and G. Brunner. 2008. Risk factors in heating, ventilating and air conditioning systems for occupant symptoms in US office buildings. *Indoor Air* 18(4):301–316.

Millennium Ecosystem Assessment Board. 2005. *Living Beyond Our Means: Natural Assets and Human Well Being.* MEA, United Nations.

Minutillo, J. 2008. Design professionals follow the physician's precept: "First, do no harm." *Architectural Record* 196(8):130.

Naess, A., and D. Rothenberg. 1989. *Ecology, Community and Lifestyle.* Cambridge University Press, Cambridge, UK.

National Oceanic and Atmospheric Agency (NOAA). 2008. *Climatography of the United States.* NCDC, Asheville, NC.

Ohrenschall, M. 2000. Green building pays. *CON.WEB* 056 August 31. www.newsdata.com/enernet/conweb/conweb56.html.

Olgyay, V. 1963. *Design with Climate.* Princeton University Press, Princeton, NJ.

Pacala, S., and R. Socolow. 2004. Stabilization wedges for solving the climate problem. *Science* 305:968–972.

Reynolds, J. 2002. *Courtyards: Aesthetic, Social and Thermal Delight.* John Wiley and Sons, New York.

Rijal, H. B., P. Tuohy, M. A. Humphreys, J. F. Nicol, A. Samuel, and J. Clarke. 2007. Using results from field surveys to predict the effect of open windows on thermal comfort and energy use in buildings. *Energy and Buildings* 39:823–836.

Rosenburg, R. 1974. *Microclimate: The Biological Environment.* John Wiley and Sons, New York.

Schmitz-Günther, T., ed. 1998. *Living Spaces: Sustainable Building and Design.* Könemann, Cologne, Germany.

Snell, C., and T. Callahan. 2005. *Green Building.* Lark Books, New York.

Socolow, R., and S. Pacala. 2006. A plan to keep carbon in check. *Scientific American* 295(3):50–57.

Sommer, R. 1972. *Design Awareness.* Rinehart Press, San Francisco.

Steen, A., B. Steen, D. A. Bainbridge, and D. Eisenberg. 1994. *The Straw Bale House.* Chelsea Green, White River Junction, VT.

Sunset Western Garden Book. Lane Publishing Company, Menlo Park, CA (including climate maps; many editions).

Thoreau, H. D., ed. by B. P. Dean. 1992. *Faith in a Seed: The Dispersion of Seeds and Other Late Natural History Writings.* Island Press, Washington, DC.

US Environmental Protection Agency. 1991. *Sick Building Syndrome.* Research and Development. MD-56.

U.S. Navy Sun position calculators. http://aa.usno.navy.mil/data/docs/AltAz.php.

van Dresser, P. 1976. *A Landscape for Humans.* Lightning Tree Press, Santa Fe, NM.

Venolia, C. 2002. Designing for vitality. pp 36–42. In J. Kennedy, M. G. Smith, and C. Wanek, eds. *The Art of Natural Building.* New Society Publishers, Gabriola Island, BC.

Wackernagel, M., and W. Rees. 1996. *Our Ecological Footprint: Reducing Human Impact on the Earth.* New Society Publishers, Gabriola Island, BC.

Wargocki, P., and R. Djukanovic. 2005. Simulations of the potential revenue from investment in improved indoor air quality in an office building. *ASHRAE Transactions* 111(Pt2):699–711.

Weisman, A. 2007. *The World Without Us.* St. Martin's Press, NY.

Wilson, A. 2008. Mandate passive survivability. *Fine Homebuilding* 196:22,24.

Wolfe, J. N., R.T. Wareham, and H. T. Scofield. 1949. Microclimates and macroclimate of Neotoma, a small valley in central Ohio. *Bulletin of the Ohio Biological Survey* 1:1–267.

Wong, I. L., P. C. Eames, and R. S. Perera. 2007. A review of transparent insulation systems and the evaluation of payback periods for building applications. *Solar Energy* 81:1058–1071.

World Commission on Environment and Development. 1987. *Our Common Future.* Oxford University Press, Oxford, UK.

www.ncdc.noaa.gov. Weather and climate data online and in reports; early paper copy reports can be instructive. Also available state and regional climate and weather reports.

Xenergy and SERA Architects. 2000. *Green City Buildings: Applying the LEED Rating System.* Portland Energy Office. www.sustainableportland.org/CityLEED.pdf.

Chapter 2. Passive Heating

Anderson, B., and M. Riordan. 1976. *The Solar Home Book.* Brick House Publishing, Andover, MA.

Augustyn, J. 1979. *The Solar Cat Book* and 2008. *The Return of the Solar Cat Book.* Patty Paw Press, Berkeley, CA.

Bainbridge, D. A. 1979. Waterwall passive solar systems for new and retrofit buildings. pp 473–478. In *Proceedings of the Third Passive Solar Conference*. American Section, International Solar Energy Association, San Jose, California.

Bainbridge, D. A. 1981. Moved in mass. Pp. 436–449. In J. Carter, ed. *Solarizing Your Present Home*. Rodale Press, Emmaus, PA.

Bainbridge, D. A. 1982. A super-insulated passive solar house. *Solar Utilization News* 6(11):5.

Bainbridge, D. A. 1980. Making insulated bifold shutters. Pp. 292–298. In W. Langdon, ed. *Movable Insulation*. Rodale Press, Emmaus, PA.

Bainbridge, D. A., J. Corbett, and J. Hofacre. 1979. *Village Homes' Solar House Designs*. Rodale Press, Emmaus, PA.

Bainbridge, D. A., K. L. Haggard, and P. Cooper. 2007. Water walls: an effective option for high performance buildings. *Solar Today* July–August:38–41.

Balcomb, J. D., ed. 1992. *Passive Solar Buildings*. MIT Press, Boston.

BASF. 2008. Intelligent temperature management in an extremely lightweight approach. BASF Aktiengesellschaft, Ludwigshafen, Germany.

Bhandari, M. S., and N. K. Bansal. 1994. Solar heat gain factors and heat loss coefficients for passive heating concepts. *Solar Energy* 53(2):199–208.

Butti, K. and J. Perlin. 1980. *A Golden Thread*. Chesire Books, Palo Alto, CA.

Chen, C., H. Guo, Y. Liu, H. Yue, and C. Wang. 2008. A new kind of phase change material for energy storing wallboard. *Energy and Buildings* 40:882–890.

Chiras, D. D. 2002. *The Solar House: Passive Heating and Cooling*. Chelsea Green, White River Jct, VT.

Feist, W. 2009. Passivhaus Institut. www.passiv.de and www.Passivhaus-info.de. Passivhaus Institut, Darmstadt Rheinstr. 44/46, 64283 Darmstadt, Germany.

Givoni, B. 1991. Characteristics, design implications, and applicability of passive solar heating systems for buildings. *Solar Energy* 47(6):425–435.

Haggard, K., P. Cooper, J. Rennick, and P. Niles. 2000. Natural conditioning of buildings. Pp. 37–69. In L. Elizabeth and C. Adams. *Alternative Construction: Contemporary Building Methods*. John Wiley and Sons, New York.

Hammond, J., M. Hunt, B. Maeda, B. Kopper, and D. A. Bainbridge. 1977. *The Davis Energy Conservation Report*. Living Systems, Winters, CA.

Lahuerta, J. 2001. *Casa Batllo Barcelona*. Triangle Postals SL, Barcelona, Spain.

Littlefair, P. J. 1998. *Site Layout Planning for Daylight and Sunlight*. IHS-BRE Publishing, Bracknell, UK.

Mazria, E. 1979. *The Passive Solar Energy Book*. Rodale Press, Emmaus, PA.

Nayak, J. K., N. K. Bansal, and M. S. Sodha. 1983. Analysis of passive heating concepts. *Solar Energy* 30(1):51–69.

Neubauer, L. W. 1968. Effect of size, shape and orientation on temperature characteristics of model buildings. ASAE Paper 68-413. Utah State University, Logan.

Neubauer, L. W. 1972. Orientation and insulation. *ASAE Transactions* 15(4):707–709.

Niles, P., W. B. Haggard, and K. L. Haggard. 1980. *Passive Solar Handbook for California*. California Energy Commission, Sacramento.

Nisson, J. D., and G. Dutt. 1985. *The Superinsulated Home Book*. John Wiley Sons, New York.

Seifert, R. 2009. On shutters. *Alaska Building Science News* 14(4):8,9.

Spring, M. 2007. Dazzling achievement. *Building*. www.building.co.uk/story.asp?storycode=3088489.

Torcellini, P., and S. Pless. 2004. Trombe walls in low energy buildings: practical experiences. NREL/CP-550-36277. www.nrel.gov/docs/fy04osti/36277.pdf.

Van Dresser, P. 1977. *Homegrown Sundwellings*. Lightning Tree Press, Santa Fe, NM.

Vitruvius Pollio, M., translated by M. H. Morgan. 1960 [1st Century BC]. *The Ten Books of Architecture*. Dover, New York.

Wright, D. 2008. *The Passive Solar Primer*. Schiffer Publishing. Atglen, PA.

Chapter 3. Passive Cooling and Ventilation

Abraham, F. F. 1960. Determination of long-wave atmospheric radiation. *Journal of Meteorology* 17: 291–295.

Allard, F., ed. 1998. *Natural Ventilation in Buildings: A Design Handbook.* James and James, London, UK.

Arizona Solar Center. 2009. Natural Cooling. www.azsolarcenter .com/technology/pas-3.html.

ASHRAE. *Handbook of Fundamentals.* www. ASHRAE.org

Aynsley, R. 2007. Natural ventilation in passive design. *BEDP Environment Design Guide* May. TEC2-Summary.

Bahadori, M. N. 1978. Passive cooling systems in Iranian architecture. *Scientific American* 238(2):144–154.

Bahadori, M. N. 1985. An improved design of wind towers for natural ventilation and passive cooling. *Solar Energy* 35(2):119–129.

Bahadori, M.N., M. Mazidi, and A. R. Dehghani. 2008. Experimental investigation of new designs of wind towers. *Renewable Energy: An International Journal.* 33(10):2273–2281.

Bainbridge, D. A. 1978. The Indio cool pool experiment. *Alternative Sources of Energy* 32:6–10.

Bainbridge, D. A., and M. Hunt. 1976. *The Indio Cool Pool Experiment.* Indio Energy Conservation Project, City of Indio, Indio, CA.

Bainbridge, D. A., J. Hammond, and B. Kopper. 1976. *Cool Pool System.* Davis Energy Conservation Report, Living Systems, Winters, CA.

Bassiouny, R., and N. S. A. Kourah. 2008. An analytical and numerical study of solar chimney use for room natural ventilation. *Energy and Buildings* 40:865–873.

Battle McCarthy Consulting Engineers. 1999. *Wind Towers: Detail in Building.* John Wiley & Sons, London, UK.

Bliss, R. W. 1961. The performance of an experimental system using solar energy for heating, and night radiation for cooling a building. S30:148–157. UN Conference on New Sources of Energy, Rome, Italy.

Bobenhausen, W. 1994. *Simplified Design of HVAC Systems.* John Wiley and Sons, New York.

Bourgeois, J.-L., and C. Pelos. 1996. *Spectacular Vernacular.* Aperture Books, New York.

Bourne, R., and C. Carew. 1996. Design and implementation of a night roof-spray storage cooling system. *Proceedings ACEEE Summer Study in Energy Efficiency in Buildings*, Washington, DC.

Brager, G. S., and R. de Dear. 2000. A Standard for Natural Ventilation. *ASHRAE Journal* 42(10):21–28.

Brooks, F. A. 1952. Atmospheric radiation and its reflection from the ground. *Journal of Meteorology* 9:41–52.

Brooks, F. A. 1959. *An Introduction to Physical Microclimatology.* University of California, Davis.

BTS. 1999. Whole house fans. www.eren.doe.gov/erec/factsheets /aircond.pdf.

Building Research Establishment. 1978. Principles of natural ventilation. *BRE Digest* Cl/SfB, Digest 210.

Burton, J., and J. Reiss. 1979. Low cost induced ventilation cooling system retrofit. *3rd Passive Solar Conference*, San Jose. Pp. 589–593.

Byrne, J. 1999. Finding the whole-house fan that fits. *Home Energy Magazine* May–June.

Catalanotti, S., V. Cuomo, G. Piro, D. Ruggi, V. Silvestrini, and G. Troise. 1975. The radiative cooling of selective surfaces. *Solar Energy* 17:83–89.

Chalfoun, N. V. 1997. Design and application of natural down-draft evaporative cooling devices. *ASES97.* http://cala.arizona.edu /research/hed/publications/ASES97/Ases97.html.

Chen, B., D. Clark, J. Maloney, W.N. Mei, and J. Kasher. 1995. Measurement of night sky emissivity in determining radiant cooling from cool storage roofs and roof ponds. Passive Solar Research Group, University of Nebraska, Omaha.

Chilengwe, N., and S. Sharples. 2003. Low and high pressure experimental analysis of ventilators for natural ventilation in buildings. *International Journal of Ventilation* 2(2):149–158.

CIBSE. 2005, 1997. Natural ventilation in non-domestic buildings. CIBSE AM 10. www. CIBSE.org

Clark, G., F. Loxom, C. H. Treat, and C. Allen. 1979. *An Assessment of Evaporative, Radiative and Convective Cooling Processes and Their Application in Selected Cities in the US.* Trinity University, San Antonio, TX, for US Dept. of Energy. Publication P.C.-1.79.

Cramer, R. D., and L. W. Neubauer. 1959. Solar radiant gains through directional glass exposure. *ASHRAE Transactions* 65:499–513.

Cramer, R. D., and L. W. Neubauer. 1959. Summer heat control in small homes. *Transactions ASHRAE* 2(1):102–105.

Cramer, R. D., and L. W. Neubauer. 1965. Diurnal radiant exchange with the sky dome. *Solar Energy* 9(2):95–103.

Cramer, R. D., and V. G. Kay. 1956. Temperature control practices. *Journal of Home Economics* 48(3):181–184.

Cramer, R. D., R. B. Deering, V. G. Kay, and L. W. Neubauer. 1958. Temperature control for houses. *Journal of Home Economics* 50(3):175–180.

Cunningham, W. A., and T. L. Thompson. 1986. Passive cooling with natural draft cooling tower in combination with solar chimneys. PLEA, Hungary.

Dai, Y. J., K. Sumathy, R. Z. Wang, Y. G. Li. 2003. Enhancement of natural ventilation in a solar house with a solar chimney and a solid adsorption cooling cavity. *Solar Energy* 74:65–75.

Davis Energy Group. Nd. Nightsky® systems cools roof tops, saves energy. www.davisenergygroup.com.

de Jaeger, D., M. Manning, and L. Kuijpers. 2005. *Safeguarding the Ozone Layer and the Global Climate System: Issues Related to Hydrofluorocarbons and Perfluorocarbons.* IPCC/TEAP Special Report. www.ipcc.ch/pdf/special-reports/sroc/sroc_ts.pdf.

Deering, R. B. 1955. Effective use of living shade. *California Agriculture* September:10, 11, 15.

Department of Defense. 2002. *Unified Facilities Criteria Design: Engineering Weather Data.* www.wbdg.org/ccb/DOD/UFC/ufc_3_400_02.pdf.

Duly, C. 1979. *The Houses of Mankind.* Blacker Calmann Cooper, London, UK.

Eley and Associates. 2003. *Hawaii Commercial Building Guidelines for Energy Efficiency Natural Ventilation.* For the State of Hawaii DBEDT 2-1.

Environmental Research Laboratory. 1986. To all those interested in cooling towers. Tucson, AZ.

Everson, G. J., L. W. Neubauer, and R. B. Deering. 1956. Effect of certain home furnishings on room temperature. *Journal of Home Economics* 48(3):165–167.

Fairey, P., S. Chandra, and A. Kerestecioglu. 1986. *Ventilative cooling in southern residences: a parametric analysis.* FSEC-PF-108-96, Florida Solar Energy Center, Cape Canaveral.

FAO. 1986. *Improvement of Post-Harvest Fresh Fruits and Vegetables Handling: A Manual.* UNFAO Regional Office for Asia and the Pacific, Bangkok.

Federal Energy Management Program. 1997. White Cap™ roof spray cooling system. *Technology Installation Review.* Pacific Northwest National Lab, Richland, WA.

Frey, C. M., and E. Parlow. 2007. Urban radiation balance of two coastal cities in a hot and dry environment. *International Journal of Remote Sensing* 28(12):2695–2712.

Givoni, B. 1969. *Man, Climate and Architecture.* Elsevier, New York.

Givoni, B. 1977. Solar heating and night radiation cooling by a roof radiation trap. *Energy and Buildings* 1:141–145.

Givoni, B. 1991. Performance and applicability of passive and low-energy cooling systems. *Energy and Buildings* 17:177–199.

Givoni, B. 1994. *Passive and Low Energy Cooling.* Van Nostrand Reinhold, New York.

Givoni, B., M. Paciuk, and S. Weiser. 1976. *Natural Energies for Heating and Cooling of Buildings—Analytical Survey.* Research Report 017-235, Building Research Station, Technion, Haifa.

Goss, J. R. 1956. *Cooling of water by nocturnal radiation and evaporation.* M.S. Agricultural Engineering, University of California–Davis.

Green, K. W. 1979. Passive cooling. *Research and Design* 11(3):5–9.

Hammond, J. 1976. The Winters House. *Passive Solar Heating and Cooling: Conference and Workshop Proceedings, Los Alamos,* NTIS-LA 6637-C.

Hammond, J., M. Hunt, R. Cramer and L. W. Neubauer. 1974. *A Strategy for Energy Conservation.* Prepared for the City of Davis by Living Systems, Winters, CA.

Hay, H. 1976. Atascadero Residence, *Passive Solar Heating and Cooling: Conference and Workshop Proceedings*. Los Alamos, NTIS LA-6637-C.

Hay, H., and J. I. Yellot. 1969. International aspects of air conditioning with movable insulation. *Solar Energy* 12:427–438.

Hay, H., and J. I. Yellott. 1969. Natural air conditioning with roof ponds and movable insulation. *ASHRAE Transactions* Part 1(75):165–177.

Heidarinejad, G., M. Heidarinejad, S. Delfani, and J. Esmaeelian. 2008. Feasibility of using various kinds of cooling systems in a multi-climates country. *Energy and Buildings* 40:1946–1953.

Heusinkveld, B. G., A. F. G. Jacobs, A. A. M. Holtslag, and S. M. Berkowicz. 2004. Surface energy balance closure in an arid region: role of soil heat flux. *Agricultural and Forest Meteorology* 122:21–37.

Hürlimann, M. 1928. *Indien*. Verlag Ernst Wasmuth, AG, Berlin.

James, P., J. Sonne, R. Viera, D. Parker, and M. Anello. 1996. Are energy savings due to ceiling fans just hot air? *Proceedings of the ACEEE Summer Study on Energy Efficiency in Buildings* 8:89–93.

Kaneko, Y., K. Sagara, T. Yamanaka, H. Kotani, and S. D. Sharma. *Ventilation Performance of a Solar Chimney with Built In Latent Heat Storage*. Department of Architectural Engineering, Graduate School of Engineering, Osaka University, Osaka 565-0871, Japan.

Kelly, C. F., T. E. Bond, and N. R. Ittner. 1957. Sky temperatures in the Imperial Valley of California. *Transactions American Geophysical Union* 38(3):308–313.

Khan, N., Y. Su, and S. B. Riffat. 2008. A review on wind driven ventilation techniques. *Energy and Buildings* 40(8):1586–1604.

Kjaersgaard, R. H. Cuenca, F. L. Plauborg, and S. Hansen. 2007. Long-term comparisons of net radiation calculation schemes. *Boundary-Layer Meteorology* 123:417–431.

Kolle, J. 2008. A buyer's guide to bath fans. *Fine Homebuilding Annual Kitchens and Baths* 199: 60–63.

Kondratyev, K. Ya, and M. P. Fedorova. 1963. The fluxes of outgoing long-wave radiation incident on surfaces at various orientations. *Planetary Space Science* 11:983–986.

Kuhn, T. E. 2006. Solar control: comparison of two new systems with the state of the art on the basis of a new general evaluation method for facades with venetian blinds or other solar control systems. *Energy and Buildings* 38:661–672.

Lai, C. 2005. Prototype development of the rooftop turbine ventilator powered by hybrid wind and photo-voltaic energy. *Energy and Buildings* 38:174–180.

Lockhart, L. 1957. *Persia*. Thames and Hudson, London, UK. P.40, plate 85.

Lomas, K. J., M. J. Cook, and D. Fiala. 2007. Low energy architecture for a severe US climate: design and evaluation of a hybrid ventilation strategy. *Energy and Buildings* 39:32–44.

Lstiburek, J. W. 2008. New light in crawlspaces. *ASHRAE Journal* May:66–71.

Macdonald, V. 2000. *Guide to Resource-Efficient Building in Hawaii* (first edition, Revision B, June), produced by the Hawaii Advanced Building Technologies Training Program.

Martin, A., and J. Fitzsimmons. 2000. *Making natural ventilation work*. BSRIA GN.

Mazria, E. 1979. *The Passive Solar Energy Book*. Rodale Press, Emmaus, PA.

McFall, D. 2001. *From FSEC—So Cool It's Hot*. Florida Solar Energy Center, University of Central Florida, Orlando.

Mirah, S. E. 2005. Innovative design—BATISO and night sky cooling. *EcoLibrium* September:30–35.

Neubauer, L. W. 1953. Summer comfort. *Small Homes Council Circular* G6.0:1–7.

Neubauer, L. W. 1959. *Cooling principles for building*. UC Davis, Ag Engineering Dept. handout 012859.

Neubauer, L. W. 1964. The sun is our enemy. *Journal of Agriculture* January:198–201.

Neubauer, L. W. 1969. Southermation: heat control for farm buildings. *ASAE Paper PCR69-117*. ASAE Pacific Coast Region.

Neubauer, L. W. 1970. Optimum alleviation of solar heat stress on model buildings. ASHRAE Paper 70-401. St. Joseph, MI.

Neubauer, L. W. 1972. Orientation and insulation: model versus prototype. *ASHRAE Transactions* 15(4):707–709.

Neubauer, L. W. 1972. Shapes and orientations of houses for natural cooling. *Transactions of the American Society of Agricultural Engineers* 15(1):126–128.

Neubauer, L. W., and R. D. Cramer. 1965. Shading devices to limit solar heat gain but increase cold sky radiation. *ASHRAE Transactions* 8(4):470–472, 475.

Neubauer, L. W., R. D. Cramer and M. Laraway. 1964. Temperature control of solar radiation on roof surfaces. *Transactions of the American Society of Agricultural Engineers* 7(4):432–434, 438.

Niles, P. W. B. 1976. Thermal evaluation of a house using a movable-insulation heating and cooling system. *Solar Energy* 18(5):413–419.

Niles, P. W. B., K. L. Haggard, and H. R. Hays. 1976. Nocturnal cooling and solar heating with water ponds and movable insulation. *ASHRAE Transactions* 82:793–807.

Noble, A. 2007. *Traditional Buildings.* I. B. Taurus, London, UK.

Olgyay, V., and A. Olgyay. 1957. *Solar Control and Shading Devices.* Princeton University Press, Princeton, NJ.

Olgyay, V. 1992 [1963]. *Design with Climate.* Van Nostrand Reinhold, New York.

Ozisik, N., and L. F. Schutrum. 1959. Heat gain through windows shaded by metal awnings. *ASHRAE Transactions* 65:311–320.

Papaefthimiou, V. D., C. O. Katsanos, M. G. Vrachopoulos, A. E. Filios, M. K. Koukou, and F. G. Layrenti. 2007. Experimental measurements and theoretical predictions of flow field and temperature distribution inside a wall solar chimney. *Journal of Mechanical Engineering Science* 308:33–41.

Parker, D. S., M. P. Callahan, J. K. Sonne, and G.H. Su. 1999. *Development of a High Efficiency Ceiling Fan, the Gossamer Wind.* Florida Energy Office, Dept. of Community Affairs, Tallahassee.

Rajapaksha, I., H. Nagai, and M. Okumiya. 2003. A ventilated courtyard as a passive cooling strategy in the warm humid tropics. *Renewable Energy* 28:1755–1778.

Reitan, C. H. 1959. Distribution of precipitable water vapor over the continental US. *Bulletin of the American Meteorological Society* 41(2):79–98.

Reynolds, J. S. 2002. *Courtyards.* John Wiley and Sons, New York.

Rijal, H. B., P. Tuohy, M. A. Humphreys, J. F. Nicol, A. Samuel, and J. Clarke. 2007. Using results from field surveys to predict the effect of open windows on thermal comfort and energy use in buildings. *Energy and Buildings* 39:823–836.

Rofail, T. 2006. *Natural ventilation in buildings.* Windtech Consultants Pty Ltd. NEERG Seminars. 11 pp.

Rohles, F. H., S. A. Konz, and B. W. Jones. 1983. Ceiling fans as extenders of the summer comfort envelope. *ASHRAE Transactions* 89(1A):245-263.

Runsheng, Tang, and Y. Etzion. 2004. On thermal performance of an improved roof pond for cooling buildings. *Building and Environment* 39(2):201–209.

Santamouris, M., K. Pavlou, A. Synnefa, K. Niachou, and D. Kolokotsa. 2007. Recent progress on passive cooling techniques: advanced technological developments to improve the survivability levels in low income households. *Energy and Buildings* 39:859–866.

Sellers, W. D. 1965. *Physical Climatology.* University of Chicago Press, Chicago, IL.

Soflaee, F., and M. Shokouhian. 2005. Natural cooling systems in sustainable traditional architecture of Iran. *International Conference on Passive and Low Energy Cooling for the Built Environment,* Santorini, Greece. 715–719.

Southern Energy Institute. ND. Whole House Fan. *Energy Technical Bulletin* 10. Georgia Environmental Facilities Authority, Atlanta.

Stavrakakis, G. M., M. K. Koukou, M. Gr. Vrachopoulos, and N. Markatos. 2008. Natural cross ventilation in buildings: building-scale experiments, numerical simulation and thermal comfort evaluation. *Energy and Buildings* 40(9):1666–1681.

Strock, C., and R. L. Koral. 1965. *Handbook of Air Conditioning Heating and Ventilation.* Industrial Press, New York.

Sustainability Victoria. ND. *Natural ventilation systems.* Melbourne, Australia.

van Moeseke, G., E. Gratia, S. Reiter, and A. De Herde. 2005. Wind pressure distribution influence on natural ventilation for different incidences and environment densities. *Energy and Buildings* 37:878–889.

Venolia, C., and K. Lerner. 2007. *Natural Remodeling for the Not-so-Green House: Bringing Your Home into Harmony with Nature.* Lark Books, New York.

Walker, A. 2010. *Natural Ventilation.* WBDG. www.wbdg.org/resources/naturalventilation.php.

Watt, J. R. 1963. *Evaporative Air Conditioning.* Industrial Press, New York.

Chapter 4. Natural Lighting

Ander, G. D. 2003. *Daylighting Performance and Design.* John Wiley and Sons, New York.

Ander, G. D. 2008. Daylighting. In the *Whole Building Design Guide.* National Institute of Building Sciences. www.wbdg.org/resources/daylighting.php. Accessed December 2008.

Bainbridge, D. A. 1978. Chapter 8: Daylighting. In *The First Passive Solar Catalog,* Passive Solar Institute, Davis, CA.

Baker, N., and K. Steemers. 2002. *Daylight Design of Buildings.* James & James Ltd., London, UK.

Boubekri, M. 2008. *Daylighting, Architecture and Health.* Architectural Press, Elsevier, Amsterdam.

British Standards Institute. 1982. BS8206 Pt 2. *Code of Practice for Daylighting.* BSI.

Building Officials and Code Administrators. 1990. *The BOCA National Building Code.* Chicago, IL.

Building Research Station. 1966. Integrated daylight and artificial light in buildings. *Digest* 76, Second Series, H.

Enermodal Engineering Ltd. 2002. *Daylighting Guide for Canadian Commercial Buildings.* Public Works and Government Services, Canada.

EREC. ND. *Daylighting for Commercial and Industrial Buildings.* DOE. EREC Reference Briefs. US Department of Energy, Energy Efficiency and Renewable Energy Network (EREN).

Evans, B. H. 1962. Solar Effects on Building Design. Publication 1007, Building Research Institute.

Evans, B. H. 1981. *Daylight in Architecture.* McGraw-Hill, New York.

Federal Energy Agency. 1975. *Lighting and Thermal Operations: Guidelines.* USGPO, Washington, DC.

Fitch, J. M. 1972. *American Building: The Environmental Forces That Shaped It.* Houghton-Mifflin, Boston.

Galasiu, A. D., and J. A. Veitch. 2006. Occupant preferences and satisfaction with the luminous environment and control systems in daylit offices: a literature review. *Energy and Buildings* 38:728–742.

Hopkinson, R. G. 1958. Model and measurement in lighting research. *Discovery* 19:232.

Hopkinson, R. G., P. Petherbridge, and J. Longmore. 1966. *Daylighting.* Heineman, Oxford, UK.

Illuminating Engineers Society, North America (IESNA). 2000. *Lighting Handbook Reference,* 9th ed. www.iesna.org.

Innovative Design. 2004. *Guide for Daylighting Schools.* Daylight Dividends, Lighting Research Center Rensselaer Polytechnic Institute. www.daylightdividends.org. Accessed December 2008.

Keighley, E. C. 1973. Visual requirements and reduced fenestration in offices: a study of multiple apertures and window area. *Building Science* 8:311–320.

Köster, H. 2004. *Dynamic Daylighting Architecture.* Birkhaüsen, Basel, Switzerland.

Kuhn, T. E. 2006. Solar control: comparison of two new systems with the state of the art on the basis of a new general evaluation method for facades with venetian blinds or other solar control systems. *Energy and Buildings* 38:661–672.

Lam, W. M. C. 1986. *Sunlighting as Formgiver for Architecture.* Van Nostrand Reinhold, New York.

Larson, L. 1964. *Lighting and Its Design.* Whitney Library of Design, New York.

Lawrence, T., and K. W. Roth. 2008. *Commercial Building Toplighting: Energy Saving Potential and Potential Paths Forward.* Prepared for the US Department of Energy, Building Technologies Program, by TIAX LLC, Cambridge, MA 02140-2390.

LBL Building Technologies Program. 1997. Tips for Daylighting with Windows. windows.lbl.gov/daylighting/designguide/designguide.html.

LBL Building Design Advisor. http://eetd.lbl.gov/eetd-software-bda .html.

Lechner, N. 2001. *Heating, Cooling and Lighting: Design Methods for Architects,* 2nd ed. John Wiley & Sons, New York.

Libbey, Owens, Ford Sun Angle Calculator, daylight overlays and booklet, *How to Predict Interior Daylight Illumination.* LOF, Toledo, OH.

Littlefair, P. J. 1998. *Site Layout Planning for Daylight and Sunlight.* IHS-BRE Publishing, Bracknell, UK.

Lynes, J. 1968. *Principles of Natural Lighting.* Elsevier, New York.

Moore, F. 1991. *Concepts and Practice of Architectural Daylighting.* Van Nostrand Reinhold, New York.

Nabil, A., and J. Mardaljevic. 2006. Useful daylight illuminance: a replacement for daylight factors. *Energy and Buildings* 38:905–913.

National Research Council/CNRC. *Model Energy Code for Buildings.* www.nationalcodes.ca.

Ne'eman, E., and R. G. Hopkinson. 1970. Critical minimum acceptable window size: a study of window design and provision of view. *Lighting Research and Technology* 2(1):57–68.

Olgyay, A., and V. Olgyay. 1976 [1957]. *Solar Control and Shading Devices.* Princeton University Press, Princeton, NJ.

Osterhaus, W. K. E. 1993. Office Lighting: A Review of 80 Years of Standards and Recommendations. LBL-35036 WG-31I. Published in the *Proceedings of the 1993 IEEE Industry Applications Society Annual Meeting,* October 2–8, 1993 in Toronto, Ontario, Canada.

Ott, J. 1976. *Health and Light.* Pocket Books, New York.

Phillips, D. 1964. *Lighting in Architectural Design.* McGraw-Hill, New York.

Phillips, D. 2004. *Daylighting: Natural Light in Architecture.* Elsevier, Amsterdam, Netherlands.

Redler, A. 2007. Let there be light. *RCIS (Royal Institute of Chartered Surveyors) Building Surveying* January:10–11.

Roisin, B., M. Bodart, A. Deneyer, and P. D'Hert. 2008. Lighting energy savings in offices using different control systems and their real consumption. *Energy and Buildings* 40:514–523.

Rosenfeld, A. H., and S. E. Selkowitz. 1976. Beam Daylighting: Direct Use of Solar Energy for Interior Lighting. *IES Conference Proceedings.*

Stein, B., J. S. Reynolds, W. T. Grondzik, and A. G. Kwok. 2006. §3.4 Direct sun and Daylight. In *Mechanical and Electrical Equipment in Buildings.* John Wiley and Sons, New York.

Thayer, B. M. 1995. Daylighting and productivity at Lockheed. *Solar Today* May–June:26–29.

Tzempelikos, A. 2008. The impact of venetian blind geometry and tilt angle on view, direct light transmission and interior illuminance. *Solar Energy* 82(12):1172–1191.

University Council of Dublin, the Architect's Council of Europe, Softech and the Finnish Association of Architects, European Commission. 1999. *A Green Vitruvius.* James & James, London, UK.

US Energy Information Administration. Annual reports. *Energy use in commercial buildings.* http://tonto.eia.doe.gov.

Villecco, M., S. Selkowtiz, and J. E. Griffith. 1979. Strategies of daylight design. *AIA Journal* 68–77, 104, 108, 112.

Webb, A. R. 2006. Considerations for lighting in the built environment: non-visual effects of light. *Energy and Buildings* 38:721–727.

Chapter 5. Harvesting On-Site Resources

Resource Inputs and Outputs

Bainbridge, D. A. 2009. *Rebuilding the American Economy*. Rio Redondo Press, San Diego. www. sustainabilityleader.org.

Bainbridge, D. A. 2006. Adding ecological considerations to "environmental" accounting. *Bulletin of the Ecological Society of America* 8(4):335–340. http://esapubs.org/bulletin/backissues/087-4/oct_web_pdfs/comment4.pdf.

ExternE. 2008. *The ExternE Project Series*. www.externe.info.

Hertwich, E. G. Accounting for sustainable consumption: a review of the studies of the environmental impact of households. Pp 88–108. In T. Jackson, ed. *The Earthscan Reader in Sustainable Consumption*. Earthscan, London, UK.

Kolpin, D. W., E. T. Furlong, M. T. Meyer, E. M. Thurman, S. D. Zaugg, L. B. Barber, and H. T. Buxton. 2002. Pharmaceuticals, hormones, and other organic wastewater contaminants in US streams, 1999–2000: a national reconnaissance. *Environmental Science and Technology* 36:1202–1211.

McDonough, W., and M. Braungart. 2002. *Cradle to Cradle*. North Point Press, New York.

Miller, C. 2005. Food waste. *Waste Age* October 1. http://wasteage.com/mag/waste_food_waste_3/index.html.

Pigou, A. C. 1920. *The Economics of Welfare*. Methuen, London, UK.

Platt, B., and N. Seldman, Institute for Local Self-Reliance, Washington, DC. 2000. *Wasting and Recycling in the United States*. GrassRoots Recycling Network, Athens, GA.

Schaltegger, S., Bennett, M., and Burritt, R., eds. 2006. *Sustainability Accounting and Reporting*. Springer, Dordrecht, Netherlands.

Young, J. E., and A. Sachs 1994. *The Next Efficiency Revolution: Creating a Sustainable Materials Economy*. Worldwatch Institute, Washington, DC.

Water Heating

Bainbridge, D. A. 2007. Build your own passive solar water heater. *Mother Earth News* October–November:78–86.

Bainbridge, D. A. 1981. *Integral Solar Water Heaters*. Passive Solar Institute, Davis, CA. www.builditsolar.com/projects/waterheating/IPSWH/IPSWH.pdf. Accessed November 2006.

Bourgoing, R. 1989. Cleaning water with sunshine. *IDRC Reports* April:21.

Brooks, F. A. 1936. *Solar energy and its use for heating water in California*. University of California Agricultural Extension Bulletin 602.

Budihardjo, I., and G. L. Morrison. 2009. Performance of water in glass evacuated tube solar water heaters. *Solar Energy* 83:49–56.

Faiman, D., H. Hazan, and I. Lauffer. 2001. Reducing the heat loss at night from solar water heaters of the integrated collector-storage type. *Solar Energy* 71(2):87–93.

Fraisse, G., Y. Bai, N. Le Pierrè, and T. Letz. 2009. Comparative study of various optimization criteria for SDHWS and a suggestion for a new global evaluation. *Solar Energy* 83:232–245.

Gil, C., and D. Parker. 2009. *Geographic Variation in Potential of Residential Solar Hot Water System Performance in the United States*. October. FSEC-CR-1817-09, Cocoa, FL.

Owens, R. 2003. Florida batch water heater. *Home Power* 93:66–70.

Reiss, J., and J. Burton. 1981. The Breadbox: a passive solar water heater. Pp. 238–247. In J. Carter, ed. *Solarizing Your Present Home*. Rodale Press, Emmaus, PA.

Schmidt, Ch., A. Goetzberger, and J. Schmid. 1988. Test results and evaluation of integrated collector storage systems with transparent insulation. *Solar Energy* 41(5):487–494.

Smyth, M., P. C. Eames, and B. Norton. 2006. Integrated collector storage solar water heaters. *Renewable and Sustainable Energy Reviews* 10:503–518.

Smyth, M., P. C. Eames, and B. Norton. 2004. Techno-economic appraisal of an integrated collector/storage solar water heater. *Renewable Energy* 29:1503–1514.

Souliotis, M., and Y. Tripanagnostopoulos. 2004. Experimental study of CPC type ICS solar systems. *Solar Energy* 76:389–408.

Electricity Production

Bell, J., and H. Honea. 2007. Electricity supply and price security in San Diego County. www.jimbell.com/mayor/Final%20Draft%20August%202007.pdf.

Endecon Engineering. 2001. *A Guide to Photovoltaic Design and Installation*. California Energy Commission. (a bit dated but a good overview). http://www.energy.ca.gov/reports/2001-09-04_500-01-020.PDF

Home Power magazine is an excellent resource. homepower.com.

Kemp, W. H. 2005. *The Renewable Energy Handbook*. New Society Press, Gabriola Island, BC.

Mehalic, B. 2009. PV performance. *Home Power* 133:50–55.

Parker, D. S., J. P. Dunlop, J. R. Sherwin, S. F. Barkaszi Jr., M. P. Anello, S. Durand, D. Metzger, and J. K. Sonne. 1998. *Field Evaluation of Efficient Building Technology with Photovoltaic Power Production in New Florida Residential Housing*. FSEC-CR-1044-98, Florida Solar Energy Center, Cocoa, FL.

Schaeffer, J., A. Berolzheimer, and B. Giebler. 2008. *Solar Living Sourcebook*. New Society Publishers, Gabriola Island, BC.

Wiles, J. 2008. *PV and NEC: Suggested Practices*. www.nmsu.edu/~tdi/Photovoltaics/Codes-Stds/PVnecSugPract.html.

Wiles, J. 2008. *PV Systems Inspector/Installer Checklist*. www.nmsu.edu/~tdi/pdf-resources/INSPECTOR_CHECKLIST_6-23-06.pdf.

Low-Impact Development— Water, Stormwater, and Gray Water

Bainbridge, D. A. 1976. *Planning for energy conservation*. Living Systems for the City of Davis, CA.

Bainbridge, D. A. 1976. *Street design for energy conservation*. Living Systems for the City of Davis, CA.

Bainbridge, D. A., J. Corbett, and J. Hofacre. 1979. *Village Homes' Solar House Designs*. Rodale Press, Emmaus, PA.

Bourgoing, R. 1989. Cleaning water with sunshine. *IDRC Reports* April:21.

Centre for Science and Environment. www.rainwaterharvesting.org/Urban/model-projects.htm.

Ciochetti, D. A., and Metcalf, R. H. 1984. Pasteurization of naturally contaminated water with solar energy. *Applied and Environmental Microbiology* 47(2):223–228.

Gelt, J. 2009. *Home Use of Graywater, Rainwater Conserves Water and May Save Money*. Water Resources Research Center. University of Arizona, Tucson. http://ag.arizona.edu/azwater/arroyo/071rain.html

Gould, J., and E. Nissen-Petersen. 1999. *Rainwater Catchment Systems for Domestic Supply*. ITDG Publications, London, UK.

Karpiscak, M.M., G.W. France, K.J. DeCook, R.C. Brittain, K.E. Foster and S.B. Hopf. 2001. Casa del Agua: Water conservation demonstration house 1986-1998. *Journal of the American Water Resources Association*. 37(5):1237-1248.

Lancaster, B. 2006. *Rainwater Harvesting for Drylands*. Rainsource Press, Tucson, AZ.

Ludwig, A. 2006. *Builder's Greywater Guide*. Oasis Design, Santa Barbara, CA.

Milne, M. 1979. *Residential Water Reuse*. California Water Resouces Center, UC Davis. Report 46.

Mollison, B., and R. M. Slay. 1997. *Permaculture: A Designer's Manual*. Tagari, Sisters Creek, Tasmania.

Ludwig, A. 2006. *Builder's Greywater Guide*. Oasis Design, Santa Barbara, CA.

Obeng, L. A., and F. W. Wright. 1986. Integrated Resource Recovery: The Co-Composting of Domestic Solids and Human Wastes. UNDP Project Management Report 7.

Ortega, A. 1977. Water saving devices for sanitation in deserts. In *UN Conference on Alternative Strategies for Desert Development and Management*, Sacramento, CA.

Pacey, A., and A. Cullis. 1986. *Rainwater Harvesting*. Intermediate Technology Publications, London, UK.

Reisner, M. 1986. *Cadillac Desert: The American West and Its Disappearing Water*. Viking Penguin, New York.

Srinivasan, R. K., and S. V. Suresh Babu. 2000. *A Water Harvesting Manual for Urban Areas*. Centre for Science and Environemnt, New Delhi, India.

Termorshuizen, J. W., and P. Opdam. 2009. Landscape services as a bridge between ecology and sustainable development. *Landscape Ecology* 24(8):1037–1052.

Texas Water Development Board. 2005. *The Texas Manual on Rainwater Harvesting,* 3rd edition, Austin, TX.

Thompson, J. W., and K. Sorvig. 2000. *Sustainable Landscape Construction.* Island Press, Washington, DC.

Van der Ryn, S. 1978. *The Toilet Papers.* Capra Press, Santa Barbara, CA.

Watt, S. B. 1978. *Ferrocement Water Tanks.* Intermediate Technology Publications, London, UK.

Green Materials and Material Life Cycles

Addis, B. 2006. *Building with Reclaimed Components and Materials: A Design Handbook for Reuse and Recycling.* Earthscan Publications, London, UK.

Aiello, A. E., E. L. Larson, and S. B. Levy. 2007. Consumer antibacterial soaps: effective or just risky? *Clinical Infectious Disease* 45:S137–47.

Applehof, M. 2006. *Worms Eat My Garbage: How to Set Up and Maintain a Worm Composting System.* Flower Press. www.wormwoman.com.

ASTM. 2007. *International Standards for Sustainability in Building:* 3rd edition. CD-ROM.

Bainbridge, D. A. 1980. Low energy materials. Pp. 98–100. In *Second Passive Solar Catalog,* Passive Solar Institute, Davis, CA.

Bainbridge, D. A. 2004. Sustainable building as appropriate technology. Pp. 55–67, 75–77. In J. Kennedy, ed. *Building Without Borders: Sustainable Construction for the Global Village.* Island Press, Washington, DC.

Bourgeois, J. L., and C. Pelos. 1996. *Spectacular Vernacular.* Aperture Books, New York.

Brigenzu, S., H. Schütz, and S. Moll. 2003. Rationale for and interpretation of economy-wide material flow analysis and derived indicators. *Journal of Industrial Ecology* 7(2):43–64.

Cascadia Group. 2006. *Detailed Characterization of Construction and Demolition Waste.* California Integrated Waste Management Board, Sacramento.

Chalfan, L. 2001. *The Case for Zero Waste.* Zero Waste Alliance. www.zerowaste.org.

Chartwell School. 2006. *Design for Deconstruction.* EPA Region 9. www.lifecyclebuilding.org/files/DFD.pdf.

Compost tea. www.uos.harvard.edu/fmo/landscape/organiclandscaping/tea_recipes.pdf.

Construction waste.www.lifecyclebuilding.org/resources.php.

CSPC. 2009. Executive summary, Chinese drywall. www.cpsc.gov/info/drywall/nov2009execsum.pdf.

Don't flush your medicines down the toilet. www.pharmacy.ca.gov/publications/dont_flush_meds.pdf.

Easton, D. 2007. *The Rammed Earth House.* Chelsea Green, White River Junction, VT.

Eisenberg, D. 2009. Resources from the Development Center for Appropriate Technology. www.dcat.net/resources/index.php.

Elevitch, C., and K. Wilkinson. 1998. Sheet mulching: greater plant and soil health for less work. Agroforestry Net. www.agroforestry.net/pubs/Sheet_Mulching.html.

Elizabeth, L., and C. Adams. 2000. *Alternative Construction: Contemporary Natural Building Methods.* John Wiley, New York.

Emmenegger, M. F., et al. 2006. Life cycle assessment of the mobile communication system UMTS: towards eco-efficient systems. *International Journal of Life Cycle Assessment* 11(4):265–276.

European Environment Agency. 2001. Total material requirement of the European Union. European Environment Agency Technical Report 55. Copenhagen. http://reports.eea.eu.int/Technical_report_No_55/en.

Falk, B., and B. Guy. 2007. *Unbuilding.* Taunton Press, Newtown, CT.

Fathay, H. 1973. *Architecture for the Poor.* University of Chicago Press, Chicago, IL.

Fernandez, N. P. 2008. The influence of construction materials on life-cycle energy use and carbon dioxide emissions of medium size commercial buildings. MBS, Victoria University, Wellington, NZ.

Fisk III, P., and D. Armistead. 2003. The emergence of Life Cycle Space™ and the Life Cycle Ratio™—a proposed planning tool for lowering our ecological footprint. *3rd International Life Cycle Assessment and Life Cycle Management Conference,* Seattle, WA.

Fisk III, P. 1982. Availability and spatial coincidence of indigenous building materials. 2nd *Regional Conference on Earthen Building Materials*, Tucson, AZ.

German waste laws. www.bmu.de/english/waste_management/acts_and_ordinances/acts_and_ordinances_in_germany/doc/20203.php.

Goodhew, S. and R. Griffiths. 2005. Sustainable earth walls to meet the building regulations. *Energy and Buildings* 37:451–459.

Green electronics made easy. www.epeat.net/SearchResults.aspx?return=stat&epeatcountryid=1&rating=3&ProductType=3.

Grossman, E. 2006. *High Tech Trash: Digital Devices, Hidden Toxics, and Human Health.* Island Press, Washington, DC.

Guinée, J. B, J. M. van den Bergh, J. Boelens, P. J. Fraanje, G. Huppes, P. P. A. A. H. Kandelaars, Th. M. Lexmond, S. W. Moolenaar, A. A. Olsthoorn, H. A. Udo de Haes, E. Verkuijlen, and E. van der Voet. 1999. Evaluation of risks of metal flows and accumulation in economy and environment. *Ecological Economics* 30:47–65.

Guy, B., and S. Shell. 2002. Design for Deconstruction and Materials Reuse. *Proceedings of the CIB Task Group 39—Deconstruction Meeting.* Ed. A. Chini and F. Schultmann. CIB Publication 272.

Haggard, K., and S. Clark, eds. 2000. *Straw Bale Construction Sourcebook.* California Straw Building Association/SLOSG, Santa Margarita, CA.

Haught, L. 2006. The planet's answers are in the soil, says BPC's green thumb. *Downtown Express.* 19(23):NP. October 20–26. www.downtownexpress.com/de_180/theplanetsanswers.html.

Huberman, N., and D. Pearlmutter. 2008. A life-cycle energy analysis of building materials in the Negev Desert. *Energy and Buildings* 40:837–848.

IEA Bioenergy Task 37. ND. 100% Biogas for Urban Transport in Linkoping, Sweden. *Biogas in the Society.* www.iea-biogas.net.

Inform. ND. The Secret Life of Cell Phones. www.informinc.org.

Karlen, C., I. O. Wallinde, D. Heijerick, C. Leygraf, and C. R. Janssen. 2001. Runoff rates and ecotoxicity of zinc induced by atmospheric corrosion. *Science of the Total Environment* 277(1–3):169–180.

Kawashima, C. 2000. *Japan's Folk Architecture: Traditional Thatched Farmhouses.* Kodansha International, New York.

Kern, K. 1975. *The Owner Built Home.* Scribners, New York.

Kernan, P. 2002. *Old to New: Design Guide, Salvaged Building Materials in New Construction.* Greater Vancouver Regional District. British Columbia, Canada.

Kershaw, S. 2008. The promise of green paint. *New York Times* May 15. www.nytimes.com/2008/05/15/garden/15paint.html.

King, B. 1996. *Buildings of Earth and Straw: Structural Design for Rammed Earth and Straw Bale Houses.* Ecological Design Press, Sausalito, CA (dist. by Chelsea Green Publishing).

King, B. 2005. *Making Better Concrete.* Green Building Press, San Rafael, CA.

King, B. 2006. *Design of Straw Bale Buildings.* Green Building Press, San Rafael, CA.

King, B. 2009. *Standard Guide for Design of Earthen Wall Building Systems.* ASTM2392. ASTM International.

Lacinksi, P., and M. Bergeron. 2000. *Serious Straw Bale.* Chelsea Green, White River Jcunction, VT.

Latch, D. E., J. L. Packer, W. A. Arnolda, and K. McNeill. 2000. Photochemical conversion of triclosan to 2,8-dichlorodibenzo-p-dioxin in aqueous solution. *Journal of Photochemistry and Photobiology A: Chemistry* 158(1):63–66.

Lerner, K., and P. W. Goode. 2000. *The Building Official's Guide to Straw Bale Construction v2.1.* California Straw Building Association, CA. www.strawbuilding.org.

Leroux, K., and N. Seldman. 1999. *Deconstruction: Salvaging Yesterday's Buildings for Tomorrow's Sustainable Communities.* Institute for Local Self-Reliance, Washington, DC.

Lorinc, J. 2009. Turning organic waste into energy. *New York Times,* Green Inc. http://greeninc.blogs.nytimes.com/2009/06/19/turning-human-organic-waste-into-energy.

Magwood, C., and P. Mack. 2000. *Straw Bale Building: How to Plan, Design and Build with Straw.* New Society Publishers, Gabriola Island, BC.

Miller, L. A., and D. Miller. 1982. *Rammed Earth Homes.* Rammed Earth Institute International, Boulder, CO.

Minke, G. 2009. *Building with Earth.* Berkhauser, Basel, Switzerland.

Musson, S. E., and T. G. Townsend. 2009. Pharmaceutical compound content of municipal solid waste. *Journal of Hazardous Materials* 162(2–3):730–735.

Nancarrow, L., and J. H. Taylor. 1998. *The Worm Book.* Ten Speed Press, Berkeley, CA.

Network of International Society for Low Exergy Systems in Buildings (LowEx.net) and the Global Climate and Energy project at Stanford. gcep.stanford.edu/research/exergy/resourcechart.html.

Neubauer, L. W. 1964. *Adobe Construction Methods.* Manual 19. University of California, Dept. of Agricultural Sciences, Davis.

New York City Compost Project. ND. Indoor composting with a worm bin. DSNY Bureau of Waste Prevention Reuse and Recycling. www.nyccompost.org/resources/wormbin.pdf.

Noble, A. 2007. *Traditional Buildings.* IB Taurus, London, UK.

Platt, B., and N. Seldman. 2000. *Wasting and Recycling in the United States.* Institute for Local Self-Reliance, Washington, DC, and GrassRoots Recycling Network, Athens, GA.

Pope, A. U. 1965. *Persian Architecture.* George Braziller, New York.

Rosen, C., T. R. Halbach, R. Mugaas, and P. Unger. 2008. *Composting and Mulching.* University of Minnesota Extension Service. BU-03296. www.extension.umn.edu/distribution/horticulture/components/3296-02.html (most states have similar bulletins).

Rudofsky, B. 1987 [1965]. *Architecture Without Architects.* University of NM Press, Alburqueque, NM.

Schmidt-Bleek, F. 1999. *The Factor 10/MIPS-Concept: Bridging Ecological, Economic, and Social Dimensions with Sustainability Indicators.* Zero Emissions Forum, United Nations University, ZEF-EN-1999-3-D.

Sunset magazine. ND. Simple DIY Recycling Center. www.sunset.com/home/weekend-projects/how-to-build-diy-recycling-center-00400000040552.

Snell, C., and T. Callahan. 2005. *Building Green.* Lark Books, New York.

Steen, A., B. Steen, D. A. Bainbridge, and D. Eisenberg. 1994. *The Straw Bale House.* Chelsea Green, White River Junction, VT.

Steen, B., A. Steen, E. Komatsu, and Y. Komatsu. 2003. *Built by Hand.* Gibbs Smith Publisher, Layton, UT.

Stingley, T. 2005. *Residential Deconstruction Manual.* Startdust Non-profit Building Supplies. Mesa, AZ. http://epa.gov/region09/waste/solid/stardust/StardustDemolitionSalvageManual.pdf.

Stulz, R., and K. Mukerji. 1988. *Appropriate Building Materials: A Catalogue of Potential Solutions.* Swiss Center for Appropriate Technology, IT, GATE.

Sutton, R., O. Naidenko, N. Chwialkowski, and J. Houlihan. 2008. Pesticide in soap, toothpaste and breast milk—is it kid-safe? EWG Research. www.ewg.org/reports/triclosan.

van Dresser, P. 1977. *Home Grown Sundwellings.* Lightning Tree Press, Santa Fe, NM.

Van Oss, H. G., and A. C. Padovani. 2002. Cement manufacture and the environment. *Journal of Industrial Ecology* 6(1):89–105.

Volhard, F., transl. by A. Haller and B. Vann. ND. *Leichtlehmbau—Straw Clay Method.* Verlag C.F. Mueller, Karslruhe, Germany.

Waste reduction—Green Schools. 2008. http://your.kingcounty.gov/solidwaste/greenschools/documents/Fast_Facts.pdf.

Wuppertal Institute. ND. Table V2. Material Intensity of materials, fuels, transport services. Wuppertal, Germany. www.wupperinst.org/uploads/tx_wibeitrag/MIT_v2.pdf.

Yepsen, R. 2009. US Residential food waste collection and composting. *BioCycle* 50(12):35.

Landscape Regeneration and Integration

Aronson, J., S. J. Milton, and J. M. Blignaut. 2007. *Restoring Natural Capital.* Island Press, Washington, DC.

Bainbridge, D. A. 2007. *A Guide for Desert and Dryland Restoration.* Island Press, Washington, DC.

Bradshaw, A. D., and M. J. Chadwick. 1980. *The Restoration of Land.* University of California Press, Berkeley.

Campbell, A., and G. Stepen. 1994. *Landcare: Communities Shaping the Land and the Future.* Allen and Unwin, St. Lenards, AU.

Ehrenfeld, J. G., and L. A. Toth. 1997. Restoration ecology and the ecosystem perspective. *Restoration Ecology* 5(4):307–317.

Franklin, J. F. 1993. Preserving biodiversity: species, ecosystems, or landscapes? *Ecological Applications* 3:202–205.

Haggard, K. 2008. *A Brief Architectural History of San Luis Obispo County: Indigenous 1500 to Green 2100*. Central Coast Books, Los Osos, CA.

Lyle, J. T. 1999. *Design for Human Landscapes*. Island Press, Washington, DC.

Máté, F. 2009. *The Wisdom of Tuscany: Simplicity, Security and the Good Life*. Albatross, London.

Naveh, Z. 1994. From biodiversity to ecodiversity: a landscape ecology approach to conservation and restoration. *Restoration Ecology* 2(3):180–189.

Naveh, Z. 2005. Epilogue: toward a transdisciplinary science of ecological and cultural landscape restoration. *Restoration Ecology* 13(1):228–234.

Naveh, Z., and A. Lieberman. 1994. *Landscape Ecology: Theory and Application*. Springer-Verlag, NY.

van Dresser, P. 1976. *A Landscape for Humans*. Lightning Tree Press, Santa Fe.

Chapter 6. Essays on Integrated Design

Bainbridge, D. A. 1972. *Man and the City: The Human Ecosystem*. Bainbridge, Behrens, and Moore, Inc., Davis, CA.

Bainbridge, D. A., J. Corbett, and J. Hofacre. 1979. *Village Homes' Solar House Designs*. Rodale Press, Emmaus, PA.

Bainbridge, D. A. 2007. *A Guide for Desert and Dryland Restoration*. Island Press, Washington, DC.

Bang, J. M. 2005. *Ecovillages: A Practical Guide to Sustainable Communities*. New Society Publishers, Gabriola Island, BC.

Bell, J. 1994. Achieving Eco-Nomic Security on Spaceship Earth. ELSI, San Diego.

Brown, A. 2009. *Just Enough: Lessons in Living Green from Traditional Japan*. Kodansha International, Tokyo, Japan.

Callenbach, E. 1999. Ecological rules of a sustainable society. Pp. 17–29. In T. Inoguchi, E. Newman, and G. Paoletto. *Cities and the Environment*. United Nations University Press, New York.

Callenbach, E. 1975. *Ecotopia*. Bantam, New York.

Corbett, J., and M. Corbett. 2000. *Designing Sustainable Communities: Learning from Village Homes*. Island Press, Washington, DC.

Corbett, M. 1981. *A Better Place to Live*. Rodale Press, Emmaus, PA.

Demers, M. 2006. *Walk for Life: Restoring Neighborhood Walkways to Enhance Community Life, Improve Street Safety and Reduce Obesity*. Vital Health Publishing.

Ehrenfeld, J. G., and L. A. Toth. 1997. Restoration ecology and the ecosystem perspective. *Restoration Ecology* 5(4):307–317.

Fisk III, P. VD. Center for Maximum Potential Building Systems. Reports and publications. Austin, TX.

Fisk III, P., and R. Ramina. 2000. Industrial Ecology as a Regional Planning Tool: A New Potential for Economic Environmental Regional Planning. *4th International Conference on Technology Policy and Innovation*, Curitiba, Brazil.

Haggard, K., P. Cooper, and C. Gyovai. 2006. *Fractal Architecture: Design for Sustainability*. San Luis Obispo Sustainability Group, Santa Margarita, CA.

Integrated Design. ASHRAE guides. http://aedg.ashrae.org.

Kretzmann, J. P., and J. L. McKnight. 1993. *Building Communities from the Inside Out: A Path Toward Finding and Mobilizing a Community's Assets*. ACTA Publications, Chicago.

Kwok, A. G., and W. T. Grondzik. 2007. *Green Studio Handbook*. Architectural Press, Oxford, UK.

Levine, R. S. 2000. Beyond Sustainability Indicators: The Sustainable Area Budget, Regional Sustainable Development: Making Sustainable Development Visible: Indicators for Regional Sustainable Development. Graz, Austria, November.

Levine, R. S., E. J. Yanarella, T. Radmard, and H. Dumreicher. 2003. Sustainable cities: a strategy for a post terrorized world. *Terrain* 13(summer–fall). www.terrain.org/articles/13/strategy.htm.

Lyne, J. 2000. Who's no. 1? Finland, Japan and Korea, says OECD education study. *Site Selection Online Insider*. www.siteselection.com/ssinsider/snapshot/sf011210.htm. Accessed December 2009.

McCann, B. 2008.Global prospects for rainwater harvesting. *Water 21.* December:12-14.

Mollison, B., and R. M. Slay. 1997. *Permaculture: A Designer's Manual.* Tagari, Sisters Creek, Tasmania.

Naveh, Z., and A. S. Lieberman. 1994. *Landscape Ecology.* Springer-Verlag, New York.

Portney, K. 2003. *Taking Sustainable Cities Seriously: Economic Development, the Environment, and Quality of Life in American Cities.* MIT Press, Cambridge, MA.

Putnam, R. 2000. *Bowling Alone: The Collapse and Revival of American Community.* Simon and Schuster, New York.

Roseland, M. 1998. *Toward Sustainable Communities.* New Society Publishers, Gabriola Island, BC.

Sassi, F., M. Devaux, M. Cecchini, and E. Rusticelli 2009. *The Obesity Epidemic.* Organization for Economic Cooperation and Development. OECD HWP#45. Paris, FR.

Schlossberg, M., and A. Zimmerman. 2003. Developing statewide indices of environmental, economic and social sustainability: a look at Oregon and the Oregon Benchmarks. *Local Environment* 8(6):641–660.

Srinivas, H. 1999. Urban Environmental Management: A Partnership Continuum. Pp 30–46. In T. Inoguchi, E. Newman, and G. Paoletto. *Cities and the Environment.* United Nations University Press, NY.

Sustainable Seattle. 1993. *Sustainable Seattle Indicators of Sustainable Community: A Report to Citizens on Long Term Trends in Their Community.* Seattle, WA.

Termorshuizen, J. W., and P. Opdam. 2009. Landscape services as a bridge between ecology and sustainable development. *Landscape Ecology* 24(8):1037–1052.

Timberg, S. 2008. The novel that predicted Portland. *New York Times,* December 12.

Waters, A. 2008. *Edible Schoolyard.* Chronicle Books, San Francisco.

Weisman, A. 1998. *Gaviotas: A Village to Reinvent the World.* Chelsea Green, White River Junction, VT.

White, R. R. 2002. *Building the Ecological City.* Woodhead Publishing, Cambridge, UK.

Znouda, E., N. Ghrab-Morcos, and A. Hadj-Alouane. 2007. Optimization of Mediterranean building design using genetic algorithms. *Energy and Buildings* 39:148–153.

Aeschylus described the barbarians: *"Though they had eyes to see, they saw to no avail; they had ears, but understood not. They lacked the knowledge of houses . . . turned to face the sun . . ."*

ILLUSTRATION CREDITS

Photos and illustrations are by the authors, Ken Haggard, David A. Bainbridge, and Rachel Aljelani, unless otherwise credited.

Fig. 0.2   Photo courtesy of Patsy Terrell, www.patsyterrell.com

Fig. 0.3   Wedge diagram data from Pacala and Socolow, 2004.

Fig. 1.12   Illustration adapted from Jim Augustyn, *The Solar Cat Book* (Berkeley, CA: Patty Paw Press, 2008)

Fig. 1.16a, b   Graph and photo courtesy of Passive House Institute Darmstadt, www.passivhaus.de

Fig. 1.18   Photo courtesy of David Miller

Fig. 1.22   Photo courtesy of Helen Taylor, www.calacademy.org

Fig. 1.25 a, b   Photo courtesy of Reflex Glass-Leicester, www.reflexglass.co.uk

Fig. 1.41a   Photo courtesy of Emily Hagopian, EmilyHagopian.com

Fig. 1.41c   Photo by Bethany Bandera, bethanybandera.com

Fig. 1.41e   Photo courtesy of Emily Hagopian, EmilyHagopian.com

Fig. 1.41f   Photo by Bethany Bandera, bethanybandera.com

Fig. 1.41g, h   Photo courtesy of Emily Hagopian, EmilyHagopian.com

Fig. 2.15   Illustration courtesy of John S. Reynolds, FAIA

Fig. 2.16a   Photo by Jeremy Marshall from *Bringing Sustainable Energy into Your School*. Energie-Cités

Fig. 2.17   Photo courtesy of Pliny Fisk III, www.cmpbs.org

Fig. 2.23a   Photo courtesy of Brian Kesner, www.ragtopstudios.com

Fig. 2.23b   Photo courtesy of Bruno Giberti

Fig. 2.23c   Illustration by Pascal Coste, Courtesy of Special Collections, California Polytechnic State University San Luis Obispo

Fig. 2.23d, e, f   Photos courtesy of Pere Vivas and Ricard Pla, Casa Batlló, S.L.

Fig. 2.24f, g   Photo courtesy of David Wright, davidwrightaia.com

Fig. 2.25b   Photo by Bethany Bandera, bethanybandera.com

Fig. 2.32a   Photo courtesy of Steve Baer, zomeworks.com

Fig. 2.32d   Photo courtesy of Solar Components, www.solarcomponents.com

Fig. 2.35a   Reprinted from Professor Edward Morse patent drawing

Fig. 2.40c   Photo courtesy of Jonathan Hammond, indigoarch.com

Fig. 3.7   Photos courtesy of John S. Reynolds, FAIA

Fig. 3.12a   Photo courtesy of Monica Renata, http://www.flickr.com/photos/insidemyworld/2851008606/sizes/o

Fig. 3.12b   Photo courtesy of Nate Robert, http://www.flickr.com/photos/naterobert/4479157796/sizes/l/

Fig. 3.14c   Photo courtesy of snikrap, http://www.flickr.com/photos/snikrap/2956781954/sizes/o/

Fig. 3.19a   Photo courtesy of Ali Vakili Rad

Fig. 3.30   Photo courtesy of National Renewable Energy Laboratory (NREL), nrel.gov

Fig. 3.33a   Adapted from Scott Clark, www.slosustainability.com

Fig. 3.36   Illustration courtesy of J. R. Watts

Fig. 3.41a   Martin Hürlimann, Fotostiftung Schweiz/Pro Litteris © 2011

Fig. 3.41c   Photo courtesy of ahisgett, http://www.flickr.com/photos/hisgett/2989350419/sizes/l/

Fig. 3.41c   Photo courtesy of srboisvert, http://www.flickr.com/photos/srboisvert/213532922/sizes/o/

Fig. 3.43a   Photo courtesy of Erin Scholl, erinscholl.com

Fig. 3.43b   Photo courtesy of Chandrika V. Jaggia, milanarchitecture.com

Fig. 3.46   Photo courtesy of Ali Zingstra

Fig. 3.47   Photo courtesy of Esme_Vos, http://www.flickr.com/photos/esme/3932192971/sizes/l/

Fig. 3.48a   Photo courtesy of Paul Miller, http://upload.wikimedia.org/wikipedia/commons/9/9d/Bedzed.jpg

Fig. 3.48b   Photo courtesy of Paul Miller, http://www.flickr.com/photos/paulmiller/65091224/sizes/l/

Fig. 3.49h   Photos courtesy of Charles (Chuck) R. Edelson

Table 4.2   Data from John S. Reynolds, FAIA.

Fig. 4.12b   Photo courtesy of http://farm4.static.flickr.com/3004/2892338411_167fe46334_0.jpg

Fig. 4.12d   Photo courtesy of Gruban, http://www.flickr.com/photos/gruban/http://www.flickr.com/photos/worldofjan/275722535/in/photostream/

Fig. 4.12f   Photo courtesy of Don Choi

Fig. 4.12g, h   Illustration by Pascal Coste, reprinted from *Monuments modernes de la Perse, mesures, dessines et decrits par Pascal Coste. Publies par ordre de son excellence le ministre de la maison de l'empereur et des beaux-arts* (Paris: A. Morel, 1867).

Fig. 4.12i   Photo courtesy of lyng88, http://www.flickr.com/photos/lyng883/4231628941/sizes/o/

Fig. 4.12j   Photo courtesy of Plutor, http://www.flickr.com/photos/plutor/319493257/sizes/l/

Fig. 4.13d   Photo courtesy of Kabacchi, http://www.flickr.com/photos/kabacchi/4365195281/sizes/o/

Fig. 4.19–4.20   Photos courtesy of Swenson Technology, rMeter.com

Fig. 4.29   Photo courtesy of calm a llama down, http://www.flickr.com/photos/samgalison/2372360442/sizes/o/

Fig. 4.30   Photo courtesy of Tripwire Interactive, http://commons.wikimedia.org/wiki/File:Red_Orchestra_Kp3.jpg

Fig. 4.31   Photo courtesy of Richard Beller

Fig. 4.32a-e   Photos courtesy of Richard Beller

Fig. 5.5b   Photo courtesy of Charles J. Sharp, http://upload.wikimedia.org/wikipedia/commons/5/5d/Angkor-Wat-from-the-air.JPG

Fig. 5 .5c   Photo courtesy of Christopher Yip

Fig. 5.6a   Painting by Thomas Buchanan, reprinted with permission of Haller-Buchanan Studios, Denver, Colorado

Fig. 5.7a   Photo courtesy of USDA, www.usda.gov

Fig. 5.7b   Photo courtesy of jimg944, http://www.flickr.com/photos/jimg944/120567428/sizes/l/

Fig. 5.9b   Photo courtesy of Eric Lee, www.Harpiris.com

Fig. 5.13   Photo courtesy of Sicco Rood

Fig. 5.14–5.22   Data and photos courtesy of Steve Heckeroth, renewables.com

Fig. 5.23   Data courtesy of Swenson Technology, rMeter.com

Fig. 5.30b   Photo courtesy of Jennifer Ferguson, watersmart.biz

Fig. 5.30c   Photo courtesy of Kingspan Environmental, www.kingspanwater.com

Fig. 5.41a, b, c Photos and illustration courtesy of Clivus Multrum, clivusmultrum.com

Fig. 5.42a   Photo courtesy of Dustin Poppendieck, humboldt.edu/arcatamarsh/index.htm

Fig. 5.43a   Photo courtesy of Yvonne Lehnhard, http://www.novaquatis.eawag.ch/index_EN

Fig. 5.45   Illustration courtesy of Pliny Fisk III, www.cmpbs.org

Fig.5.47   Illustration courtesy of National Park Service

Fig. 5.48   Illustration courtesy of Pliny Fisk III, www.cmpbs.org

Fig. 5.49a-b   Photos courtesy of Athena and Bill Steen, www.caneloproject.com

Fig. 5.51   Photo courtesy of David Eisenberg, www.DCAT.net

Fig. 5.53   Illustrations courtesy of Pliny Fisk III, www.cmpbs.org

Fig. 5.57b   Photo courtesy of Bonnie Lippitt

Fig. 5.58   Photos courtesy of Rachel Aljilani, www.quickcompost.com

Fig. 5.64a   Photo courtesy of Joseph Kasperovich

Fig. 5.66a   Photo courtesy of Joseph Kasperovich

Fig. 5.67e   Photo courtesy of Emily Hagopian, EmilyHagopian.com

Fig. 6.0   Photo courtesy of City of Davis, California

Fig. 6.13a   Photo courtesy of Shelly Danko-Day, www.GrowPittsburg.org

Fig. 6.13b   Photo courtesy of Thomas Heinser, www.thomasheinser.com

Fig. 6.15–6.21   Illustrations courtesy of Pliny Fisk III, www.cmpbs.org

Fig. 6.22–6.24   Illustrations and photos courtesy of Richard Levine, www.centerforsustainablecities.com

Fig. 6.26–6.27   Illustrations and photos courtesy of Richard Levine, www.centerforsustainablecities.com

Page 259   Photos courtesy of Emily Hagopian, EmilyHagopian.com

ACKNOWLEDGMENTS

Every book reflects the work, contributions, and influence of many people. We would particularly like to thank our partners, Polly Cooper and Laurie Lippitt, for their support and assistance over the years. And we'd like to thank our clients, who believed in us and had the wisdom and courage to build more sustainable buildings. Over the many years of our collective experience, we have also benefited from the advice, support, and inspiration of many colleagues and co-workers. Their energy, enthusiasm, and good humor have helped make the sustainability trail a more enjoyable experience. We have both learned from traditional craftsmen and -women around the world as well.

We would especially like to thank Phil Niles, Lynne Elizabeth, Pliny Fisk III, John Reynolds, Margot McDonald, Scott Clark, and our many colleagues at ASES, ISES, the New Mexico Solar Energy Association, and the Northern California Solar Energy Association.

And too many others to include them all, but special thanks from KH to:

Harold Hay, Jim Augustyn, Lori Atwater, Steve Baer, Maurice and Joy Bennett, Don Cutter, Francis de Winter, Nancy Florence, Liz Barber, Christine Gyovai, Emily Hagopian, John Liu, Jennifer Rennick, Anthony and Victoria Stoppiello, Paul and Marion Wolff, Alfredo Fernandez-Gonzalez, Ron Swenson, Mark Dure-Smith, Richard Beller, Steve Heckeroth, Piret Harmon, Richard Levine, Christopher Yip, Brian Kesner, Bruno Giberti, David Wright, Mikel Robertson, Gudrun Grell, Gale Day, John Edmiston, Jake Feldman, Henry Hammer, Liz Scott Graham, and everyone else who helped along the way.

And from DB to:

Loren W. "Tod" Neubauer, Peter and Florence van Dresser, Mike and Judy Corbett, Jon Hammond, Marshall Hunt, Denny Long, Betsy Bainbridge, David Eisenberg, Matts Myhrman and Judy Knox, Bill and Athena Steen, Catherine Wanek, Bob Bolles, Kelly Lerner, Bob and Chris Sowers, Bruce King, Bruce Haglund, Bill Roley, Drew George, Josh Marcengill, Jim Wilson, and David Springer. Many other friends and colleagues have provided ideas, wisdom, and support over the years. My students at William Carey International University, UC Riverside, San Diego State University, and Alliant International University have also added insight and wisdom far beyond their years. Jim Goodrich, the founding dean of the Marshall Goldsmith School of Management, kindly provided the time and opportunity for me to complete this work and offered his support along the way. I would also like to thank Kodak for making Kodachrome II such a stable medium for storing images, many thirty-plus years old and all in excellent condition. Ritz Camera and Chrome scanned old slides and negatives.

A special thanks from both of us to Rachel Aljilani, who made this book possible with her exceptional organizing, writing, and design skills. And thanks to Erin Scholl for layout and design work and guidance with the mysteries of Pages. Cannon Labrie helped wrangle the text into shape. And special thanks to Chelsea Green's Patricia Stone who provided invaluable support and assistance. Her hard work and initiative helped bring this complex layout to completion and to market. Thanks!

INDEX

NOTE: page numbers followed by t refer to tables.

Index content